Society in Zimbabwe's Liberation War

Edited by

NGWABI BHEBE
Professor of History
University of Zimbabwe

TERENCE RANGER
Rhodes Professor of Race Relations
University of Oxford

JAMES CURREY
Oxford

HEINEMANN
Portsmouth, N.H.

UNIVERSITY OF ZIMBABWE PUBLICATIONS
Harare

James Currey Ltd
73 Botley Road
Oxford
OX2 0BS

Heinemann
A division of Reed Elsevier Inc.
361 Hanover Street
Portsmouth, NH 03801-3912

University of Zimbabwe Publications
P.O. Box MP 203
Mount Pleasant
Harare

ISBN 0-85255-660-8   (James Currey cloth)
ISBN 0-85255-610-1   (James Currey paper)
ISBN 0-435-07411-3   (Heinemann cloth)
ISBN 0-435-07412-1   (Heinemann paper)
ISBN 0-908307-37-3   (University of Zimbabwe Publications)

1 2 3 4 5 00 99 98 97 96

British Library Cataloguing in Publication Data
Society in Zimbabwe's Liberation War. –
1. Zimbabwe – History, Military – 1965-1980 2. Zimbabwe –
Social conditions – 1965-1980
I. Bhebe, Ngwabi II. Ranger, T.O. (Terence Osborn), 1929-
968.9'104

Library of Congress Cataloging-in-Publication Data applied for

Typeset by University of Zimbabwe Publications
and printed in Britain by Villiers Publications, London N3

Contents

Religion and the War

Ideology, Education and the War

Legacies of the War

Contributors

Jocelyn Alexander completed her doctoral thesis for Oxford University – 'The State, Agrarian Policy and Rural Politics in Zimbabwe' – in 1993. She is Junior Research Fellow of Somerville College, Oxford, and holds a three-year Leverhulme Foundation award for field research in Nkayi and Lupane districts.

Ngwabi Bhebe is Professor of History and Pro-Vice Chancellor of the University of Zimbabwe. He is the author of many books and articles on the history of Zimbabwe, the most recent being *ZAPU and ZANU Guerrilla Warfare and the Lutheran Evangelical Church in Zimbabwe* which is now at press.

Anthony Chennells teaches English at the University of Zimbabwe. He is the author of many articles on White Rhodesian fiction and has made a particular study of writing on the liberation war.

Fay Chung worked in the ZANU Education Department in Mozambique and after independence served in the Ministry of Education, eventually becoming Minister of Education. She is now Chief, Education Cluster, UNICEF, New York.

Janice McLaughlin completed her doctoral thesis for the University of Zimbabwe – 'The Catholic Church and the War of Liberation' – in 1991. It is being published in revised form by Baobab. She taught with the ZANU Education Department in Mozambique and after independence worked with the Zimbabwe Institute for Education with Production. She is now at Maryknoll in the United States.

David Maxwell completed his doctoral thesis for Oxford University – 'A Social and Conceptual History of North-East Zimbabwe, 1800–1990' – in 1994. It is being published by Edinburgh University Press. He is Lecturer in International History at the University of Keele.

Paulos Matjaka Nare was a teacher at Manama Secondary School in south Gwanda when its teachers and pupils went into Botswana with ZIPRA. He was appointed as organizer of ZAPU's schools in Zambia. After independence he became headmaster of the J.Z. Moyo School in south Gwanda.

Mark Ncube is Oral Historian and Chief Archivist of the National Archives Records Centre in Bulawayo. He has worked particularly on the Mwali shrines in the Matopos and has recently been involved with the project for the reconstruction of Old Bulawayo.

Terence Ranger is Professor of Race Relations at the University of Oxford. He has written many books and articles about the history of Zimbabwe. Studies of the liberation war include *Peasant Consciousness and Guerrilla War in Zimbabwe* (London, James Currey, 1985).

Richard Werbner is Professor of Social Anthropology in the University of Manchester. He is the author of many books and articles about Zimbabwe. Work on the liberation war includes *Tears of the Dead* (Edinburgh, African International Institute, 1991).

Abbreviations & Acronyms

AIC	African Independent Church	NUF	National Unifying Force
ANC	African National Congress	OAU	Organization of African Unity
AZTREC	Association of Zimbabwe Traditional Ecologists	OCGC	Officer Commanding Ground Cover
		OCSB	Officer Commanding Special Branch
BMATT	British Military Advisory and Training Team	PSBO	Provincial Special Branch Officers
		PSYOPS	Director of Psychological Operations
BSAP	British South Africa Police	RA	Republican Alliance
BSS	Bureau of State Security	RAP	Rhodesian Action Party
CCJP	Catholic Commission for Justice and Peace	RENAMO	Mozambique National Resistance
		RF	Rhodesia Front
Cde	Comrade	RIC	Rhodesian Intelligence Corps
CID	Criminal Investigation Department	RLI	Rhodesian Light Infantry
CIO	Central Intelligence Organization	RNP	Rhodesian National Party
COIN	Counter Insurgency	RP	Rhodesian Party
COMOPS	Combined Operations	RRA	Rhodesian Republican Army
COMPOL	Commissioner of Police	SACP	South African Communist Party
CP	Centre Party	SADF	South African Defence Force
CSM	Church of Sweden Mission	SASCON	Southern African Solidarity Congress
DAI	Directorate Air Intelligence	SAS	Special Air Service
DAPP	Development Aid from People to People	SB	Special Branch
DDG	Deputy Director-General	SFA	Security Force Auxiliaries
DEX	Director External	SRANC	Southern Rhodesian African National Congress
DG	Director-General		
DIN	Director Internal	SRC	Students Representative Council
DMI	Directorate of Military Intelligence	SWAPO	South West African Peoples Organization
DP	Democratic Party		
DSBO	District Special Branch Officer	UAC	Union Administrative Council
ELCZ	Evangelical Lutheran Church of Zimbabwe	UANC	United African National Council
		UDI	Unilateral Declaration of Independence
FISBY	Federal Intelligence and Security Bureau	UNIP	United National Independence Party
		USSR	Union of Soviet Socialist Republics
FNLA	National Front for the Liberation of Angola	ZANLA	Zimbabwe African National Liberation Army
FRELIMO	Front for the Liberation of Mozambique	ZANU	Zimbabwe African National Union
FROLIZI	Front for the Liberation of Zimbabwe	ZANU/PF	Zimbabwe African National Union Patriotic Front
GC	Ground Coverage		
GPSO	Government Protective Security Officer	ZAPU	Zimbabwe African People's Union
HNP	Herstigte Nasionale Partie	ZCC	Zimbabwe Council of Churches
INTAF	Ministry of Internal Affairs	ZDI	Zimbabwe Defence Industries
ICC	Intelligence Co-ordinating Committee	ZIMA	Zimbabwe Medical Aid
JHC	Joint High Command	ZIMFEP	Zimbabwe Foundation for Education with Production
JMC	Joint Military Command		
JOC	Joint Operation Commands	ZINATHA	Zimbabwe National Traditional Healers Association
LWF	Lutheran World Federation		
MAF	Mission Aviation Fellowship	ZIPA	Zimbabwe People's Army
MCP	Malawi Congress Party	ZIPRA	Zimbabwe People's Revolutionary Army
MNR	Mozambique National Resistance		
MPLA	The People's Movement for the Liberation of Angola	ZIRCON	Zimbabwe Institute of Religious Research and Ecological Conservation
NDP	National Democratic Party	ZIS	Zambian Intelligence Service
NIS	National Intelligence Service	ZLC	Zimbabwe Liberation Council
NRP	Northern Rhodesia Police	ZNA	Zimbabwe National Army
NSO	National Security Organization	ZP	Zambian Police

Acknowledgements

The editors wish to thank the Ford Foundation and the Swedish Agency for Research Co-operation with Developing Countries (SAREC) both of which supported the International Conference on the Zimbabwe Liberation War held in Harare on 8–12 July, 1991, at which most of the papers appearing in these two volumes were presented. We are also grateful for the generous subsidy the two organizations have provided for the publication of the two books.

We are further grateful to Professor Carl F. Hallencreutz and his colleagues, the organizers of the Seminar on Religion and War in Zimbabwe and Swedish Relationships held at Uppsala on 23–28 April, 1992, for their permission to publish Ngwabi Bhebe's paper on the Healing of the Scars and Jeremy Brickhill's chapter on the Mafela Trust. The conference gave us an opportunity to finalize our editorial work.

We are thankful for the academic sponsorship we have enjoyed from the University of Zimbabwe and the Oxford University African Studies Committee during the conference itself and throughout our editorial work.

For the unstinted and efficient secretarial and administrative support, we are grateful to Phyllis Ferguson, who worked hard for the success of the conference from our Oxford end; to Miss Emerencia Naka, of the University of Zimbabwe, who provided the conference with all its secretarial support; Mr Bryan Thomas Callahan of Swarthmore College, Pennsylvania, who ran around to ensure that conference papers were produced in the right amounts and that they were delivered to the participants timeously; and to Mr Dumisani Vuma, who ferried participants between the airport and the conference venue at the University of Zimbabwe.

Finally, we are indebted to the University of Zimbabwe Publications Committee and the then Publications Officer, Roger Stringer, and the Director of Publications, Samuel Matsangaise, and the entire staff for well produced publications.

Edited by
NGWABI BHEBE & TERENCE RANGER

*Soldiers in
Zimbabwe's
Liberation War*

*Society in
Zimbabwe's
Liberation War*

General Introduction
NGWABI BHEBE
TERENCE RANGER

In July 1991 the University of Zimbabwe was host to an international conference on Zimbabwe's War of Liberation. Two speakers at once threw down a challenge. The first was the Vice-Chancellor, Prof. Walter Kamba, who insisted that the conference was meeting at just the right moment:

> For us the war is still a living reality. But it is also history . . . We can look at it now clearly; look at it whole. The unity agreement makes it possible, and makes it necessary, to include the role of ZIPRA as well as the role of ZANLA, to extend the grassroots studies of the war from Manicaland and Mashonaland into Matabeleland. Ten years and more of independence make it possible and make it necessary to look back and ask questions about the effect of the war and its legacy for what has followed. For the sake of Zimbabwe's understanding of itself we need to raise questions about social conflict during and after the war, about gender, about terror and counter-terror, about mobilization and demobilization, about combatants and ex-combatants, and even about dissidents.

> Zimbabwe needs to remember and to understand the war: to understand it at the level of high analysis and to understand it at the level of suffering and trauma. We need to understand it for reviewing policy, for making the record more complete, for healing memories. At the University here this week you can discuss everything and anything, raise challenging questions, dispute comfortable stereotypes. This is part of what we mean by academic freedom, a freedom for which this university firmly stands . . . Zimbabweans need knowledge about the war. It is your job to learn from them and make available what you have learned.

His challenge was pushed further by Dumiso Dabengwa, who urged that conditions be created for a new breed of social scientists to emerge in Zimbabwe.

> We urge the emergence of a class of scholars capable of withstanding threats and intimidation and rising above racial, ethnic and tribal considerations . . . The new breed of Zimbabwean social scientists ought to stand up against the suppression of any information and should develop an ever-critical mind with respect to the facts, especially purported facts, and actions of political leaders. Anything short of cultivating a tradition of selfless enquiry and exposure of the truth will certainly lead to a nation of sycophants and robots without the necessary powers of independent thought which we should all cherish. A conference on the history of the liberation war is an excellent beginning.

It is a hard task for any conference — or for any subsequent publication — to live up to these demands for courage and rigour and independence of mind. But at least the conference attempted to do so. It brought together, for the first time and in an atmosphere of frankness, leaders and members of ZANLA, ZIPRA and the Rhodesian Security Forces; it brought together cabinet ministers from both ZAPU and ZANU/PF backgrounds, Zimbabweans and non-Zimbabweans, professors and graduate students, those who have already published books on the war and those who are setting out to write them, historians and anthropologists and literary critics and educationalists and theologians. Over four days of discussions this varied group remembered and probed and questioned.

These two volumes present most of the papers given to the conference, and the volume introductions draw on the conference discussions. We hope that their publication will mark another stage in our understanding of the war. However, it should at once be made clear that they do not set out to offer a full coverage of all aspects of the war or a full commentary on what has already been published. It is their intention to move on: to look at questions which have hardly yet been raised and to suggest others which are just beginning to be defined. So in order to make the best use of these two volumes, it is necessary to begin with a brief account of the existing literature on the liberation war.[1]

There is an odd paradox about this literature. Writing about most wars usually begins with descriptions of battles, accounts of armies, biographies of generals and autobiographies of soldiers. Only later do historians turn to the impact of those wars on civilians, on society, on older men and on women and children. But as far as Zimbabwe's war of liberation is concerned, the reverse has been true. The major studies of the war from an African perspective do not deal with armies or military tactics or the experience of fighting men and women. Instead they deal with the impact of the war on Zimbabwe's peasantries;[2] with the war experience of African women;[3] with ideology and religion;[4] and with the need for healing after the war.[5] Only from the White Rhodesian side of the war has there been a flood of books about soldiers and fighting — whether general accounts of the war,[6] or boasts of the triumphs of the Rhodesian Intelligence services,[7] or glorifications of the 'special forces',[8] or picture-books,[9] or White autobiographies.[10] Many of these have been published in South Africa. So it would be true to say that we know a great deal on the African side about civilians and about religion; a great deal on the Rhodesian side about military operations and 'dirty tricks'. But we still know very little about the guerrilla armies or guerrilla intelligence services, just as we know hardly anything about Rhodesian ideology and religion, or about the effect of the war on White civilians.[11]

There are several reasons for this imbalance. To quote again from Dumiso Dabengwa's contribution, from the perspective of the liberation movements 'the armed struggle was only part of the struggle'. The guerrillas always had a keen appreciation of the supreme importance of the social, ideological and political 'fronts'. But on the Rhodesian side — both during the war and in the retrospective literature — it often appears as if military factors only are significant: as if the war could (and should) have been decided purely by military superiority. Indeed, much of the literature published in South Africa claims that the Rhodesian forces could have 'won' the war in battle had they not been betrayed. The almost exclusively military focus of ex-Rhodesian literature on the war is a sign of continued failure of understanding.

But there are also research reasons for this imbalance. When academic work began on the war after 1980, researchers in Zimbabwe did not have access to the records of any of the armies. ZANLA's files were unsorted and closed to scholars.[12] ZIPRA's files were seized by the police.[13] Rhodesian army and police files were either burnt in a great holocaust of documents or smuggled to South Africa. So researchers in Zimbabwe went out into the rural areas, where the war had been fought, and interviewed the people who had experienced it. As a result they paid a great deal of attention to peasant grievances, or to peasant religion, or to the cleavages in rural society. But they interviewed few guerrillas since those who had fought the war were rarely any longer to be found in the areas where they had been combatants. However, at least some of those writing in South Africa had access to the smuggled Rhodesian army files.

Finally, there has been the strange silence of the guerrillas since 1980, with only one autobiography published.[14] Many reasons have been suggested for this. Some scholars — such as Richard Werbner in south-western Zimbabwe — have found ex-combatants reluctant to talk about traumatic war-time experiences. Others have argued that for ZIPRA veterans, at least, and even for former members of ZIPA or the 'left' groups within ZANLA, it has not until recently been safe to do so. Yet others speak of the marginalization of even ZANLA ex-combatants (a marginalization reflected in these volumes in Teresa Barnes's interviews with former guerrillas), and of the creation of an 'official' version of the war which gives all the glory to political leaders and to generals, many of whom are safely dead. For whatever reason, publishers have been reluctant to accept guerrilla life-stories. The result of all this has been that the guerrilla experience has come to us through fiction rather than through history and autobiography.

As we have suggested, there have been some positive benefits of this silence about the military aspects of the guerrilla war. It is no bad thing to *begin* with the experiences of civilians, peasants or women. It is important to see the war in social, political and ideological terms rather than just as a military operation. But, clearly, this imbalance has had many negative effects. We have been stuck with an orthodoxy — one version of the war which gives all the credit to ZANLA and none to ZIPRA, and which highlights some elements within ZANLA while denigrating others.[15] The time has certainly come, as Walter Kamba insisted, to look at ZIPRA as well as at ZANLA, and to look at ZIPRA and the 'Nhari' rebellion and the 'Vashandi' within ZANLA. The time has certainly come to review contrasting military strategies; to hear the voices of the combatants at least as clearly as those of the peasants or of 'the mothers of the revolution'. Even the Rhodesian side of the military struggle, about which so much has already been written, needs to be made into history rather than myth.

For these reasons our first volume will focus on 'Soldiers', bringing together chapters on ZIPRA, ZIPA and ZANLA; discussing the 'Nhari' rebellion and the 'Vashandi', the Fifth Brigade and the 'dissidents'; comparing Rhodesian Intelligence Services with guerrilla intelligence services; exploring the effects of Rhodesian 'dirty tricks' and poisoning on the guerrillas; looking at the integration of the armies after 1980; and giving a voice to ex-combatants.

Nevertheless, there is still much to be said about the social, political and ideological aspects of the war and these are the topics of our second volume, on 'Society'. This volume, too, will focus on questions which have not yet been explored in the social historical research already done. Thus there is no chapter on spirit mediums — so effectively discussed in David Lan's *Guns and Rain*. Instead there is a chapter exploring the hitherto neglected subject of the interaction between guerrillas and the Mwali shrines of the south-west. There are no chapters making the sort of generalizations which have already been established about the role of the Christian churches in the war. Instead there are detailed case studies which modify or complicate those generalizations or bring to the fore hitherto neglected denominations. There are no chapters on peasant ideology (about which so much has been written by Ranger and Kriger and Manungo); instead there are contributions on education and ideology in the camps in Zambia and Mozambique, and on Rhodesian ideology as reflected in fiction. Finally, there are three chapters which open up an important new topic: the continuation of the war after 1980 in some places and its continuing impact in others. These chapters look at the war of the 'dissidents' in Matabeleland; at the impact of the war on gender relations; and on what patterns of patriarchy have emerged from the war in the rural areas.

Yet we hope that in focusing on different topics in these two volumes we have not lost sight of the insights of the work that has already been done. Even in a volume on 'Soldiers' it is not really possible ever to forget civilians. Thus if Jeremy Brickhill's first chapter in the first volume deals with 'pure' military history, discussing ZIPRA's development of a conventional war capacity, his second chapter on the work of the Mafela Trust relates the documentation of the guerrilla dead to the sorrows and traumas of the whole of rural society. Moreover, there are many interactions between the two volumes, between 'soldiers' and 'society', which we seek to bring out in the two individual volume introductions. These volumes are not a repudiation of the best work of the first decade but are designed to add to and deepen them.

Finally, the conference was intended to be a stimulus to further research, so it may be useful to set out what does *not* appear in these volumes and which topics still need to be explored. So far as the first volume is concerned the main group of 'soldiers' missing are the 'Auxiliaries' of Abel Muzorewa and Ndabaningi Sithole. We make some initial comments on them in the volume introduction but the whole subject of the Internal Settlement and of the auxiliaries badly needs to be researched. We suspect that such research will add not only to our understanding of the war on the ground but also of gender and generation issues and of witch-killings during the war.

So far as 'Society' is concerned, the greatest absence is of urban society. Urban links with rural insurrection is a topic well explored in studies of the Mau-Mau but hardly touched upon for Zimbabwe. Were there urban supply networks? Were there urban sabotage cells? What about the refugees who flocked into the towns from the countryside? What of the urban unemployed youth recruited as auxiliaries? What of the 'traditions' of urban violence, beginning with the riots of the mass nationalist period, through the clashes between ZAPU and ZANU supporters in 1963 and 1964, to urban violence during and after elections in the 1980s? Is there any urban equivalent to rural religious developments during the war? Given the centrality of urban violence in South Africa and the sophistication of the studies made of it, this is a serious gap in the Zimbabwean literature.

There are also areas of the country about whose wartime experience we knew hardly anything. There has been no study, for example, of the war history of the peasant societies of Northern Matabeleland, which we badly need to balance Jeremy Brickhill's account of the fighting men and women in that province. Nor do we know much about civilian interactions along and across the Mozambique border, either during the war or in the post–1980 period of RENAMO raids. There is the lowveld — Tonga country in the north-west, or Hlengwe and Shangaan country in the south-east — a study of which would help break down the exclusive focus on the 'Shona' and the 'Ndebele'.

And even in those areas where studies *have* been carried out on the civilian experience in the war we need more attention to *class* as well as to gender and generation. Now that the 'indigenous businessmen' (or women) are coming into their own, we need studies of their role during the war. Of course, even now that indigenous businessmen and women are coming into their own, Whites still dominate much of the economy and possess the most productive areas of the land. We need to know much more about White society and ideology in the past and especially during the war.

Another conference in ten years time will be able to throw light on all these questions — and generate yet new ones in its turn. In the interim we offer these two volumes as, we hope, a provocative report on the state of the debate about Zimbabwe's liberation war.

Volume Introduction:
Society in Zimbabwe's Liberation War

NGWABI BHEBE
TERENCE RANGER

INTRODUCTION

Our first volume dealt with soldiers and with armies. That theme needed no explanation. The theme of 'Society' is different. Society can mean many things and we need to explain what it means here. In this volume we deal with people's beliefs, ideas and experiences. We look first at religion, both African religion and Christianity, and ask what happened to religious belief during the liberation war and after it. Next we look at how people were educated so that they could understand the war and prepare themselves to change society after it. We also look at the ideas used by White Rhodesians to justify fighting the war with such brutality. (Later we also examine civilian experience of brutality at the hands of guerrillas, dissidents and the Fifth Brigade). In our third section we examine some of the consequences of the war. What impact did it have on people's sense of identity — as 'Shona', as 'Ndebele', as women? How far did new ideas and new identities carry on after the war ended? And even if there has not been the 'revolutionary' transformation that was promised, we show that what happened in the war is still shaping Zimbabwean society and the ways in which Zimbabweans think and feel. As in the first volume, the chapters are written both by leading participants in the war and by research academics; as in the first volume, we are more concerned with the realities than with the comfortable myths of the war. Some heroic deeds are recorded here and some terrible ones; some idealistic hopes and some cynical compromises. All are part of the experience of the war and all need to be understood.

RELIGION AND THE WAR: THE MWALI SHRINES

This volume begins with three chapters on religion — one dealing with south-western Zimbabwe and two with north-eastern. Of course, we do not claim that

6

this is a new theme. David Lan has told us about the spirit mediums of north-east Zimbabwe and their assistance to ZANLA; Ian Linden has told us about the war history of the Catholic Church.[1] But we do claim to show some new things about this old theme. Thus we do not have a chapter on mediums, but we do have a chapter on another important African religious system — the Mwali rain-shrines of the Matopos. We do not have a chapter generalizing about 'the church'. Instead we have two case studies of particular missions, one Protestant and one Catholic, based on very detailed documentary and oral research. These studies show the fascinating and sometimes unexpected particulars which underlie the generalizations. In combination with previous (and forthcoming) work we think that these chapters show that 'religion' was not just important to specially 'religious' people. During the war religion of one kind or another was important to almost everybody.

The opening chapter by Mark Ncube and Terence Ranger on religion and the war in southern Matabeleland helps to link this volume to its predecessor. Discussing 'Soldiers', we looked at a series of suggested contrasts between ZIPRA and ZANLA and found some of them more convincing than others. Ncube and Ranger begin by reviewing these suggested differences to see if they help to explain another apparent contrast. Up to now it has seemed that there was little if any interaction between ZIPRA and any form of religion. There were no *mhondoro* mediums in Matabeleland and nothing has been written about ZIPRA's use of any other sort of African religion. There was open hostility between ZIPRA and most of the Christian missions in southern Matabeleland. This seems very different from ZANLA's use of mediums and its positive relationship with many missions and individual priests. On the face of it, it appears that ZIPRA fought a 'secular' war and ZANLA a 'religious' one. Discussion of these apparent differences has played with various explanations — perhaps 'the Ndebele' are less spiritual than 'the Shona'? Or maybe ZIPRA was more proletarian and rational than the peasant-based ZANLA?

Ncube and Ranger do away with such speculation. They find that the alleged contrast between ZIPRA's 'secular' war and ZANLA's 'religious' one is not true. The Mwali shrines were just as important to people in Matabeleland as the mediums were in other parts of the country. They were used by Joshua Nkomo and other NDP and ZAPU cultural nationalists; rural nationalists revived the Mwali ideology; the cult's view of history and of the transition of regimes helped provide a sense of meaning to all the confused events of the war and the first years of Independence. African religion *was* important in Matabeleland; ZIPRA and ZANLA were not very different. Nor was the Mwali cult by any means the only African religious element in the war in Matabeleland. When after Independence one of the history teachers at J. Z. Moyo School in southern Gwanda deployed her students to collect oral evidence about the war, many of them came back with stories about the key importance of the *madhlozi* ancestral spirits.[2]

Ncube and Ranger show that both ZIPRA and ZANLA guerrillas operated in the Matopos and both sought support from the shrines. This suggests that we need to try to fill a gap in our knowledge of the war. ZANLA guerrillas went to Mwali shrines as well as to *mhondoros*. But what did ZIPRA guerrillas do in Shona-speaking areas when they were beyond the influence of the Mwali cult but where there were spirit mediums? It is strange that we do not know the answer because there were ZIPRA guerrillas in the area where David Lan did his research — indeed, some of them arrested him for a time! But in his *Guns and Rain,* Lan says nothing about ZIPRA interactions with the mediums, focusing entirely on ZANLA. Yet unpublished anthropological research on Nemakonde district — a Shona-speaking area in which ZIPRA was active — has shown that ZIPRA guerrillas certainly worked closely with mediums there during the war and returned to them for healing after it. Both guerrillas and local people saw this as a revival of pre-colonial relationships, when Lobengula sent tribute to the senior mediums of Nemakonde. Moreover, we know from South African ANC guerrillas who entered Zimbabwe with ZAPU soldiers under the ZAPU/ANC alliance that one of the issues which divided them was the ZAPU men's readiness to consult mediums and the ANC men's mockery of the idea.[3]

It seems likely, then, that if ZIPRA had opened up the north-eastern front in the early 1970s, as it so nearly did, its guerrillas would have responded to offers of assistance from spirit mediums just as positively as ZANLA was to do. In short, it is important not to think of ZANLA as 'Shona' and 'spiritual' and of ZIPRA as 'Ndebele' and 'secular'. We ought to see both guerrilla armies as responsive to the beliefs and institutions of the people among whom they were operating.

However, if ZIPRA and ZANLA, Ndebele and Shona, do not look so different after reading Ncube and Ranger's chapter, some contrasts do emerge. The priests of the rain-shrines did not behave exactly like spirit mediums, and guerrillas and nationalists did not use them in exactly the same way. Priests of the shrines did not accompany guerrilla bands into the field; they did not go into exile with the guerrillas. There were no Mwali shrines in ZAPU camps in Zambia as there were spirit medium 'locations' in ZANU camps in Mozambique. The rain-shrines seem to have been important in the long-term rather than in an immediate emergency: they offered a view of history which provided a pattern for the total struggle rather than advice on what to do in any particular combat.

SPIRIT MEDIUMS IN THE WAR

Now, as we have said, this volume contains no chapter on spirit mediums. But many of its chapters mention mediums; so do some of the chapters in our first volume, and so did many of the participants in the conference discussions. Moreover, highly relevant work by Dr Martinus Daneel and by Dr Janice McLaughlin has recently become available. So it may be helpful before leaving the question of African religion and the war to sum up what has emerged from all this discussion of the role of mediums.

To begin with, it is clear that the major adversaries in the war looked at mediums in quite different ways. As Anthony Chennells shows in his chapter in this volume, Whites saw mediums as an aspect of the unchanging, 'primitive' character of Black society. From the White point of view the influence of mediums could either be 'bad', with the *mhondoro* acting as a 'witch-doctor' to whip up barbaric violence, or it could be 'good', with the medium speaking for the conservative views of traditional rural society against Marxists and modernizers.

During the war the Rhodesian Front regime used both arguments: Ian Smith explained initial guerrilla successes in the north-east as the result of the use of 'witch-doctors', but at the same time District Commissioners were instructed to use every effort to bring senior mediums 'on side'. Chennells shows how Rhodesian novelists reflected this same ambivalence, mediums appearing in some stories as cackling demoniacs and in others as guardians of true tradition. Chennells thus summarizes the argument of Peter Stiff's *The Rain Goddess:*

> The spiritual authorities in Shona society are finally more significant than the guerrillas will ever be. The latter work for change; the *mhondoro* wants only to reproduce the social formations and the social practices which have remained intact and been sanctioned over the centuries. In the novel the 'rain goddess', opposed as she is to the violence and death that the guerrillas have brought, withholds the rain until the people themselves are willing to turn against these disturbers of traditional stasis . . . By suggesting that the *mhondoro* does actually have power over rain, Stiff raises to a mystical truth what was political strategy by Internal Affairs . . . to ensure that traditional spiritual authorities sided with the regime.

Josiah Tungamirai's chapter in *Volume One,* while denying that ZANLA accepted *mhondoro* as spokesmen of 'mystical truth', also speaks of the use of mediums as a 'political strategy', this time by 'pragmatic' ZANLA guerrillas. He too sees the mediums as representing 'tradition', though this time a tradition of protest rather than of stasis:

> The tradition of the spirit mediums, who had participated effectively in the first *Chimurenga War* of 1896/7, was still alive in the 1970s and the new generation of mediums was equally opposed to the Whites and their colonial oppressive system.

But others who encountered the mediums during the war came to see them very differently — as flexible and adaptive to change, while at the same time not easily captured by any political strategies. Fay Chung, at the end of her chapter, describes the co-existence of different ideological tendencies within ZANU:

> One group asserted its adherence to democracy, nationalism, modernism, and later, Marxism-Leninism, while the larger group of peasants clung to their traditional ideology dominated by traditional resistance figures such as Nehanda, Kaguvi, Chaminuka, and the ancestral spirits . . . ZANU did

not try to destroy traditionalism in the way that FRELIMO tried to do, but instead tried to win the traditionalists' support for the liberation struggle. The traditional leaders, the spirit mediums, on the other hand, also tried to understand and accommodate modern trends. At a meeting held between the spirit mediums and myself, for example, in early 1978 at Pungwe III military camp, the subject of discussion was the reasons for the participation of such countries as the United States, China and the Soviet Union in the Zimbabwe liberation struggle. Whilst the spirit mediums remained the upholders of traditional values, such as respect for life and preservation of the environment, they were able to accept modern trends such as the use of sophisticated modern weapons and education.

Moreover, Fay Chung told us in discussion, their insistence on 'respect for life' and on morality made the mediums inside the Mozambican camps uneasy allies for the guerrilla 'chefs'. Mediums began to speak against the 'Veterans', condemning their exploitation of women and their imposition of violent punishments. In fact, said Chung, there was a surprising amount in common between the puritanical, idealistic mediums and the puritanical, idealistic Marxist 'Vashandi' who were the other thorn in the side of the 'Veteran' old guard.

But whether we see the mediums as static or as flexible traditionalists, the question remains — how important were they during the liberation war? David Lan's work has been criticized by Michael Bourdillon and others for overstating the influence of the mediums. And fresh research has restated this division of opinion, with Martinus Daneel making perhaps the most far-reaching assertions yet about the liberation role of the mediums, and Janice McLaughlin seeking to document deep-seated ZANLA suspicion of their influence.

Since 1988 Daneel — author of an impressive series of books on Karanga Independent Churches — has been involved in the formation of the Zimbabwe Institute of Religious Research and Ecological Conservation (ZIRCON). One of its constituent bodies is the Association of Zimbabwe Traditional Ecologists (AZTREC), whose nucleus 'consists of spirit mediums, chiefs and ex-guerrilla fighters'. Daneel explains:

> Traditionally the chiefs and spirit mediums, representing the official link between the senior tribal ancestors and their living descendants, together wielded considerable tribal political power. During *chimurenga* the mediums were responsible for a renaissance of traditional religion. They conveyed the directives and inspirational messages of the senior 'guardians of the land' to both ZANLA high command in Mozambique and the fighters at the war front in Zimbabwe. These guardians were believed to be united in a spirit war council *(dare rechimurenga)*, presided over by Mwari, the traditional high-god. Thus all of Zimbabwe's spirit powers, via their spirit mediums, were directly involved, guiding the struggle and influencing guerrilla tactics at the front.[4]

Daneel's informants on the war are drawn largely from the mediums collaborating in AZTREC, some of whom were themselves ZANLA guerrillas. In a recent conference paper, Daneel elaborated at some length the accounts of these informants. He sees the senior *masvikiro* as consistent opponents of colonialism, first leading the struggle in 1896, and then under Rhodesian rule

> bringing communal frustrations into the open and voicing criticism against the oppressor in the name of the mystical guardians of the land. In defiance of White rule the *masvikiro* were reinforcing the bonds between the living and living dead, thereby encouraging peasant communities to bear oppression with dignity and to keep up the resolve to seek liberation. In this respect the *svikiro* was a key mobilizer of resistance.

During the second *chimurenga* the mediums stimulated a revival of African religion, and this 'in turn inspired the guerrilla fighters' and 'in many cases informed and even gave direction to strategic operations at the war front and contributed greatly to close co-operation between rural communities and fighters'. Daneel draws upon the testimonies of 'a large number of ex-combatants' to assert that there was a general guerrilla belief in the spiritual war council, with 'the national ancestors' — Chaminuka, Nehanda and Kaguvi — at the highest level, followed by the 'founder ancestors' of the chieftancies:

> In the spirit world the final authority behind the ZANLA and ZIPRA high commands and probably more effectively in charge of the entire war effort throughout the country, was the *dare re chimurenga*. The link between the spiritual war council and the fighting cadres was the spirit mediums.

Some fighters were themselves possessed by 'ancestral spirits at the war front'; some mediums 'were integrated into guerrilla detachments'. These proclaimed the claims of the ancestors to the lost lands and helped to discover 'through ancestral intervention' who were the real traitors to the cause. Daneel adds the fascinating detail that guerrillas in Masvingo never used *n'angas* to divine 'witches', thus avoiding any form of magic and relying on the pure spiritual power of the mediums.[5]

One could hardly imagine a more extensive set of claims for the centrality of the mediums than these: readers will have noticed that Daneel thinks that the mediums were more in control of the war effort than ZIPRA's and ZANLA's high commands. Janice McLaughlin, however, has drawn on very different evidence and to very different effect. She has had access to the ZANLA archives, where reports from spirit-possessed guerrillas are not to be found and where there are instead the cool and rational assessments of the political commissars.

To begin with, McLaughlin's account is not all that different from Daneel's. It credits a woman spirit medium of the Dzivaguru cult, living near a FRELIMO base at Gungwa mountain in Mozambique, with formally introducing traditional religion into the war, and describes how she called a 'Congress of Traditional Spirits' in July 1972 'to bless the relaunching of the war', which was attended by mediums from many parts of Zimbabwe and also by 'a senior delegation of ZANLA guerrillas in training'. McLaughlin cites a Marxist guerrilla as crediting the mediums with 'natural bush lore, sound military strategy, human psychology and practical morality'. So far, so similar to Daneel. But thereafter the story changes.

By 1975 there were fierce debates between the radicals and the 'Veterans' about the use of spirit mediums. In 1976 the Zimbabwe People's Army (ZIPA), which briefly asserted the dominance of younger, educated guerrillas, 'found the Rhodesian forces were using mediums to lure many guerrillas to their deaths', and so banned 'all contact with mediums'. In 1977, as they regained control of the war, ZANLA 'Veterans' reinstated contact with mediums inside Zimbabwe. But from then on there was constant criticism by political commissars of over-reliance on mediums.

In the Tete, Manica and Gaza 'provinces' especially, guerrillas were said to be obeying mediums rather than the ZANLA rules of conduct. McLaughlin quotes one political commissar writing in 1979 that 'the killing of members of the masses' was 'being directed by spirit mediums', while guerrillas had 'lost the art and science of war' and merely followed the mediums' instructions. She quotes another rebuke, this time to women guerrillas who had obeyed the injunction of mediums not to carry weapons during menstruation: 'We are not under the rule of spirit mediums . . . No medium has ever liberated a country . . . You want to create your own Medium Spirit Policy instead of the Party.'[6]

In her chapter in this volume McLaughlin spells out the implications of all this. Whether or not there were close relations between mediums and guerrillas depended, she suggests, on the period. 'In the early days of the war, 1972–4, traditional religion seemed to be the dominant mode of mobilization and guerrilla recruitment'; on the other hand, 'neither European missionaries nor guerrillas had developed patterns of interaction, viewing each other with suspicion if not downright hostility'. There was a halt in the war in the mid-1970s and when it resumed the radical Marxists of ZIPA were in command. They 'held a much more negative position towards religion in general and traditional religion in particular'; they looked down on traditional religion as 'peasant superstition'. At first they were also hostile to Christianity, but McLaughlin argues that as they were themselves the product of mission schools, they were much more ready to see missions as part of the modern world and as a source of useful services.

The violent retaliation by the Rhodesian government against Bishop Lamont convinced the guerrillas that the Catholic Church was on their side. When ZIPA was disbanded 'there was a revival of the use of traditional religion in some areas of the country by some groups of guerrillas'. But the balance had shifted for good, and 'Christian missions continued to play a vital role'.

David Maxwell's chapter in this volume suggests a third approach, adopting neither Daneel's assertion of the dominance of mediums throughout the war, nor

McLaughlin's argument of a shift away from mediums towards missions. In Maxwell's view, what determined relations was the state of popular religion in any particular area. In some places:

> The perception by some guerrilla élites of the strength of popular Christianity caused them to take up Christian idioms in order to mobilize support. In areas where the brokers of popular religion were Christian, guerrillas were forced to seek legitimacy from priests and Black pastors rather than spirit mediums.

In areas where mediums were 'the brokers of popular religion', on the other hand, guerrillas worked with them. This could have paradoxical effects. Maxwell shows that around Avila in Nyanga — the very mission which McLaughlin sees as emblematic of the new, close alliance between the guerrillas and Catholicism — a local spirit medium continued to dominate popular religious imagination and to act as the guerrilla's main ally, while around the Pentecostal Elim Mission, with its conservative politics and ecclesiology, the destruction of tradition by the missionary offensive left the guerrillas with no option but to work with local Christian leaders.

How are we to reconcile these fascinating findings? The extremes of the various arguments seem equally implausible. One cannot believe, as Daneel's informants maintain, that some sort of spiritual high command really directed the war. On the other hand, it does not seem likely that ZIPA leadership was so much in control in 1976 as to be able to ban effectively all interactions with mediums. (Fay Chung commented that the radicals failed to win majority support in the camps in Mozambique at least partly because of their contempt for grassroots religion. For their part, the mediums refused to be drawn into debate with the radicals, saying merely that events would show who had the support of the ancestors. The overthrow and suppression of the ZIPA leadership thus seemed to many people a judgement upon them). What seems likely to be the way forward is to combine Maxwell's emphasis on context with McLaughlin's emphasis on chronology.

One further point needs to be made to conclude this discussion of traditional religion. David Lan's work has taught us to separate mediums from chiefs, the former coming to represent the heroic ancestors, the latter dwindling into bureaucratic puppets. Recent research has challenged such dualism. Daneel remarks for Masvingo that:

> The sharp distinction (made by Lan) does not apply in equal measure to Masvingo Province. Ex-combatants indicated that they were aware at the time of the difficulties confronting chiefs, and the inevitability of their playing virtually double roles. Yet they were satisfied that the majority of the chiefs in the province were supportive of their struggle. In a few cases detachment and section commanders even considered accompanying supportive chiefs to the relative security of Mozambican camps.[7]

David Maxwell has attacked 'dualism' in his account of Katerere local politics,[8] and Jocelyn Alexander's chapter in this volume admirably makes the case for the importance of chiefs since 1980 and by implication for reconsideration of their role in the 1970s.

CHRISTIAN MISSIONS DURING THE LIBERATION WAR

As well as much discussion of African religion during the conference, there was also a good deal of attention paid to the role and experience of Christian missions during the war. We have already begun, in fact, to explore the different perspectives of David Maxwell and Janice McLaughlin. The former stresses the depth or shallowness of popular Christianity as the critical factor; the latter stresses the political position of the church hierarchies and their readiness, or lack of it, to put the material services of their missions at the disposal of the guerrillas. As we have suggested, the contrast between their approaches can readily be seen in their treatment of Avila Mission. For McLaughlin 'Avila was the new Church for a new society, changing Church-State relations irrevocably'; for Maxwell it was a place with very little local support, a mission which had failed to create a deep popular Christianity.

It emerged in discussion that both perspectives could be — and probably were — true. Avila was 'the new Church' for McLaughlin not because of its relations with the local people, but because events there had brought about Bishop Lamont's historic decision that the Church should assist the guerrillas: 'From 1976 the liberation forces knew that they could get assistance from Catholic missions. Appeals to traditional religion and Marxism declined as Christian missions became reliable and trustworthy partners.' Yet, as Maxwell argued, on the ground Avila was more vulnerable to guerrilla suspicions and local indifference than the other missions in the area, whether Catholic or Protestant.

Maxwell states his case thus:

> It seems to me that a mission's war-time standing with its local community cannot simply be understood in terms of the ability of its leaders to construct meaningful relations with the comrades, but also its success in founding a popular Christianity which allowed it to continue to operate with the consent of local people. The relative strengths and weaknesses of this popular Christianity can be explained by tracing the patterns of interaction with indigenous culture and religion since the mission's founding . . . It remains my contention that popular Christianity in the vicinity of Avila Mission was weaker than at both Elim and Regina Coeli Missions.

By 'interactions with indigenous culture and religion' Maxwell does not mean a passive tolerance. The priests at Avila tolerated the local spirit medium, Diki

Rukadza. But in Maxwell's view they did nothing to create a vital popular Catholicism and so left Rukadza to speak for 'the land'. The Avila priests made no use of the long-established ingredients of Manyika folk-Catholicism — pilgrimages and holy places and healing grottoes — by which earlier missionaries had Christianized the landscape. Their up-to-date Catholicism was intellectual and abstract, with little attraction to the people. By contrast, Regina Coeli did manifest 'elements of folk-Catholicism'.

As for Elim, its form of popular Christianity was paradoxically founded on intolerance:

> The Pentecostals had a unique way of sacralizing the landscape. It occurred through contestation. The local spiritual landscape was to be possessed through power encounters. Those held by evil spirits were to be exorcised, charms and bracelets burned and medicines destroyed . . . A zone of popular Christianity was carved out by means of Pentecostal fire and brimstone. In the process spiritual power relations were altered considerably. Razau Kaerezi, the medium living just outside the mission, was completely undermined . . . During the armed struggle the comrades came and moved him to a distant and isolated village where he *could be more* help to them. Around Elim, the Pentecostals held spiritual sway.

By this, of course, Maxwell means local Black Pentecostals. It was with these men and women that the guerrillas worked around Elim, while at Avila they worked particularly through the medium.

This case-study nicely complicates all generalizations. We might have supposed that pilgrimages and Lourdes shrines were patronizing importations from peasant Europe or that Pentecostal confrontation with traditional religion represented nothing more than White cultural arrogance. Maxwell shows that in both cases they had been taken over and made alive by African Christians themselves. Just as in our discussion of spirit mediums we quoted those who were impressed by their creativity rather than their mere traditionalism, Maxwell argues that Black popular Christianity showed an equal creativity:

> The liberation war saw the death of the Old Mission Church and the birth of the new Zimbabwe Church . . . The vacuum caused by the exodus of missionaries was filled by Black Christians [who] grasped that wider social relations were also in a state of flux, as guerrillas tried to win constituencies from women, youth, ethnic groups and ruling and common lineages . . . The war finished with the Church in the hands of the rural people. Once again in the hands of local agents, free to use their own creativity and imagination, the post-war rural Church saw a period of rapid expansion . . . Rural Christians' experience of the war affected the content of popular theology . . . Rural Christians found it easier to theologize their experiences of the war than to historicize them. Indigenous

Christian theology readily offers meaning to suffering in story, song and symbol.

In work like this, historians of mission churches are not just writing 'church history', nor only relating the contacts between mission stations and guerrillas. They are probing what happened to rural society, or at least to rural society in its 'folk Christian' zones.

The other chapters which relate to mission Christianity in this book deal with Matabeleland rather than with Manicaland. Here the contrast between eastern and western Zimbabwe looks more real than it did in terms of African religion. As Ncube and Ranger show, Protestant and Catholic missions alike in southern Matabeleland were regarded with uniform and consistent hostility by the guerrillas. To explain this we can draw both on McLaughlin's and Maxwell's explanations. In Matabeleland church hierarchies never imagined it possible to work with guerrillas, so the Avila transformation never took place. But no more did Maxwell's transforming popular Christian creativity.

Ncube and Ranger document the political conservatism of the Catholic hierarchies in southern Matabeleland. As for Protestantism, Carl Hallencreutz in his conference presentation on western Zimbabwean missionary Christianity, set up a pattern not unlike Maxwell's. The heads of what he calls 'regionally-based' Protestant mission churches (such as the Lutheran Evangelical Church) lived in the towns and were heavily involved in the 'moderate nationalism' of Muzorewa's ANC, 'at a time when their parishioners had to adjust themselves to the new challenges of guerrillas from both ZIPRA and ZANLA'. There is little evidence at present that either these parishioners or rural Black Catholics responded in Maxwell's creative and dynamic way. Maxwell himself suggests that the deeply rooted popular Christianity of Manicaland 'can be contrasted with Matabeleland, an area of very different cultural heritage. Popular Christianity seemed slow to take root among the Ndebele people. This is doubtless part of the reason why ZIPRA were able to knock out with great rapidity the whole succession of missions in Matabeleland.'

As Ncube and Ranger stress, there were many material reasons for the weakness of popular Christianity in Matabeleland. There was the hostility to mission-educated entrepreneurs, which found expression in revived African religion. There were the deep-seated grievances of the African tenants on the huge mission farms, long exposed not only to moral regulation but also to destocking and agricultural rules. (Neither factor operated in the area of Avila and Elim, which did not possess farms and whose educational provision was warmly welcomed by local Hwesa anxious to catch up with the skills of immigrant Manyika.)

But despite all this, it may nevertheless be that the impression of 'popular Christian' east and an 'indifferent Christian' west is also a misleading one. We have not had a detailed case-study like Maxwell's for southern Matabeleland. It may be that popular Christian creativity there should be sought in apolitical churches like the Seventh Day Adventists, who claim to have expanded greatly during the war in Matabeleland. Or it may be that we need to look at the totally unresearched African Independent Churches of southern Matabeleland, and in particular at Matabeleland Zionism.

Martinus Daneel — who *has* written at such length about Zionism in Masvingo — is now working towards a book on the role of Karanga Independent Churches during the war. Some of the Karanga churches have joined his ZIRCON, grouping together as the Association of African Earthkeeping Churches.[9] Daneel writes of 'the close assistance given by the ZCC congregations to the guerrilla fighters'. He goes on:

> But it was not only the ZCC which was actively supportive of the liberation struggle in Zimbabwe. *Ndaza* Zionists and Maranke's Apostolic prophets . . . played an increasingly prominent role at the war front as *chimurenga* escalated geographically into a full-blown bush war. In the same way that the traditional spirit mediums were providing the guerrillas with mystical ancestral guidance, prophets were also moving around with the fighters at the front, prophesying to them in the name of the Holy Spirit about enemy movements and other security matters . . . Like the traditional *varidzi venyika*, the Holy Spirit was experienced as a kind of 'guardian of the land' against the White intruders. Much depended on the predilections of Christian or non-Christian guerrilla commanders whether they opted for traditionalist or Christian prophetic guidance. Many of them made use of both, cross-checking the one against the other . . . Possibly the most important *chimurenga* function of some AIC prophets — similar to that of their *svikiro* counterparts — was to assist in community cleansing operations during *pungwe* meetings.[10]

This gives an additional dimension to the question we have discussed above as to why and when guerrillas chose African religion or Christianity. It also suggests that a study of Matabeleland Zionism would be richly rewarding. As we have said, the topic of Christianity in the war is not a new theme, but it is clear that much more research needs to be done in western Zimbabwe before we fully understand it.

Meanwhile, Ngwabi Bhebe gave the conference an oral report of his own research on the war-time experience of the Lutheran Evangelical Church in the Midlands and Matabeleland.[11] (The first part of his chapter in this volume is a condensed version of his oral presentation.) Among many other things, this provided an ironical commentary on the debate between Maxwell and McLaughlin. Bhebe showed that the Lutheran Church took its own 'Avila' decision when its mission fell into ZANLA's Gaza province of operations. The church leadership decided that there should be full co-operation. ZANLA guerrillas drew on the mission stations for cash, clothing and footwear; the missions responded by self-taxation of salaries and the appointment of buyers who used their own trucks to fetch supplies for the guerrillas from town. Yet in the end all this did not save the mission stations from the wrath of the people, and after closure during the height of violence many of them were looted and destroyed by the peasantry. Why was this?

The Lutheran missions may have had their own 'Avila moment' but they certainly did not have their own zones of Maxwell-style popular Christianity. Indeed, in Bhebe's oral presentation, the stations seemed less like rural missions and more like urban enclaves. They had hospitals, schools, highly paid African nurses, teachers and doctors, who employed cooks, gardeners and cleaners. They were centres of affluence and adjacent to them were commercial townships where local African businessmen, also Lutheran, ran stores and other enterprises. The mission élite were linked to Bulawayo by reliable transport services and often spent their week-ends in town; in any case they were linked to urban culture through their transistor radios and newspapers. One of the consequences of the war was that by 1977 all mission personnel were Black Zimbabweans but this made them no more integrated with surrounding rural society. The stations were petty-bourgeois communities which might be tolerated by the peasantry because of their services but which were also disliked because of their wealth. As Bhebe remarked, laborious and horny-handed peasants had no love for siesta-taking headmasters.

On top of all this, the mission stations' collaboration with ZANLA won them few local friends. Mission personnel were exempt from attendance at *pungwes* and guerrillas made a point of not entering mission premises so long as money and supplies were provided. Peasants deeply resented this exemption from their own sufferings and dangers. Moreover, if the area was a ZANLA war zone it was also a ZIPRA recruiting ground. ZIPRA did not engage in operations there but in desperate need of recruits it drew from the Lutheran schools and sometimes, as at Manama Mission, abducted whole school communities. Popular support for the guerrillas was expressed as much in volunteering for ZIPRA as in supplying ZANLA. In a very different way from Maxwell's, Bhebe's case study is as much social history as church history.

THE WAR, EDUCATION AND IDEOLOGY

Religion is in itself ideological. But religious innovations certainly did not exhaust the ways in which Zimbabweans tried to equip themselves to understand the war and prepare for post-war society. Nor for all their loudly proclaimed 'Christian civilization' did religious creativity have much to do with White Rhodesian war-time ideology.

This thematic section of our second volume groups together Anthony Chennells's chapter on 'Rhodesian discourse, Rhodesian novels and the Zimbabwe liberation war' with chapters by Fay Chung and Paulos Matjaka Nare on the creation of educational services in ZANU and ZAPU camps. The grouping seems incongruous but in fact Chung's and Nare's chapters might have been designed as an answer to the White Rhodesian myths which Chennells sets out.

As we have already remarked, Chennells shows that Whites saw Black society as fixed in unchanging attitudes. Whites could fit spirit mediums into this picture, for good or ill, and even attempt to make use of them. But they could not fit in Marxists or even professionally educated Africans. To most Rhodesian Whites, 'the war could not be a war. It could only be a rebellion, which meant, in settler mythology, primitive space attempting to re-absorb civilized space, and it was as a battle against this reassertion of the primitive that the war was described and indeed fought.'

Black Christians, well-clothed professionals and African Marxists all seemed extraneous to African society while at the same time unable to enter into and share the values of Europeans. They were pre-destined trouble-makers, able only to whip up and exploit rural resentment without being able to understand or control it. Thus, in Rhodesian novels, leaders of the Black rebellion are imagined sometimes as African Independent Church preachers, sometimes as 'fat-cat' politicians in exile, sometimes as ruthless Marxist ideologues. None of these, however, was thought to have anything to do with 'real' African society. So the White heroes of these novels might be able to frustrate the rebellion by themselves capturing 'tradition' and rural ideology and turning them against the agitators. It was beyond White Rhodesian imagination to conceive of an indigenized Marxism, an indigenized capitalism, or even an indigenized Christianity.

Now, we have already seen that rural 'tradition' was itself innovative, that Africans had indeed indigenized Christianity, and that Ngwabi Bhebe's Lutheran businessmen had gone far to indigenize capitalism. As Chennells insists, White Rhodesians were 'victims of their own discourses [and] had few means of correctly analyzing the situation in which they found themselves'. They could not have imagined the range of interactions between religion and the war which we have been discussing. Nor could they have comprehended that balance between 'Veterans', the radical 'Vashandi' and the spirit mediums which Fay Chung described for the ZANU camps in Mozambique.

What Fay Chung's and Paulos Matjaka Nare's chapters in this volume describe is yet another development beyond the Rhodesian imagination — the evolution by Zimbabweans themselves (rather than by Soviet ideological commissars) of a progressive education appropriate to the conditions of a new Zimbabwe. The frankness and humanity of their accounts reveal how much a Zimbabwean experiment this creation was.

At first sight, thought, it is disconcerting that in both ZAPU and ZANU camps the establishment of formal educational services came so late in the day — not until 1977. And it is perhaps also disconcerting that the new Zimbabwean education seems to have been so much 'constructed', by trial and error, by borrowings from here and there, and that it was hardly in place as an effective system by the time of Independence. Perhaps there is even a danger of confirming rather than shattering Rhodesian prejudices about the shallowness and eternality of radical ideas!

To understand these two chapters we need to understand why 1977 was the year of initiation of camp schools. It was as late as this because until then neither

ZAPU nor ZANU had enough teachers to staff a school or adult-education system, and because ZAPU in particular did not really have enough pupils. These chapters are not talking about ideological education for guerrillas. They are talking about education for the thousands of boys and girls who were too young to fight, and the thousands of men and women who were too old. In one sense ZIPRA's abduction of Manama school provided both pupils and teachers at a stroke and constituted a model for those extraordinary youth camps which developed in Zambia. In Mozambique, too, though there had been need for attention to the young and old for some time, it was only in 1977 that it became possible to provide it. Moreover, the chapters are about education provided by parties, and in Mozambique the power of ZANU as a party rather than of ZIPA as an army really only dates from 1977.

Thus before reading these chapters we need to go back to our first volume and to remind ourselves of the development of ideological education among the guerrillas prior to the setting up of these school systems. David Moore there describes how the young radicals of ZIPA 'under the impression that the war was now advancing under a qualitatively new mandate, hastened to construct the liberation movement's most important ideological initiative', Wampoa College at Chimoio. Wampoa was designed to enable a guerrilla élite to study 'Marxist works which had been denied the ZIPA cadres under the old regime'. It was also designed to construct an ideological 'line' on which ZANLA and ZIPRA guerrillas could unite. One hundred selected candidates were to come to Chimoio for an intensive four-months course in the basics of Marxism-Leninism. In the event the first (and only) four-months course offered a cultural nationalist 'geography' syllabus, stressing traditional religion and culture, as well as syllabi in historical materialism, dialectical materialism, political economy and formal logic. The hundred graduates of Wampoa were expected to return to the guerrilla camps to become teachers in their own right. Moore thinks the Wampoa experiment was full of promise but he admits some weaknesses also. The College was confessedly élitist. Many of the uneducated guerrillas were suspicious of this new élite and alienated 'from the apparently select and restricted democracy of the academy'. Moore argues that ZIPA intellectuals did not regard the uneducated as incapable of learning or of ideological transformation. On the contrary, the whole idea was to diffuse the ideology of Wampoa so as to transform the whole army. But there was no time: cleavages within ZIPA itself and the hostility of the ZAPU and ZANU 'old guards' brought the experiment to an end.

The developments of 1977 must be seen against this background. The Wampoa experiment had made the 'Veterans' suspicious of the whole idea of progressive education — so Paulos Matjaka Nare tells us that guerrillas in the Zambian camps suspected him and other teachers of being spies. In her doctoral thesis Janice McLaughlin provides two illustrations of the ZANLA 'Veteran' response to the Wampoa experiment:

When the veterans returned to Mozambique in early 1977 [after their release from prison in Zambia] they reasserted their leadership, causing some upheaval within ZANU. Their re-instatement resulted in the detention of some of the ZIPA commanders and political commissars . . . In July 1977 Chitepo College [as Wampoa College was later called] was closed. The oral evidence given by Josiah Magama Tongogara, ZANLA's Commander-in-Chief, to a committee investigating the closure of Chitepo College, provides some insights into the ideological divisions that had arisen. 'I went to Chitepo on 25 July 1977 and there were 258 comrades. I attended a lesson there. I spent the whole day. The lesson was about "Space and Time" . . . I told them to concentrate on the situation we have now, teaching Party line, not philosophy . . . I said we must not teach about space and time.'[12]

As for the Wampoa syllabus itself, McLaughlin tells us that its mere possession became 'a serious offence' and that 'as far back as early 1977' the ZANU Commissariat ordered that all Wampoa materials be surrendered to 'the Security Department of the respective camps'.[13]

It was against this vexed and sensitive background that progressive school education had to be developed. Fay Chung's chapter takes up the story after the collapse of ZIPA and the re-assertion of ZANLA. The first school was also set up at Chimoio but under very different auspices from those of Wampoa. Although ZANU's first Secretary for Education was Ernest Kadungure, 'a trained teacher as well as a veteran guerrilla', ZANU's more organized educational input developed in the context of 'a flood' of university lecturers and students into the party's ranks. Their Marxism, comments Chung, was more a function of 'the fashion for Marxism-Leninism in Western universities' than of the guerrilla ideology of Wampoa. Their educational aim was also wider — 'to establish an education system in the Mozambican camps that would incorporate ZANU's political agenda of national unity and national consciousness; socialism, anti-imperialism, anti-colonialism and anti-racism'. It was not a programme for an élite but was directed mainly to refugee children, together with adult literacy classes using the 'Paulo Freire method'. Nor was it designed to destroy tradition. Fay Chung ends her chapter by stressing that 'at no time [did] the spirit mediums oppose modern education, many of them having received primary education themselves'.

Her chapter describes the extraordinary practical difficulties and appalling dangers amidst which these camp schools were established in Mozambique. Paulos Matjaka Nare's describes the yet more difficult establishment of the ZAPU camp schools. There was a crippling shortage of teachers and books. The ZAPU schools never went beyond primary level and were far removed from the élite atmosphere of Wampoa College. Yet they, too, evolved a curriculum 'that would neatly address the socio-economic transformation required in the future independent Zimbabwe'. They stressed production, self-reliance and political education against 'suppressive and exploitative types of ruling systems'.

There was agreement among the participants at the conference that the creation of these camp schools had been a remarkable achievement. Preben Kaarsholm described the creativity of drama, dance and music in the ZAPU camps, where students were taught Sindebele, Shona and English, where praise-poems were performed to Mzilikazi and Lobengula, topical satirical plays were produced, and all this co-existed with a 'radically modernist' insistence on scientific socialist rationalism. McLaughlin described how impressed she had been by ZANU schools in Mozambique in 1978 with their atmosphere of 'real mental decolonization'; Carl Hallencreutz described his visit to ZAPU camps in 1979 and his impression that they constituted reconstructed societies of high morale. Jeremy Brickhill felt that Paulos Matjaka Nare had been too modest; in his view the ZAPU schools had saved a potentially lost generation by replacing parents and communities with a new collective identity. In contrast to the White myths of polarization set out in Chennells's chapter, the camp schools had instilled both 'traditional' and 'modern' ideologies. As Fay Chung pointed out, before their arrival in the camps urban child refugees had been as unfamiliar with spirit mediums as with Marxism and had to learn about both. There was little disposition to question this positive 'myth', save perhaps for Ngwabi Bhebe assuming the role of devil's advocate and asking whether so much could possibly have been achieved in barely over two years. Could an alternative system possibly have been built up in so short a time?

ZIMBABWEAN SOCIETY AFTER 1980: LEGACIES OF THE WAR

All the discussions at the conference — whatever the topic — raised the question of what happened after the war. What happened to progressive alternative education? What happened to African Christian initiatives? Was there a continued revival of African religion? What were the longer term results of war-time mobilization of peasants or of women? And have there been negative legacies of the war — continuities of terror, failures to restore the moral order?

The three chapters in our third and concluding section deal with some of these questions. Ngwabi Bhebe's examines the legacies of the war for the Lutheran Evangelical Church; Jocelyn Alexander's takes up the themes of mobilization and demobilization; Richard Werbner's describes the negative legacies of the war in Matabeleland. Conference discussions — not represented by any chapter in this volume — explored other issues, particularly the post-war history of progressive education, of African religion and of gender relations. It seems useful to summarize briefly first these discussions and then the three chapters.

PROGRESSIVE EDUCATION AFTER THE WAR

The conference asked why the Mozambican and Zambian models of revolutionary education had not been imported wholesale into independent Zimbabwe. Was Ngwabi Bhebe right to suspect that they did not really constitute an effective alternative structure? Or had they been undercut by the continuing power of conservative bureaucracy?

Fay Chung and Janice McLaughlin, who worked for many years with the Zimbabwe Foundation for Education with Production (ZIMFEP), were frank about the difficulties of implanting the camp system of education into Zimbabwe after 1980. McLaughlin described the return of 10 000 children from Zambia and Mozambique; their dumping on wrecked mission stations (including some of the southern Matabeleland stations discussed by Ncube and Ranger); the suspicion felt by educational bureaucrats for what they saw as 'military training camps preparing terrorists to invade South Africa'; the attempts made by these bureaucrats to starve the pupils out by cutting off their food supply, or to drive the teachers out by refusing to pay them or to give them demobilization grants. All this had a severe effect on morale.

Moreover, there were serious difficulties inherent in the evolution of the camp schools themselves. They had been very much party schools, and since ZAPU and ZANU/PF were so much opposed to each other after 1980 it was difficult to unite all the schools to form a single lobby for progressive education. They had also been very much military schools. As Paulos Matjaka Nare told the conference, ZAPU schools in Zambia had been under military discipline — 'after all, they punish also in socialist countries'. When ZIMFEP took over the schools, they had to continue with military discipline, 'otherwise they didn't think we were serious'. It had been difficult to move from military structures and ceremonies to participatory and co-operative patterns more appropriate to civil education.

Fay Chung writes in her chapter that in Mozambique 'plans were made regarding the take-over of the education system after Independence'. But in discussion she spoke of how such plans had been frustrated. When Dzingai Mutumbuka was appointed Minister of Education in 1980 he found himself entirely surrounded by the educational old guard. In their eyes he might just as well have 'come from Mars as from Mozambique'; there was weeping and gnashing of teeth for fear he should seek to introduce 'guerrilla education'. He was faced with a dilemma. Should he try to work with this old guard or should he replace it by bringing in all 600 members of his Education Department from Mozambique? In the end he brought in only Fay Chung; the rest of the 600 felt 'very great bitterness' and many left education altogether.

This was a comprehensive demobilization. McLaughlin argued that despite everything ZIMFEP had managed to keep the traditions of camp education alive and that these were likely to gain more relevance in the current crisis of unemployment. But most members of the conference felt that ZIMFEP was only marginally significant. How, then, are we to account for what happened — or failed to happen? Not, surely, in terms of White Rhodesian beliefs that transforming education is incompatible with African 'traditionalist' society. The explanation lies rather in that other aspect of Rhodesian discourse, which Chennells's chapter shows as having been constantly in tension with the notion of the unspoiled 'primitive', namely the sense of professional obligation to 'educate' Africans for their role in the economy. The educational bureaucracy inherited in 1980 prided itself on its 'professionalism' — just as we saw in our first volume that the criterion of professionalism has been applied to the integrated Zimbabwean National Army. This ideal of professionalism has been one of the real continuities between Rhodesia and Zimbabwe. It is this which has smothered the creative impulses of war-time radical education.

Perhaps, then, we should raise the question of continuity about Chennells's chapter as well. It ends: 'Both the discursive space and the literal geographical space in which racist legislation had been embodied over the years were smashed by war. With Mugabe's victory at the polls both the discourse and the Rhodesia which produced it were simultaneously swept away.'

But were they, utterly and completely? We refer here not to the little knots of rural White racists, muttering in the country club bar. We refer to the continuities of official thinking. It is possible to argue that class has replaced race in official discourse but that its terms otherwise remain much the same.[14] Do not urban 'experts' still regard peasants as locked in unchanging and irrational traditionalism, despite all the counter evidence of the war? Has there not been an unbroken continuity of thought (and projects) between colonial and Zimbabwean development experts? Even if Rhodesian novelists no longer thrive, the dichotomy between 'civilized' and 'primitive' lives on.

AFRICAN RELIGION AND INDEPENDENT CHURCHES AFTER THE WAR

Since Independence the great spirit mediums of the first *chimurenga*, Nehanda and Kaguvi, have become the pre-eminent national heroes. Histories of ZANLA's campaigns have paid tribute to the role of the mediums in the second *chimurenga*. Nevertheless, there has been no continuation of the war-time alliance. McLaughlin's doctoral thesis shows that even during the war Robert Mugabe himself was sceptical about the mediums, telling Father Traber in April 1979 that 'there are just too many *midzimu* . . . far beyond the traditional Shona belief. It's all too much for my liking.'[15] After the war, the government sought to define the *mhondoro* out of any political role. It allocated an exclusively healing role to them, lumping them together with *n'angas* as members of the Zimbabwe National Traditional Healers Association (ZINATHA). This blurred the key distinction which the guerrillas had observed between mediums and diviners.

Daneel, whose ZIRCON involves defining the mediums differently — as ecological guardians — tells us that:

> The imposition of a socialist-Marxist model of local government in the rural areas curtailed the land allocation and customary judiciary powers of chiefs. Consequently, both chiefs and *masvikiro* — offices which were always integrally related to tribal politics — were weakened and lost some of their prestige. The *masvikiro* in particular, after their rise to national prominence as *chimurenga* heroes, soon became frustrated with

their relative obscurity in the post-war period. Modern politics, they felt, did not accord them sufficient recognition for the key roles they had played in the liberation struggle. Nor could they effectively bring their spiritual authority to bear on modern processes of land and community development.[16]

Hence mediums in Masvingo and elsewhere blamed drought on the new government's failure to recognize the spiritual authority of the ancestors. African religious movements offered rural populations one way to criticize professional modernization projects imposed from above.

Ncube and Ranger's research in Matabeleland has revealed a yet more intense sense of post-war crisis — military, political, economic, ecological. The dominant idiom in which this sense of crisis has been expressed is a search for explanations of the drought which has afflicted Matabeleland in most years since Independence. In this context the rain-shrines of Mwali have been increasingly influential. The ZAPU leaders had regular recourse to the shrines prior to the Unity Agreement and the amnesty; ZANU-PF ministers supported Shona-speaking claimants to the Njelele priesthood; new or revived shrines have begun to operate in northern Matabeleland. In these ways, the nationalist interaction with African religion continued in Matabeleland after 1980 while there was a rupture elsewhere in Zimbabwe between the nation-state and populist African religion. Now that Joshua Nkomo and other ex-ZAPU leaders are part of the government, however, we may expect a similar cleavage to develop in Matabeleland too.[17]

African Independent Churches have had mixed fortunes since Independence. Those which oppose vaccination, hospital treatment, formal education and raising the national flag have come under constant criticism from government and the press. Press editorials have accused Zionists and Vapostori of being stuck in the negative anti-colonial nationalism of the 1930s rather than having graduated to national developmentalism. But Daneel has a different report about Zionism:

> The focus of the AICs in the post-war situation shifted significantly from political to socio-economic liberation. The Holy Spirit was now seen more as the liberator from poverty and economic despair, intimately involved through the AICs in nation building. In this phase development projects and even educational training centres at AIC headquarters — such as the multi-million college erected by Bishop Nehemiah Mutendi (son and successor of the late Samuel Mutendi) at Zion City — became signs of God's blessings on his people, his concretized salvation in black holy cities.[18]

From this perspective, African Independent Churches (like African religion) are not so much hostile to 'development' as engaged in a dispute over who should define and implement it.

GENDER AND STATUS IN POST-WAR ZIMBABWE

There have not so far been any fully satisfactory gendered accounts of the war and its aftermath.[19] Instead there have been too many attempts to produce a heroic 'herstory' of the war: attempts which have over-estimated the number of female guerrillas and over-stated the emancipatory mobilization of women. Nor was there any presentation at the conference which succeeded in giving such a gendered account. Heike Schmidt issued a necessary challenge to the participants in her 'Gender and status: Implications for the Zimbabwean liberation war'. She pointed out that in much recent academic literature gender has been in the text but not in the analysis, and she went on to propose some analytical questions that need to be asked about gender relations and the war. With her agreement we have not included her presentation in this volume. It was made before she had conducted her own field research in the Honde Valley, refined her questions, and begun to come up with answers. For the moment the best that we can do is to alert the reader to the forthcoming appearance of Heike Schmidt's work and that of other current researchers.[20]

During the conference, however, there were many scattered references to gender, and to the experience of women, just as there are in recent theses. These need to be set in an analytical framework such as Schmidt proposed in order to bear fruit. Still, they were stimulating and it seems worth-while to bring them together here.

Fay Chung suggested that faction disputes with ZANU in Mozambique had a gender dimension. In particular, she suggested, the Nhari rebels against the 'Veterans' attracted the support of women because many of the 'Veterans' forcibly commandeered women as part of their proper privileges. There was also a gender dimension in the struggle between the 'Veterans' and the 'Vashandi'. As we have seen, Chung described what she called 'puritanical' oppositions of two sorts: one from the young left radicals who proposed a new set of gender relations, the other from spirit mediums who accused the 'Veterans' of breaking traditional prohibitions. This, of course, was a debate which raged inside Zimbabwe itself during the war. As David Lan has shown, mediums imposed stringent sexual prohibitions upon guerrillas; at the same time radical political commissars sought to enforce rules of conduct for interaction with civilian populations. But there were many breaches of these prohibitions, as some guerrillas exercised the same 'rights' over young women which the 'Veterans' enjoyed in Mozambique. (Needless to say, there were also many examples of rape by members of the Security Forces and the Auxiliaries, often as an assertion of 'status' against guerrillas).

Women were also particularly, though by no means exclusively, affected by witch-finding and witch-killing during the war. While a good deal has been written about guerrilla interventions to improve the status of rural women, too little has been said about the contrary effects of the vast increase in witchcraft accusations and executions. Meanwhile, even if, as they claimed, Auxiliaries did not hunt witches, their 'disciplining' of the young rural assistants to guerrillas often fell disproportionately on the girl *chimbwidos*.

At the same time it was clear that during the war women were not merely the objects of exploitation or of protective taboo. There were, of course, women guerrillas (of whom too little was heard at the conference), though these had to contend with the confused sexual and gender morality of the liberation war. Moreover, as Norma Kriger has suggested, and as Heike Schmidt argued, some rural women were able to make use of guerrillas to further their protest against patriarchal oppression. And in Zimbabwean rural areas, from which so many men were absent, women came to take on 'masculine' roles and characteristics. Richard Werbner's chapter in this volume describes how in south-western Matabeleland 'some older women, unarmed yet driven to resistance in defence of their homes . . . had acted with that heroic quality usually attributed to men, of *chibindi*, fierceness, reckless courage'.

Maxwell's chapter argues that women also took on male roles even in that bastion of patriarchy, the Catholic Church:

> At Avila Mission the local Carmelite Sisters came into their own as [Father] Peter Egan's flight was followed by the arrest of two Black priests at the end of 1976. Rural African women in Manicaland had struggled for half a century for the right to enter holy orders and had finally gained recognition in 1959. Now they, too, had a chance to prove themselves and . . . conducted priestless services, taught the faith and ran the institution.

McLaughlin's thesis has a section entitled 'Religious Women — Invisible Heroes' which makes the same point in more detail. She points out that African sisters suffered 'from the racism in the Church and in the society, as well as from sexism', but that the 'liberation war propelled [them] into the forefront for change'. Much more numerous than Black male priests, and locally based, they constituted the Church's major point of contact with the guerrillas. 'The war made us stay alert', one told McLaughlin. 'We were united by the suffering in the war . . . We didn't want to be comfortable while other people were suffering. We stayed on in the rural missions.'[21]

Similar points have been made for the Protestant churches. Thus Crispen Mazobere, now Bishop of the Methodist Church, writes:

> The Manyano/Ruwadzano with their black skirts, red blouses and white head-gear should be truly expressive of the redemptive path . . . The work of outstanding women of faith and sacrificial service to Christ, like that of Mrs Mazila Maliposa of Siabuwa, points to some of the merit Zimbabwean Methodists should uphold. This woman of no academic attainment, only equipped of Christ's spirit, held her people together almost single-handed during the most dangerous times during the armed struggle. Ordained ministers were moved to security while she stood the ground of Christian witness and kept the Lord's flock going.[22]

At the same time, examples were given during conference discussions of continuities of particularly female roles. Carl Hallencreutz remarked that when he visited the ZAPU camps in Zambia in 1979 he was struck by the social role of older women, to which Paulos Matjaka Nare replied that in Victory Camp social and familial relationships sprang up spontaneously between *omasulu* older women and the girls, while in the boys' camps there were few older men and no real creation of social relations between the generations. Richard Werbner's chapter shows how Kalanga women, once the key participants in *shumba* cults of possession by 'domestic demons', have become major figures in the *sangoma* healing cult of ancestral possession which memorializes and activates the war dead.

Even without an over-arching analytical framework, these scattered references show that no simple model of 'mobilization' or 'emancipation' of women during the war is tenable. They also suggest that we cannot discuss the legacy of the war for gender relations simply in terms of the fulfillment or non-fulfillment of the emancipatory promise.

This has, of course, been attempted. In his recent doctoral thesis Ken Manungo argues for the importance of what he calls 'guerrilla justice', both during the war and after it. He holds that this can best be shown in the case of gender. During the war, he writes:

> Women found that the charge of adultery against local men fell on sympathetic guerrilla ears far more readily than they would if laid before local officials in the context of a tradition which condoned extra-marital relations. Because of the breakdown of the chief's traditional court, the guerrillas presented themselves as the new adjudicators of civil cases in the rural areas. They claimed a system of justice which listened to everyone, regardless of gender.

After the war, he argues, 'a brief look at the post-colonial Zimbabwean application of social justice, particularly in the realm of women's affairs, reveals the continuity between ZANU's war-time patterns of guerrilla justice and the present system.' Manungo cites the Legal Age of Majority Act, the Maintenance Act and the Ministry of Women's Affairs as proof of the continuation of the sensitivity to gender discrimination first revealed in the 'war-time guerrilla courts'.[23]

There have been many others who have totally discounted the Zimbabwe government's intentions and maintain that rural women have reverted to all the disadvantages and oppressions of colonial Rhodesia. So far as gender relations are concerned, the revolution has been betrayed.

Neither of these extreme positions seem plausible. As Heike Schmidt argued at the conference, and as her recent work amply demonstrates, the wartime experience of women was so varied and contradictory that no simple discontinuities or continuities can be discerned. The 'spaces' opened by the war for women have been closed for some but not for all. The ambiguities of the war have helped to produce the present confused and contradictory state of gender relations. As

Josephine Nhongo's current research is demonstrating, there was no straight-forward mobilization of women even in ZANLA areas of Mozambique. The present situation cannot be seen simply as a result of 'demobilization'. These seem to us sensible conclusions, far removed from the usual extremes of judgement on post-war Zimbabwean society, where everything is either marvellously transformed by the revolution or terribly untransformed by the revolution's betrayal. The effects of the war are more contradictory, pervasive and long-term than such judgements can accommodate.

MISSION CHRISTIANITY AFTER THE WAR

We turn now to the issues raised by the three chapters which deal with post-war Zimbabwe. Ngwabi Bhebe's account of how the scars of war have been healed in the Evangelical Lutheran Church of Zimbabwe (ELCZ) is certainly richly full of contradictions and ambiguities. We have already summarized his account of the tensions between the urban leaders of the church, the mission-station élite, the peasant parishioners; between the claims of Muzorewa's UANC on 'moderate' Protestants, of ZANLA guerrillas on teachers and nurses and businessmen, of ZIPRA recruiters on boys and girls. To these class and ideological cleavages he adds ethnic tensions.

During the war itself these ethnic tensions were present but were not decisive. Gwanda and Mberengwa — the Lutheran zone — were multi-lingual and multi-cultural. Before the war the whole area supported ZAPU; during the war ZANLA's omnipresence gave ZANU more influence than ZAPU. But both guerrilla armies operated easily in this culturally mixed zone. *After* the war, however, a political struggle replaced the military. ZAPU recruited among Ndebele-speakers, ZANU among Shona-speakers. The Venda-speakers were caught in between and divided between the two parties. As Bhebe writes: 'The ELCZ parishes too became ethnically divided and these divisions tended to harden during the civil war in Matabeleland. Because the church mirrored national divisions it was virtually impossible to overcome the church's divisions until a national peace was arranged.'

But it was made yet more difficult by the other cleavages in the church. During the war Bishop Shiri was stranded in Bulawayo and cut off from the sufferings of rural Lutherans. His nationalism expressed itself more in his insistence that the church should be independent of the Church of Sweden Mission than in any attempt to ensure that rural lay people, who had borne the brunt of the war, had a voice in its affairs. The totally African church hierarchy was alienated from the local mission élites, from the peasantry, and from the Ndebele-speaking Western Deanery. The war had brought about the indigenization of the ELCZ and the radicalization of rural Lutherans. But it also left the church in total and scandalous disarray.

Bhebe's chapter confirms Maxwell's emphasis upon the tensions between church structures and the Christian grassroots which everywhere emerged as a legacy of the war. But it does not confirm Maxwell's prediction that grassroots Christian creativity will win the day. When in the end the disarray of the ELCZ became too scandalous and party politicians intervened, they did not insist on the autonomy of the parishes. Instead they refurbished the bureaucratic structures of the church.

In 1991 many of the mission-founded churches celebrated their centenaries. There were many professions of appreciation by President Mugabe. But it seemed to be the institutional rather than the inspirational church to which this appreciation was directed — its schools, hospitals, development schemes. For their part the mission-descended churches have sought to collaborate with the government in 'nation-building' and 'development' and have played down their prophetic and spiritual role. The church hierarchies, now fully indigenized, have regained and increased their old power and become part of the Zimbabwean establishment, manifesting an ecclesiastical professionalism to go along with military, educational and developmental professionalism. There has not seemed much room for the creativities of popular Christianity or for further expressions of law and female initiative.

But here, too, it is not a simple matter of the revolution betrayed rather than consummated. The dialectic of the war has not yet worked itself out. The rise of the discourse of 'civil society' may reactivate the emphasis upon mobilization and the grassroots. As an editorial in the August 1991 issue of the *Southern African Political and Economic Monthly* put it:

> On the part of the Church [there is an] inevitable feeling of guilt and therefore an overzealous attempt to exonerate itself from the colonial legacy . . . On its part the post-colonial state seeks to capitalize on this feeling of guilt . . . The Church is, more often than not, a status designation confined to those established denominations that have been part and parcel of the various socio-economic and political orders that have variously characterized Africa's modern history: and less representative of the masses that constitute its following. For the Church to become the kind of social force that it should be in the broader Civil Society, it is imperative that it, too, seeks to establish the democratic framework that will ensure that all the various elements — big and small, hierarchy and rank and file — are fully represented and reflected in whatever is said to be the voice of that which is recognized as the Church. This would render the Church even more effective as it seeks, as it should, to constrain and restrain the excesses of the state in post-colonial society.

THE GRASSROOTS, THE PARTY AND THE STATE

These questions have not arisen, of course, only in the post-war churches or in relation to gender. The rural population as a whole was 'mobilized' during the war. When the war ended initiative seemed to lie with local party branches and tribunals or with peasant committees occupying and allocating land. Jocelyn Alexander's chapter is primarily about what happened to 'guerrilla justice' and to these local structures of mobilization in the ZANLA district of Chimanimani. Her story is perhaps predictable. There was never a very realistic hope that power could continue to reside with these grassroots bodies. But the details of how this possibility came to an end are surprising and paradoxical and relate to many of the issues raised in the introductions to these volumes.[24]

It is unexpected that after so much debate about the one-party state in Zimbabwe she is able to show so convincingly that the main loser in Chimanimani since 1980 has been the local party, which now hardly exists as an instrument of policy making or of mobilization. It is also unexpected, after so much has been written on the decline of chiefs, that she is able to show chiefs and other 'traditionalists' as important players in Chimanimani's politics of competitive patriarchies. Tungamirai's chapter in our first volume follows David Lan in arguing that authority passed from chiefs to mediums in eastern Zimbabwe. Alexander has never been able to believe this. Both in Chimanimani — and in her second case-study district, Insiza — the most powerful chiefs have been nationalist activists who play an influential role today. She is able to show, moreover, that leadership of the opposition to state bureaucratic power in Chimanimani has passed by default into the hands of the chiefs. Since there is no locally dynamic party and no effective peasant organization, only chiefs and mediums, by appealing to 'tradition', can oppose villagization or tenurial 'reform' and continue to demand the restoration of the lost lands. In this way, the chiefs keep open some of the space which the war gave to local peasants; but they do so at the expense of closing some of the space which the war gave to women. Dr Manungo's 'guerrilla justice' and its embodiment in legislation favourable to women's rights finds short shrift in the newly restored chief's courts.

Like Heike Schmidt, Alexander is not arguing that all has been betrayed. Chimanimani since 1980 is very different from what it was in colonial times. Many of the aspirations of the elders who dominated anti-colonial mass nationalism have been achieved, and even popular demands have been to some extent assuaged by land transfer. But as the land frontier closes in Chimanimani, as elsewhere, Alexander's work poses the question whether the blocking of spaces opened by the war will mean the confirmation of the dominance of bureaucrats and patriarchs or whether other elements will compel the opening of new spaces.

NEGATIVE LEGACIES: MATABELELAND AFTER THE WAR

The developments we have so far been discussing — the recovery of hierarchy, bureaucracy, professionalism — can be seen as socially conservative but they have been one way of restoring order and normalcy after the violence of war. Yet the war left destructive legacies of continuing terror and abnormality. These are the subject of Richard Werbner's disturbing chapter. As Werbner shows, in south-western Matabeleland appalling violence came to an end only with the amnesty of 1988. The traditions which had been established during the liberation war — ZIPRA, ZANLA and Security Force traditions — fell into the different pattern of 'dissidents', Fifth Brigade and professional army during the 1980s. The result was a violence yet more arbitrary and unendurable for the civilian population than that of the war itself.[25]

Like Ngwabi Bhebe's discussion of the ELCZ, Werbner's chapter describes the development of ethnicity after 1980. In the introductions to these volumes we have been consistently arguing for the similarities rather than the differences between ZAPU/ZIPRA and ZANU/ZANLA. Both were nationalist movements, making their appeal to the whole Zimbabwean nation. Their attitude to rural culture was very similar. They simultaneously developed very similar systems of progressive education in the refugee camps in Zambia and Mozambique. Both guerrilla armies were able to operate in more than one language zone. While Ncube and Ranger show that there was a specifically 'Matabele' rural cultural nationalism, they also show that there existed in Matabeleland a series of overlaying identities — from 'Kalanga' to 'Ndebele' to 'Zimbabwean' — with none an obstacle to participating in the others. In short, there is much to argue against any idea that from the beginning ZAPU/ZIPRA represented 'the Ndebele' and ZANU/ZANLA represented ' the Shona'.

Nevertheless, however fortuitously, the two guerrilla movements came to operate out of different front-line states — ZIPRA from Zambia and ZANLA from Mozambique — and hence entered, dominated and recruited from different regions. In their intense interactions with local culture, guerrillas necessarily mobilized local senses of identity and were not always able or concerned to generalize them. The 'working cultures' of the ZAPU and ZANU camps came to be markedly different. As Masipula Sithole repeated in his address to the conference, factions within the parties and armies often mobilized support by making ethnic appeals. In all these ways the war intensified ethnic identification and self-identification as well as intensifying the sense of Zimbabwean nationhood. Moreover, the war involved an inevitable dehumanization of opponents, who were stigmatized as 'the other.'

Ngwabi Bhebe makes the point that in Gwanda and Mberengwa ethnic differences became much more dangerous *after* the war. Richard Werbner shows the tragic working out of this war-time legacy in south-western Zimbabwe after 1980, a working out in which ethnic identifications were accentuated to the point of caricature and in which the techniques and slogans of national liberation were abused and dishonoured on both sides. Werbner writes:

> The nationalist struggle [had] fed and in turn was fed by its antithesis, the polarization of two quasi-nations or super-tribes, the Shona against the Ndebele . . . The catastrophe of quasi-nationalism is that it can capture the might of the nation state and bring authorized violence down ruthlessly against the people who seem to stand in the way of the nation being united and pure as one body . . . It is as if quasi-nationalism's victims, by being of an opposed quasi-nation, put themselves outside the nation, indeed beyond the pale of humanity.

He argues that such quasi-nationalist ferocity was displayed in Matabeleland after 1980, in murders by dissidents and in the operations of the Shona-speaking Fifth Brigade, 'a punitive army which, along with the police, behaved like an occupying force come down upon an alien people'. Yet the Fifth Brigade also played out 'certain parts created in the liberation war'. It held *pungwes*, where Kalanga-speakers were made to sing Shona *chimurenga* songs. It acted as though it was the true maker of Zimbabwe as a nation. The effect upon the Kalanga-speaking people of the south-west, confronted by a state army which behaved like a guerrilla army, and which through 'political education' told them that they were 'really' Shona, was to confirm yet more strongly their own complex sense of identity. It made them feel simultaneously more 'Kalanga' and more 'Ndebele'. Now, after unity and amnesty, the work has to begin all over again to make them feel more Zimbabwean.

What needs to be done is to deploy the truly nationalist, progressive and liberationary legacies of the war rather than the quasi-nationalist and coercive ones. The conference — itself only made possible by the unity agreement — was one example of such a process. It sought to bring into view all the participants in the struggle and to give each a place in a complex, plural movement for liberation. In this way, it might be hoped, the history of the war could be uniting rather than divisive, while in its complexity such a history would at the same time caution against single 'pure' identities and single, simple solutions.

CONCLUSION

We should end this introduction by reflecting on a theme which emerges from many of the chapters in this volume — the theme of healing. The war was a time of terror and trauma; the period after the end of the war has been for many a time of frustration or of continued guilt and grief. Many of the chapters in this volume record attempts to deal with such disruptive pain.

African religion has been deeply involved. Maxwell compares post-war healing by *n'angàs* to healing of memories within popular Christianity, stressing the centrality of confession in both; Richard Werbner emphasizes the 'need to be cleansed from wartime acts of violence and violation' and the consequent 'great revival' of *sangoma* cults, with 'their specially costumed embodiment of the dead, their revelatory messages warning people against forgetting the past, their fixing of blame for neglect of the dead, their herbal prescriptions for cleansing and protection, their dancing and drumming, their blood sacrifices and other ritual acts of therapy.' African religious spokesmen call for the healing of society and of the environment as well as for individual cleansing. Ncube and Ranger quote a priest of Mwali lamenting that after the war the guerrilla armies had not been sent to the shrines *en masse* to be cleansed of blood; Daneel writes that spirit mediums in AZTREC 'call for the ravished land to be clothed once more with trees'.[26]

The Christian churches have also been deeply involved in healing. Maxwell describes how the Elim massacre has been transformed into triumph by the healing conversion of its perpetrators. The centenary volume of the Methodist Church describes how in 1980 a predominantly Black Methodist group came together to heal 'Europeans who [were] deeply spiritually and psychologically disturbed as a direct result of the war'.[27] Independent Churches prophets have healed those against whom there were still unresolved suspicions of witchcraft.

We would ourselves see history as a form of healing. In his opening address to the conference, Professor Walter Kamba declared that Zimbabweans need to understand the war 'for healing of memories'. He expressed his pleasure that the conference was to end with presentations on 'popular history' and went on:

> We must make good the claim that there is no barrier between university history and popular history . . . We [must not] claim academic freedom as a privilege, just for us, so that we can enjoy clever discussions above the head of the mob. Academic freedom is a *duty* to set all one's gifts unsparingly in the service of the people. And that is nowhere more obvious than in the business of this conference. Zimbabweans need knowledge about the war. It is your job to learn from them and to make available what you have learned. I believe that in doing so you serve and vitalize not only academic research here but also . . . everywhere where there are self-serving myths to contest and where men and women of the mind need to share in the passion of the people.

Quoting Pamela Reynolds's work on healing by *n'angas*, Maxwell writes that 'unless the patient tells the truth the ritual is ineffective'. There is no one truth about the war. Still, unless each historian tells the truth as best they can, this historical remedy will also be ineffective. We think that the contributors to this volume, as to the first, have told the truth as they see it, to the best of their ability. We hope that the two volumes will provoke yet further confessions and explorations so that the healing truths about Zimbabwe's liberation war, in all their complexity and ambiguity, all their glory and terror, become yet more plain.[28]

1

Religion in the Guerrilla War: The Case of Southern Matabeleland

TERENCE RANGER
MARK NCUBE[1]

INTRODUCTION

There is a striking contrast in our present picture of the guerrilla war between a 'religious' eastern Zimbabwe and a 'secular' south-west. In eastern Zimbabwe we possess David Lan's remarkable study of the interaction between guerrillas and spirit mediums.[2] In eastern Zimbabwe, too, though some Christian churches were attacked by guerrillas, others worked closely with them.[3] In the south-west, by contrast, it seems that 'traditional religion' played no part in the war, while almost all the large mission stations in the region were attacked or abandoned.

If this contrast survives further research, there are two possible broad explanations, one to do with differences between the guerrilla movements and the other with differences between the religious systems of east and west. Thus Jeremy Brickhill has argued a series of propositions for ZIPRA which bear upon our question. His analysis of questionnaire material on recruitment to ZIPRA suggests that it was a force drawn from largely urban sources, often from young men in industrial employment. He proposes a contrast between the 'proletarian' army and ZANLA's 'peasant' forces — a contrast likely to predispose ZIPRA to secular ideologies while ZANLA was likely to respect rural 'traditional' culture. He also suggests a contrast on the ground. After the banning of the nationalist parties in 1964, ZAPU branches continued to exist underground in most parts of the country. Hence when ZIPRA guerrillas entered an area, they were able to work with the ZAPU elders, draw recruits and auxiliaries from the ZAPU Youth League, and food and supplies from the ZAPU women's organizations. ZIPRA guerrillas, in short, did not 'need' to construct a new political ideology but drew upon already established rural nationalism. By contrast, ZANLA guerrillas did not inherit existing party committees and had to construct their own networks. They needed to create a combined ideology of guerrilla and peasant beliefs and to work in each place with the legitimate religious leaders of the people.

It would be possible, on the other hand, to explain the contrast between eastern and south-western Zimbabwe in terms of differences between the religious systems themselves. Thus while David Lan has shown how spirit mediums could speak for the original conquering ancestors and express their support for the guerrilla war, most scholarship on the Mwali/Mlimo cult of the south-west has emphasized its total commitment to peace and fertility. Perhaps the Mwali shrines and their officers were just not 'available' to guerrillas. Moreover, it is arguable that Christianity was less deeply rooted and 'popular' in rural Matabeleland than in eastern Zimbabwe. Missionaries who had experienced the flowering of African Christianity in Manicaland often bemoaned the comparative indifference of their congregations in Matabeleland. And in any case the Christianity of the Zimbabwean south-west was divided between a fundamentalist and apolitical Protestantism and the conservative paternalism of the Mariannhill Catholics. Perhaps south-western Christianity was also not 'available' for alliances with the guerrillas.

In short, if the apparent contrast between 'secular' Matabeleland and 'religious' eastern Zimbabwe turns out to be real, there are plausible combined explanations for it. The aim of this chapter, however, is to test both the contrast and the explanations. Its finding is that the contrast is only partly true and that some of the explanations are more plausible than others. It must be stressed that this chapter is in itself very preliminary, based as it is on a selection of indicative material rather than a decisive mass of data. If seems useful, nevertheless, to raise questions for further research.

AFRICAN RELIGION AND CULTURAL NATIONALISM IN MATABELELAND

Let us suppose, to begin with, that Brickhill is right to emphasize that the ideology of the guerrilla war in Matabeleland reflected rural nationalism. The question then is how secular was that nationalism? A tentative answer is that political nationalism in Matabeleland had been accompanied by an ever more influential cultural nationalism, and that this cultural nationalism increasingly appealed to religious ideas. It seems that there were two currents at work — one in the rural areas where a symbiosis of 'Ndebele' identity and 'pre-Ndebele' religion was being worked out from the 1950s onwards; the other in the towns, and especially in Bulawayo, where urban nationalist intellectuals articulated a broad 'Ndebele' identity and sought to draw on the whole historical and cultural tradition of Matabeleland. These two currents were linked particularly through the figure of Joshua Nkomo. By the time of the guerrilla war, it can be argued, the 'heritage' of African religion had become an integral part of western Zimbabwean cultural nationalism — part of a composite rural ideology — which it would be difficult for guerrillas to override, however proletarian and secular their own attitudes might be.

A brief account of these two currents is necessary. The 1950s were a critical period of conceptual transformation in rural Matabeleland. Up to that time protest against threats of eviction, destocking, enforcement of agricultural rules, forced labour, etc, had been articulated by a local Christian 'progressive' leadership. Thus in the area of the Matopos themselves — despite the fact that they were the site of the main Mwali shrines — opposition in the late 1940s and early 1950s did not draw at all on claims of antiquity vested in traditional religion. In the National Park the Sofasonke protest association, led by the London Missionary Society radical, Nqabe Tshuma, held its meetings at the London Missionary Society church and school in Whitewaters. In Wenlock the Sofasihamba protest association was led by members — or ex-members — of the Brethren-in-Christ mission at Mtshabezi. Opposition in the Matopo Reserve drew upon the African Christian élite of the Matopo Mission. These linked protest movements appealed to the 'promises' implicit in the colonial moral economy — the 'promises' of Cecil Rhodes to allow 'the Ndebele' undisturbed occupation of the Matopos; the 'promises' of the absentee owners of Wenlock Ranch, whose agent, Richardson, had ruled over the area in patriarchal style; the 'promises' of the missionaries that African entrepreneurial farmers would be rewarded rather than evicted. When there was a Commission of Inquiry into African rights in the Matopos, Sofasonke's lawyer, Paddy Lloyd. took it upon himself to stress the antiquity and importance of the Mwali shrines and their historic links with the population threatened with eviction. But Sofasonke spokesmen themselves relied upon 'Ndebele' identity, Christian progressivism and the 'promises' of Rhodes. And even when Sofasonke members began to seek links with radical proto-nationalist organizations, like Benjamin Burombo's African Voice Association, their message laid more stress on universal African proletarianism than on cultural nationalism.[4]

After the failure of Sofasonke and Sofasihamba, evictions from the Matopos, destocking in Wenlock and enforced agricultural rules in the Matopos Reserve, there was a rapid abandonment of appeals to colonial moral economy and a movement into nationalism. The earliest rural branches of the revived African National Congress in Matabeleland were established in the Matopos or the African areas to the south of them. But the leaders of the new nationalism were still educated entrepreneurs, traders and store-owners in particular. These men had been part of the mission Christian élite, and still revealed many mission values, but many of them were now at odds with the missionaries, critical of the inadequacies of mission education, resentful of the authoritarian rule of missionaries over the tenants on church farms. Under their leadership, therefore, rural nationalism in Matabeleland was taking on the character of a critique by frustrated modernizers of colonial restrictions on African enterprise.

So far, so secular — or, so far, so plainly on the way from Christian progressivism to secular modernist nationalism. Bu then, at the end of the 1950s, another note enters the story of rural anti-colonial ideology. The rural entrepreneurs themselves came under pressure from a more radical rejection of colonial ideas and forms; large numbers of small peasants began to express a rejection of their own modernization as well as of colonial destocking, eviction and agrarian rules. This rejection partly took the form of a revival of the influence over agriculture of the Mwali shrines of the Matopos.

Striking instances of this revival — together with the scandalized reaction of rural modernizers — can be found in that journal of the progressives, the *Bantu Mirror*.

On 27 December 1958 the *Mirror* carried a rather garbled story from Insiza, describing how an 'evangelist' had called together all villagers at Vizhe school 'for the purpose of praying for rain . . . at the foot of one of the mountains'. It was announced that 'all Wednesdays would be observed as a day on which prayers will be said to the 'God of Rain' . . . a decision was taken that those people who do not obey the rule of not working on Wednesdays be dealt with. Villagers were allowed to work on Sundays at their fields but not on Wednesdays.' Plainly the 'evangelist' was an emissary of one of the Mwali shrines and the issue at stake was the highly visible and symbolic one of whether the Christian progressive Sunday or the 'traditional' Wednesday should be observed as the day of rest. Progressives who ignored the Wednesday prohibition were to 'be dealt with'.

On 10 January 1959 the *Mirror* recorded the horrified response of the teacher at Vizhe School, R. M. Mhlanga, who expressed 'my greatest horror of my life about what I see here':

> People here at Insiza have chosen to keep Wednesday holy. The reason, I am told, is that on Wednesday the goddess at the Matopo Hills ordered them that should they plough or cultivate on Wednesdays they will have offended her and as a result she will not send them rain. The result is that people have taken to ploughing on Sundays. Worse still, the chief has made it a rule, no let me call it a law, that no one should do field work on a Wednesday.

Mhlanga attacked 'uneducated chiefs' who did not know how to read the Bible. 'There is only one God — Jehovah — and not Ngwali.'

What was really striking about this Insiza case was that the chief was very much 'Ndebele' but that he was now enforcing the commands of the 'Kalanga' Mwali cult. Clearly a symbiosis of rural cultural traditions was taking place. And even more strikingly by the middle of January 1959 the 'Wednesday Movement' had spread to the very stronghold of progressive nationalism and of self-conscious Ndebele chiefship, the Simukwe Reserve, south of the Matopos. Simukwe was Joshua Nkomo's home area; he had opened a branch of Congress there as early as February 1958; the branch had campaigned vigorously against inadequate schooling, destocking and land shortage. The secretary of the Simukwe branch was a progressive store-keeper, John Mano Dube, who had previously been Secretary of the Matopo South Reserve Council. In short, early nationalism in Simukwe was typically focussed on demands for modernizing self-help by Christian educated men who were now falling out with the missionaries. Dube attacked the limitations of mission schools and demanded recognition of elected school committees. At the same time Congress saw itself as speaking for the interests of the impoverished majority. Meanwhile Chief Bidi Ndiweni was himself moving into opposition of the regime over destocking and Land Husbandry. Ndiweni was assertively determined to uphold Ndebele authority over any possible Kalanga cultural assertion.[5]

The arrival of the 'Wednesday Movement' in Simukwe polarized all these contradictions. The *Mirror* of 17 January 1959 reported that Chief Bidi had told

> a gathering of teachers, church deacons, demonstrators, Christians and non-Christians and ordinary villagers, that he was one of the people who used to plough on Wednesdays some time back. Chief Bidi Ndiweni said that some time back a delegation went to a mountain near his Reserve where it is believed a goddess lives, to ask for rain. The goddess of rain is reported to have told the rain seekers that their chief cultivated his land on Wednesdays. They should go to him and ask him to supply them with rain. The Chief added that in that year he experienced a great phenomenon which proved to him that he was doing wrong and that for many days rain never came until he had to observe Wednesday as a holy day . . . . Finally Chief Ndiweni warned those who cultivated their lands on Wednesdays to stop it and observe this day as a holy day. He said those who did not observe this day will be made to pay five shillings for the messenger who arrests them.

There was an immediate response from Congress. J. M. Dube called a meeting of the branch to denounce the Chief. 'Congress did not discourage or despise African customs', he said, but Christians should not be compelled to observe the chief's order. 'Enough blood was shed in the Middle Ages', he declared, and he did 'not want to see that happen today'. He instructed Congress members to defy the Chief and 'to continue cultivation on Wednesdays'. Another outraged progressive wrote to the *Mirror* on 31 January to demand that 'they must work on Wednesday, one of the days when a man should sweat in labour'.

Victory was not to go to Dube or to his view of nationalism. Shortly after his protest meeting he was detained under the 1959 Emergency legislation — and the Wednesday observation spread through Simukwe, not as an anti-nationalist manifestation but as the expression of a different kind of nationalism. At this point the issue fell out of the pages of the *Mirror* but it certainly did not die away on the ground. The peoples of the Matopos reserve were facing at this time a renewed threat of eviction and their intensive cultivation of the vleis and wetlands so as to produce vegetables for the Bulawayo market was being prohibited by the Land Development Officers. Yet controlled cultivation of the vleis was permitted by the ecological doctrine of the Mwali shrines. The people of the reserve came increasingly to express their opposition to colonial agrarian intervention in terms of their loyalty to the injunctions of the three or four shrines which operated in the Reserve, Wednesday observance among the rest.

Just to the south of the Matopos Reserve, in Wenlock Ranch, the Wednesday commandment was also spreading. On 30 August 1990 we interviewed Mark

Dokotela Ncube at his prize-winning vlei farm in northern Wenlock, in the southern foothills of the Matopos and only a mile or two from Dula shrine. Ncube comes from a Kalanga family which has farmed the same land for generations, but he had accepted 'Ndebele' identity as a member of Chief Sigombe's 'tribe'. A teacher for the Brethren-in-Christ mission, he was a member of the Sofasihamba association which lobbied against the threat of eviction from Wenlock; later, when he had resigned as a teacher and begun to transform his farm he acted as an adviser to Sigombe in the Chief's ambitious modernizing projects. Ncube cared for the Chief's pedigree bulls, drove Sigombe to meetings in his truck and explained items in the *Bantu Mirror* to the Chief's *indaba*. Sigombe encouraged him to join Congress and he became Secretary to the Matopos Branch in late 1958. Like Dube in Simukwe, Ncube was detained under the 1959 Emergency legislation. He was very plainly an archetypical example of the Christian progressive nationalist.

Up to this point his relationship to the Mwali cult had been one of contemptuous curiosity. In the early 1940s, when he was at Dula School which is situated just opposite the shrine, people told him that a miraculous bell rang in the cave. Ncube explained that 'I wanted to see the God myself', so he went into the cave and found two pieces of metal which when struck together rang like a bell; 'An old lady used to go into the cave. She would strike the metal. It was she who spoke as the God, in Kalanga, in a foreign language. Her son would translate. They are both dead now.' Thus although the founding priest of Dula was buried in the kopje next to his land, Ncube ignored the commands of the cult. However, as he returned from detention and set about developing his remarkable system of irrigated banana-groves, fish-ponds, maize-fields and rich grazing, he discovered that the cult was neither dead nor impotent. His father told him that the observation of Wednesday as a rest-day, which had not previously been observed, had now become universal, 'as a result of confusion'. Ncube soon clashed with the neighbours whose interests he had presumed to speak for as an officer of Congress. When windows at the local school, which he had founded and of which he was Chairman and Treasurer, were broken by birds the people said that this was because he did not honour the shrines and obey their rules. They demanded that he brew beer and do penance. He refused. As for the Wednesday observation:

> Everyone else around here believes in it. They do not farm on Wednesdays and they demand that I do not. I refuse and they call me a Tshombe [traitor]. I say to them: stores do not close on Wednesdays; businesses do not close. If they close then I will close. My farm is a business. They hate me for that.

As this example shows, the issue of the Wednesday observation was not merely a public and visible sign of commitment. What was at stake was a repudiation of the expertise of the Land Development Officer; a repudiation of the 'gospel of the plough'; a repudiation of an African agrarian entrepreneurial élite for who a farm was a business. This evidence confirms the chronologically vague assertions of shrine priests and adepts of their growing influence during the nationalist period. Even when the nationalist parties were banned in 1964 the Mwali shrines continued to thrive. They were, after all, still able to hold public meetings. Thus on 23 October 1967 even the *Bulawayo Chronicle* noticed a large gathering at the new shrine at Bembe in the Shashe hills, near the historic Indaba site in the Matopos Reserve. The 'rain-goddess', Mdingene Ncube, held a 'traditional ceremony' in which 'she communed with the ancestral spirits on the subject of rain'. 'Hundreds' attended, including officers and members of the N'anga Association of Central Africa who 'were promised extra healing powers'. Three black oxen were slaughtered, there was 'singing and dancing' throughout, and at evening the 'rain-goddess led the visitors to the traditional cave'. As we shall see, Bembe was a particular shrine of resort for guerrillas during the 1970s.

While the influence of the cult was expanding at the grassroots, a second development had been taking place in Bulawayo. This was the rise in the late 1940s and 1950s of a cultural nationalism which emphasized language, history, culture and religion. The Bulawayo cultural nationalists argued for true demotic Sindebele against stiff, archaic Zulu; others argued for recognition for the Kalanga language. Often these were the same men because in Bulawayo in those days there was a doctrine of the hierarchy of identity — one could be a Kalanga cultural nationalist so far as local Bulilima-Mangwe affairs were concerned; an Ndebele cultural nationalist as far as the affairs of Matabeleland were concerned; and a territorial nationalist where the interests of all the Africans in the Colony were concerned. In this way Joshua Nkomo's brother, Stephen, could write to the *Bantu Mirror* on 10 February 1951 in praise of chi-Kalanga — 'this is a time of nationalism and of pride in one's language and Kalangas should wake up'; could become in 1960 Chairman of the leading Ndebele cultural nationalist association, the Matabeleland Home Society; and also in the same year become chairman of the Bulawayo branch of the mass nationalist National Democratic Party.[6]

So far as religion was concerned, Bulawayo cultural nationalism had nothing public to say about the Mwali cult. Its emphasis was rather on the great shrine of the Ndebele nation, Mzilikazi's grave at Entumbane in the Matopos Reserve. The Matabeleland Home Society had long sought to make Entumbane as much a centre of pilgrimage as Rhodes's grave in the Matopos was for Europeans; the *Bulawayo Home News* regularly rebuked European missionaries who countenanced Westminster Abbey as a shrine of the British ancestors and who were prepared to preach at Rhodes's grave, but who rebuked Africans for 'ancestor worship'.

A key figure in the cultural nationalism of the early 1950s was that son of Simukwe, and product of mission entrepreneurism, Joshua Nkomo. In the Wednesday observation controversy in Simukwe, Nkomo might have been expected to be on the side of Dube rather than on the side of Chief Bidi Ndiweni. Yet Nkomo had been struck in his overseas visits by the respect paid to the past. The *Bantu Mirror* of 30 August 1952 reported that he had called a meeting in Bulawayo in order to set up a society 'to preserve all the African culture and heroes of Africa'. In London, he said, people drew upon their past. 'He spoke at length of Chaminuka,

Mzilikazi and Mambo.' Nkomo carried these ideas out into the countryside. The *Mirror* of 17 April 1954 reported his address to teachers in Matobo, urging them to preserve 'customs, language and the tilling of the land' and to 'remember African heroes of long ago'. Nkomo joined the Kalanga Cultural Society because, as the *Home News* remarked on 12 January 1957, 'he is also a Kalanga and is keen that Kalanga customs should be kept'. But he was also a keen Ndebele traditionalist. He went on pilgrimage to Inyati to the royal praise-singer, Ginyilitshe, to ask him 'about various matters of Ndebele national interest'. He accompanied Matabeleland Home Society delegations to the *Indunas* where he urged that Entumbane should become a burial place for all who deserved well of the Ndebele nation.

Much of this seems very intellectualized and remote from grassroots concerns. While Nkomo was urging teachers in Matobo to preserve customs and the tilling of the land, the Mwali cult's emissaries were undercutting those very teachers and calling for a return to older ideas of ecology. But in fact Joshua Nkomo represented a living link between the cultural nationalism of the towns and the grassroots developments which we have been describing. And nowhere is this more clearly seen than in his relationship to the Mwali shrines.

In 1953, as is now well known, Nkomo visited Dula shrine in the Matopos Reserve. This visit was kept secret for a long time and became legendary in ZAPU circles. But in 1984 Nkomo himself described it in his autobiography. In his account, he, Grey Bango and William Sivako were received at the shrine and all other petitioners sent away. The Voice of Mwali then prophesied that 'the people of this land' would regain power in 'a big war in which many will die', but only after 30 years. Nkomo adds that 'for thirty years I kept the secret that the Voice had foretold a long and costly struggle'.[7] In our interview with him in 1988 Grey Bango elaborated on the meeting, describing it as a moment when the straying Kalanga/Ndebele children of modern education and the city returned to their roots and were given the true wisdom. In his version the elders at the shrine had rebuked the young citified men and denied them access to the cave. But when they nevertheless presented themselves, the Voice wept for half an hour over its prodigal sons and then dismissed the elders, so that it could speak for hours to Nkomo and Bango. During this time the Voice not only predicted the future but even more importantly revealed the whole secrets of the past, of divine history, and the secrets of the transition of regimes.[8] We are a long way from Dokotela Ncube's almost contemporary mockery of the mystical bell and the old woman pretending to be God in the Dula cave.

We are even further in the account we were given, also in 1988, by Mrs V. Lesabe. Mrs Lesabe, who lived as a girl in Whitewaters in the National Park during the heyday of Sofasonke resistance to eviction; who belonged to a leading African Methodist Episcopal family; and who was Head Girl at the London Missionary Society School at Hope Fountain, has since become an adherent of the Mwali cult. Though an aristocratic Ndebele by descent, she has come to accept the cult's control of the region's history. In her version of the 1953 visit, Bango and Nkomo inserted themselves into the queue of supplicants going up to the cave after dark:

Once they were in the queue and in the dark nobody was seeing who was who. Then a Voice from the shrine began calling the two young men. Nobody knew they were there except the Voice from the shrine . . . And the Voice said to Joshua, 'You, son of Nyangolo, great-son of Maweme, you will lead this nation. When you go into the river, I'll be with you, into the seas I'll be with you. When you climb trees I'll be with you. When you hide among the small shrubs I'll be with you. Wherever you are I'll be with you until this war is over. Nobody will touch your body. I'll fight with you, let's go to the war together.'[9]

It is hard to tell, of course, exactly when this version of the 1953 visit gained currency. It is also hard to tell when stories of Nkomo's divinely ordained birth began to spread. In Mrs Lesabe's 1988 version both Joshua's father and he himself were born only at the intervention of the shrine. Joshua's grandfather and grandmother, in this account, visited Njelele and were told by the Voice that from them would descend 'a grinding stone to lead my children'. Then Joshua's father was born; he grew up, married, had two children but could achieve no more. 'They tried *everything*. They've got no children. They went back to the Shrine' at Njelele. The Voice told them that it had stopped them having any more children because it wanted them to accept the responsibility of bearing the saviour of its people. 'I want you to give me a grandson who is going to lead my people, that small grinding stone I told you about is going to come from you. Then the woman gets pregnant. Joshua is born.' In this way, concluded Mrs Lesabe, although both Joshua's father and mother were mission-educated teachers, 'Joshua was born only because of the shrine.' Perhaps this story is a product of recent years. But it seems likely to have arisen out of the fusion of urban cultural nationalism and the rural revival of the Mwali cult during the early 1960s. Certainly Nkomo's nationalist nickname, which dates from those years — the little slippery rock — draws perfectly clearly upon the metaphors of the Mwali cult.[10]

Mrs Lesabe's 1988 testimony was important, too, for revealing how at the nationalist intellectual level the same process of symbiosis between Kalanga divinity and Ndebele identity was being effected. She argues that Mwali brought Mzilikazi and the Ndebele to Zimbabwe in order that pre-existing human sacrifice to the spirits could be replaced by cattle sacrifice. Thereafter, while most of those possessed by the shrine spirits were Banyubi or Kalanga or Venda, nevertheless *some* significant Ndebele were also possessed. In particular, as we shall discuss more fully below, the spirit of the Dula shrine possessed one of the leading Ndebele warriors during the 1896 rising. At Dula, the shrine to which Nkomo went in 1953, there was thus believed to be a fusion of the Zansi military tradition and the prophetic powers of the Mwali cult.

Our argument, then, is that ZAPU's nationalist ideology in Matabeleland had come to incorporate — and to incorporate at many different levels — the power and the discourse of African religion. At the grassroots, populist nationalists observed the Wednesday rest-day; at their head stood a man who not only inherited

the military prowess of the Ndebele kings, but whose birth had been foretold by
Njelele and whose eventual victory had been promised by Dula. Our argument is
also that this was not a one-way process; not merely a co-option of the reputation
of the cult by myth-making nationalists. The dispatch of the Wednesday movement
messengers from the shrines was certainly the work of priests and not of politicians;
we have the testimony of other visitors to Dula, including some of Nkomo's Shona
allies in the nationalist movement of the early 1960s, that when they were taken to
the shrine 'it was really hot' and rebuked them for being so slow to challenge the
government. Moreover, there could be a direct interaction between priests and
politicians. Grey Bango claims that he and Joshua Nkomo were responsible for
placing the controversial Sitwanyana Ncube as priest at Njelele in the 1960s. In
short, nationalism in Matabeleland was less secular and African religion more
available than has often been suggested.

The fusion of religion and nationalism in the rhetoric of the early 1960s is
caught in the *Bantu Mirror's* report on 20 January 1962 of a speech by a National
Democratic Party activist, Amos Mazibisa. In December 1961 the NDP was banned;
the government sent troops into the Matopos, where they demanded the surrender
of NDP cards and beat those who would not produce them. Meanwhile there was
serious drought. 'Looking very furious', Mazibisa explained the drought in a
nationalist adaptation of the Mwali idiom:

> In the days of old when drought sapped all the life from crops and stock
> and the community was facing imminent hunger, tribal leaders consulted
> their ancestors to find out what had gone wrong in the lands. But in the
> 20th century Matabeleland droughts do not come just because ancient
> Gods are angry. It is the fury of the people that drives away the rain-
> carrying clouds from the skies. You see, we have been praying to our
> Gods for years that we must be united. The Gods allowed us to unite. We
> formed a political party. The party was banned. Then we formed a new
> party. But we could not be allowed to meet. And during that time we
> prayed to our Gods at Matopos to show us some visible expression that
> our anger and frustration were being appreciated by the Gods. So long as
> the ban on meetings lasted we had no rains . . . Next time there is a ban
> on meetings we shall tell our Gods to stop the rains indefinitely so that
> we shall all (Africans and European farmers) suffer together.

AFRICAN RELIGION AND THE WAR IN MATABELELAND

We have set out at some length the nationalist background to the guerrilla war in
Matabeleland in order to show that at both the grassroots level and at the level of
ZAPU ideology there were strong interactions with the ideas and symbols of the
Mwali cult. This being so — and especially if Brickhill is right about the continuing
influence of rural ZAPU branches — we might expect ZIPRA guerrillas at least to
show respect to the shrines and perhaps themselves to turn to the cult for support.

But such an argumentative inference is no longer enough. We must now turn to the direct evidence of the interaction of African religion with the guerrilla war.

There is, of course, a well-established literature documenting the importance of Shona spirit mediums to the liberation war in eastern Zimbabwe. In particular, David Lan, in his study of the Dande valley, has argued that young guerrilla strangers were transformed into 'sons of the soil' by the ritual and mythic skills of the mediums. But until recently there has been no such evidence of the influence of the Mwali cult during the war. In September 1991, however, Martinus Daneel presented his own findings on the role of the Mwali shrines in resistance, nationalism and guerrilla war. He argued that for the Masvingo district and the whole of the Shona-speaking south the shrines, and in particular a shrine in the Matopos Reserve known variously as Matonjeni, Wirirani or Zhilo, have played a critical part.

Going back to the 1896 risings, Daneel asserts that the cult provided 'the all-important mystical legitimation' for the uprisings, and that 'the creator god of ecology' mutated into 'a militant deity', 'the god of war and peace and the god of justice opposing oppressive rule'. After the defeat of the risings, cult messages 'emphasized the unique identity of the culture and entrenched a solid tradition of resistance to white interference'. As nationalist resistance stiffened in the 1960s there was 'a revival of traditional religion'. In turn traditional religion 'inspired the guerrilla fighters, in many cases informed and even gave direction to strategic operations at the war front and contributed greatly to close co-operation between rural communities and fighters'.

Daneel cites 'cultic messengers throughout Masvingo Province and the priestly colony at Dzilo' for the fact that Mwari

> did eventually change from a message of resistance to white rule to a full declaration of war. Mwari is reported to have engaged in oracular intervention, the essence of his/her pronouncements being: full condonation and support of the ZANLA . . . fighters in their struggle to regain the lost lands . . . divine confirmation that this time *chimurenga* would succeed in replacing colonial rule by black majority rule.

Messengers constantly carried these injunctions from the shrines and 'as the crisis grew, more regular contact was established between district communities and the Matopos priestly colonies'. Even the ZANLA operational headquarters at Chimoio — according to Daneel's informants — sent emissaries to Zhilo shrine 'to obtain mystical directives for the conduct of the war'.[11]

Daneel's fascinating material seems to confirm that the Mwali cult was as influential during the liberation war as were the Shona spirit mediums — indeed he shows the cult and the mediums working closely together. But this still does not answer our question concerning the war in Matabeleland. Daneel's work has always depicted the Matopos shrines as 'Shona' survivals in the zone of Ndebele conquest; for him, as for Gelfand, Matonjeni/Wirirani/Zhilo has been the shrine particularly for the Karanga of Masvingo.[12] Perhaps the shrines were active in the war but only in Shona-speaking areas or with ZANLA guerrillas.

Indeed, this possibility seems to arise from one of our own interviews. By the end of the war ZANU guerrillas were operating in the Matopos Tribal Trust Land itself, adjacent to its shrines, and in rivalry with ZIPRA. ZANLA could not easily claim legitimacy from Mzilikazi's grave at Entumbane, or claim support from surviving party committees. On the other hand, the shrines had drawn pilgrims from Shona-speaking areas for many decades, and probably for centuries. It seemed likely, then, that ZANLA would turn to the shrines.

On 23 July 1989 we interviewed the shrine-keeper at Bembe shrine in northern Matopos Communal area. The keeper is a priestess, 'Daughter of Rain' Minye Ncube, who runs the shrine with her husband, Melusi Sibanda. Bembe is a 'new' shrine, set up by Minye Ncube in 1964, after the fall of a great rock from Bembe Hill. 'I had dreamt of a white rock that spoke all the languages. When this rock fell they came to see me and brought me to live at this place. They said I must cause the rain to fall.' Minye Ncube had been born at Zhilo as a member of the priestly family there. Her new shrine was a spectacular success and attracted pilgrims both from Matabeleland and from western Mashonaland to the 'white rock that spoke all the languages'.

The liberation war, said Minye Ncube in July 1989, was a time of great danger, as both guerrilla armies and the 'Security Forces' struggled to control Matopos: 'We were not certain if we would reach the place safely. We were afraid all the way. We had difficult times.' But this was not because of the guerrillas:

> They had respect because they wanted to be blessed through ancestral ceremonies until the country became independent. When the ceasefire was declared they came, but the majority were not Ndebele. It was those that came from the east, it is those who came here. They never gave me problems. When war ended they came in very large numbers. Locals were surprised up to today . . . They heaped their guns together . . . the size of that house. They wanted me to find out if it was true there was a ceasefire. They wanted to consult the shrine and ancestors that genuine freedom had come or if it was a plot to massacre them in camps . . . I told them that independence would come but that there might be problems, that is what I had been told. They filled the whole village. It was during Christmas time. I had brewed some beer and there were many locals. The guerrillas asked for my radio to dance and say good-bye.

This public appearance at the shrine by ZANLA guerrillas who had been operating in the hills all around it revealed the shrine's spiritual collaboration with them. Many of the locals disliked ZANLA so that 'even today many people don't like me'. Government soldiers, alerted by the gathering, alleged that the priestess was still hiding guerrillas in the hills, and 'threatened to kill me'. [13]

Up to this point we might still be in the world of Jeremy Brickhill, with ZANLA 'needing' to use the shrines and ZIPRA confident in its rational ideology and its local public support. But things were not in fact so clear cut. After all, there were many locals at the Bembe Christmas beer-brewing; the very emergence of this Bembe shrine had been part of the revival of the Mwali cult in Matabeleland; its grassroots nationalist significance should have led ZIPRA guerrillas too to show 'respect'. And there are indications, both in our interview at Bembe and in Daneel's September 1991 paper, that ZIPRA guerrillas drew on the shrines as well as ZANLA. At Bembe, Melusi Sibanda told us the ZIPRA units operating to the north of Matopos had sent gifts of black cloth to the shrine in exchange for protection. The shrine has been much used since 1980 by ZAPU members seeking to understand and reverse the electoral defeat and threatened suppression of their party. Daneel tells us that Mwali cult messengers expressed 'full condonation and support' for both ZANLA and ZIPRA and that 'ZIPRA fighters, operating in the Matopos area regularly consulted with shrine officials.'[14]

Since we were carrying out field-work in the Matopos very soon after the end of the 'dissident' war, it was perhaps not surprising that we were given little direct information about either ZIPRA or 'dissident' recourse to the shrines. But what we *were* given in abundance was information about the ideological context in which such recourse made sense.

Let us return to David Lan and the mythic legitimation which Dande spirit mediums gave to ZANLA guerrillas. To discover whether there was any equivalent to this in Matabeleland we need to focus especially on Dula shrine. It was Dula which Nkomo visited in 1953, Dula to which he took Chikerema and other Shona nationalist allies, and Dula which has remained into the 1980s a regular place of resort for ZAPU leaders. Why Dula?

The Dula shrine was one of several shrines operative in the Matopos Reserve, each with its own special function. On 27 July 1989, while driving towards Zhilo shrine, we gave a lift to an elderly woman pilgrim, Mrs Mpofu, who told us: 'I was given to you by God to come and explain.' She went on to describe the special roles of each of the shrines:

> What I learnt is that it was at Dula that they went when they went to war, to take instructions, predictions and how they should conduct themselves. This one, Zhilo, they came to ask for rain, springs. The rain from the shrine at Magubu was associated with lightning.[15]

This explanation echoed an earlier response when, on 10 September 1988, we interviewed a group of cult adepts at Kumbudzi in Matopos Communal Area. They told us that although shrine priests were Venda or Nyubi or Kalanga, some 'Nguni', or aristocratic Ndebele, could be possessed by the shrine spirits: 'Look at Dhlo-Dhlo who brings messages to Dula when they are going to war.' Dula, they said, was masculine; Zhilo was feminine.[16] Other cult respondents told us that the 'war shrine', Dula, was known as the shrine of the Red Axe.

How then, to interpret these assertions of a link between Dula and war, when the Mwali cult has been so often interpreted solely in terms of peace and fertility? We did not get the impression that the idea of the shrine of the Red Axe was a recent one, invented as a result of the guerrilla war itself. Indeed, Mrs Mpofu explicitly told us that the division of roles among the shrines — and Dula's special link with war — was what 'the old people' had described and that 'nowadays' the specializations were much less clear cut. The adepts at the group interview were talking of a sequence of members of the Dhlo-Dhlo family coming to Dula as messengers of war. In view of the association of Mwali with war and cattle-raiding in published Kalanga legends, collected in south-western Zimbabwe, it is even possible that the dualism of a masculine 'war' shrine and feminine 'fertility' shrine goes back a long way.[17] But there seems no doubt that in more recent times there has been developed a specific notion of a link between Dula, as the shrine of the Red Axe, and the aristocratic Ndebele warrior tradition.

Our best informant for this was Mrs Lesabe, the aristocratic Ndebele convert from Protestantism to the Mwali cult, member of the ZAPU Central Committee, and a close associate of Joshua Nkomo. According to her, in 1896 the spirit of Dula shrine fell on Mtuwane Dhlo-Dhlo, one of the leading Ndebele military commanders (and the man whom Cecil Rhodes called 'the Mlimo's mouth-piece').[18] The shrine of the Red Axe gave Mtuwane the power to wage the 1896 war against the Whites — which is known in Matabeleland as the war of the Red Axe. It also gave him the power to negotiate an end to that war. Mrs Lesabe told us:

> Mtuwane was Nguni, the son of Ugogo; he was given the power of war by the shrine, by Dula, but when referring to the war you don't call it Dula. You call it the Red Axe. This was when they were fighting against the whites in the 1890s . . . At Dula there are two powers there. One is for the war and the kingdom of the Ndebele people . . . This Mtuwane Dhlo-Dhlo was given the power of war, really of war . . . This spirit never dies because just now there is Mtuwane's great-grandson who is possessed by the same spirit. So that it will never die. Not ever.

According to Mrs Lesabe, it was to the shrine of the Red Axe that Nkomo went in 1953 — hence its power to promise him protection in the forthcoming war. According to her also, it was because Mtuwane, hero of the 1896 war, was possessed by the shrine spirit, that Dula was able to give 'the power of war, really of war' to ZIPRA guerrillas in the 1960s and 1970s and this was why 'ZIPRA was so much powerful'.[19]

Thus if Matonjeni/Wirirani/Zhilo — which features in Karanga myths as the focal point of creation and the source of fertility[20] — was the obvious source of legitimacy for a struggle to regain Karanga land, Dula/The Red Axe was in the minds of Ndebele cultists the obvious source of power for ZAPU's guerrilla army. It was in this ideological context that interactions between ZIPRA guerrillas and the shrines made sense.

However, the bulk of the evidence connecting ZIPRA guerrillas to the shrines during the war deals with another subject — support given by the guerrillas to the religious cultural nationalist programme of the locals. This could take three forms — denunciation to the guerrillas of 'sell-outs' who refused to obey the injunctions of the cult; pressure by adherents of the cult upon the congregations of the Christian mission centres which had been deliberately sited close to the shrines; and disciplining of cult priests whose misconduct had led the people to fear that the protective power of the shrines was being undermined. We can cite examples of all three.

When we interviewed Mark Dokotela Ncube in northern Wenlock in August 1990 he told us that the 'hatred' of his neighbours had continued into the war. As each new band of guerrillas came into the area, he said, he was denounced as a man who despised the commands of the cult, who ran his farm as a business, and who had a licence for a shot-gun (the only one in the area) from the Smith regime. Time and time again the guerrilla groups came to kill him, to lay waste his crops and to carry off his gun. (Indeed, a few miles to the north in the Matopos Communal Area, resident entrepreneurs were killed by guerrillas). According to Ncube he managed to persuade the guerrillas that it would be irrational to kill him, telling them that the only reason there were bananas growing to feed them was because he could guard the crops with his gun. If they killed him and took the gun they would have plenty of bananas for the moment — but thereafter none. At any rate he survived the war on his land.[21]

As for Christian churches and schools close to the shrines, on 30 August 1988 we interviewed Japhet Ngwenya, headmaster of the Seventh Day Adventist School at Tshatshani, Matobo. Ngwenya was born to a Seventh Day Adventist family at Njelele. His grandfather still used to attend ceremonies at the shrine, and he himself led a black ox for sacrifice there when he was a boy. But when he grew up and became politically active he insists that the shrine was not regarded as important:

> What people were saying really was that the traditional God at Njelele had left, long left. Since he had left there was no more Voice there . . . Nobody really paid too much attention to that shrine in relation to the political movement . . . People meant politics. We did not find anything like what actually happened after independence, that you find people making feasts there and so on and so forth. We didn't have anything of that nature. We never did that. We went straight to politics.

What lay between his youthful secular nationalism and the current political uses of Njelele was the guerrilla war. 'When the war was heating up' says Ngwenya, 'they began to pay attention not only to the shrine but to the spirits in general.' And in the end the Seventh Day Adventist school at Njelele felt the backlash of revived traditionalism:

When the school was put up there, up until very late really there was no opposition or hostility between the Seventh Day Adventists and the traditionalists. Late 40s there was no problem, early 50s there was no problem. You know the problem came very recently. During the War. When there were some people who were patronizing the shrine there and they passed by Njelele school and the church there, and they would say a few nasty comments as they passed by. Well, up to the point that some people were beginning to say that church should not be here as the whole place belongs to Njelele shrine. It went on until somewhere in 1978 even the guerrillas got involved. I was actually there and on a Sabbath day one day soon after church, they had been at Mayabu's place [the village of the shrine priest], they arrived at my house and they were told that we were in church. Now, after church some of our church members passed by, they were quite old people, and their books were burnt, and after that they came straight to the church and school there, where they found us, they gave us a bit of a beating and burnt our books, saying we were foolish, colonized.[22]

But if the guerrillas worked closely with an approved shrine priest, Ngwenya told us, they were much harder on priests whom they believed to be betraying the traditions of the shrine than they were on Christians. 'If they found that somebody was abusing certain spirits and certain traditional rules than they, they didn't like this person.' So ZIPRA guerrillas chased Sitwanyana Ncube away from Njelele, even though he had originally been placed there by Nkomo and Bango.

There were a lot of people who were saying quite a lot of nasty things about him . . . He had to run away from the freedom fighters, because they didn't like him, they knew he had no right to be there . . . He said he was running away from Smith's soldiers because they wanted to kill him. But the story is heard that he was actually running away from the freedom fighters. They didn't want him there. He had introduced wrong things.

It was held that Sitwanyana's fee-charging, relations with women, and so on, endangered the powers of the shrine. So the guerrillas responded to the requests of the people and chased away the imposter.[23]

Sitwanyana himself claimed in July 1988 much more friendly relation with the guerrillas. The shrines had protected the freedom fighters in the war. The problem was that after the war the ritual necessities had been forgotten.

We communicated with the shrine during the ceasefire period. During the ceasefire when a lot of rain fell. When the leaders came from outside the country. We communicated. But things were not properly handled. It was supposed that after the fruits of independence came, the shrine had to be informed so that even the guerrillas who had fought should be cleansed. They had fought hard. Traditionally a lot of beer was brewed when the *amabutho* came back from war; they were cleansed. That ceremony was not performed. Up to date that has not been done.[24]

We were told in 1989 that some guerrillas were being sent to Njelele for cleansing, in particular some National Army men, ex-ZIPRA guerrillas, who had been driven mad by the spirits of those who had been killed and who had been sent to the shrine.

In all these ways, then, there is evidence of the role of the Mwali shrine during the guerrilla war in southern Matabeleland. In addition, it seems that during the war the influence of the cult spread into, or revived in northern Matabeleland. In July 1991 Dumiso Dabengwa told Terence Ranger how at some time in the 1970s an emissary from the Njelele shrine established himself at Pu Pu in Lupane district, close to the Shangani Memorial. ZIPRA forces established a strong base nearby; their Political Commissar visited the Mwali shrine and received its blessing and endorsement; he then ordered other guerrillas not to visit the isolated kraal so as to protect it from Security Force reprisals. After 1980 Pu Pu Mwali kraal remained a zone of tranquility in the midst of the atrocities of the 'dissident' war: 'Even the Fifth Brigade fell calm when they came there.' Today there is a plan to establish the first 'shrine' to the ZIPRA dead near Pu Pu so that the heroic spirits of the guerrillas can overcome the spirits of the Shangani Patrol. Dabengwa sought permission from the Pu Pu priest, who gave it in person but said that he must seek the approval of Mwali at one of the major shrines.[25] This 'revival' of the Mwali cult in northern Matabeleland as a result of the war, has also been documented by the recent research of Marieke Clarke. As she has shown, the Mwali shrine at Manyanga/Taba Zi Ka Mambo has become active for the first time since 1896.[26]

In some ways for southern Matabeleland too, the most impressive evidence of the importance of the shrines during the war has been their significance in the 1980s. As Ngwenya explained to us, before the war public and political use was never made of Njelele in the way that has happened since 1980. It was the war, he said, that had made the difference. At any rate, in 1980 the old cultural nationalist, Joshua Nkomo, held his electoral rally at Njelele and was rewarded with rain; thereafter he sought to make Njelele a national — even an international — pilgrimage centre on the model of Jerusalem or Rome. ZAPU formed a National Shrines Committee to ensure that the legitimate keepers were in place at the Mwali shrines and at Entumbane. The Ndebele chiefs in a further development of the symbiosis of Kalanga and Ndebele culture, were recognized as the custodians of the shrines and as responsible for mobilizing people, food and tribute for the annual rain rituals. All this was public. But in private, as ex-ZIPRA soldiers clashed with ex-ZANLA and as ZAPU itself seemed threatened with extinction, members of the ZAPU Central Committee visited the shrines for prophetic guidance. Meanwhile, the dissidents out in the hills interacted with the shrines and their congregations, among other things once again chasing Sitwanyana Ncube away from Njelele. The cult's explanations of drought and its attitudes towards the environment were drawn upon for an understanding of the plight of Matabeleland in the 1980s. There can be little doubt that the shrines have been more intensely and variously used in the 1980s than at any other time in the twentieth century. This contemporary history plainly derives partly from the events of the guerrilla war.[27]

Equally plainly the conventional view of a 'secular' war in Matabeleland has to be modified. But what of the conventional view of the experience of the Christian missions in the south-west?

A BRIEF DISCUSSION OF THE MISSION STATIONS OF THE SOUTH-WEST

There is not much time for a discussion of mission Christianity in as much detail as our account of African religion. Fortunately the outlines of the mission experience during the war are much better known. Briefly, the years 1977/8 were the climax. In 1977 the London Missionary Society school and station at Dombodema and the Methodist school and mission at Tegwani closed down; in 1978 the Anglican school and mission at Cyrene closed and became an army base; Catholic missionaries were killed at Embakwe; the school at Empandeni closed (the mission itself being abandoned the following year); St Joseph's in Simukwe was abandoned as was the mission at Makwe in Gwanda. By 1979 the missionary presence in the rural south-west had almost completely vanished. These experiences left a bitter legacy for mission-descended Christianity in southern Matabeleland. As late as 1987 the official booklet published to celebrate the centenary of Empandeni still spoke of 'terrorists' rather than of guerrillas.[28]

How are we to account for this? Some missionaries themselves did so in terms of the anti-religious secularism of the guerrillas. The history of the Mariannhill missions which was published in Bulawayo in 1980 thus described an incident at one of Empandeni's Mass centres, Silima, on 30 December 1979. Fr. Rudolf Anders went out to say mass; he was suddenly surrounded by armed men who threatened to shoot him; he survived and returned to Empandeni to report that 'the indoctrination of the people in the Mass centre was pure and simple Marxism'.[29] But even if Fr. Rudolf was correct in this assessment, it cannot be used to make a contrast between 'secular' ZIPRA and 'religious' ZANLA — the armed men in this case were themselves members of ZANLA, who by the end of 1979 dominated the area around Empandeni.

The one account we have of discourse between ZIPRA guerrillas and Catholics gives a very different impression. In the files at Empandeni is an account by Fr. Pius Ncube of two raids by ZIPRA on St Joseph's Mission, Simukwe, the first in November 1977 and the second in March 1978. The four guerrillas took money, drugs and equipment and on the second occasion ordered the school to close. Their discourse was that of populist nationalism. They had once been Catholics — one said that he had been born in the clinic at St Joseph's and another, picking up a rosary, 'remarked piously: "how much I liked this thing in my youth" '. But they had come to see the Catholic church as foreign and exploitative. They told the

African sisters that they would not harm them 'since they were daughters of Zimbabwe' but also told them that 'We shall come back one day and burn this mission which belongs to Ian Smith.' When the sisters told them that the money was for the poor they replied, 'We are poor also.' Sarcastically they took things belonging to the priest and quipped 'since the priest is not paid but given these things we also have a right to them'. In the sitting room they saw the Bishop's portrait and asked 'Have you ever seen any African priest putting on such finery?' They said 'God and the angels are always painted white but the devil is painted black.'[30]

This sort of thing might strike the Mariannhill fathers as 'communistic' but it can equally plausibly be traced back to the cultural nationalist upheavals of the early 1960s, with their reassertion of 'black' religion and the repudiation of entrepreneurial inequality. We have described above the spread of the Wednesday movement in Simukwe and its imposition on Christians by Chief Bidi. There are significant echoes of this in the Mariannhill account of what happened at St Joseph's, Simukwe, during the open nationalist period:

> The time between 1960 and 1965 were years of unrest in this whole district on account of African nationalism. A woodshed of the mission was set on fire. Christians were intimidated and prevented from attending Mass on Sundays by the threat of physical violence, such as beatings with knobkerries, and of arson, such as the burning of the homes of those who dared to fulfil their Sunday obligations.[31]

There seem convincing enough links between this nationalist violence and the discourse of the ZIPRA guerrillas in the late 1970s. And if we were to want to push our argument, perhaps beyond conviction, we might suggest that from the early 1960s to the late 1970s there was an input from the Mwali cult — focusing in the nationalist period on those who 'dared to fulfil their Sunday obligations' rather than the holy Wednesday rest day; extending during the guerrilla war to attempts, like that at Njelele, to remove Christian churches and schools from the territory of the shrines; and even finding expression at St Joseph's in 1978 in the vindication of 'black' spirits against 'white' angels. (And if we were really to venture into speculation we might point out that through much of its early history Empandeni/ Embakwe had been locked in struggle with the Mwali cult, the priests driving off the cult's emissaries and suffering dreadful drought in return).[32]

But although these are intriguing speculations, our real argument about the missions of southern Matabeleland is a very different one. The reasons for their predicament *were* largely secular, but they arose from the secular grievances of peasants and tenants rather than from the secular ideology of guerrillas. Just as we have argued that guerrillas had to take the Mwali cult seriously because the people did, so we argued that the guerrillas were hostile to the missions largely because the people were. (The same ZANLA guerrillas whom the missionaries thought were teaching pure Marxism around Empandeni in 1978 also inquired from the people on Empandeni farm which members of the Catholic community *they* regarded as sell-outs).[33]

We have seen from studies of guerrilla interactions with missions in other parts of Zimbabwe (including David Maxwell's chapter, this book) that the attitude of the local people to the mission was critical. In southern Matabeleland there were several reasons why relations between the people and the missions were marked by tension. As we have seen, during the earlier nationalist period there were tensions over primary schools, and even later, when such schools had been taken over by local Councils, there remained criticism of the basic and unintellectual approach of mission secondary schools. But the major grievance was over land. The Mariannhill history puts the matter clearly:

> Considered at one time essential for getting established in the country and evangelizing the people, mission farms proved more and more a heavy burden. Empandeni-Embakwe farm, nearly as big as Luxembourg, was no exception. As holder of the title deeds . . . the Bishop of Bulawayo was made responsible for conserving soil, reducing overstocking and fencing the land . . . Laws had to be enforced to make Africans reduce their livestock, and unauthorized squatters had to leave the farm. All this caused unpleasantness.[34]

Even when in the late 1970s most of the Empandeni Farm was declared Tribal Trust Land (T.T.L.), tension between the mission and the people did not relax. For decades the missionaries had used their power as landlords to hammer 'polygamists, Protestants and pagans'; now the effect of the transformation from mission farm to T.T.L. was 'immediate, in so far as the people considered themselves free of church laws, as for instance, with regard to marriage'.[35] The Empandeni area, once a Catholic zone, became in this sense a 'liberated zone', a readily available base for guerrillas and still full of old resentments against the mission.

Other Catholic missions in southern Matabeleland aroused resentment because of other grievances over land. Minda Mission, at Antelope Mine in Matobo, was deliberately built adjacent to the Antelope Irrigation Scheme and had irrigated plots and grazing land. Its aim was to 'raise' its pupils 'from subsistence farming to cash farming'. But the whole of the Antelope Scheme became very unpopular; its expansion took land away from Simukwe T.T.L.; its authoritarian discipline drove many of the peasant settlers away; the scheme became in essence a state farm. The result, in the words of the Mariannhill chronicler, was that

> there was much intimidation of the mission labour force and our Christian people. This resulted in the tribes-people turning against the mission . . . and against the Water Development Department of the Government . . . Many of those engaged in farming on the irrigation plots have left. In 1977–78 twenty-two tribes-people and five Europeans were murdered.[36]

We have cited the well-documented Catholic experience. But land problems bedeviled Protestant missions too. The London Missionary Society farm at Dombodema (where oral tradition postulates a brotherly relationship between early missionaries and the local priest of the Mwali shrine) was wracked by disputes between the church and its tenants, which resulted in sympathy for the guerrillas. (The problems of tenants and 'squatters' at the London Missionary Society Hope Fountain farm continued into the 1980s, assuring support for the dissidents).

In addition to continuing cultural nationalist feelings and acute grievances over land, another factor affected the great mission farms of the south-west — their closeness to the border with Botswana. Guerrilla groups, having raided the mission, could retreat into Botswana, often taking volunteers from among the pupils with them. This in turn led to constant Security Force and Police incursions. And the final factor in the plight of the south-western mission lay precisely in their attitude to the authorities. So far as we have been able to determine, the Whites in charge of the missions, whether Catholic or Protestant, did not contemplate for a moment working with guerrillas, as many missionaries did in eastern Zimbabwe. They regarded the guerrillas as 'terrorists' and looked to the police and army for protection against them. Father Pius Ncube in Simukwe might declare: 'I am not convinced about armed self-defence, since Christ did not do so. If it is God's will that in this situation I should depart this world his will be done', but elsewhere there was ready resort to armed protection.[37]

Thus *The Chronicle* of Ekusileni Mission in Filabusi is full of references to the good relations of the priests and the police. At Christmas 1977, when celebration at a festive matins took the missionaries away from their radio-alert so that the police received no answer to their calls, a police patrol 'at great risk to their own lives' set off to 'rescue' the mission. In the event the police 'joined the missionaries in happy greetings and some refreshments'. After guerrilla pressure in 1978 and the closure of the school, 'the police took over the mission as a security base' which 'indeed proved most beneficial to the station'.[38]

This reliance on police protection of property rather than reliance on the goodwill of local Christians (as at Maxwell's Elim) seemed a clear indication of where the missionaries stood in the struggle. Hence they were desperately exposed when the police could not or would not assist. A document in the Empandeni files reveals the predicament:

> Owing to the political unrest, especially to the north of Empandeni at Dombodema and Tegwani Missions, where abductions of pupils to Botswana took place, which led ultimately to the closure of these schools towards 1977, a certain unrest also prevailed at Empandeni among the girls and boys of the Secondary School and the Homecraft School. On 17.10.77, the very day our Bishop H. Karlin administered the Sacrament of Confirmation to Empandeni Boarder boys, 20 boys and 10 girls, without any previous warning, went to 'Geneva', as we jocosely called their departure for Francistown to join the 'liberation' forces.

On 23 April 1978 five guerrillas visited Empandeni and ordered that the school close. The two White priests at once visited the police at Plumtree, 'asking them whether the school could be kept open under police vigilance and protection'.

They received a lesson in reality. The Chief Inspector said that 'it might have repercussions on Empandeni by the come-back of the terrorists' and that in any case 'staffwise the police could not do it'. With great reluctance, the Bishop and the mission priests decided to close the school, having learnt from the police that 'the terrorists seem more or less in control of the district'.

Having thus revealed his closeness to the police, Fr. Andrew Bausenwein stayed on after all the other Whites had left. 'I announced in Church', he wrote on 13 October 1978, 'that I would stay on even at the risk of being shot, as long as they appreciate Holy Mass and the Sacraments . . . So far we have survived, but one can never tell whether one or the other of the Empandeni people bears a grudge against one or the other of us and instigates the terrorists to avenge him/her.' Too late to do much good the Catholic missionaries were now solely dependent on the people.[39]

The mixture of police absence most of the time and police presence some of the time was equally undermining to the Protestant missionaries. Thus in January 1977 the Methodist minister J. S. Gordon, wrote to the Senior Assistant Commissioner of Police, Matabeleland. He explained that from September 1976 there had been severe unrest in Nata T.T.L. and on Tegwani Mission Farm. Church buildings had been burned down; young men 'were disappearing' from the mission farm to join the guerrillas; the Plumtree Police rounded up most of the remaining youngsters between 17 and 20, some of whom worked for the mission and held for an appropriately biblical 40 days and 40 nights; 'in the school itself the boys and girls were becoming jittery'; there was no regular police protection but Security Force units suddenly arrived at the school without warning, 'with guns pointing in every direction', and entered the girls' dormitory at bed-time; then on the night of 9 November 1976, 35 boys defected. 'A team of police officers came to investigate at the school'; several remaining boys were carried off for interrogation; the rest of the school, having posted notices reading 'All Else Has Failed. Let Us to the Church Today', and 'There are no Gods in the Beit Hall', assembled in the church to pray for their fellows in police custody. Since the police continued to hold pupils once examinations had begun, the remainder of the school boycotted the examinations. Then, as a bizarre climax, the police returned to arrest Reverend E. M. Musa, 'Thirty-five years a Chaplain to the Military Forces'. Gordon proclaimed his own loyalist credo: 'We have to prove to and win over the minds of these boys and girls — first of all *God* is in *control*; second, this Country is given to us to *develop* and serve Him in, under a Government which can be *trusted* to protect the interests of good citizenship and the best development of all our resources.'[40]

Gordon certainly regarded the guerrillas as terrorists. Musa, protesting his own arrest at gun-point, the calling 'by all sorts of names to make me feel that I was nothing', his detention in the cells, and his feeding from a dustbin lid, described himself as 'a loyal Rhodesian citizen'.[41]

> I am a registered voter. I put the government in power by my vote. I am a Chaplain to the Military Camps. Why should I be arrested like a man who has murdered . . . and be labelled a liar, a Communist, and what not?

Are there no respected people in this country? If I do not deserve respect
— who should be respected?[42]

As Gordon commented, Musa 'wonders where is *his protective security now* —
when he has trusted so much to the Law and Order Maintenance Force'.[43]

And this was the overall thrust of Gordon's letter to the Senior Assistant
Commissioner. 'Since we do not seem to have the police protection at Tegwani
necessary for the easy pursuance of the purposes of educating the children placed
in our care, we come to you to ask.' He then posed several questions — did the
police not realize that mission schools were very sensitive places where their
conduct should seek not to provoke *'fear* and *distrust of normal law and order and
discipline'*; did they not sympathize with the missionary aim not to aggravate
further relations between the students and the Security Forces; did they not think
the school should remain open? If so, 'we must be protected from *outside irritation'.*
If the police could not protect it was better they did not 'irritate'.[44] The police could
not protect Tegwani and it was too late to rely on the people to do so. The school
closed.

CONCLUSION

We can rapidly summarize our conclusions. We have found that there *were* special
characteristics of southern Matabeleland Christianity — a theological conservatism,
a reliance on the government, an inability to imagine collaboration with the
guerrillas; all coupled with particular tensions over land. We have found that
there *were* special characteristics of African religion in southern Matabeleland — a
capacity to symbolize the people's antipathy to state interference with agriculture
and cattle-raising, their suspicion of entrepreneurship, and also to provide a
symbolic and ritual language for cultural nationalism. We have found that there
were special characteristics of nationalism in Matabeleland, with it complex
interaction with regional history and religion. We have not explored in this chapter
whether there were also special characteristics of the ZIPRA guerrilla army. Perhaps
there were, but we feel the story of religious interaction in southern Matabeleland
during the war can be explained without invoking them. The factors described
above are enough in themselves to offer as an explanation. Above all, how the
people valued African religion and assessed the missions determined what
happened to both during the war.

2

Christianity and the War in Eastern Zimbabwe: The Case of Elim Mission

DAVID J. MAXWELL

To discover how religion moves from hapless cry to effective protest, from opiate to stimulant, is a matter of great urgency.[1]

INTRODUCTION

Cox's above injunction specifies a particularly pertinent task for historians of religion, especially those investigating the role of Christianity in Zimbabwe's war of liberation. The context of poverty and injustice out of which this agenda to harness a liberatory Christianity emerges has already given rise to fertile enquiry amongst theologians in Latin America. Here, many Christian denominations have clearly taken a preferential option for the poor in the latter's struggle to redress gross economic and social inequality. They have also adopted a prophetic stance against repressive and authoritarian states which legitimize and perpetuate such injustices. Latin America is a sub-continent to which African theologians look with great envy, dismayed by what they see as the seeming passivity of African religious movements which render their practitioners incapable of bringing about meaningful structural change.[2] Yet it seems to me that a good deal of these African theologians' dismay is misplaced. In this chapter on Christianity and the War in Eastern Zimbabwe, I will explore a dynamic religion capable of offering effective and practical support to ZANLA guerrillas, and of transforming itself to contain a revolutionary content. This is a religion which does not subject peasants to historical forces beyond their control but renders them co-agents in the making of their own history. Admittedly, their Christianity is not as blatantly 'political' as their Latin American counterparts who have benefited from a Marxist methodology which has enabled them to reflect critically on their society. Nevertheless, I will

Map 1
Northern Nyanga District

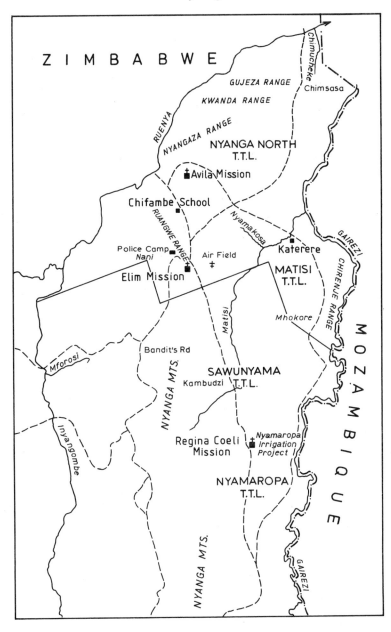

demonstrate a Zimbabwean Christianity equally reflexive in nature and able to respond not only to the crises and needs of the liberation war but which also continues today to help Africans face the struggles of post-independence Zimbabwe.

In fact, a considerable historiography has already developed concerning the role of Christianity in Zimbabwe's liberation war. Ngwabi Bhebe has done a number of case studies of the Evangelical Lutheran missions in southern Zimbabwe; Terence Ranger has written about Catholic and Anglican Churches in Makoni District; Michael Bourdillon and Paul Gundani have attempted to reconstruct the experience of rural Christians in central Zimbabwe in the vicinity of a number of Catholic missions; and Sister Janice McLaughlin is writing four case studies on Catholic missions as part of a doctoral thesis.[3] Out of this body of work a number of issues of common interest have arisen. The most obvious questions concern the contribution of the Church to the armed struggle, and the response of the liberation armies to the Church. In relation to the second question, Terence Ranger has recently noted that so far all published accounts of the war have been based on the testimonies of African civilians rather than those of the guerrillas themselves. He suggests that the seemingly positive contribution of many churches may be part of 'an oral tradition which has hastened to claim a connection with the victorious side of the war'.[4] Here then historians of the war must go to the records of the liberation armies themselves to begin to reconstruct a range of guerrilla mentalities towards the church during the armed struggle. Sister Janice with her access to ZANLA archives has begun to embark on this task although this is not the only intention of her work. Like Ian Linden, she is asking how the experience of the war shaped both Catholic theology and practice, though whilst he wrote from the perspective of the national and institutional church, his inquiry focused on the grassroots.[5] The issue of war-time experiences has recently opened up a new problematic as scholars have begun to investigate how Zimbabweans have sought to give meaning to, and bring about healing of, their memories of violence during the armed conflict.[6]

In this chapter I will explore three issues which emerge from the body of scholarship cited above. Firstly, I will look at guerrilla-church relations. Secondly, I will investigate how experience of the war shaped both the production and content of popular theology. Thirdly, I will look at how post-war Christianity has mediated the tensions and healed the wounds caused by the violence of the struggle.

Although all themes will be developed with reference to my case study of Elim Mission, the third historiographical trend is of particular relevance. It was here at Elim, in June 1978, that White missionaries and their children were massacred in an act of notorious violence so horrific that it sent reverberations around the international community. The case study will thus investigate how the Elim Movement has dealt with that violence as well as reconstruct the specific conditions that led to the massacre. The chapter's concerns usefully divide into three sections. The first two form a descriptive narrative as is the convention for this type of study. Firstly I trace Elim's missionaries' relations with the guerrillas and local community both in Katerere, northern Nyanga District, and in the Vumba, where they were massacred. I will then shift the focus to Elim's Black Christians and their endeavours to maintain and defend a popular Christianity which had become integral to their rural identity. In the third section I widen the focus, drawing some conclusions as to how the experience of the war shaped the form and content of rural Christianity in Manicaland.

For the purpose of comparative analysis I will occasionally refer to the Catholic missions, Regina Coeli and Avila, that flank Elim, but the dominant focus of the study remains on the latter. I do so for two reasons. Firstly, I am making a conscious effort to redress the balance which still leaves a paucity of work done on Protestant Christianity (no less Pentecostal Christianity) and the war. Secondly, my connection with Elim Mission, Katerere, where I taught for three years, has given me access to a remarkable archive. Once again, with the commencement of the war, the missionaries became historically conscious. In the early 1950s their predecessors had realised that they were part of a heroic age — the age which saw the founding of a popular Christianity. Aware that they were part of a process which was radically transforming the society they engaged with, they sent back streams of correspondence to mission headquarters in London, including articles for missionary journals describing what they were seeing. In the 1960s and early 1970s the quantity of this correspondence greatly diminished. However, the late 1970s saw the dawn of a new missionary age — an age of testing. Diaries began to be kept, the flow of correspondence dramatically increased and international delegations came and went, writing lengthy reports on their investigations. This archive when combined with oral sources provides a remarkable opportunity to reconstruct Elim Mission's war-time history. It is arguable that my dominant focus on the war-time history of just one mission makes this study too narrow. Yet it seems to me that it is only at the micro-level that we can begin to identify and trace the interactions which explain guerrilla-church relations at a wider, more general level.

From community to tragedy: Elim missionaries and the Vumba massacre

In this first section I seek to explore Elim missionaries' relations with guerrillas in Katerere, northern Nyanga District. I set these relations in the context of their relationship with the local community, many of whom they came to depend on for protection and information. I will then show the tragic irony of their move to the Vumba where they believed they would be safer. Here they had no relations with the local community and relations with the guerrillas rapidly deteriorated. This led to their horrific massacre in June 1978.

The coming of the war to Manicaland caught missionaries by surprise. It precipitated forced theological responses to moral dilemmas they never would have dreamed existed a few years previously. In northern Nyanga, amongst the local Hwesa and Barwe peoples, the war hit Avila Mission first in April 1976. Close to Chifambe, it was *en route* from ZANLA's border crossing at Chimsasa. When one evening they arrived asking for medicines, Father Peter Egan was totally unprepared for what happened next. He told me:

Three guerrillas with machine-guns took me outside and put me up against a wall. It was very traumatic . . . I hadn't done anything to the people. I had lots of Black friends and those guys came with machine-guns. It scared me. The whole world was going mad.[7]

Egan reported the incident to the authorities, fled to Salisbury and emigrated to Ireland for the rest of the war. Father David Weakliam, head of Egan's sending Province in Southern Ireland at the time, described Egan as 'very unfortunate'. His was one of the first interactions between Carmelite priests and guerrillas in their Manicaland Diocese. At that stage he had felt compelled to obey the law and had now effectively banished himself from his vocation. The incident precipitated a crisis within the order and prompted Weakliam — accompanied by Carmelite theologian, Father Paul Lennon — to embark on a tour of their mission stations. Following the tour, Carmelite missionaries gathered to devise a policy which would enable them to continue their work whilst at the same time limiting the degree to which their staff and local community were exposed to danger. The final policy was both 'complex and pragmatic', and 'sympathetic to not reporting the presence of guerrillas'.[8] Here the Carmelites were not only making a practical response to Vatican II Theology which had influenced many of the second generation of priests who arrived in Southern Rhodesia in the 1960s, but they were also expressing a sense of Irish nationalism which had always manifested itself in the Order's distance from the colonial state.[9]

On the 27th of April, 1976 a group of 21 heavily-armed guerrillas arrived at Elim Mission and requested food and medicines from the missionaries.[10] The missionaries were just as unprepared as Peter Egan. When Sister Joy Bath, a young nurse, found a group of guerrillas on her doorstep she was more annoyed at her loss of sleep than anything else. She listened to their speeches with an innocent disinterest: 'Look here, I'm very tired. I've been delivering babies all day, and I'm worn out. I've to be up early in the morning, and I need my sleep. Why don't you come back some other time?'[11] Phil Evans, a sober young school teacher, talked with the guerrillas for some hours. He was particularly interested in one of them who confessed to have been a lay Methodist preacher. God had not answered his prayers for the political liberation of Africa and hence he had sought liberation by means of the gun.[12] Evans was so struck by this conversation that when he later learnt that this guerrilla had been caught and sentenced to death, he attempted to write to him.[13]

The Elim missionaries were by no means antagonistic towards the comrades. Phil Evans and his wife Sue had initially been refused entry into Rhodesia because they had described themselves as conscientious objectors — a detail which had impressed the guerrillas.[14] The correspondence files received from missionaries in Rhodesia show that a number of the older ones who had cut their teeth in the 1950s were hostile to the early nationalist movement.[15] One in particular had come into conflict with ZAPU in his attempts to intervene in the prospective marriages of African school teachers.[16] But by no means did all the older missionaries take such a stance. The mission's pioneers, the Drs Brien, although intensely conservative in many respects, had a strong pragmatism which led them to visit missionaries in Nyasaland in late 1962 to learn from the situation there.[17] The late 1960s saw a transition from health to education as the mission's central activity. This was accompanied by an influx of younger missionaries who accepted the prospect of majority rule and sought to educate a missionized élite in preparation for it. The missionaries' intellectual response to the war, however, was limited by their conservative evangelical theology which focused their energies on individual transformation to the exclusion of social justice and structural change. There was a tendency to depoliticize issues. Thus Evans later commented on his conversation with the ex-Methodist guerrilla: 'Do we talk about Rhodesia in political terms? The fundamental problem is the heart of man — the revolution must occur there. Only God's message of repentance will remove the hatred and bitterness and distrust.'[18] This comes close to what the sociologist Bryan Wilson saw as the Elim Movement's general disdain for and disinterest in social and political questions.[19] At times some missionaries lapsed into accepting the Smith regime's portrayal of the struggle as Christianity and capitalism versus atheistic communism.[20] When expressed in spiritual terms the political issue had more appeal.

After the shock of their initial encounter with the guerrillas the missionaries withdrew from the station for a few days. They quickly returned, developing a doctrine of neutrality which they saw as the most likely means of keeping the mission open. In February 1977, Brian Barron, a journalist with more nerve than most, made the dangerous journey to Elim Mission to interview Peter Griffiths, the Principal of the secondary school. Griffiths told him that the missionaries had made a deliberate decision to refuse government protection. He went on to elaborate their position:

> We are very conscious of the fact that there are groups of guerrillas all around us, those mountains are in Mozambique and they come in all the time. Around us too are the police camp and army groups are camped on the airfield, but we stick to a strict neutrality. In fact we had a couple of guns here sometime ago for shooting snakes and leopards and so on, we handed these in because we have come to tell people about Jesus Christ.[21]

But there was more to this neutrality than just the handing in of a few guns. The missionaries constructed a concrete policy in dialogue with local Black Christians and an international delegation. Four major points emerged:

1. That mission personnel did not fraternise with the [Rhodesian] army or [Rhodesian] security forces.
2. That mission personnel did not travel in [Rhodesian] army or [Rhodesian] security vehicles.
3. That mission personnel endeavoured to keep good relations with local people.
4. That mission personnel did not keep guns.

Missionaries were also encouraged to make greater effort in the learning of Shona.[22] In practice, the policy often led to difficult moral dilemmas. Thus on one occasion Griffiths refused to allow mission transport to be used to help move the furniture of a family who had been attacked by ZANLA, for fear of allying the mission with the government.[23]

As the war encroached further and further into the lives of the missionaries their correspondence and diaries reveal that they were intensely aware of how it was affecting missionaries elsewhere. Whatever the denomination, the deportations, arrests and massacres shocked all missionaries alike and stimulated a growing ecumenism. In Inyanga District the old animosities and distrust which had typified relations between the Southern Irish Catholic missions of Regina Coeli and Avila and the Northern Irish Protestant Elim Mission rapidly subsided into one of mutual support and solidarity. Along with the Carmelite Father Tony Clarke and Anglican Bishop Paul Burroughs, Griffiths went to court in Umtali to testify on behalf of Father Lawrence Lynch of Mount Melleray Mission and Michael Pocock of St. Mary's Mission, as to the dilemmas of missionaries caught in the crossfire. Both were being prosecuted for failing to report the presence of guerrillas.[24] Another example of this growing ecumenism was the formation of the aid organization Christian Care.

Conditions around Elim Mission deteriorated and images of war became common in the art of even the primary school children.[25] The Land Rover-cum-ambulance was mine-proofed and patients in need of urgent medical attention were airlifted to Inyanga to avoid travelling on the roads. As fewer patients dared to travel in to the mission hospital so the nurses were forced to go out to the people to treat them at clinics. Such journeys were fraught with danger.[26]

From the period April 1976 to July 1977 the missionaries had no direct contact with the guerrillas. As seen below, Griffiths would receive information concerning mined roads and guerrilla movements which again placed him in great moral dilemmas, but the guerrillas never did return to the mission whilst the missionaries were there. However, two events occurred which caused Griffiths to approach the comrades himself. Firstly, on 16th July 1977, Pastor Ephraim Satuku was brought to the mission having been severely beaten by the comrades. He had been falsely accused of being a sell-out. A few days later nurses visiting a clinic were given the following letter requesting money from the secondary school:

Forward With Revolution!
Z.A.N.L.A. Forces 1.
Hello Sisters
Well this must not be a surprise to you. We met your priest over this side and dealt with him. We treated him accordingly. We taught him a lesson he was intruding in our affairs. If you ask him he can explain to you in a good way. We have ordered him to be driven to hospital. We are waiting for good results from that patient of ours. You must not get worried on your side you are excluded out of the case. Do not fear to come to this side , we welcome you each time.

We are sorry to send you. If you can communicate with the Teachers at Emmanuel School tell them that we ask for help from them. Can they help us with the sum of $100. They can give you the money so that you may bring it tomorrow as you are coming for your services at the church. You will give the money to the person we shall send to meet you tomorrow. Hoping you are fine and keep on with your duties alright, From Comrades.[27]

Griffiths attended an Elim Church service in the vicinity and with the help of Pious Munembe, the primary school headmaster, met the guerrillas at their mountain base 4-5 km from Kambudzi clinic.[28] Griffiths was very apologetic on the money issue and told the comrades that he would not be able to give them any as he would have to debit it to the freedom fighters and he was sure that they would not want this. They asked if his staff would be willing to contribute but Griffiths replied that he did not trust them all and that they would leave the school. He added that he came from a democratic country himself and wanted to see a Black person ruling Zimbabwe. The comrades accepted his position. He then mentioned that the mission was considering moving the secondary school to keep it going, and they tried to persuade him to stay.[29]

When the school did eventually move in August 1977, Griffiths was able to tell the *Manica Post* that Elim Mission: 'had never been threatened by terrorists'.[30] It is noteworthy that the letter from ZANLA cited above, although containing veiled threats against Ephraim Satuku, seemed to go to some lengths to reassure the missionary community. It is important to understand why. Many of the answers are found in earlier patterns of mission interaction between missionaries and local people in the 1950s. I have traced and analyzed these patterns in great detail, highlighting the role played by local migrant Apostolic Faith mission leaders in helping Elim's Pentecostal missionaries gain legitimacy from the community.[31] The successful planting of a Black-led church half a decade before Elim's pioneers, the Drs Brien, emerged on the scene, meant that the latter were able to benefit from the Pentecostal ambience already created by it. The Elim missionaries had other allies too. One group was that of local women who were highly responsive to Pentecostal Christianity. This was due to their ritual and symbolic exclusion from Hwesa traditional religion which is highly patriarchal. The arena of Pentecostal Christianity not only provided them with a means of rural solidarity but also the opportunity for self-expression and creativity in the spontaneity of the service. The movement's hostility to the Hwesa spirit world which it 'demonised' gave local women the opportunity to subvert it through exorcisms and Pentecostal power encounters. The women were particularly loyal to the Drs Brien whose unique blend of medical science and divine healing helped stem a crisis in infant mortality which had been as high as 60%. The final collection of allies was a migrant élite of Manyika people evicted from Bonda Mission in the southern part of the district where they had been heavily missionized. Once in the north of the district they rapidly took up the opportunities Elim offered for literacy and bio-medicine and characterized as 'uncivilized' the local Hwesa and Barwe, who were slow to appreciate them. The latter when struck by the Manyika's prosperity and greater opportunity in the labour market began to imitate them in their mission adherence. Thus in this context of Elim's good standing with the local community, Elim missionary, Phil Evans could write: 'It is significant that although the freedom fighters are very present in the area the Mission has not been involved. We pray that the respect and goodwill built up over the years will help us to weather the storm.'[32]

The actions of the missionaries there during the war obviously had an equally important part to play in maintaining good relations with ZANLA. Although always keen to keep up the appearance of neutrality, they closely identified with the plight of the local people. Their continued presence in Katerere was a testimony to this. Increasingly, Griffiths found himself representing the complaints of local people, often church members, to the police. Such complaints were about the harsh treatment they received from the security forces. On one occasion his action led to the arrest of soldiers responsible for the rape of two girls; on another, the early release of a man suspected of aiding guerrillas. He also protested about the behaviour of 'uncouth' Grey Scouts who terrorized the mission whilst looking for terrorists. In the last case he also wrote a letter of complaint to Colonel Norman Wood, Chaplain-in-Chief of the Rhodesian forces.[33] In July 1977 J. C. Smyth, a representative of Elim's International Mission Board, visited Katerere and interviewed Black and White staff there. Concerning Griffiths he wrote: 'Peter is in good standing with the terrorists. He has given himself so fully to the local people representing them before the Security Forces and by virtue of the fact that he was a witness in the defence for a Rev. [sic] Michael Pocock . . .'[34] However, Griffiths's response to the exigencies of the war was not to the taste of all his missionary colleagues. In the previous year's report, Smyth and his companion, Wigglesworth noted 'a sharp cleavage between senior staff on the station on the political issue'.[35] In this case Griffiths seems to have won the power struggle for the other senior missionary in question, who wished to keep arms, never returned from leave. However, in Smyth's 1977 report he went on to note how Griffiths's sympathetic stance again brought him into conflict — this time with the Field Superintendent: 'This aspect of the mission's alignment with the terrorists was against R. B. Chapman's conscience and I believe would, had we continued in Katerere, brought considerable tension.'[36] Nevertheless, as long as Griffiths headed the mission community, their relations with the comrades had most chance of working.

Lastly the role of Black Christian staff on the mission and the local community in protecting the missionaries was vital. When the guerrillas arrived at Elim Mission in April 1976, they visited all the missionaries except Roy Lynn who they knew had a gun. It was obvious that the comrades interrogated the local people about the missionaries. Pious Munembe confirmed this, stating that with the exception of the missionary couple who never returned from leave, 'A lot of the local people supported the missionaries.'[37] But it was not just the local people; often more clout was needed. Pastor Ephraim Satuku elaborated for me:

I went and spoke on their behalf . . . I took the Elim Constitution to them (the guerrillas) and I said this is what Elim is. They don't believe in politics in such a way . . . I said this is their stand and they are here to help poor Africans like myself. And they were impressed.[38]

Ian Linden in his book *The Catholic Church and the Struggle for Zimbabwe*, puts the point well:

The daily life and safety of rural missions increasingly depended on the good-will of the population to the point where traditional dependence relationships had been turned on their heads. Missionaries survived by the Grace of God and the grace of their parishioners who recommended them to guerrillas, or condemned them.[39]

This new role of 'broker' between guerrillas and missionaries that the African staff found themselves in was not an easy one. In 1977 J. C. Smyth wrote: 'It would appear that the presence of the European puts them in considerable difficulty with their own people especially ZANU. They are continually having to protect the European and this does not make it easy for them.'[40]

Remote and on the border, Katerere had many groups of guerrillas based there or passing through it on their way to commercial farms and other targets. By no means were all of these groups benign towards White missionaries or for that matter towards even their own people. As I will later show, the process by which Black Christians sought out and established successful working relations with the comrades was an extremely delicate one. Thus, they were intensely aware that both the local community and ZANU sat in judgement on them and that the precarious balancing act they were playing had many dangers. Hence they were very assertive in their desire to shape missionary response to the war and particularly to help distance them from the security forces.[41] However, despite the tensions within the mission community, relations with both guerrillas and local people did remain satisfactory. The reality of this was seen in the reduction of ZANLA activity on the days surrounding the beginning and ending of school terms and the detailed information Griffiths received concerning mined roads and guerrilla movements.[42]

Despite the missionaries' determination to stay in Katerere, circumstances beyond their control began to impinge, making it very difficult to keep the secondary school open. Two valued African staff resigned, unwilling to risk their lives any longer; new enrolment figures dropped dramatically; and finally the mission's five-ton truck which supplied the school was blown up on its way to Salisbury. The driver's mate was killed. The driver had failed to take the longer but safer route along the border. Logistically it was becoming impossible to keep the school open.[43]

In May 1977, Bonda Girls School made the decision to move into the Convent in Umtali. The premises of Eagle School in the Vumba also lay vacant and the missionaries believed it would be sensible to move there for a number of reasons. Although it was only six miles from the Mozambique border, there had been no evidence of guerrilla activity. It was only one-and-a-half miles from the tarmac road to Umtali and hence it would be easy to keep the school open and attract qualified African staff.[44] A few lines in J. C. Smyth's preliminary report of 1977 somewhat ominously put the counter argument:

> They (the missionaries) recognise that there is no safety in Rhodesia that can be guaranteed. They see that in Eagle School there maybe a possibility of greater danger. They will be in an area of European farmers who are targets for ZANU whereas in Katerere they are only in an area of transit where ZANU are concerned.[45]

The site for the school in the Vumba was very different from its previous one in Katerere. No longer was it part of a compound open to the local community but blatantly separate. As missionary Joyce Lynn wrote: '. . . it isn't quite the same as Katerere; being away from Africans is difficult when you are trying to win them. We long for the day when the differences will be sorted out and we can go back . . .'[46] The missionaries had leased the premises of the Eagle Preparatory School for European Boys. It thus had strong associations with the White minority regime. The problems the White staff were to encounter were greatly compounded by the loss of Peter Griffiths, the headmaster, who returned to Britain on leave. A shrewd Welshman, until his untimely death in October 1993 a senior civil servant in the Zimbabwean Ministry of Education, Griffiths and his wife, Brenda, had built the school around themselves since the 1960s. The loss of their experience was to weigh heavily. Further, the Eagle School had been built to accommodate about 150 small boys. Now it had to take twice that number of boys and girls — all teenagers.

Many of the youngsters had arrived at the school deeply traumatized by an event which had marred their departure from Katerere. On the 29th of July 1977, three buses had come to take the students at the end of term. The drivers were unwilling to follow Griffiths' advice about which road to take and two of the buses detonated landmines. Two boys were killed and a third lost his leg. One bus driver was burnt to death.[47] A good many of the children lost all their belongings. In their new surroundings many experienced fear and others 'unpleasant physical symptoms'.[48] Food strikes and a general breakdown of order ensued. The Black and White staff were divided in their response. Six boys crossed the border and the boarding master fled when three of them threatened to sell him out to guerrillas for punishing them.[49] In all this Phil Evans, the acting headmaster, found his work very hard. A gifted young man of just 28, he had been in the country for less than two years. Strict and inflexible, he was often misunderstood.[50] Griffiths returned to Rhodesia briefly and seemed to defuse the situation, but the following term Evans encountered new problems. An anonymous letter arrived telling him to raise the level of the manual workers' wages on pain of death. This was followed by another, appearing to be from guerrillas, telling the missionaries to clear out.

These threats coupled with the massacre of two Salvation Army missionaries on the border with Botswana was enough to persuade the missionaries to follow the example of their counterparts at St. Augustine's Penhalonga and move into Umtali, commuting to work each day.[51] At a special meeting on the 13th of June, the missionaries made public their intention to move into the city. They began the search for accommodation.[52]

On the 23rd of June 1978 a band of 20-30 guerrillas visited the school in the Vumba. They broke open the school stores and distributed food and new uniforms to many of the school children and let them have a 'bean feast'. They then went to round up the missionaries. The following morning their bodies were found on the sports field. Catherine Picken, Wendy White, Roy and Joyce Lynn, Peter and Sandra McCann, Phil and Sue Evans, all dead, the bodies of their four children lying beside them; one a three-week old baby girl. Three of the women had been raped. Some yards away lay Mary Fisher, critically ill from her wounds. She never regained consciousness. The nature and degree of violence meted out on the victims defied all imagination. They had been stabbed, bludgeoned and hacked to death; their bodies severely mutilated.[53] 'No other single event in the war — at that time', writes Martin Meredith, 'led to such universal condemnation of the guerrillas'.[54]

Martin and Johnson in their account of how the ruling ZANU élite came to power, generously entitled *The Struggle For Zimbabwe*, attempt to slant their material towards suggesting that the massacre was committed by Selous Scouts. Their contention is that near the time of the Internal Settlement, the government was seeking to discredit ZANU. Their argument is a plausible one; the lengths to which the Rhodesians were prepared to go with their playing of dirty tricks are by now well-documented. Indeed, a White resistance literature, whose only market is the South African one, has emerged out of Rhodesian soldiers' reminiscences.[55] However, the testimonies of the African students and staff present at the school at the time of the massacre, point to ZANLA.[56] The strongest evidence comes from the guerrillas themselves.

In the early 1980s Elim's International Missions' Board began to hear rumours that a number of the guerrillas involved in the massacre had remarkable conversion experiences. Griffiths was directed to investigate the rumours and was able to meet the platoon commander who had led the attack on his colleagues. I will deal more fully with the context and meaning of this story in the final section of this chapter but at this point it is only necessary to say that in the interview, this ex-combatant told Griffiths that it had been his decision to close down the school and kill the missionaries. He gave three reasons. Firstly, he wanted to undermine White morale in the country. Secondly, he sought to close down institutions in the area to facilitate more effective routes for guerrilla infiltration. Thirdly, the missionaries had not instantly responded to his directive to leave the site.[57]

Once on the school site the guerrillas seemed to have a detailed knowledge of its lay-out and there is potentially a long list of people, either staff and students inside the school or locals outside, who could have sold the missionaries out. A few weeks prior to the massacre, four boys had been abducted into Mozambique and then released back into the school.[58] One thing, however, becomes patently clear: the missionaries had suffered from the loss of the community in Katerere which had given them so much support. The two church leaders who remained there had no doubt whatsoever about that. Pious Munembe told me:

> The mission had moved to a new place and the people there didn't know the missionaries, neither did they know the Africans who were there. And I think that, when asked questions by the comrades operating in the area, they would not have given good reports.[59]

Ephraim Satuku told me: 'They did not have someone who could speak on their behalf to explain to the person who organized it that they were only there to teach and to help Africans.'[60]

Although guerrilla relations with missions could exhibit a ruthless unpredictability, a number of factors could ease relations. In northern Nyanga District, both Catholic and Pentecostal missionaries were forced to make theological and practical responses to safeguard the future of their work. Missionaries of all denominations shared common dilemmas which stimulated a growing ecumenism. The relative strengths of popular Christianity around mission stations also influenced their standings with guerrilla bands coming into the area. Insights into this popular Christianity can only be gained through tracing patterns of interaction made by missionaries since the inception of their work. The standing of missionaries in the eyes of local communities was another ingredient. All of these factors safeguarded Elim's work in Katerere and were absent after the move to the Vumba. Here there was a breakdown of consensus within the school and no relations with a sympathetic local community. The above quotations are undoubtedly the key. Local Christian leaders and their flocks had become the brokers with the comrades. Their cooperation with Christian missions could make or break them.

From mission to church: Black Christians and guerrillas in northeast Zimbabwe
It is now time to shift the focus to the Black Christians in the northern Nyanga District of Zimbabwe. I begin by describing the rapid process of indigenization that took place during the war years. Secondly, I look at the dynamics of the church's relations with guerrillas while its leaders and members struggled to maintain a rural Christianity. Lastly, I explore how in the process of this struggle, both the form and content of their Christian religion changed.

As the liberation war ground to an end, back in Britain, the Drs Brien were writing to another pioneer, Father Peter Egan of Avila and Regina Coeli. Their letters are a chronicle of despair and disillusionment. Mrs Brien wrote:

> They are in for an awful time. The Whites can get out. Poor Blacks and yet after all we helped them with, churches, schools, hospitals and clinics. How many wanted to repent and believe in the Lord Jesus Christ? . . . We

get very disturbed at times especially Cecil but all we can do is pray for them.[61]

They blamed themselves for not preaching the gospel more effectively[62] and at times their letters had a millennial flavour:

Isn't it a tragic ending to it all, all the hard work of the years has been worked out. The Marxists don't want any churches or any religion to be witnessed to in their Marxist state. Well the bible says it will be like this before the return of the saviour and the 24th Matthew describes it.[63]

Their letters marked the end of an era. The old missionary world was indeed coming to an end but others did not share their pessimism about the future of the Church. As J. C. Smyth remarked in his final report after the massacre: 'I do not believe we should write off Rhodesia . . . The day of planting has been done. There must follow a harvest. In due season we shall reap if we faint not.'[64] Indeed there was much to substantiate Smyth's optimism — even his triumphalism — which many outside observers at this juncture would have thought misplaced. For although Smyth's reports, like missionary diaries and correspondence, factually document the end of an era, they contain another sub-text which ran parallel to this — a sub-text which reveals the rapid rise of a Black-led church.

The international delegation which arrived in Rhodesia in late June 1978 expressed surprise at the speed at which R. B. Chapman, Elim's field Superintendent, handed over control of its institutions to local African personnel. They assumed that his decision-making had been clouded by the shock of the massacre.[65] Yet in many respects Chapman was simply acknowledging what had been a reality in much of Elim's work there during the previous two years.

My interviews with Black Christians connected with Elim's work in Zimbabwe revealed that they had a great respect for many of the missionaries who had lived and worked with them. But one thing had irked them — the slowness of the missionaries to allow them to take up positions of power and responsibility in the leadership. At the onset of the war all this began to change as Africans began to risk their lives for the survival of the mission. Satuku proposed a joint executive position and new clauses in the constitution allowing for joint committees and lay representation.[66] Work commenced on a new Shona Constitution and on the 9th of July 1977 it was presented to 23 African men from local churches.[67] The withdrawal of the missionaries from Katerere in August 1977 presented many of them with new opportunities. J. C. Smyth wrote: 'All hope of the future must be entrusted to the leaders . . . Some of the African brethren appeared to welcome the unexpected responsibility. The distinct impression was gained that they wanted to prove something to themselves.'[68]

Others, unwilling to take up responsibilities while missionaries were still present, were now propelled into leadership. Already by mid-1977 it had been noted that only Africans were in a position to do the church-based work, much of it being done by Ephraim Satuku, who continued to visit churches and preaching points on his motorbike.[69] Thus, when the missionaries left, a new and direct link was established between Elim headquarters in England and the African mission management committee in Katerere.[70] The Missionaries themselves realized that old relations could never be the same again. As Phil Evans wrote: 'I feel that missionaries will have to change their image considerably to service.'[71]

The shift in Black-White power relations that I have detailed for the case of Elim Mission was indicative of a much wider process which swept across Rhodesian missions. From the 17th–19th of May 1977, the Rhodesian Catholic Bishops held a symposium at Driefontein to discuss 'the Church in the New Order'. They found that:

> Among Christian communities there is a deepening sense of solidarity and suffering together and striving for the future. Because priests are unable to visit certain areas and their communities, great reliance has to be placed on catechists and lay leaders for the work of evangelisation.[72]

The Catholic Church also found that new structures were appearing within it. Its School of Social Work at Silveira House reported: 'The building of Christian Communities is the rule of the day.'[73]

At Avila Mission the local Carmelite sisters soon came into their own as Peter Egan's flight was followed by the arrest of two Black priests at the end of 1976. Rural African women in Manicaland had struggled for almost half a century for the right to enter Holy Orders and had finally gained recognition in 1959.[74] Now they too had a chance to prove themselves, and in the absence of Black and White male authority conducted services without priests, taught the faith and ran the institution.[75]

Ian Linden, a scholar who possesses not only the training of an historian of religion but also acute theological insight, has written on the above profound transformations which occurred at the level of individual missions and nationally saw the birth of a new Zimbabwean Church. Reflecting on the standing on the Catholic Church in the throes of war he vividly writes:

> . . . a terrible emptiness seemed to fill the ecclesiastical superstructure. Authority lay elsewhere, in the suffering of the rural Church and in those clergy and laity who shared it. More than ever the ecclesiastical world of the institutional Church appeared like a hard shell containing new and different sources of power and growth.[76]

Linden rightly points to the sufferings of the rural Church as the motor of change for the institutional Church's theology and structures, yet the binary oppositions he is inclined to perceive between grassroots and hierarchy, and ecclesiastical centre and rural periphery, seem difficult to maintain in the context of Manicaland. Here Southern Irish Carmelite priests had consistently identified with the rural people and their Bishop, Donal Lamont, was swift to support them and their flocks in their struggles. The case of Fathers Ignatius Mhonda and Patrick Mutume who were arrested at Avila Mission in November 1976 is much to the point. Lamont was quick to order legal and medical cover and organize priests and nuns to line the streets of Rusapi in a show of solidarity as they were marched handcuffed through the streets for their court appearance.[77] Although many of Lamont's priests resented their Bishop's seigneurial style, they appreciated that his pastorals did at least go some way towards reflecting the needs and aspirations of rural Catholics. Similarly, the yearly delegations to Manicaland led by their Southern Irish Provincial gave the Carmelite authorities in Ireland a good grasp of the issues their missionary priests faced. My repeated reference to the annual reports of Elim's International Missions' Board shows how this was equally true in the Pentecostal case. On the ground in Rhodesia, Peter and Brenda Griffiths, the only remaining Elim missionaries there, not only helped Black Christians gain legal representation but also used the resources of the Mission Aviation Fellowship (M.A.F.) to fly in supplies to the rural church in Katerere which at times seemed in a state of siege.[78]

It was in the hands of local Christian communities like those in Katerere that rural Christianity was to live or die. I now shift the focus back to Elim to illustrate the intricate way in which workable relations with the guerrillas were constructed. When the Elim missionaries left for the Vumba in July 1977, control of the mission was left in the hands of a new board of management run by Africans: three men and two women.[79] Pious Munembe remained head of the primary school and his wife Evelyn took charge of the hospital, helped by Leonard Katerere, a relation of the chief. Even before the missionaries had left for the Vumba, the Black Christians had established working norms with the guerrillas. In response to the comrades' requests, a support committee was established by African staff. Each working person gave $20 for the purchase of soap, toothpaste, toothbrushes, clothes, medicines and food. It was understood that the comrades should stay away and only communicate by letter. Meetings were held a good distance away from the mission, at certain appointed villages. Griffiths was aware that the African staff were supporting the guerrillas and even at times assisted them, taking watches to be mended and as already mentioned, after the massacre, flying in guerrilla supplies. It was this alternative supply to the guerrillas which again allowed the missionaries to remain in Katerere unhindered.[80]

However, the relationship established between Elim's Black Christians and the comrades was more complicated than that. Munembe and Satuku actively sought out and cultivated friendships with guerrillas with whom they could work. Such guerrillas Munembe described as 'reasonable fellows'. Most significant here was Comrade Rangarirai Mwana We Povo, ('Ranga' for short). Son of an Anglican primary school headmaster in the southern part of the district, Ranga had left school in search of adventure. He ended up in prison in Zambia and was adopted by Herbert Chitepo who became like a second father to him. Ranga joined the armed struggle after Chitepo's assassination. Someone with knowledge of Nyanga district was needed after ZANLA extended operations and opened up the MMZ (Mozambique-Manicaland-Zimbabwe) province. Thus Ranga, platoon commander and political commissar, entered the northern part of the district in 1976.[81] Seen as a reasonable and diplomatic man, to this day he is remembered as a hero. Munembe described him as a man who wanted to 'save as many lives as possible'. Ranga's own war-time record seems to confirm this. He told me how he had saved from certain death Chief Nyamaropa who had mistakenly supported Ndabaningi Sithole; he moved him out of the area. On another occasion he saved Pastor Ephraim Satuku from a beating. Satuku had been called to a meeting with the comrades. When given tea, he bowed his head to say grace. This caused offence to some guerrillas who suggested flogging him. Ranga intervened pleading tolerance. Satuku admitted to me that Ranga helped save the mission. Evelyn Munembe made cakes for Ranga .[82]

There were other guerrillas besides Ranga who were sympathetic towards the mission. One was Howard Chaka who was related to a mission primary school teacher, John Sithole, from Chipinge. He was one of those comrades present when Griffiths explained that he was unwilling to give them school money. One night, Evelyn Munembe accompanied her husband a great distance in order to extract one of Comrade Chaka's aching teeth by the light of a hurricane lamp. Another reasonable fellow was Comrade Bhudi, a sectional commander who operated in the area for a long time. He helped Munembe create a workable system for supplying the comrades.[83]

Amongst the guerrillas it is possible to discern differing mentalities towards the church. Comrade Ranga described himself as a Christian. Like those who gained self-legitimation through the spirits, so Ranga found legitimation through the Christian faith. He told me:

> I've seen how hard life can be, my experience as a combatant in the front.
> When we first came to operate on this MMZ side we were 63 and from 63
> we are now three today surviving. And I believe it's a blessing from God.
> I've been involved in too many big battles and survived by chance. I
> believe it is the love of God.[84]

When confronted by Jehovah's Witnesses at Mapani who refused to cooperate with the war effort, Ranga argued with them, citing the Prophets in support of his case. He spoke of his colleagues also at commanding levels who shared his understanding and approach. He mentioned Comrade Marovha, a member of the Salvation Army and Comrade Wolf, a relation of Bishop Muzorewa and UMEC member. The latter has also come to the attention of Sister Janice McLaughlin in her work on Avila Mission. In the vicinity of the mission, Comrade Wolf opened *pungwe(s)* (political education rallies) in prayer and recruited one of the nuns to cross the border into Mozambique.[85] Ranga believed that many of what he called the 'talented comrades' had a Christian background.

I would suggest that there was a strata of guerrilla commanders who were sympathetic to the Church due to their mission education. Indeed some of these commanders recognized the potential for mobilization in the power of Christian symbolism and mediums of expression. Through the many church services I attended during my stay in Zimbabwe (1986–1989), I became aware that a number of *pungwe* songs had originally been Christian hymns. Their words had been changed in a very simple fashion. Comrade Ranga explained this to me, telling of times when he and his comrades sat down and rewrote hymns. He gave the example of a song about Martha and Mary crying to Jesus that, if only he had been there, Lazarus would not have died. This he transformed into the people crying to Comrade Machel that, if only he had been there Comrade Chitepo would not have been killed. Another *pungwe* song about ZANLA's Maoist code of conduct had been adapted from a hymn based on Luke vi.31. — 'Do unto others as you would have them do unto you.'[86]

In an article on the history of Shona protest song G. P. Kahari traces a long tradition of different forms of song being transformed for the purpose of protest. He shows how pre-colonial forms such as the folk-tale, the *bembera* or praise song and the traditional religious song were all used to this end. To this list he adds the Christian hymn.[87] Kahari alludes to hymns being used in *pungwe(s)*, mentioning the second example I give above, but he does not explore this idea in depth.[88] I suggest that it was a natural progression from the same village school choirs he mentions, which, in the 1940s, sang songs in front of Native Commissioners voicing, in a covert form, grievances about destocking, forced-labour and bad policing.[89] The effect of these politicized hymns would have been striking. They carried resonances of the authoritative religiosity of the original message yet had been subsequently transformed to emphasize the sacrificial nature of the struggle.

Apart from being able to identify reasonable individual guerrillas, another vital component in the Black Christians' working relationship with guerrillas was their ability to win confidence. Much of this was down to the person of Pious Munembe, the primary school headmaster. He not only secured their material aid but also ran their messages. At one time he fooled local police officers by smuggling letters past them concealed in an old inner tube attaching packages to his motorbike. In some respects Munembe seemed to fill the vacuum left by Griffiths. On one occasion he was confident enough to go to the local police camp to complain about the beatings nurses had received from the security forces.[90] In interview Comrade Sam Zvaitika picked Munembe out as 'very helpful'.[91] The last component needed to establish this working relationship was trustworthy local people, who would act as the mission's representatives to the guerrillas and, when the need arose, as 'go-betweens'. These two men were from the Sapramango family, living near the Chief's village. Munembe elaborated for me:

> I think they were Apostolic Faith Christians. They were very helpful. We worked out a system with the comrades, where they could only send those guys and no one else. So we knew who we were speaking to. We trusted them and they trusted us . . . When there was a problem with supplies and we could not supply all the groups, they helped us talk to the comrades.

Thus the Black Christians were not at the mercy of over-zealous *mujiba(s)* as were so many other missions in that period.

However, this picture I have drawn of good working relations between guerrillas and Black Christians around Elim Mission was by no means replicated in all of Elim's churches throughout Katerere. By the 1st of January 1977 the church at Chifambe was closed and another at Mbiriyadi 'shaken to its foundations'.[92] Only a year later it appeared that only two churches, the one on the station and another nearby at Bhande, remained open.[93] There were a number of reasons for the demise of rural churches. As Bourdillon and Gundani stress, fear was a dominant factor.[94] In areas like Gotekote and Mazurura, in the early stages of the war, it was more of security force beatings than of guerrilla activity.[95] Others feared that their movement would attract unwanted attention from either side, whilst still others listened to the preaching of certain guerrilla groups. Their utterances varied greatly in their degree of subtlety, from denying the existence of God and asserting that Christianity was a White man's religion, to more sophisticated word plays.[96] In the latter case some informed the people that: 'The Whites brought *Mwari* (God) and took your *mari* (money).'[97] Another reason for church closure was that people simply stopped believing and turned instead to the spirits, as indeed many guerrillas did.[98] My interviews in Katerere indicate a considerable revival of traditional religion during the war, particularly belief in *mhondoro* or clan spirits.

As I have indicated, by no means did all the guerrilla commanders have a benign attitude towards Christianity. In 1977 Elim's most distant outlying church at Chiwarira, on the border, was closed by a ZANLA commander who forbade locals to attend.[99] Sister Janice in her case study on Avila Mission mentions the guerrilla who opened *pungwe(s)* in prayer. Yet one of my informants who operated as a *mujiba* in the area told of how other comrades went out of their way to compel mission staff to blaspheme and say: 'Down with the Lord.' Nevertheless, the priests there persevered.[100]

It is now appropriate to make some attempt to explain the similarities and differences between the war-time experiences of the three missions located in northern Nyanga district: Elim, Regina Coeli and Avila. Sister Janice's continuing work on Avila Mission has proved very revealing. Her sources — both ZANLA archives and confidential Catholic material — show a vital interaction of priests and nuns with guerrillas which she claims consolidated the Church behind its leadership. Yet it seems to me that a mission's war-time standing with its local community cannot simply be understood in terms of the ability of its leaders to construct meaningful relations with the comrades, but also in its success in founding a popular Christianity which allowed it to continue to operate with the consent of the local people. The relative strengths and weaknesses of this popular Christianity can be explained by tracing the patterns of interaction with indigenous culture and religion since the mission's founding. Having described and traced these interactions with respect to the three missions in question in a previous paper, it remains my contention that popular Christianity was weaker in the vicinity of Avila Mission than both Elim and Regina Coeli Missions.[101]

Although an Irish Carmelite mission like the famous Triashill and St Barbara's in the southern part of the district, Avila possessed a profoundly different religious history. Terence Ranger has done much work on these former two missions which border Makoni district and shown that by the outbreak of the liberation war they had, through the agency of priests, catechists and local people, created a strong folk-Catholicism which had its roots in the early years of this century. Here German Trappists and then German Jesuits took great pains to seize hold of the local spiritual landscape by its sacralization. They imported 19th century Ultramontanist peasant cults from Europe, such as the Lourdes grotto and miracle-working statues of Our Lady of Fatima. Pilgrimages and perambulations — organized to these shrines in the hills surrounding the missions — were events of such religious significance that they brought the labouring men home.[102] In 1949 the Irish Carmelites took control of the region which soon became the Umtali Diocese. Once again there was continuity with their emphasis on the Virgin of 19th and 20th century apparitions which was at the heart of Carmelite spirituality. My own research from their archives in Dublin shows that in 1950 the Manicaland Catholic identity was further enhanced with a new Carmelite flavour with the founding of Brown Scapular Confraternities at Umtali, St Barbara's and St Killian's. Along with the Rosary, the Scapular was eagerly taken up by young and old, supplanting the bracelets which had hitherto been used to ward of evil spirits.

However, the Carmelite missions established in the northern part of Nyanga District saw a rapid departure from the symbols, rituals and texts used to build this highly distinct folk-Catholicism. The new Catholic missionaries who did much of the work in the 1960s and 1970s had been heavily influenced by Vatican II Theology. They were mildly horrified by what they encountered at Triashill and dropped what they considered the non-essentials — the shrines, pilgrimages, possessions, Scapulars and Rosaries — failing to realize the extent that these forms had been seized upon and indigenized by local peasants. The new emphasis was on Africanization and inculturation. At Avila Mission, Africanization was fulfilled in Peter Egan's architectural masterpiece — the round church with thatched roof in Hwesa style. At Regina Coeli catechists introduced African music and drums in the worship. The priests in the north, keen to foster inculturation, greatly assisted the ethnographer, Michael Gelfand, in his work on the Hwesa and Sawunyama dynasties.[103] At Avila, Gelfand identified and extensively interviewed Diki Rukadza, medium of the great Hwesa *mhondoro* Nyawada.[104] Living close to the mission station at Chifambe, the priests made no attempts to challenge his spiritual authority or disrupt his work. In one interview Peter Egan even remembered him as a drinking partner.[105] On his opinion of the mission at Avila, Rukadza himself told me: 'They are very careful. They respect the spirits of the area.'[106] His clan spirit, Nyawada, was to become a significant source of inspiration and legitimacy to comrades entering the area during the war.[107]

At Elim Mission all was very different. The founding missionaries, the Drs Brien, made no attempt at dialogue with the local traditional religious leaders. Instead, as I have already indicated, they welcomed the alliances formed with them by groups hostile to traditional religion. The Pentecostals too had their own unique way of sacralizing the land. It occurred through contestation. The local spiritual landscape was to be possessed through power encounters. Those held by evil spirits were exorcised, charms and bracelets burnt and medicines destroyed. Local villagers were chided for their 'heathen practices' and a zone of popular Christianity was carved out by means of Pentecostal hellfire and brimstone. In the process, spiritual power relations were altered considerably. Drums used to appease the ancestors fell silent and Razau Kaerezi, the medium living just outside the mission, was completely undermined. Not only did his wife and children convert but the pools in the Manjanja associated with his spirit were seized by the Pentecostals to become places of baptism and open-air testimony. Kaerezi was known to fall into trance and his clan spirit Chikumbirike cursed the missionaries. During the armed struggle, the comrades came and moved him to a distant and isolated village where he would be more help to them.[108] Around Elim, the Pentecostals held spiritual sway.

Regina Coeli Mission was closer to Elim in the strength of the popular Christianity that had fostered. Elements of a folk-Catholicism had developed there by chance. The mission was situated in a fertile valley of the Nyamaropa reserve adjacent to a large irrigation project. The project had greatly altered the social structure being populated by Manyika master farmers on six-acre plots, who were very much more modernized than the local Hwesa and Barwe.[109] The area in general had witnessed the settlement of many Manyika evicted from the south of the district in the 1950s where they had been extensively missionized. Those evicted from the Carmelite mission at Triashill brought with them their Scapulars and Rosaries. Extremely assertive and aware of the benefits mission education and bio-medicine gave them in the Rhodesian economy over other ethnic groups, some Manyika demanded the mission facilities they were used to in the south.[110] Like the Manyika around Elim Mission, they formed alliances with the local missionaries and protected Regina Coeli from looting by other local ethnic groups.[111] Avila had no such groups of Manyika move into its vicinity and this had made the initial task of missionization relatively more difficult.

One of the biggest Catholic missions in the country, Regina, had a large and effective hospital and its doctor, Fr. Robert MacCabe, had made a concerted effort to dialogue and work with traditional healers and stay on good terms with the local people. On one occasion in 1977, guerrillas watched him celebrating mass in a very remote place and did nothing to stop him. He told me:

> I was known to them. Over the years I visited their homes and was very friendly with them and never acted in a high handed way . . . I think they liked and respected me . . . They had nothing against me and one guerrilla even said that to me.[112]

Another of the priests there on good terms with the comrades was Father Martin whom David Weakliam, his Provincial in Ireland at the time, described as a 'cute man from Cork' possessing a natural shrewdness.[113] This priest actively helped the guerrillas with supplies and at times warned them of Rhodesian troop movements.[114] On his tour of Carmelite missions in 1976 Weakliam's impression was that Regina was the safest one he visited describing it as an 'oasis'. Yet ironically, the price Regina was to pay for such good relations with the comrades was an indiscriminate attack from the security forces.[115] Father Martin remained at Regina throughout almost the entire period of the war.

At Elim the Black Christians were able to exploit the strength of their popular Christianity to protect the station's site. Aware that many stations had been looted or destroyed by the community when the missionaries had left the mission, the local church moved to prevent this. Munembe explained their strategy:

> Pastor Satuku called a meeting of kraalheads *sabhuku(s)* [village heads], the chief and prominent people in the villages. We killed a goat, cooked *sadza* and fed them well. And then we said that we were asking them to look after the station, the buildings and everything. And we told them that we did not think the war would last for ever and that peace was just around the corner. We said that it would be nice to gain Independence when all these buildings are still standing, because we would use them to continue the secondary school. Then we took them around the whole mission — the buildings and what we wanted them to look after, and we all agreed that this was the best thing to do.

Regina Coeli Mission did see some damage to its site and Avila suffered the looting of doors and window frames. But in the case of the latter there was one notable exception. Its beautiful round church in traditional Hwesa style remained completely intact. This successful symbol of Africanized Christianity was sacred to the local people and no group of guerrillas dared touch it.[116]

Likewise, where priests and African church leaders were on good terms with the local people, the comrades were loathe to prevent them from preaching or carrying out their duties. I mentioned the example of Robert MacCabe above and the point is made even more vividly with the case of Pastor Ephraim Satuku. As I mentioned earlier, Satuku had been beaten, having been falsely accused as a sell-out. In July 1977, he had accused a woman working at Kambudzi clinic of selling the mission's medicines and of stealing a watch. Angered at her exposure she told the comrades that Satuku was preventing her from giving them drugs. Satuku, an Elim pastor who had worked at Kambudzi Church for some years, was summoned to a guerrilla tribunal. He denied the charges but the consensus was that he should be executed. At this stage the commander intervened arguing that the accused had done nothing wrong. The guerrillas decided to beat him with big sticks instead. However, once the beating began it became apparent that Satuku would be killed. In a remarkable turn of events the commander (Comrade Howard Chaka) again intervened, saying that he was willing to die with the innocent victim if the beating did not stop. During the tribunal Satuku let it be known that whatever happened he would continue to preach the gospel. The comrades later told him they had no quarrel with this.[117] Around Elim Mission itself, the guerrillas visited only three times in three years and never interfered with its functioning.

One last dimension is vital in understanding why Elim and Regina Coeli Missions were able to continue to function in the period 1977–80. Increasingly the area around them was becoming a semi-liberated zone. The correspondence and diaries of the Elim missionaries enable the historian of the war to reconstruct guerrilla strategy with remarkable accuracy. Firstly, the comrades seized control of the communications network. As early as September 1976 the guerrillas had blown up the Inyangombe bridge and were attacking farms in the Chikore and Tanda area. Thus the shortest route from Salisbury to northern Nyanga via the Mutoko road was effectively closed down.[118] Other bridges were destroyed too.[119] The next shortest route into the area was from the town of Inyanga — two hours' drive across dirt roads which soon became mined. The latter part of the journey was through passes surrounded by steep valley edges, rocks and plenty of vegetation, making excellent sites for ambushes. The route became known as the *Bhinya* road (Bandit's road). The alternative route via Troutbeck and Regina Coeli, which wound across countless mountains, through thin openings in rocks and over flimsy bridges, was even more treacherous for security forces. The geography, which had made the Native Commissioners of old complain bitterly about administering the northern part of the district, once again began to assert itself.[120] By 1976 all the roads surrounding Elim Mission had been mined, and the comrades controlled all civilian movement by forcing them out along the road on the border.[121] The only other option was to travel in military convoy — an unwise move for those wishing to stay in the area.

Besides securing control of movement, the comrades also sought control of the peasantry. Local headmen with strong associations with the Rhodesian state were killed.[122] Resources were channelled to the guerrillas and uncooperative store-owners killed or their stores burnt down.[123] The international delegation which visited Elim in 1976 recorded that a local man who had reported the first visit of guerrillas to the mission had been shot as soon as he had returned from Salisbury a few weeks later. They noted: 'The whole of the African population in the area is in sympathy with ZANU and there is evidence that the school children are in contact with them.'[124]

At the end of 1976, the Rhodesian forces made a concerted effort to prevent the area from becoming a point of guerrilla infiltration and numerous contacts ensued. The government declared their operation a success.[125] However, in the period of relative quiet that followed, infiltration continued and J. C. Smyth, who returned in mid-1977 wrote of ZANLA: 'It now appears that their domination of the people is complete in bush areas where the people will do that which they are directed to do by them.'[126] From the beginning of 1977 the dominant focus of Brenda Griffiths's diary was no longer on guerrilla activity but security force harassment of people whose allegiance lay elsewhere. ZANLA had entered the area in 1976 already in possession of names of families known to be sympathetic to their cause. They initially went from homestead to homestead mobilizing these pockets of support. Only after building on this constituency did they begin to mobilize on a wider scale by means of the *pungwe*.[127] As time went on, the *pungwe(s)* grew in size.[128] The security forces now no longer dared to camp there. Instead, they would travel in from Inyanga for brief sorties before fleeing again. By 1978, the people of the area were able to sing their very own *chimurenga* song:

> The Boer has gone,
> I saw him go with white water,
> He has gone with the water of the Gaerezi,
> I saw him go, he went with white water.[129]

This issue of geography, I believe, partially explains the different pictures myself and Norma Kriger paint of guerrilla relations with the people. A strong sub-theme of her work on the war is the need of the comrades to use violence and coercion to mobilize the local population of Mutoko. Through Mutoko, her district of study, runs a wide tarred road, stretching from Harare to the border at Nyamapanda. Such a road would have given the security forces rapid access to the four wards upon which she bases her study. With the capital just over an hour's drive away, the guerrillas would indeed have had little opportunity to win the hearts and minds of the people. Kriger raises the issue of geography or accessibility herself but does not seem to grasp its significance. She writes: 'The greatest proportion of adult "refugees" — those who fled their rural homes because of the war and had nowhere to go and no one to support them — came from Murewa district (30%) with the next biggest percentage from Mutoko (13%).'[130] Murewa is also on the Mutoko road, only closer to Harare. On the other hand, Katerere, once the comrades seized control of communications, could be as much as seven hours' drive from the capital along deserted bush roads for much of the journey.[131] Within the space of a year the guerrillas had turned it into an area of transit through which they moved to attack commercial farms further south.

Finally, one brief case study will serve to illustrate how geography could ease relations with guerrillas. Between Elim Mission and Regina Coeli Mission lies the area of Kambudzi. It is approached through steep mountain ranges and across many rivers whose bridges were destroyed in the war. It was almost impossible for the security forces to get there.[132] Comrade Sam Zvaitika described it as 'liberated zone' run by a chairman, vice-chairman and treasurer. He remarked that: 'We were so many comrades that we could not get all our things in one go.'[133] Right in the middle lay an Elim church, which the people had proudly built with their own hands. It had its own clinic and primary school and had been the site of a very successful convention in 1973. The local headman was an Elim member. In many respects Elim Kambudzi could be seen as a sub-station of the main mission. Its leader was not a missionary but Ephraim Satuku, who had lived there for a while. He had instructed his flock well, warning them to form 'cells' in time of war. Ready when it came, they met in homes when afraid and openly in the church when safe. This "people's church" remained open throughout the war, a monument to the popular Christianity which had survived its full horrors and metamorphosized in the process.[134]

The liberation war saw the death of the old mission church and the birth of a new Zimbabwean church. The closure of the rural areas to Whites rendered much of the old-style mission work obsolete. The vacuum created by the exodus of missionaries was filled by Black Christians. Some were reluctant, but others showed initiative. The latter grasped that wider social relations were also in a state of flux, as guerrillas tried to win constituencies from women, youth, ethnic groups, and ruling and commoner lineages. Such Black Christian leaders with foresight worked hard to establish good working relations with guerrillas whilst not compromising their faith. Sympathetic guerrillas were courted and Christian 'go-betweens' elicited by these leaders. The perceptions by some guerrilla élites of the strength of popular Christianity caused them to take up Christian idioms, such as song, in order to mobilize support. In areas around Regina Coeli and Elim Missions, where the brokers of popular religion were Christians, guerrillas were forced to seek legitimacy from priests and Black pastors, rather than spirit mediums. In areas where guerrillas were strong enough to found semi-liberated zones, and Christianity possessed a deep enough rural base, it was allowed to coexist with the new revolutionary order.

From massacre to martyrdom: Mending hearts and finding meaning in violence in post-war Manicaland

Zimbabwe's liberation war did not just reshape the Church's structures and dictate the content of its popular theology in some impersonal deterministic manner. As I have shown, the Church's relations with both comrades and community during the armed struggle was a two-way process. The ability of guerrillas to come to terms with the representatives of popular Christianity influenced their standing with local communities. Likewise in post-Independence Zimbabwe, the Church's relations with wider society exhibits a similar dialectical nature. In the 1980s it has played a central role in mediating the tensions and healing the wounds brought about by memories of violence experienced in the previous decade.

The most visible impact of the war on the Church occurred at the level of personnel. Satuku and Munembe were to emerge as the Executive Chairman and the Executive Secretary of the Elim movement they had fought so hard to preserve. Patrick Mutume of Avila Mission, who had suffered imprisonment for his role in the struggle, was made a Bishop. But the Church had not changed only at the level of individual personnel. The war had seen a whole Catholic Order come into its own. The local Carmelite sisters, The Handmaids of Our Lady, had done much of the mission work at Avila in the absence of Black and White male authority, and had made 'remarkable progress'.[135] They were to retain much of their new-found responsibility after Independence.

Other changes at the level of faith and popular theology were perceptible. Elim missionaries talked of a 'sifting process' in which only the 'true Christians' would stand.[136] Indeed as the pressures of war increased, many churches were whittled down to a committed core. And as both oral and written archives indicate, these core members did stand as Christians in the face of violence and intimidation whether from guerrillas or security forces.[137] Many of those who remained committed to the Church did so of course in the absence of priests and missionaries. The war finished with the Church in the hands of the rural people. This was a situation reminiscent of the early days of the founding of popular Christianity in Manicaland, where a handful of over-stretched missionaries, often no more than station administrators, were forced to leave much of the evangelism to African teachers, evangelists and catechists.[138] Once again in the hands of local agents, and free to use their own creativity and imagination, the post-war rural Church likewise saw a period of rapid expansion. This process has been best documented in the extensive archives of Zimbabwe's Catholic Church which show that this appropriation of religious authority by the people made itself felt almost immediately.[139] In April 1980 a National Pastoral Consultation took place. On its deliberations, the commentator, J. Kerkhofs wrote the following:

> The local Church showed itself aware of the signs of a changed time. And in the face of many challenges it described its position very assertively 'as the need to adapt to change as a work of reconciliation and reconstruction' and visioned a place in this process as being 'a church of the people, listening to the people, at the service of the people'.[140]

This new 'rural dynamism' had a great influence on the shape of the meeting's recommendations on pastoral priorities. After reiterating an emphasis on evangelism and community building, it resolved that:

1. Priests must be free to concentrate on basic pastoral work . . . the aim is a self-reliant Church in which the life of the faith is truly incarnated as that of the local Church loyal to its communion.
2. To promote fuller involvement of laity in pastoral work of the Church.
3. To promote catechists for the above purposes.[141]

Increasingly the Zimbabwean Catholic Church was waking up to the fact that it was experiencing a revival in the hands of a previously powerless laity. Only two years later a report on the Church's pastoral efforts noted that:

> The recognition of lay vocation in the Church continues to grow more and more appreciated . . . Each diocese now has a training centre. Mutare's has only begun to function this year, but has already provided 26 seminars and courses on leadership, women's skills, youth and development . . .[142]

This process of constructing 'a new ecclesiastical division of labour and religious power'[143] had the assent of many of Manicaland's missionary priests who, when caused to reflect on their war-time experiences, realized that they had not been as deeply in touch with the aspirations of their flocks as they had previously believed they were. Hence they were more willing to assume a more supportive role in church work.[144] The case of the far smaller Elim Church was obviously very different. Although the Black church leaders there had expressed irritation at the slowness of the mission to give them responsibility, in actuality they received complete institutional control far too rapidly in June 1978. The disjuncture caused by the massacre of one missionary generation led to a void of administrative continuity which left the church's institutions reeling for the early years of Independence.[145] However, despite institutional problems, Elim's rural base pressured for both the re-opening of old churches closed down during the war and the founding of new churches.[146] The late 1980s saw a response to this with leadership-training workshops, and expatriate missionaries stressing partnership rather than paternalism.

Although the massacre of Elim's missionaries in the Vumba caused much hardship for those who survived them, the way those actors involved in the tragedy came to terms with its full horror gives insights into the dynamic nature of African Christianity with its continued ability to respond to crises. I have mentioned earlier in this chapter the conversion of a number of those involved in the attack on the Elim missionaries. It is now time to explore this remarkable event in some detail. Shortly after the war had ended, eight members of the platoon were in an army camp at Entumbane. Together, they experienced a vision in which they saw the cross and the hand of God coming against them in judgement. Seven of them immediately left the country and enrolled in Bible colleges in East and West Africa, whilst the eighth, not having a passport, joined a Pentecostal Bible College in Harare. Griffiths, sceptical of the rumours of this story he was receiving, was encouraged by Elim U.K. to investigate. He arranged a visit to the college and was introduced by the principal to the man who had led the attack on his colleagues. His appearance matched the description given by a lawyer working in Harare who had been a student at the school at the time of the massacre. The ex-combatant went by the pseudonym of Gary Hove. He had left Goromonzi School at the age of 14 to become the youngest platoon commander in ZANLA, operating under the Chimurenga name of Devil Hondo — War Devil. He expressed great concern about the relatives of the Elim martyrs. Griffiths was greatly moved by the encounter, and maintained a friendship with Hove from that day. A ninth member of the platoon had an equally remarkable conversion. An African pastor by the name of Mpofu, from Harare Intercessors, was invited to preach at a rehabilitation centre for ex-combatants in Troutbeck, Nyanga. Whilst preaching, a paraplegic man screamed and cried out for mercy. He later told the pastor that he had been one of those responsible for the killing of the Elim missionaries. All the guerrillas had been deeply struck by the sight of their victims praying for them as they were being slaughtered.[147]

Although particularly dramatic in Elim's case, this conversion to Christianity by ex-combatants was not an isolated event. In the period 1986–89 I came across the example of three White ex-security force members who had converted. Like

Werbner's ZAPU ex-combatants, they too were unable to talk about their wartime experiences, but in a similar manner to that of Elim's guerrilla converts, were involved in acts of restitution — in this case mission work in Mozambique.[148] Terence Ranger records a similar phenomenon. In 1981 he was told by Archdeacon Alban Makoni how ex-guerrillas who had killed African Christians came to confess to him that Christ and the Devil waged war in their hearts with AK rifles.[149] What all this reflects is the need of the war's principal actors to deal with both their guilt and memory of their victims.

This desire to come to terms with the past was shared by other groups who participated in the war. During the struggle the comrades were assisted by teenage *mujiba(s)* who gathered information for them, helped carry weaponry and organized *pungwe(s)*. These *mujiba(s)*, who now possessed a degree of power, actively turned traditional relationships with elders on their head. One *mujiba* described to me how he took strong drugs and beat old people slow to support the comrades. He went on to explain how he could exploit his new-found power over his elders: 'Since we were young boys we would go with girls. And if we found out that the father was refusing his daughter to go with us, that's the very time we would find ways of creating enmity between that man and the Boys (comrades).'[150] The war had not only exposed but also heightened generational tensions already deep in Shona society; Christian conversion again offered a means to ameliorate them. This *mujiba* told me:

> During the war I had become a notorious guy and had forgotten all about the Bible. But after the war, when the Word was preached to me again, I could see that I was wrong and I had backslidden. And I had to repent and after repenting I can say that all that happened in the war had nothing to do with me.

These post-war religious reprieves are also mirrored in the traditional idiom. In a recent article on trauma and healing, Pamela Reynolds explores this issue in a very detailed manner. She notes that on returning from the war, men and women who had fought on either side sought out traditional healers for 'rituals of expurgation'. Many came fearing retribution from *ngozi*, the avenging spirits of those they had wrongly killed as witches.[151] This form of healing differed from the Christian examples I have given in that it involved external cleansing as well as internal, and exhibited no evidence of acts of restitution. However, they both possessed a striking similarity in the central importance of confession. Reynolds observes that unless the patient tells the truth the ritual is ineffective.[152]

Christianity in post-war Manicaland has not only addressed the need for healing; it has also offered meaning to the violence many experienced during the struggle. Once again I shall illustrate this through the very specific case of the Elim massacre before widening the focus to popular Christianity in general. Very rapidly after the Vumba massacre the Elim movement struggled to make sense of the violence that had shaken it to its foundations. Out of the response from its local membership the idea of martyrdom soon developed. R. B. Chapman, the field superintendent found himself deluged with letters from students and ex-students from Emmanuel Secondary School horrified at the fate of their teachers. Yet, inspired by their example they promised to persevere in their faith.[153] When they transferred to new schools, many founded Christian groups at them and invited Peter Griffiths to come and preach.[154] As Bishop Donal Lamont pointed out to me, the sufferings of White priests and missionaries in the war had the effect of strengthening the Church. The people now knew that White Christians were committed to them.[155] The martyrdom had an impact on Elim's African leadership too. In July 1978 a meeting was held to review the future of the work in Katerere. Pious Munembe spoke strongly in favour of keeping it open. He told me: 'I said if aliens are prepared to come into a foreign land like this and work for God until their lives are taken in the war, how much more should the indigenous people be expected to work?'[156] Since the late 1980s northern Nyanga has been subject to a number of attacks from RENAMO who slaughter their victims in a frighteningly similar manner to the way the Elim missionaries were killed. The martyrdom of the missionaries gives the next generation courage in the present situation.

The martyrdom of the Elim missionaries has implications for the government's policy of national reconciliation introduced immediately after Independence. After the massacre in the Vumba it became apparent that the Elim movement had antagonized the White population of Umtali. The missionaries had refused police protection and alarms and fences had not been installed to increase security. Women and children had been left in vulnerable situations.[157] In its desire for neutrality, Elim seemed to have let the White side down. Worse still at the funeral service in Umtali, the movement offered prayers of forgiveness for the missionaries' killers. On the 30th of June 1978, the British *Daily Mail* published an article entitled: 'Grave side row over revenge.' It reported that Umtali's mayor, Douglas Reed, had taken offence at Elim's response to the killers. He told journalists: 'There have been prayers for the inhuman savages who did this. While I have no wish to take issue with those who preach this gospel, I would be less than honest if I did not state that the Old Testament teachings have more appeal to me than turning the other cheek.' Meanwhile in Britain, much to the distaste of the Elim Church, the neo-fascist National Front was distributing a leaflet showing a photograph of massacre victims in an attempt to discredit the World Council of Churches.[158] On the tenth anniversary of the Vumba massacre in 1988, the Zimbabwean press were still claiming that the act had been perpetrated by Selous Scouts. If Elim's relationship with the ex-ZANLA guerrilla who led the attack on their missionaries were allowed to be made public, it would have the potential to become a powerful symbol of reconciliation.

As in the case of the Vumba massacre, the wider search for the meaning of violence began during the war. Sister Janice notes that the staff at Avila Mission met regularly to share about the situation and plan strategy. Similar sharing and reflection processes existed at Elim Mission. Pious Munembe told me:

We often met for prayers and to thank God for protecting us from the security forces and the comrades themselves, because our fellow Africans were dying, being accused of being sell-outs and so on. And we thanked God for the food supplied by the Mission Aviation Fellowship and so on.[159]

Munembe's account of the mission's war-time history gives insight into the reflexive theology formulated by Zimbabweans at grassroots level which Victor Kwenda, speaking in 1981 at the Buriro/Esizeni Reflection Centre, assured seminarians was already taking place.[160] It was a contextual theology but not of the South American type, which Linden writes about but never finds, or indeed of the South African *Kairos* kind.[161] Rather, it was a theology that provided the faithful with hope and a concrete response to their sufferings. Munembe once again elaborated the point for me: 'We read often from the Psalms of David, when he was running away from his son Absalom and it looked like any time he might catch up with him. And he described God as his refuge — Psalm 23 especially.'

Ultimately, rural Christians' experience of the war affected the content of popular theology. In a recent paper entitled: 'The Meaning of Violence in Zimbabwe', Terence Ranger remarks that his initial readings of his oral material on Makoni district revealed ordinary men and women had been unable to grasp the historic importance of their sufferings because they seemed to lack public significance. On re-examination of his data, however, he realized that many people had been able to see their experiences as publicly significant by patterning them on traditional war myth stereotypes and heroic legends.[162] It strikes me that in a similar manner rural Christians found it easier to theologize their experiences of the war than to historicize them. Indigenous Christian theology readily offers meaning to suffering in story, song and symbol. Sister Janice in her case study of Musami Mission quotes a priest disappointed at the Catholic Church's failure to build on the experience of the armed struggle: 'I do not think they learned the lesson because the powers-that-be remained in town. They were never out there.'[163] If the analytical focus is moved away from the ecclesiastical centre to the rural base, a more encouraging picture emerges. Here, as other scholars have found, those seen as heroes were not the guerrillas themselves but ordinary people, who survived the war and at times against seemingly impossible odds.[164] Even today, rural Christians often find recourse in memories of the struggle and draw inspiration from the fact that they survived in their struggle to overcome the hardships they face today. This process can be seen at the level of song. Since Independence, many of the clumsily translated Western hymns have now been discarded. The rural Church has gone one stage further down the road of Africanization. Numerous *pungwe* songs have been transformed into Christian hymns. Thus:

Boys,
Boys, let's be courageous,
Until we take Zimbabwe,
Until we take it. — becomes:

Boys,
Boys, let's be courageous,
Until we get to heaven,
Until we get there. — Thus:

Heroes, heroes of Zimbabwe, died at Chimoio,
Sit down heroes of Zimbabwe,
So that we may remember those who died for Zimbabwe. — becomes:

Heroes, heroes of the gospel, died on the cross,
Sit down heroes of the gospel,
So that we may remember those who died on the cross.[165]

In yet another song, the figure of a sell-out called Nyathi is transformed into both Judas and the Devil. Thus popular Christianity in Manicaland possesses a remarkable internal dynamic which enables it to continually respond to crises which affect rural Christians. It has not just provided the means of giving meaning to, and healing of the traumas of the liberation war but has also reinterpreted the past to help ordinary people make sense of the present.

The war left the Church in the hands of local people. They had not simply appropriated its structures but also its religious authority. The new structures of the Zimbabwean Church reflected this with greater emphasis on lay vocation and an indigenous leadership. This renewed closeness with its base made it responsive to the needs of rural people in post-war society. The church has offered them the chance to come to terms with and heal memories of the war through acts of confession and restitution. Christians have found meaning for the pain they experienced through concepts of reconciliation, sacrifice and, in the specific case of Elim, martyrdom. This dynamic continues today as Christians draw inspiration from the war through the idioms of testimony and song as a means to help them overcome the hardships of the present.

CONCLUSION

To conclude, I believe the approach of this chapter has proved a vindication of the micro-study. The wealth and richness of written sources generated by one mission, corroborated by means of interviews with those who retain their history in oral form, provides the historian with a remarkable opportunity to reconstruct perceptions and experiences of the war. Although these are traced at a very local level, they nevertheless offer deeper and surer insights into processes which shaped religious history in rural Zimbabwe. In summary, Elim missionaries suffered from being disengaged from a sympathetic community and placed in a hostile environment, where they were to encounter hostile guerrillas. On the other hand, the Black Christians in Katerere survived the war with their mission intact through their sheer determination and ability to construct networks of information and understanding with both the local community and groups of guerrillas operating within it. Often these networks comprised Christians or people sympathetic to the Christian faith. Such networks with the local community have recently had to be reconstituted in order to deal with the threat of RENAMO bandits who have been more successful than expected in infiltrating the area. During the later stages of the war, it was no longer possible for missionaries to operate in rural areas and the vacuum of authority was filled by Black Christian leaders. This brought about a rapid indigenization of the church and the growth of self-sustaining base Christian communities. Thus, the outcome of the war left a legacy of an African church leadership and greater lay vocation. These are signs of a reappropriated religious authority.

This chapter has consistently shown that popular Christianity in Manicaland has taken deep root in the lives of rural people. This can be contrasted with Matabeleland, an area of very different cultural heritage. Missionaries who had worked in the former region and were later transferred to the latter, often contrasted with bitterness the spiritual fertility of Manicaland with Matabeleland's seeming spiritual dryness.[166] Popular Christianity seemed slow to take root amongst the Ndebele people. This is doubtless part of the explanation as to why ZIPRA were able to knock out with great rapidity the whole succession of missions in Matabeleland.

In the arena of ideas Christians met regularly during the armed struggle to reflect on their daily trials and sufferings. The content of their theology inevitably changed to become a theology of hope, action and endurance. Its content, expressed in the idioms of song and testimony, and in the concepts of sacrifice and martyrdom, continues to help rural Christians make sense of the many struggles they face in a post-Independence regime which has failed to fulfil the expectations they had of it. This new theology enables them to draw inspiration from their heroic survival of the trials of war. But it has not just offered meaning to their lives; it also contains the means to heal the trauma of violence many experienced through acts of confession, reconciliation and restitution. Thus, rural Christians have allowed their faith to interpret and be interpreted by their experience of the liberation struggle. This dynamic nature of Manicaland's rural Christianity explains its continued relevance in post-Independence Zimbabwe.

Map 2
Mutare Diocese

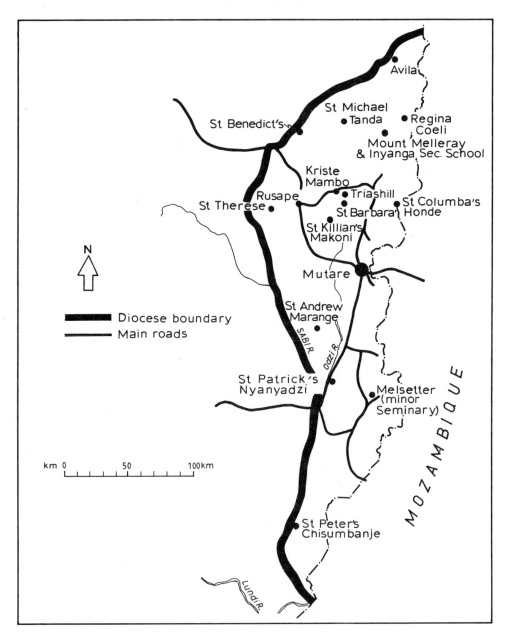

Avila Mission: A Turning Point in Church Relations with the State and with the Liberation Forces

JANICE MCLAUGHLIN

Bishop Lamont was really a thorn in our side . . . We saw him at the time as a person who was using the church to support terrorism. That was the official attitude . . . The sort of picture I think our security forces were trying to portray to the public and to the world was that the Roman Catholic Church in particular was actively involved in supporting terrorism in every aspect — from weapons, safe houses, information, supply of medicine.[1]

INTRODUCTION

The above admission by a former member of the Rhodesian Special Branch, who asked to remain anonymous, indicates the hostility that had grown between the Catholic Church and the Rhodesian Government during Zimbabwe's war of liberation.

It also indicates the central role which Bishop Donal Lamont played in destroying the partnership that had previously existed between the church and the settler state. An incident which took place at Avila Mission in northern Nyanga in April 1976 was the turning point which led to changes in the church's relations with the government and with the liberation forces.

This chapter will examine these changes. In particular it will look at the role of Bishop Lamont and the role of the local priests, sisters and laity at Avila Mission, as well as the consequences which events at one remote rural mission had for the entire Catholic Church in Zimbabwe.

THE WAR COMES TO AVILA

David Maxwell has done extensive research on Christianity in northern Nyanga and the impact of the war on popular theology in the area.[2] He has traced the histories of Elim Pentecostal Mission and Avila Catholic Mission, describing their rivalry as well as their similarities and differences. The chapter will not delve into the history of the mission, which was established by the Irish Carmelites in 1953, but will proceed immediately to the coming of the war to the area in early 1976.

Significant changes had taken place within the liberation forces by that time which were to have a bearing on subsequent events at Avila. In 1976 a combined army composed of forces belonging to both the Zimbabwe African National Union (ZANU) and the Zimbabwe African People's Union (ZAPU) was set up through the intervention of President Julius Nyerere of Tanzania and President Machel of Mozambique.[3] This army was known as the Zimbabwe People's Army (ZIPA), and was made up of younger, better educated guerrillas with a more radical socialist orientation. This group introduced scientific socialism into the curriculum of ZANU's ideological training centre which had previously concentrated on the 'national grievances' and on lessons from China's Red Army.[4] The radicals called themselves the *Vashandi* (Workers) because of their emphasis on a revolution led by the working class. They were opposed to the use of religion in the struggle, be it Christianity or traditional religion.[5] In view of Jeremy Brickhill's work on the ZAPU army, the Zimbabwe People's Revolutionary Army (ZIPRA), it would be interesting to know whether the ZIPRA cadres within ZIPA influenced this ideological development.[6]

ZIPA was able to take advantage of the new situation brought about by Mozambique's independence in 1975 and opened up two new fronts: Manica Province along the eastern border and Gaza Province in the south. Avila Mission was located just a few miles from the Mozambique border and was to become a transit station for the ZIPA forces on their way to and from Mozambique. In early April 1976, Sister Vianney, an Irish Presentation Sister who ran the clinic at Avila, received a handwritten note via a local resident, asking for medicine. When the Bishop of Umtali Diocese, Donal Lamont, arrived at the mission a few days later, Sr. Vianney showed him the note. Interviewed in Dublin in 1989, Bishop Lamont explained what happened:

> The sister showed me this dirty piece of paper asking to give the bearer medicine for malaria and diarrhoea. I said to Sr. Vianney, 'Oh, come off it, you know quite well who it is.' And she said, 'Yes, I know. What do we do?' I said, 'Well, give, give.' She said, 'That's alright but what about reporting? We are supposed to report.' Because, you see, the penalty was death for collaboration and the penalty was death for not reporting. I said to her, 'How could you possibly stay having informed? You're simply associating yourself with an illegal regime that is not recognized by any state in the whole world. You couldn't possibly do it.' And of course, it was alright for me to say that and then to go back to Umtali, but I regarded this as the only possible thing one could do. And they were extraordinarily brave women.[7]

When the guerrillas arrived a few days later, Sr. Vianney gave them the medicines. The ZIPA forces used the occasion to lecture the sister and the parish priest, Fr. Peter Egan, on Marxism. They spoke of 'the glories of communism and the evils of capitalism as represented by the Kennedys, the Rockefellers and the Catholic Church'.[8] They also ordered Fr. Egan to reduce the fees at the school and the clinic and asked him to get them watches and radios.

The next morning Fr. Egan reported the incident to the government authorities in Nyanga, and left the country a few days later, not to return until after independence.[9] Mr Wilson Martin Chiutanye, the mission driver and handyman known to the mission staff as 'Heavy Duty', explained why he thought that Fr. Egan acted as he did:

> Before Fr. Egan left, he was approached by the boys, Joboringo and Ruware and others. They demanded 12 watches and 12 wirelesses. The next day, the priest Egan called me and said that if we were to give . . . to the comrades it was a threat to him. If the government soldiers were to hear of this, he would be accused of supporting the comrades. If he didn't follow the wishes of the comrades, they would blame him for lying that he really loved the Blacks. He did not want to be in danger with both groups, soldiers and comrades. He decided to leave the mission.[10]

The security forces took their revenge on the mission almost immediately. Truckloads of soldiers arrived at Avila the day after the ZIPA forces had been there. They interrogated and beat people at random. Other soldiers shot at people from helicopters which hovered over the mission. They seriously wounded Mrs Maida Nyamapfeni, whose case was reported to the Justice and Peace Commission by Bishop Lamont.[11]

After this tragedy the Bishop called an emergency meeting of all his priests to develop a common policy. In spite of the outspoken leadership of their Bishop, who was also the Chairman of the Catholic Commission for Justice and Peace (CCJP), the diocese was not prepared to respond to the war. Though the Irish background of the Carmelite priests made them naturally hostile to the colonial government and sympathetic to the aspirations of the people, they did not know how to behave when armed men, shouting anti-Christian slogans arrived on their doorstep. Yet at the diocese meeting, they agreed to give the guerrillas whatever they requested and not to report their presence to the authorities.[12]

Bishop Patrick Mutume said that the decision was unanimous with the exception of one priest who left the country.

> . . we were going to take a common line of action, the whole team. We advised everybody who did not agree with this to leave the country . . . We decided at that meeting that whatever you do, you must think of your neighbour mission because the people in the next mission will suffer from your mistakes.[13]

Most of the rural missions in the diocese were visited by the guerrillas before the end of the year. Few, if any, experienced difficulties. Lectures on 'the glories of communism and the evils of capitalism' were expected and received with good humour if not agreement. The diocesan policy together with the Irish predilection for the underdog led to cordial relations between the guerrillas and the Irish missionaries, often bordering on partnership. Terence Ranger has shown several examples of this partnership at Triashill, St. Barbara's and St. Killian's Missions in his work, 'Holy men and rural communities in Zimbabwe'.[14]

Looking back on this period with a certain amount of satisfaction, Bishop Lamont mentioned the Irish connection:

> And it was total commitment and involvement and it was just taken for granted, the boys are coming and that's that. Incidentally, we had this experience here in Ireland and it was the same thing. The boys, you knew who the boys were. As a small boy, I remember being called one morning early by my mother and I was serving Mass. 'Go down and tell so and so that the Tans are here.' And it was always the boys and so we'd been through it. I think you could go to any mission station and you'd find that they all knew the lads.[15]

Bishop Mutume concurred, recalling with a laugh that to be Irish was a sure sign of acceptance by the guerrillas.

> What struck us in the Umtali Diocese, is that each time they (guerrillas) would come to a place for the first time, they would ask us, 'Are you Irish?' And when you said yes, they'd put down the guns against a wall and they would ask for a drink . . . They immediately were at home. The relationship was quite good . . . Some of our priests were so much on their side that you sort of had to warn them that . . . you could not show that visibly. It could be dangerous.[16]

Thus, in spite of the bad beginning at Avila, the missions throughout Umtali Diocese developed good working relations with the liberation forces. The common policy which they had adopted united them and enabled them to know what to do, regardless of the attitudes and behaviour of the various guerrilla groups which visited them. As we shall see, the guerrillas also adopted a common policy in response to church support and to government persecution of the church, and modified their slogans and behaviour accordingly.

GOVERNMENT RETALIATES AGAINST THE CHURCH

The Rhodesian authorities were not unaware of the collaboration between rural missions in Umtali Diocese and guerrilla forces. They saw Bishop Lamont as the mastermind behind this 'subversive activity' and looked for a way to silence both the Bishop and the Justice and Peace Commission which he chaired. The same former Special Branch Officer quoted at the beginning of this chapter, who happens to be a Catholic, described the official attitude at the time.

> Bishop Lamont was really a thorn in our side. He seemed to enjoy it and he was quite open in his criticisms and his assistance to the nationalist cause . . . And we saw him at the time as a person who was using the church to support terrorism.[17]

An Irish nun, who was a great friend of Bishop Lamont, inadvertently gave the government the information it needed to move against him. Sr. Susan McGrath, the superior of the Presentation Sisters, who had sisters at Avila and other missions in Umtali Diocese, was asked by police officers whether she knew that her sisters were assisting 'terrorists'. She acknowledged that she was aware of their activities, adding, 'The Bishop told us to do it.'[18] This offhand remark was the evidence the government had been seeking. The Bishop was arrested at the end of August 1976 just as *Civil War in Rhodesia,* a second Justice and Peace compilation of security force war crimes, was released and just as the Bishop issued a strong statement disassociating the Catholic Church from Rhodesia Front claims to be defending Christianity.

> Far from your policies defending Christianity and Western civilisation, as you claim, they mock the law of Christ and make Communism attractive to the African people . . . On whatever dubious grounds you may one time have based your claim to rule, such argument no longer has any validity. You may rule with the consent of a small and selfish electorate, but you rule without the consent of the nation, which is the test of all legitimacy.[19]

The Bishop's trial in September 1976 was an international event witnessed by a host of foreign journalists and observers. In order to spare Sr. Susan from being called to give evidence against him, Bishop Lamont pleaded guilty and delivered an unsworn statement. His *Speech From the Dock* traced his own personal history, the development of the diocese and pertinent Church teaching on social issues, including excerpts from his own pastoral letters. He went on to recount the incident at Avila Mission which led to his arrest, explaining the 'missionary dilemma' of whether to report and face retaliation from the guerrillas or not to report and face retaliation from the government.[20] The Bishop was found guilty of failing to report the presence of 'terrorists' and of counselling others to do likewise and sentenced to ten years in prison, reduced to four on appeal. In March 1977 he was deported. Meanwhile the local priests, sisters and laity at Avila Mission also faced the wrath of the government forces. In mid-1976, a furious Rhodesian soldier pinned Father Patrick Mutume against a tree in the mission yard. Putting a gun to his head, he shouted, 'You black bastard, speak up. One dead missionary is as good as one hundred dead terrorists'.[21] This threat quickly spread through the mission grapevine.

Patrick Mutume was taken from Avila to Ruangwa Camp in October 1976 where he was beaten and tortured for five days. Mr 'Taffy' Evans of the Special Branch, who became notorious for arresting priests, put him through the 'ordeal', telling him frankly that he might be dead or permanently maimed at the end of it.[22] Bishop Mutume, who rarely speaks of this experience, described what took place in an interview in his office in 1989.

> Each day you had to take a special course. You had to go through this course when they put your head inside water; when you are tied to a jeep and the jeep is driven; the electric shocks when they connect you to the battery of a jeep. And they do all these things and many other things like that.[23]

Fr. Ignatius Mhonda was taken by police from Avila to Nyanga Camp on the same day as Mutume. The government tried but failed to get him to act as a witness against Mutume. A blow to the head perforated one of his eardrums.[24] Both priests were detained in Rusape. In February 1977 they were tried and sentenced to five and a half years for failing to report the presence of 'terrorists'. They won the case on appeal, convincing the court that the law of reporting was unjust since it was an automatic death sentence.

> . . . if you did not report the government will sentence you to death. If you did report, the freedom fighters will sentence you to death. In each case you are dead. The church wanted to prove that this law could not be kept — you only keep it and die.[25]

The lay staff were also arrested, beaten and tortured continually. The headmaster of the school, Mr Constantine Munyaka, co-ordinated the collection of $10 each month from each of the 20 teachers to buy supplies for the liberation forces.[26] One of the priests usually co-ordinated the purchase of goods. 'Heavy Duty' was often sent to collect the supplies, risking arrest at numerous roadblocks on the way. The mission used to treat wounded guerrillas, not only from the immediate vicinity but from other missions in the diocese as well. On several occasions Fr. O'Sharkey from Tanda Mission used ingenious methods to get through the roadblocks. One diocesan legend tells how Fr. O'Sharkey hid an injured freedom fighter under a bench in the back of his pick-up truck. Five young women were seated on the bench, singing at the top of their voices as if they were going to a wedding. They would increase the volume at roadblocks and be waved through.[27] There are other diocesan legends about how these guerrilla patients miraculously escaped detection each time the security forces searched the mission, even looking under the nuns' beds.[28]

At Avila Mission, for the first time church personnel had become the victims of security force brutality. This heightened the conflict between the church and the government to such an extent that when missionaries were killed at the end of 1976 and the beginning of 1977, many sectors of the church believed that the security forces and not the guerrillas were responsible.

GUERRILLA RESPONSE TO THE CHURCH

When ZANU launched its mobilization campaign in the north-east of Zimbabwe in 1972, its policy was to win as many friends and as few enemies as possible. With this goal in mind, community leaders were to be approached first, be they headmen, spirit mediums, Christian clergy, businessmen or teachers, in order to use them to help win over the wider community.[29] Hudson Kundai, who was ZANLA's Provincial Political Commissar for Tete Province, explained how the mobilization strategy worked.

> The official position was that we had to respect the culture of a community of which religion was also a part . . . The official position of the Party was that we had to mobilize all the forces against the common enemy . . . When you got into a new area, you would either approach the local *mudzimu* or the Church that was the most influential in the area.[30]

At the same time as ZANU practised this pragmatic and ecumenical approach toward religion, it took a more critical stance towards Christianity in the political education which each freedom fighter received. In the 'national grievances' series of lessons, Christianity was presented as an adjunct of colonial conquest. It was also viewed as divisive and destructive of African culture.[31]

In the early days of the war, that is, 1972 to 1974, traditional religion was drawn upon to mobilize popular support for the guerrillas.[32] Not much work has been done on guerrilla relationships with Christian missions during that period. My own study of St. Albert's Mission in Centenary indicates that relationships were strained at best. Neither European missionaries nor guerrillas had developed patterns of interaction, viewing each other with suspicion if not outright hostility and mistrust.[33]

The détente exercise brought the war to a temporary halt in the mid-1970s. When it resumed in 1976 under the ZIPA leadership, a much more negative position toward religion in general and traditional religion in particular was adopted. Though they considered themselves to be Marxists, many of the ZIPA guerrillas were products of mission schools and saw missions as potential sources of assistance. On the other hand, they felt that traditional religion was being used by the Rhodesian forces to lure them into ambushes.[34] Possibly their mission education also made them look down on traditional religion as 'peasant superstition'. Though they advocated scientific socialism, they too were pragmatic. While shouting anti-Christian slogans and telling priests and sisters that they would be forced to marry after independence and that churches would be turned into public halls, they asked the missions to give them food, medicines, clothes, radios and watches.[35]

However, the events at Avila Mission which we have just described, changed the outlook of these young radicals towards Christian missions. The violent retaliation by the Rhodesian government against Bishop Lamont and the mission convinced the guerrillas that the Catholic Church was on the other side. They reasoned that the enemy of their enemy must be their friend, explained one of the ZIPA ex-combatants.[36] With this in mind, they revised their critical position, regarding missions as allies in the struggle.

A former ZANLA provincial commander for Tete province, Air Vice-Marshall Perence Shiri, described how his own views were changed by the witness of Bishop Lamont and some of the missions during the war.

> Bishop Lamont fought very hard. Actually, he was a hero in his own right for the cause of the Zimbabwe people . . . When I came home where the actual battle was being fought, I had to slightly sideline Marxism and look at the actual situation in Zimbabwe . . . it became very clear that religion wasn't all that much of an opium of the people . . . The image that was given by the Roman Catholic Church had to force even a lunatic to realize that the Church was behind the struggle, so we became allies.[37]

Major-General Constantine Chiwenga, another former senior ZANLA commander who was also in ZIPA, expressed a similar opinion.

> . . . the missionaries were part and parcel in revealing the evil which was being done . . . through organizations like the Justice and Peace Commission and other forums where they could denounce the regime for illegal detentions or torturing people and killing people. So it was clear, ZANU and the Church were one. We were fighting the regime through the armed struggle and yet they were fighting the regime through their own front. But the end result was the same.[38]

We have seen that at about the same time that the ZIPA leaders were revising their attitude towards Christianity, the Irish Carmelites were meeting to determine a common policy and outlook towards the guerrilla forces. Their policies converged. The Carmelites and diocesan priests in Umtali agreed to assist the guerrilla forces, regardless of their anti-Christian rhetoric or threatening behaviour, thus averting potential conflict between the Church and the liberation forces.

When ZIPA was disbanded at the beginning of 1977, there was a revival of the use of traditional religion in some areas of the country by some groups of guerrillas. Christian missions, however, continued to play a vital role as logistics centres. When the first Christian missionaries were murdered at the end of 1976 and the beginning of 1977, the liberation forces went out of their way to clear their name, drawing closer to missions in the field and publicly expressing their alliance with the Christian churches.[39]

A PRIEST AND SISTER CROSS THE BORDER

A sequel to this story of interdependence between guerrillas and Avila Mission involves the local religious superior, Sr. Helen Nyakupinda, and a diocesan priest, Fr. Maximan Muzungu, who crossed the border to Mozambique. Such identification with the liberation forces would have been unthinkable a few years previously. Helen left the mission in mid-1977 after she had been threatened with death by the Rhodesian forces. Her cousin, Batahana, who was the ZANLA detachment commander for the area, offered to rescue her by taking her to Mozambique. She gave the matter serious thought before boarding the bus to Nyamaropa where the catechist's wife took her to a nearby ZANLA base. The guerrillas took her to the Catholic mission at Catandica. She remained in Mozambique until independence, working at both mission hospitals and FRELIMO government hospitals.[40]

Fr. Muzungu, who grew up at Katerere and was a graduate of Avila Mission, had been arrested and detained several times by the Rhodesian government. He is mentioned in a ZANLA field report of an attack on Nyamaropa Camp on 8 January 1978:

> As for the attack on the enemy side, a Father Muzungu — a reliable source of ours who stays near the camp, informed us. He pretended to sympathise with one black soldier he saw . . . The soldier told him only two of them managed to flee.[41]

He also played a role in organizing a meeting between Red Cross officials and ZANLA forces after three Red Cross workers had been killed near Regina Coeli Mission in May 1978.

> I went to see the comrades and asked them what had happened and so forth. They said they would apologize for that. After some time, we organized a meeting with the comrades and the Red Cross personnel . . . The Red Cross people came. Then we drove them in my car to the spot and they then started discussing all that had happened and then an apology from the comrades was heard.[42]

Fearing re-arrest for violating his restriction order, Fr. Muzungu crossed the border to Mozambique in September 1979. He spent four months at ZANLA bases in Tete Province, receiving political and military training. He was assigned to ZANU's Chitepo College as a political commissar just as the war ended. He spent the next five months in Dendera Assembly Point in Mutoko before being demobilized to return to the priesthood.[43] His impression of life in the camps and the place of religion shed further light on the subject.

There was really a good spirit of sharing. When you buy a pack of cigarettes, you have to give nearly everyone . . . it was really a hard life. Sometimes we could spend three to four days with little or no food and we could only moralize ourselves by singing and talking, just trying to encourage one another. I made quite a lot of friends there. Some knew me from the missions and surprisingly some days the girls would sing Church hymns . . . As regards my prayers there, I only had the rosary with me. We had to surrender everything . . . but I asked them to give me back my rosary . . . so it was returned to me . . . They didn't prevent me from praying. I used to say my rosary every morning, walking in the camp back and forth, and in the evening . . . They didn't have any services in the camp because they said it would sort of divide them. There would be Catholics coming for services and non-Catholics won't be coming. So a misunderstanding may be caused there, thus dividing the camp.[44]

CONCLUSION: AVILA MISSION — A TURNING POINT

Avila was the first Catholic mission to be visited by guerrillas in Umtali Diocese. It was also one of the first missions in the whole of Zimbabwe to be visited by the ZIPA forces. It can therefore be seen as a test case.

The first contact with guerrilla forces precipitated a diocesan crisis. The act of reporting the presence of the guerrillas and the swift and brutal reprisal by government forces against the civilian population galvanized the entire diocese into action. Belatedly, the religious personnel prepared themselves to take a common stand. In spite of the ambiguity caused by ZIPA's Marxist orientation, the priests and sisters unanimously agreed to assist the guerrillas and to defy government regulations requiring them to report the presence of guerrillas to the authorities.

The brutality of the Rhodesian forces was most likely one of the strongest factors influencing the decision. If government forces had not responded so cruelly and so destructively against the peasant population, the Church might have tried to remain neutral. The myth of a church-in-the-middle was shattered at Avila. No doubt the persecution of church personnel by the government was also a decisive factor. By arresting, trying and deporting Bishop Lamont and arresting and torturing Father Mutume, the government had declared war on the Church. The ill-treatment of bishops, priests and the religious at the hands of the government signalled a radical change in church-state relations.

The church at Avila was found guilty of assisting one side in the war. This antagonized the government to such an extent that it viewed the Church as a traitor and the incidents at Avila were the turning point. The 'cordial relations' that had existed between the Church and State since 1890 were extinguished. The Catholic Church and the State were now on opposite sides of the fence. Instead of supporting government forces as the Church had done during the African resistance campaigns of 1893 and 1896–97, the Catholic Church stood with the African majority.

This re-alignment was recognized by the liberation forces as well. Unbeknown to the Church, its changing of sides came at a critical juncture in the liberation struggle. Just as a leftist group espousing Marxist-Leninism had assumed leadership of the nationalist forces, bishops, priests, sisters and lay Christians were being arrested, tortured and deported. Faced with the reality of a church with the people, some ZIPA leaders revised their attitude towards religion in general and Catholic missions in particular. They came to be seen as allies rather than as enemies. The rift between Church and State was so deep that when the first missionaries were killed at the end of 1976, few rural missionaries believed that the guerrillas were responsible for the murders.

The guerrillas had gained a new source of support, both moral and material. From 1976, the liberation forces knew that they could get assistance from Catholic missions. Spirit mediums were now joined by Christians as motivators and mobilizers. Appeals to traditional religion and Marxism declined as Christian missions became reliable and trustworthy partners. Avila was the new church for the new society, changing church-state relations irrevocably.

Many points raised in this case study require further research. For instance, the full history of ZIPA and the *Vashandi* Movement has yet to be written. ZIPA's attitude towards Christian missions also requires deeper study. I may have accepted assurances from former ZIPA leaders that events at Avila changed their attitudes and behaviour towards Christian missions too readily, especially since other former ZIPA members expressed the fear that their 'extremism', as they called it, might have led to the murder of some missionaries.

While both Linden and I speak of the divisions in the church during the war, we do not go into them in any depth. Further research on the opposition to Bishop Lamont from within the church itself might provide some interesting contrasts and show the other church which continued to take sides with the government. In my thesis I have examined the role of ideology and traditional religion in relation to the church, but both of these topics require additional study in light of the new material available in the ZANU Archives. The subject of religion and the war is a vast one, that can open up new insights in theological, political and military studies.

4

Rhodesian Discourse, Rhodesian Novels and the Zimbabwe Liberation War

ANTHONY CHENNELLS

On 4 July 1964 a Melsetter farmer was stabbed to death after his car was stopped at a road block.[1] He was the first Rhodesian White to be killed by African guerrillas since 1897. For nearly 70 years settler novelists had from time to time titillated their readers with the prospect of another rising. When it came, most novelists did not recognize that another rising had indeed begun. Much less did they realize that the rising of settler mythologies had been transformed into a modern revolution which could end only in their defeat.

There is an assumption underlying what is usually said about the war that the whole Rhodesian cause was sunk in its own iniquity; that black was white, and white black; that White Rhodesians made clear moral choices towards evil which could be answered only by justifiable violence. I do not propose to defend the Rhodesian state on moral grounds but it may be true that a moral analysis, a division into categories of vice and virtue, does not get us very far in trying to penetrate the substructures of the Rhodesian state or the Rhodesian mind which reproduced itself in the specifically cultural discourses of Rhodesia. It is beyond the scope of this chapter to link the Rhodesian discourses at its point of origin with other late-nineteenth-century discourses which liberal historiography continues to read as progressive. But it is surely now reductionism to see the British South Africa Company's expansion into the north simply as some mechanical process of British and Cape capital. Rhodes was not a conservative; the grab for the north was not a conservative action. It was an attempt to create a radically new space. This means that another way of reading Southern African history is to take its own discursive space seriously. For Whites who came to Rhodesia, like their contemporaries who went to Canada or New Zealand, Rhodesia was, at least in part, ideological space and the economic structures they created were, at least in

102

part, subservient to ideological ends. Rhodesia, as a space, defines an English race that discovers through the process of conquest and appropriation the nature of its own civilization. The English become a race only through relation to their empire; Rhodesians as spokespeople of the discourses of empire are also naming their own identity. Any social discourse proclaims within itself the space which has produced it, and which it has appropriated and named. In the case of this country, the name Rhodesia proclaims its difference from both South Africa and the rest of Africa to the north of it.

It is in his struggle to discipline both the perceived unruliness of African nature and the nature of Africans that the Englishman becomes his true self, and the Rhodesian who in turn has appropriated that discourse becomes his or her true self. The problem of African nature is relatively easily solved: it can be shot or preserved, exploited, developed or cherished. It can certainly be categorized and therefore named. The problem with Africans is that they escape such discursive location. While the discourse insisted that Englishness by itself would eternally define Africanness as other, what finally placed natives in their relations to English was their location in juridically enforced space. It is valid to read the enclosure of a Reserve, at least partially, as the closure of an irrelevant or hostile discourse. But it is closure only in White perception. Whites believed they had closed Black discourse to prevent Blacks from producing an open discourse capable of appropriating new items and therefore of transforming Blacks themselves. The reserve, then, is space which will be for Europeans outside the missions, and perhaps at some periods the Native Department, a space which will remain eternally primitive.

One of the complexities of the settler discourse, however, is that while it has fixed the relationship between Black and White in stasis, it also demands the enactment of justice, commerce and freedom upon both Black and White. In the case of Blacks this means their raising from their savage slumber to the dignity of farm or mine worker, house or garden 'boy'. Progress breaks constantly into the closed parameters of primitiveness and the fixity of the paradigm is constantly under threat. To put it another way, the demand for unskilled and later more skilled Black labour created a tension between the closed primitive discourse and the settler discourse which, because it claimed progress as its distinguishing character, was open. Contradicting the very primitiveness which Whites had claimed for them, Blacks were brought into a discourse which was open and whose end, because of that openness, could not be predicted. When Blacks are increasingly forced to encroach on White urban space, it becomes necessary for Whites to hold as an article of faith that there is always somewhere else which Blacks can call home where they are the primitives of the discourse.

The settler discourse always claims to be able to read under the appurtenances of Christianity or the veneer of civilization and to see what is really there: the genetically, racially determined nature of the Black. This has several consequences. One of them was the desperate attempt by the Native Department after 1927 to resurrect a dying past. The past is a text of which the Native Commissioner has become the true author and which, as the past is remembered only by the Native Commissioner, exists only in the Native Commissioner's mind. The Rhodesian settler novels show again and again how closure operates differentially between these two discrete spaces: White Rhodesia because it is progressive refuses closure and at the end of a characteristic novel Whites are looking forward to a future in a highly developed White country; Black Rhodesia because it is primitive is closed and the narratives write of Blacks as denizens of stasis. If novelists choose to show progressive Blacks, they are shown not as entering into White space but into a limbo of false appearances, immorality, debauchery and brutality.

The discourse as I have described it presupposes subject Whites and object Blacks. What happened with the founding of the Youth League in the 1950s was that for the first time Whites were aware that Blacks were writing themselves as subjects of a discourse which could no longer be accommodated within the closure effected by White discourse. As successive nationalist organizations were banned (and each banning can be read as an attempt at closure through silence of an inadmissible discourse), the settler discourse became increasingly more rigid in its categories. The war, when it came, could not be a war; it could only be a rebellion which meant, in settler mythology, primitive space attempting to reabsorb civilized space, and it was a battle against this reassertion of the primitive that the war was described and indeed fought. Their failure to understand what was happening around them was entirely predictable. Victims as they were of their own discourses, fostered over the years and kept ignorant by their media of developing ideologies among Black nationalists, the settlers and their novelists had few means of correctly analyzing the situation in which they found themselves. Perhaps the most striking feature of the novels which I shall look at in this chapter is their limited understanding of both the motives of the nationalists and the progress of the war.

The Blacks in Rhodesian war novels are in consequence the comic buffoons, the savages or the people with a veneer of civilization, easily stripped aside to reveal the essential savagery beneath, which they have been in the novels since the occupation. The Whites are still the men and women of the frontier, stern or kindly as the occasion warrants with people whose essential childishness is only rendered dangerous by their adult physicality. In some novels they are still the young men and women of a new world, actors in a colonial pastoral which, as with so many colonial literatures, rebukes the decadence and staleness of Britain with its youthfulness, its fresh optimism and vigour. All the items of the discourse which have informed the settler novel from its inception at the end of the nineteenth century continue to appear in these levels: Great Zimbabwe whose ruined state is a salutary warning of the fate of settlers who lose the will to rule; the Ndebele as natural allies of the settlers against the Shona; these are present together with the more obvious accounts of White Rhodesian sovereignty.

There are differences. As the war progresses and the discourse becomes more difficult to sustain, a hint of hysteria enters the novels. This sometimes can be sensed in the more strident assertion of the uniqueness of the Rhodesian identity than would have been necessary 20 years before; sometimes in the ingenious solutions the novels propose to bring the war to a victorious conclusion and which have little bearing on the practical realities of the fighting; and sometimes in the very complexity of the international conspiracies which are ranged against Rhodesia.

A feature of these novels, as I have suggested, is their ignorance of who or what the settlers were actually fighting. ZANU and ZAPU are mentioned by name in some of the earlier and later novels and Merna Wilson makes something of the divisions between the nationalists in her imaginary political parties in *Explosion*, but only in 1977 in Robert Early's *Time of Madness* do the rivalries between the parties become an issue which the settlers could exploit to their own advantage. Where the novels do note differences between the parties, these are shown to arise from ethnic antagonisms and merely confirm the myth of the Ndebele trying to recapture their lost kingdom. For most novelists the 'terrorists' belong to amorphous organizations, headed by leaders living outside the country who are in turn controlled by international communism. Ideological differences between the parties are largely irrelevant for the discursive framework disallows Blacks from extending — opening — primitive discourse to include a Western ideology unless some White is there to open it on their behalf. This makes it impossible for Blacks to produce sophisticated ideologies which would be the basis for factional differences.

Nevertheless the novelists register an unwilling, sometimes unconscious, awareness that this Rhodesia is a subtly different place from the country that for 70 years had so easily accommodated settler discourse. Since any particular discourse requires a constant relation between its dominant signifiers, during the war these had either to be rejected or strained to embody a new situation. Wilderness, animals and savages possess that constancy; wilderness, savages, AKs, grenade-launchers, land-mines and Marxist-Leninism do not. White Rhodesian discourse had written the first half of the set, but the second half, whose signs have been created outside that discourse, cannot be contained by it, particularly as they exist as a negation of the discourse. The signifiers have been extended with weapons and ideology and the discursive set has ceased to be closed. Ideally Blacks have to remain in a metonymic set which signifies the natural and the primitive and which are entirely at the disposal of the Whites. As it became impossible to ignore that the war was being enacted with the strategies and tools of modern warfare, weapons and Marxism are mentioned but the novels attempt to absorb them into savagery. Marxist-Leninism is written as an import, creating a metonymic link between the alienness of Godless communism with its own peculiar barbarities and the otherness of primitive Africa. Those who are recruited to fight are written as being driven both by the force of others and their own atavistic lust for cruelty. The signs which should have aroused the settlers to a recognition of their own predicament are written as belonging only to a savage past which had been closed in 1897 and which would inevitably be closed again.

In 1966, W. A. Ballinger's *Call It Rhodesia* shows a group of Whites gathering to discuss UDI. They are told that even if the 'Pan-Africanists' decide to invade Rhodesia,

'We could beat the living day-lights out of them.' Even if they have guns, it will not be an issue: 'It's not the guns, it's the man behind the guns. Are we afraid of black invasion? I say no.' Listening to the discussion, one of the settlers realizes that liberalism is 'sweet surrender . . . The world belonged to the strong. The future, God help us, belonged to her and her breed.'[2]

Twelve years later in Emily Dibb's *Spotted Soldiers*, the war is being described in terms like this:

[The guerrillas] operated like phantoms, stealing down the mountains during the nights, and then melting away again before daylight. The farmers were goaded to fury, and [the Rhodesian soldiers] became progressively more fatigued and frustrated as the attacks intensified.[3]

As I have suggested, settler discourse always attempted to externalize Blacks from White-controlled space — literally through the creation of Reserves and through the Land Apportionment Act, discursively through terms like 'savage' and 'child' which made them alien in civilized or adult space. Ballinger through the conceit of 'Pan-Africanism' insists that the threat will come not from within but from outside Rhodesia's borders — for while Rhodesian Blacks armed with spears might rebel, Blacks armed with rifles could come only from some space over which Rhodesians had no control. By 1978 this reassuring fantasy was no longer tenable. Dibb externalizes Blacks by making them creatures of the night, a malevolent spiritual presence, 'phantoms . . . stealing down . . . melting away', removed from human space. Still some change is registered. 'Farmers' is subject to a passive verb, and fatigue and frustration suggest that Whites have been objectified by the war. The Whites in this passage are far removed from 'strength and her breed'.

Since the novelists were looking into their own mythologies to explain Black dissidence, it is not surprising that the first war novel published after 1965, Robin Brown's *When the Woods Became the Trees* should have an Ethiopian-type movement as the organizing force behind the militants. As early as 1907, Cullen Gouldsbury's *God's Outpost* attributed a rising to an Ethiopian church leader in collaboration with traditional spiritual leaders and in several novels of the 1930s the leaders of independent churches instigate risings. Unlike most Rhodesian novelists, Brown is willing to accord some sort of value to the mainstream mission churches. Blacks can only be the losers when in place of texts from the mission, they start to carry booklets 'written by the Chinese in patronizing Shona'.[4] Maoism and Ethiopianism are offered in the novel as a set which lies in opposition to the sets which are produced by a liberal White Rhodesia in which the established missions are an important item. Uniquely among these novels, a White priest mediates African opinion, and one of the more important themes of the novel is that the Black

Messiahs, as the Ethiopian movement is called, is able to find a constituency among Blacks only because of the failure of White Rhodesians to exemplify Christianity in their dealings with Blacks. The teenage narrator, Gentleman, who is struggling to think his way clear of racial prejudice, has to move from a discourse which produces remarks like, 'The Kaffir regards kindness as a weakness',[5] to an understanding of the priest. Gentleman observes a ritual murder where a Black woman painted white is hacked to pieces and the priest explains that what the boy has witnessed is not 'just animal brutality. What you saw was an act of racial symbolism.'[6] The West, he explains later in the book is 'losing out by pure default' in its decadent secularity,[7] and the teachings of Christ 'are in sharp contrast to the manners of behaviour of the majority of Europeans in this country'.[8] At the end of the novel, Salisbury is encircled by barbed-wire entanglements through which the armies of the Black Messiahs break. As they are about to overrun the city, the priest arranges for himself to be crucified in their path. Overcome by the sight both Black and White join in racial harmony around the cross. Only in Christ can true peace be found.[9]

In 1965 it was still possible to write of Black militancy but be chiefly concerned with the spiritual welfare of the settler community. It was also possible in 1965 to claim that in the discursive space of Christianity lay a genuine liberation for both Black and White Rhodesians. For all the racial tolerance implicit in the novel, Brown can conceive of Black nationalism as having no other content than a perversion of Western spiritual traditions which is made possible precisely because those traditions have been perverted by the racism of the settlers themselves. The messianic oratory of the Messiah's leader is not indigenous; it does not derive its authority from an African experience of resistance to colonialism. Instead it is produced out of the space which lies between the discourse of missionaries represented by the priest and the quite contradictory practice of the settlers. In the context of the other novels, *When the Woods Became the Trees* seems at first sight surprisingly radical. In fact it is merely eccentric. Settlers loathed the missionaries precisely because they were aware that Blacks emerged from the missions who could not be accommodated within the normal racial taxonomies around which the settler discourse was shaped. The educated Christian Black, who for so many years had been reduced to the 'cheeky' mission 'boy,' was feared because he could write himself as subject of a discourse which denied his objective status as child or savage. The Black Messiahs are merely a more complex rendering of the type. Settlers wanted only to return Blacks to the subservience of White control. Brown's novel which seeks to return them to the control of the missionaries is another writing of the same paradigm.

A much more conventional response to nationalism is to show that its authority over Blacks is achieved by a combination of magic and thuggery which serves to confirm that they are contained within a closed discourse of irrationality and timidity. In Merna Wilson's *Explosion*, there is a scene where Petros, the Z. U. organizer in the novel, is recruiting supporters and collecting party dues at the

Polyphemus mine. When the mine sergeant dutifully pays, Petros remarks scornfully,

> He knows which side to back . . . Although his job is telling tales to the white men, he is afraid of Z. U. . . . he knows that his white friends will not protect him from the wrath of Chimuzu [the party leader] . . . the wrath of Tobiradzai, the witch-doctor.[10]

Only John Mbale on the mine refuses either to join the party or give it any money and there is a debate at the Z.U. headquarters as to the appropriate means of dealing with him. 'As he is uneducated', Chimuzu ponders, 'perhaps the *tagati* approach might work?' But Petros reminds the reader that Mbale's son, Ben, is at university and will therefore be in a position to reassure his father.[11]

Ben Mbale is as unwilling as are most of the Blacks in the novel to have anything to do with politics, but he is under pressure of a different sort. He has already been forced to join sit-in strikes, organized by a Professor Granger, who sneers at those who refuse to go along with his plans and is quite capable of failing them in their examinations. While magic and thuggery will not work with such a man, academic pressures and promises will. Chimuzu realizes that the best way of dealing with him is by offering him a scholarship to Moscow. Another perspective on educated Blacks is being developed here. The missionaries' role in sowing sedition has been taken over by men like Professor Granger and 'Exeter Hall' has been replaced by a world press corrupted by socialism. One of the reasons why Ben Mbale is uncertain what to do is that the British Government influenced by the press might suddenly decide to hand Rhodesia over to Chimuzu. Chimuzu knows only too well that his path to power lies not only in manipulating the fears of the people but in playing on the prejudices of a naïve world. 'We are dealing with a world that is all on our side!' he says. 'Have you forgotten that? Whatever we tell these fools, they will believe so long as we appeal to their idealism.'[12]

As I have mentioned *Explosion* shows some awareness of the fighting between the main nationalist parties. In the novel this is translated into Chimuzu's strategy of keeping the attention of the world press focused on Rhodesia while the strategy of the rival People for Action is simple terrorism. One of the dissidents in Chimuzu's party dismisses his strategy as 'stupid ideas'. 'Violence! Watch!' he says to Chimuzu. 'You will see blood run in the streets of every town. The blood of the White people! The blood of the Black people who will not co-operate with us!'[13] In 1966 these remarks could be shown to be mere rantings. By centering the novel on Chimuzu rather than on the P.F.A., Wilson is emphasizing that the threat to Rhodesia comes not from Black-initiated programmes of violence but from a Europe which has lost its political will to maintain African empires. As Wilson writes it, nationalism is no more than a struggle for power among ambitious men and its targets are Blacks rather than Whites.

When *Hold My Hand I'm Dying* was published in 1967, John Gordon Davis had every reason to know that Black militancy was a great deal more than another manifestation of unrest in the reserves. During 1966 he had been on the prosecuting team during the trial of ZAPU soldiers who had undergone training in the Soviet Union and subsequently infiltrated northern Matabeleland. Davis would therefore have had access to information which was not available in the heavily censored local press. This trial becomes an incident in the novel.[14] It is perhaps for this reason that *Hold My Hand I'm Dying* is more aware than most of the novels of the strategies employed by the nationalists in the mid-1960s. It is also more impatient than most with White complacency and obduracy. It is also very confused as to the appropriate reactions to the events that it is describing — which is hardly surprising since in view of the trial in the novel and references to UDI, the last quarter of the novel at least must have been written during 1965 and 1966. To place events in a fictional narrative almost as soon as they happened would have tested a more competent novelist than Davis.

Mahoney, the narrator of *Hold My Hand I'm Dying*, is capable of outbursts like: 'For Chrissake, what the bloody white Rhodesian can't realize is that the wog is going to rule Rhodesia'.[15] He advocates partnership but not the Partnership of Federation which meant that 'We just sailed on being Bwana.' Partnership for Mahoney means according a person his or her dignity and civilizing 'the African youth so that they can take their place in a modern commercial society'. There will be a future for Whites only when they've created 'a middle-class of munts, who are conservative and suburban and reasonable', indifferent to the 'swaggering, power-drunk, ignorant political hoods'.[16] Mahoney realizes that this is a game of cynical self-survival. Educated Africans will be kept happy with a few carefully selected appointments and promotions and the masses contented with 'brass bands and fire-work displays and free kaffir beer'.[17]

Passages like that reveal Mahoney's view that the people he intends to accommodate exist low on some scale of inferiority which, for all their stupidity, has White Rhodesians near its top. 'I looked around at the wogs jabbering in the bus and picking their noses and spitting, black and wooly-headed and ignorant and primitive, and I liked them. I realized I loved Africans . . . but I do not want to be ruled by them.[18] This is perhaps as honest a statement as any which occurs in the novel and that the sentiments are Davis's is suggested by that ungrammatical shift to the present tense. If a man loves Blacks, wooly-headed and primitive, it is understandable that he will have no love for those who aspire to rule him. The proclaimed love for the primitive does, however, serve to introduce another discourse which to an extent developed during the war. Rhodesian novels from the very beginning employ primitivist, romantic anti-capitalist, or pastoral discourses which lie in awkward contradiction with the more obvious and more dominant discourse of a new and progressive White nation in the making. The novelists were always torn between allowing their characters to live in harmony with the wilderness as a means of recovering their essential humanity and transforming the wilderness into a space where agricultural, mining and industrial capital could flourish. Invariably the very presence of Blacks created problems for the novelists: primitivism made little sense where a White was surrounded by

Blacks whom he believed were more successfully primitive than he could ever aspire to be. It was the very absence of civilization among Blacks which justified his presence in the country. During the war, however, what had been awkward and contradictory before became asserted with more confidence. Blacks were indeed primitive and more contentedly close to nature. Whites had unfortunately passed beyond that stage but the very sophistication which civilization accorded them allowed them to see the value of the primitive. Primitive people and primitive places must be preserved.

The first parts of *Hold My Hand I'm Dying* centre around the flooding of the Zambezi Valley by the dam at Kariba, which is registered in terms of hysterical regret that a sophisticated technology has destroyed a wilderness whose metonymies are elephant and the Tonga. Elephants, lions and 'Batonka', all mount 'their willing womenfolk' in spring for example[19] and as an extension of that set 'black men trust you and call you elder father'.[20] In those parts that deal with the war the opposition between advanced technology and the primitive are displaced by an opposition between, on the one side, civilized Rhodesia and, on the other, primitive Blacks and ideologies produced from Moscow and Peking, as artificial as the dam and as alienating to the people of the plateau as the lake waters were to the valley Tonga. The discourse of White nation builders is not entirely lost. A friend of Mahoney can assert his identity in terms which have been used for seventy years: 'I am a Rhodesian, this is *my* country . . . Sixty years ago it was a desert occupied by a handful of savages, now it's a good little country [sic] . . . I'm not going to let Britain sell us down river for a bunch of half-baked savages to wreck.'[21] This is an acceptable discourse although one of the strengths of the novel is that it also registers with some cynicism the heroic talk which greeted sanctions. In a Bulawayo bar, Mahoney realizes that no other White there has ever been into the bush. Their tans come from swimming pools, 'not from taming the wilds of Africa'. And he ironically dismisses them: 'The bush-tunicked, felt-hatted, leopard-skin-banded, bush-breaking, belt-tightening Rhodesian pioneers who'll happily eat sadza, my poor aching ass.'[22] Whatever else these people are they are improbable custodians of the wilderness.

Hold My Hand I'm Dying remains an interesting novel because of the very confusion of the discourses it employs. Sometimes Mahoney is siding with the Whites because Moscow and Peking can only destroy what is most valuable in Africa which is its primitiveness. This is localized in the narrative when Joseph Ndhlovu, Mahoney's Ndebele servant and companion, is press-ganged into leaving for the Soviet Union for training. He is the faithful Ndebele whose type appears in many Rhodesian novels as a reassurance that the more discriminating primitive will submit to the will of the strong White man. At other points in the novel Mahoney's decision to fight has no more complex motive than a determination to help Whites preserve what Whites have built. As Mahoney explains to his girl-friend:

There is only one important thing left to do. And that is to fight. There is
no more time for moderation. There is no more room left for moderation
and moderates. The black nationalists don't want moderation in Rhodesia.
Peking and Moscow don't want moderation in Rhodesia. Moderation is
compromise, and, therefore, moderation is weakness . . . That is the
tragedy, that is why there was UDI, that is the tragedy of UDI — you are
forced to choose between black and white . . . The Rhodesians have made
a stand. Now they must fight for it.[23]

There is little in the first three-quarters of the novel to justify such a conclusion.
Instead it should be read as a response to developments during 1965 and 1966 and
shows how a more belligerent White nationalism developed after the early
incursions. It also shows how the earlier affection for Blacks which is located in the
primitive cannot survive when articulate Blacks with a coherent political ideology
propose to use arms to create a modern state which is not Rhodesia. A White may
perhaps love 'wogs' and 'munts' when those contemptuous terms signal distance
which ensures that the object of love remains objectified. When the Black refuses
to remain objectified and be written as primitive, love becomes an inconvenient
emotion. Whatever else the guerrillas are going to do they are not going to call you
'elder father'. This is confirmed in the ending of the novel. An attempt is made to
blow up the Kariba wall. In a startling shift of significance, the wall is no longer
the signifier of civilization destroying primitive Africa. Now it signifies settler
creativity which the nationalist armies simply want to destroy in a blind lust for
power. The attempt on the wall is foiled and Mahoney's baby is born during the
fighting. Now that the war has begun in earnest, White Rhodesia requires as its
most important sign an intact Kariba rather than a White who is at one with the
intact primitiveness of the valley.

The exploration of a White civilization which can, if it chooses, benefit from a
primitive Africa recurs in Alan Burgess's *The Word for Love* which was published
in 1968.[24] Its dating is confused for although UDI has taken place, the Union Jack
still flies and ZAPU has not been banned. Ndabaningi Sithole and Joshua Nkomo
are mentioned by name but they have nothing to do with the nationalist
organization in the novel, the Zambezi Independent People's Party. The local
leader of this organization is the voice of nationalism in the novel and he has
received his training in the United States where he assumed the name of Ali
Hassim Khan. If Rhodesians refused to believe that Rhodesian Blacks could produce
their own political agenda, the Black Muslims or Moscow or Peking or indeed all
three could be made the instigators. In the novel a British South Africa Police
Inspector, Bill Field, is accused of raping a 'rain goddess', Lupin, whom he has
rescued after a ritual murder in the Sabi Valley. Only towards the end of the novel
is it established that Lupin seduced Field and was instigated into laying charges of
rape against him by Khan who recognizes the propaganda value of a rape charge
against a senior policeman. Rhodesians had begun to appreciate that there are
more political advantages to themselves than a paradigm which proclaimed

difference if Blacks were contented primitives. The corollary to this, however, is that without the defences of European rationalism, primitives can be manipulated by ruthless politicians, who recognize, like Merna Wilson's Chimuzu, that if they can appropriate the spiritual powers in rural societies they have a unique control over the people. By playing on the fears that Lupin is heir to, a man whose name and training make him sinisterly international sets out to destroy Field who is a suitable representative of the rational stability of settler rule. Earlier novels regard with some amusement White policemen who sleep with Black women, an inevitable occurrence in a society where there were not enough White women to go round. In this novel inter-racial sex is made an important item in the discourse which seeks to bring the primitive and the sophisticated into a mutually informing relationship. Field's wife is sterile; the 'rain goddess' represents fecundity. Field is in love with a settler woman but custom forbids that he leave his wife and marry her and thus he has no chance of having children. The 'rain goddess' is the medium between the spirits who will guarantee a harvest and the community and it is her spiritual function which recalls Field to the cycles of Nature which are more imperative than social conventions. The political and erotic themes are tenuously linked. Nationalism and Western marriage conventions are both artificial impositions on Africa which knows only the seasonal cycles of birth, fruition and death. In allowing himself to be seduced by the 'rain goddess', Field has responded to archetypical urges and is nearer to his essential nature in consequence. An Africa which turns to someone like Khan will have turned its back on the source of its vitality. In the end, however, the order which the novel directs the reader towards is not those indigenous systems of belief which have managed to remain intact despite the settler impact. Efficient descriptions of homestead burnings in the Tribal Trust Lands and riots in Harare, which are in fact based on the rural and urban unrest following the ZANU and ZAPU split, locate order very firmly in the settler government and the British South Africa Police. Rhodesians probably did believe in some vague way that the youthful vitality they saw as their distinguishing characteristic owed something to an untouched wilderness but the discourse which attempts to incorporate the primitive as an item has problems in incorporating as other items in that set the gloomily respectable Rhodesia Front Cabinet and the starched, efficient police. The value of the primitive to the settlers, their government and police lay in the ease with which it could be controlled. Beside that the recovery by a police inspector of his fecundity had to remain a very secondary consideration.

It was not until 1969 that a novel was written by a Rhodesian which claimed to deal explicitly with the war. Daniel Carney's *The Whispering Death* announces on its title page that 'This book is set in Rhodesia sometime after the Declaration of Independence when the population faces an ever increasing rise in acts of terrorism.' Carney had been a member of the British South Africa Police between 1963 and 1967 and with that background and the information he presumably had access to, he might have provided a novel which at least attempted to reconstruct something of the reality of that 'terrorism'. But items within the discourse were more real to

Rhodesians than the events which were becoming part of their daily lives yet which clearly refused discursive itemization. The discursive space which Carney's narrative occupies is made up of those fragmentary understandings of Black history and Black politics with which Rhodesians have from their earliest novels justified their claim to know the native. An albino, claiming to be the spirit of Lobengula, who will lead the Blacks against the settlers, is the leader of the guerrilla band. Later novelists such as Peter Stiff were able to draw considerable consolation from Ndebele-Shona rivalries. Carney's historical imagination is fixed on the Rudd Concession and its assumption that the Khumalo kings were sovereigns of Mashonaland. Like the Mashonaland settlers in 1896, he sees an Ndebele arm behind every Shona spear.

> But if a man were to go into the reserve and claimed he was Lobengula's spirit, [Terick, the novel's protagonist, argues] if he could perform a few tricks, hold a few impressive ceremonies, he might be able to sway them or at least terrify them so much that they couldn't hand him over.[25]

Carney's Blacks are produced not only from the Rhodesian discourse but from two centuries of imperial writing: they are the savages able to be beguiled by tricks and ceremonies and the White, in imperial romances at least, is a past-master of both.

The albino kills Terick's wife and all thoughts of tricks and ceremonies are forgotten as the novel sets primitive emotions of love and revenge against the imposed structures of law and order. Much later in the war the novelists show senior officers in the police and army responding to savagery with savagery. In 1969, although the District Commissioner and Member in Charge indulge in childish games, for this is still a Rhodesia where all the world is young, they are both men upholding the highest standards of justice and equity among a savage people. This point is made clear when Terick is arrested and condemned to death for hunting and killing the albino. Official Rhodesia, inhibited by standing orders and a determination that justice should be seen to be done, tries orthodox methods in pursuing and arresting the killers of Terick's wife. Terick and his faithful Ndebele companion, Katchemu, set out to hunt down the albino. 'Oh Mambo', Katchemu said softly, 'I will follow you unto death. She was my madam and it was my farm too . . . We'll go hunting you and I, my Mambo.'[26] The good primitive, who almost without exception in the novels is Ndebele, claims equality within shared interests even while acknowledging in 'madam' and 'Mambo' the essential hierarchy of white over black.

Novels like *The Whispering Death* show how necessary it was for Rhodesians to be able to enter into primitive discursive space when they wanted to, to allow themselves to be written within the primitive discourse, although as leaders of both settler and primitive space they are also able to author the primitive. By the fact of authorship, they remain in control of both spaces and as the novel demonstrates the dominant signifiers of Rhodesia as a whole are not those which signify the atavistic but instead the police and law-courts. Terick's narrative is framed by prologue and epilogue which are located in the prison cell where he awaits execution. The albino manifests a nationalism which has escaped from the present to a primordial discursive paradigm. Whites can move into that paradigm if they wish and there is something profoundly satisfying in adopting the ethics of the primitive. In the end, however, the civilized and the progressive will exact its price and necessarily so because in the end it is these that Rhodesia signifies.

No novel shows more clearly the security the settlers derived from primitive and untouched Africa than Antony Trew's *Towards the Tamarind Trees*. It is one response to the war that in Trew's untouched Zambezi Valley only man is vile: 'Into this wilderness had come from time to time . . . terrorists, insurgents, guerrillas; they were called all these things but if their nomenclature was in doubt their purpose was not — they had come to kill.'[27] They are not the only bloodthirsty men in the valley. A prospector has found gold and is concerned that the guerrillas will bring soldiers into the area of his claims and the mining companies will force him out. American and South African hunting parties are filled with the murderous obsessions which popular novelists like to attribute to the very rich. Only the Game Ranger, Rufus Richards, who has devoted his life to the animals of the valley, is free of avarice or political ambition.

The guerrillas in the novel are thus another manifestation of man's reckless desire to disrupt nature. As is suggested by his apparent indifference as to what they should be called, Trew is indifferent to their political motives or indeed to the rights and wrongs of their cause. Rufus Richards has made the preservation of the valley's wild life his absolute and in his eyes at least the activities of the human characters in the novel are imperfect when measured by that standard. Trew does, however, seem to be making some political judgement on the nationalist leadership. The ZAPU official, who has no intention of crossing the Zambezi is fat, 'with shiny briefcase, gold wristwatch and gold-rimmed glasses'.[28] Several subsequent novels — *The Rain Goddess, Game for Vultures* and *A Time of Madness* — draw a comparison between the life-styles of the political leadership in Lusaka or Maputo and the men in the bush and much was made of this discrepancy in the Rhodesian government's propaganda pamphlet. In the novels the venom with which clothes and accessories of the political leadership are described is part of a discourse which is almost as old as the novels themselves. The well-dressed Black is obnoxious and dangerous because he lies in some unexplored space between the comfortingly secure spaces of civilization and savagery. This particular official makes an impassioned speech on the privileges of those who lead the way for the thousands who will follow. Even if they should die, 'what finer glory than to spill your blood for Africa',[29] a remark which is particularly ironic in a novel where all human activity has no other end than the destruction of Africa's animals and by implication Africa itself. In novels like this the most important signifier of Africa is its animals and only secondarily its people and then only if they can be written as primitive. The very absence of any ideology in Trew's guerrillas prevents a political or economic or social agenda from becoming another of Africa's signifiers. Such an agenda can exist only in another set whose signifier is the destruction of Africa. In justice to Trew he does make the point that the Johannesburg tycoon in the South African hunting party 'has made a great deal of money from the sweat of under-paid African labour'[30] Any glory that the ZAPU official attains will be paid for in the blood and sweat of the guerrillas. There is little to choose in their effect on Africa between the Rand capitalist and the Zimbabwean nationalist leader.

In 1972 Wilbur Smith published *The Sunbird*. There had already been substantial incursions into Rhodesia and the willingness of Blacks not only to organize but to fight against the settler order had become apparent to any observer of the Rhodesian situation. At the end of 1972 the liberation war started in earnest. As the prospect of war loomed before White Rhodesians they felt the same insecurities that they had felt in the 1890s and as they had done in the 1890s the novelists turned to Great Zimbabwe, recognizing the lessons which an embattled settler society could learn from the ruined city. On a site on the Rhodesia-Botswana border, Kazin, the novel's archeologist hero discovers the remains of an ancient Carthaginian city, which his excavations show to have been destroyed by Black hordes sweeping down in their southward migration. As the first carbon-datings from the site confirm that Kazin's theories of an early date for Great Zimbabwe were correct, Kazin reflects, 'Somewhere between A.D. 200 and A.D. 400 an armed Phoenician warrior led his armies and elephants across this beloved land of mine.'[31] An invading army in a beloved land might well be expected to arouse hostility. The unconscious, and revealing, irony of the remark is that Kazin is thrilled at the idea. For throughout *The Sunbird* an explicit parallel is being drawn between the Carthaginian colonizers and the Whites of Southern Africa and the fate of the older civilization becomes the possible fate of the new. All the major characters in the contemporary section of the novel have their counterparts in the City of the Moon or Opet, whose history Kazin finds written out on scrolls of gold. The Emperor of the old city becomes in his twentieth-century incarnation a ruthless Rand industrialist, who is offered as a type of contemporary capitalist glamour, while the Bard of Opet becomes Kazin himself, a scientist-historian performing the function of bard in modern society. The Black king who sacks Opet becomes the Moscow-trained, Johannesburg-based academic who leads the guerrillas fighting in Rhodesia.

Throughout *The Sunbird* Africa is invoked as a uniquely brutal continent and it is an easy movement from the images of, and allusions to, savagery to the contention that only Carthaginians or White Southern Africans can contain the impulses to savagery around them. After Kazin and his party have fought their way out of a guerrilla ambush, they drive to Bulawayo. Kazin immediately thinks of Opet:

> A great civilization, a nation which held dominion over an area the size of Europe, a people who built great cities of stone and sent their ships to trade to the limits of the known world. All that remained of them were the few poor relics we had so laboriously gleaned. No other continent

was so fickle in the succour it gave to men . . . A cruel land, a savage and merciless land.[32]

In its perverse refusal to acknowledge that social and economic conditions may provide motives for political action, *The Sunbird* is a remarkable addition to a tradition of novels not notable for their political understanding. So intent is Smith on emphasizing the innate savagery of Africa that he does not recognize that the comparison between Opet and Bulawayo is profoundly subversive. In a fickle continent all attempts to build are purposeless whether Carthaginians, White Rhodesians, Afrikaners or indeed Blacks are the builders. The novel emphasizes that the Blacks in the City of Moon are slaves or serfs but seems to be unconscious of the irony that if the parallels are followed through these have their counterparts in the Black workers of Southern Africa. In any case, the Black hordes sweep down from the north. Mageba, the guerrilla leader, leaves his office each day to live with apartheid. If it is a benevolent order that his inherited savagery drives him to destroy, it is at least an order with which he is intimately acquainted.

As the parallel characters in the old and the new hegemonies indicate, history repeats itself, and the only constant feature is Africa's savagery. Whites establish their states which are characterized by technological skill, a love of beauty and the delights of leisured living, only to have them destroyed by savages unable to appreciate what they have created. If Blacks rise against South Africa or Rhodesia, then, like their predecessors, they can have no other motive than to destroy.

Great Zimbabwe was an important item in settler discourse because it seemed in its ruined state to recall the settlers to the destructive savagery surrounding them and remind them that any lapse in vigilance might bring about the same fate which had befell their colonizing predecessors. Smith is only too aware of the ease with which Whites, surrounded by their smiling land, can lapse into a state of foolish complacency. He hammers the point home by making his academic colleague the mysterious leader of the incursions. Timothy Mageba has had a brilliant academic career and runs the African Languages Department of Kazin's institute with phenomenal efficiency — seven 'authoritative dictionaries in five years'. But these are merely the trappings of civilization and the savage is still active in Timothy Mageba:

> The nose broad and flat with flaring nostrils, the lips a thick purple black and behind them strong white animal teeth. From behind this impassive mask a chained animal ferocity glows through eye slits . . . There is a dark satanical presence about him, despite the white shirt and dark business suit he wears.[33]

Initiated into the mysteries of his traditional religion by his 'witchdoctor' grandfather, even in his Johannesburg office he is liable to lapse into a trance as the spirit of his grandfather possesses him. His academic achievements should have transformed his natural bestiality. Instead as this passage suggests they are no more than an imperfect mask through which the primitive animal can be glimpsed, satanic and bestial. His Marxist-Leninism and his leadership of a band of sophisticatedly armed guerrillas are denied the status of transforming signs. They are merely extensions of what, it is implied, is the irreversibly savage nature of all Blacks.

In the same year that Wilbur Smith published *The Sunbird*, Laurens van der Post published *A Story Like the Wind*, the first part of a two-part novel, the second part, *A Far-off Place*, being published in 1974. Nowhere in these novels is Rhodesia mentioned by name and it is part of the novels' intention that Hunter's Drift, the farm that the guerrillas overrun, should not be able to be located with any accuracy in either time or space. Historical and geographical precision would be mere vulgarity in novels which are concerned to allow 'the flow of a primitive world . . . to help thaw the frozen imagination of our civilized systems so that some sort of spirit can come again to the minds of men.'[34] In fact Hunter's Drift can be located without difficulty in northern Matabeleland and the action of the novel takes place some three or four years after the first massacre of Whites in northern Angola which marked the beginning of the Angolan revolution. The point is worth making that however much van der Post should choose to disdain the exigencies of contemporary ideologies and political boundaries in favour of some primordial world spirit, not only do these possess an authority of their own but require that the fiction takes a stand in relation to them. No discourse will remain neutral towards them.

Thus although Francois Joubert, the central character, whose growth from childhood to manhood the novels describe, grows up in harmony with the nature around him, it is necessary that van der Post should distort Africa in order to allow him this spiritual intimacy. It is a central contention of both novels that no Blacks with whom we are invited to sympathize aspire to the life of modern Africa, but have to be held like flies in the amber of van der Post's imaginary continent. Inevitably the signifiers within the novel contradict one another. Hunter's Drift is a curious mixture of feudal hierarchy, socialist commune and reservation which will keep its inhabitants unspotted from the world. In fact it is an idealized version of some nineteenth century Boer frontier farm which is signified by the baroque gables of Cape Dutch architecture on the farmstead. Even then the modern cannot be prevented from smashing through this idyll. The farm's irrigation systems and range of crops deny the primitive, even as the routines of back-breaking labour which such farming demands remove Hunter's Drift from a contented integration into the rhythms of nature.

When the first guerrillas come into the vicinity of Hunter's Drift, their presence is indicated to those accustomed to listen to the messages of the bush by changes in the calls of the birds showing that something unnatural has come among them. The chief medium of the area begins to prophesy disaster for God has appeared to him in a dream telling him of the great trouble which is about to come over the land: 'Could not all see, the dream asked, how young men had forgotten the praise names of Umkulunkulu and no longer spoke of him but only of things that were useful to them?'[35] Clergymen arrive at the house and announce that they are from the 'World Council of Christian Churches' on a mission to look into 'the exploitation of the innocent black people of Africa by you settlers, and to advise on the extent to which it was a Christian duty to help the "freedom fighters" of Africa in their battle against imperialism and neo-colonialism.'[36] This is perhaps an attempt at satire for the clergymen's faces are 'pink' and 'well-fed', a telling condemnation of their lack of commitment to the real and primitive Africa for at Hunter's Drift all Whites are lean and tanned. But if it is satire, the order from which it derives its authority to mock is not primitive Africa. Primitive Africa is one polarity; the other is a profoundly conservative Europe which has as its local sign in Africa a Cape Dutch farmstead. The other polarities in the novel are that Europe on the one hand and on the other the leaders of the guerrillas who are not Black but a Chinese with Scottish and French mercenaries as seconds-in-command. Radical clergymen, dissident Europeans, a Chinese chairman are the strange amalgam of forces which will undermine Europe. Primitive Africa may be foregrounded in the novel but its foregrounding serves only to restore to Europe its spiritual health. Significantly the Black revolutionaries are almost silent in the novel. *A Story Like the Wind* contains the most sustained discourse celebrating the primitive of any of these novels. By registering Black revolutionary ideology only as silence, the novel allows the primitive an integrity which is totally closed. If Africa should ever turn its back on its essential self, it will be at the promptings of people who are alien to it and who are driven by philosophies of destruction and death, antithetical to the primitive which kills only to preserve.

One other novel was published in 1972 which showed that there were novelists who were not content to see Rhodesians entirely within their own discursive terms — the victims of international conspiracies or Africa's inherent savagery. Meredith Cutlack's *Blood Running South* was promptly banned in Rhodesia as a result. The Whites fighting in the novel belong to a mercenary group, the Association of South Africa, Portugal and Rhodesia — ASPRO. ASPRO's plan is to disrupt the Zambian economy and the internal security of the country so that it will become impossible for the nationalist forces to maintain either training camps or staging posts north of the Zambezi. This was in fact to become Rhodesian strategy later in the war. The brief glimpses that the novel provides of the nationalist leadership against which ASPRO fights does not instill much confidence in their ability to overthrow White Southern Africa. Great Zimbabwe, which so inspires Ibwe, one of the leaders, was according to Payne, the journalist narrator of the novel, built by people 'of whom nothing was known'.[37] Ibwe is relying on a myth in order to pursue a dream.

The Blacks who disarm the mercenaries and disrupt their plans are men who are members of neither ZAPU, ZANU, nor the ANC. As one of their officers explains to Payne:

'We are none of these. Our aims are often similar. We are, it is true, associated with all three organizations . . . I am an African,' he said with an air of dignity. 'An African, and that is all that is of importance. One day, Mr Payne, that will mean something.'[38]

When I first read this novel, as with Robin Brown's *When the Woods Became the Trees*, I thought that something new was being attempted which resolutely broke with the settler discourse. It seemed that by ignoring both the settler armies and the main nationalist parties, Cutlack was deconstructing the ideologies of the opposing forces to arrive at some essential element in each. The Blacks assert a pride of race which the settlers have refused them for 80 years; the settlers destroy Black political structures in order to maintain an economic power so that mercenary becomes a synecdoche for the entire settler ethos. But in fact Cutlack is caught up in one item of the discourse: Blacks cannot act effectively without Whites directing them.

A man called McNeil appears throughout the novel, a composite perhaps of Sir Robert Tredgold and Sir Garfield Todd. Like Tredgold he resigned a senior judicial position in protest against racist legislation and the description of his farmstead recalls Todd's Zvishavane ranch. Like Todd he has moved from being a leading member of the liberal establishment with all its hopes of compromise to a recognition that the future of the country lies in the hands of the Blacks. At the end of the novel it transpires that he and his sons are organizing the guerrillas who destroy ASPRO. Payne sees McNeil 'as one of the old-style benevolent men of the Empire'.[39] He attributes part of Rhodesia's problems to the immigrant who came in after the war, and who was handed an 'unearned position of authority . . . simply because he was white . . . Many . . . are less educated, less intelligent, certainly less decent than their servants they pick up at the labour pool for a few shillings a week, the day after they arrive.'[40] Unlike McNeil, Ian Smith and the majority of the settlers are common little people incapable of exercising the authority that circumstances have thrust upon them.

Despite his role as guerrilla leader McNeil is the ideal settler or administrator both in imperial fact and fiction. What seemed new in the novel is in fact an early item within the settler discourse. Empire is in the hands of the educated, the intelligent and the decent. Without rejecting racial difference one of its ends is to allow Blacks to share at least in that decency. The novel silences both the nationalists and the settlers except to allow the fatuousness of the first and the mediocrity of the second to reveal themselves. Present and articulate are Blacks who have been produced by an imperial discourse and who without loosing pride in self are able to defer to a man like McNeil. In 1972, to return us, as this novel does, to the ideals of an empire is in its anachronism a striking evasion of the actual issues which had made the liberation war both morally necessary and inevitable. Empire provides a discursive space where Africans can embark on their liberation with both dignity and moderation. It is a space controlled by imperial benevolence and lies somewhere between the unacceptable discourses produced by Rhodesia's settlers and the nationalists.

Peter Stiff's *The Rain Goddess* which was published in 1973 attempts a far more sustained guerrilla perspective on the war than any previous novel had provided. Stiff rose to the rank of Superintendent in the British South Africa Police and for anyone in that position, it must have become perfectly clear by the end of 1972 that Blacks were refusing to exist contentedly within the closed discourse the settlers had written for them. The scale of ZANLA incursions into the Chiweshe and Rushinga areas and the organization of the forward bases surprised all those who were concerned with Rhodesian security. Nevertheless there is little in the novel to alarm the settlers. Men who have left Rhodesia to join the guerrillas in Zambia are disillusioned by the incompetence of the military commanders in Lusaka. When they return across the Zambezi, they soon realize that the significant military victories claimed in Lusaka are mere clashes where small bands of their comrades are annihilated.

Nevertheless the detail in the narrative which would have offered the most consolation to Stiff's White readers is the insistence that the guerrillas are able to recruit youngsters only by accident or deceit. Kephas Ndlela, the guerrilla on whom much of the novel focuses, attends his first nationalist meeting more because he is frightened of being denounced as a 'sell-out' than because he is taken in by nationalist claims. 'All these men can do for us is to bring us trouble with the police', he says. 'I have heard they live with fat whores in big houses in Salisbury and Bulawayo on the cash they collect from uneducated people in the tribal areas.'[41] His cynicism is shown to be correct. Simon Gumede, the nationalist leader from Salisbury, is a cowardly crook exploiting the primitive bloodlust of simple peasants. In the first flush of enthusiasm the people who attended his meeting turn into a savage mob and attack a village whose inhabitants are suspected of indifference to the nationalists' cause. 'Fire, fire, fire', they chanted, their eyes glazed with savage excitement, each man hypnotized by violence. Kephas is no different. His instincts respond to the brutality around him and he sets fire to the thatch of a hut, his eyes staring . . . from madness'.[42] Inevitably, the police catch up with him and he flees to Salisbury, where Gumede persuades him to leave the country, promising him that he will be trained as a doctor if he does. Only when he is outside Rhodesia does he realize that he has been recruited for military training.

What Stiff fails to explain is why Kephas, who has every reason to hate the nationalists, should become one of their more dedicated fighters. He, in fact, makes no attempt to account for the dedication of any of the guerrillas entering a country where according both to the novel and the propaganda at the time they will almost certainly be killed. Instead, contradicting the very evidence of his narrative, Stiff insists that not only is the Black discourse as firmly closed as Whites always claimed it was, but makes the author of that closure the *mhondoro* of the title, the medium who controls rain in an area. As Burgess showed before him, the spiritual authorities in Shona society are finally more significant than the guerrillas will ever be. The latter work for change; the *mhondoro* wants only to reproduce the social formations and the social practices which have remained intact and been sanctioned over the centuries. In the novel the 'rain goddess', opposed as she is to the violence and death that the guerrillas have brought among the people of Senga, withholds rain until the people themselves are willing to turn against these disturbers of traditional stasis. When Kephas is finally killed there is a bolt of lighting and rains begin to fall. By suggesting that the *mhondoro* does actually have power over rain, Stiff raises to a mystical truth what was a political strategy by Internal Affairs which was to ensure that traditional spiritual authorities sided with the regime.

In 1973, *The Rain Goddess* was the most informed book written about the war but whether because it was inhibited by censorship or by the propaganda which gave continuing life to the settler discourse, its narrative is built around a number of fixed perceptions about Rhodesian society which appear in various novels over the years. Hopelessly idealistic missionaries get raped and murdered for their pains; tough farmers protect their land which they or their fathers hacked from virgin bush; and inevitably a Ndebele, Kephas's father, remains consistently faithful to White authority. The guerrillas may have trained in Moscow and have learned to use modern weapons but most of the Blacks in the novel are, as they have always been, in superstitious awe of their spiritual leaders. Only when some outside influence is brought to bear on them do they lapse from traditional ethics into mindless savagery. Most Blacks are content that traditional discourse remains closed. Only crooks like Gumede, who live far from traditional constraints, will attempt to open it and an open Black discourse will lead inevitably to disaster and death.

Michael Hartmann's *Game for Vultures* shares with *The Rain Goddess* some authenticity of detail but differs from it in showing a scepticism about the very discourses which created such stereotyped characters and situations in the earlier novel. A guerrilla victory is allowed on several occasions to be a possibility, which no Rhodesian author had hinted at since Robin Brown's *Messiahs* broke into Salisbury. A character in the novel, David Swansey, remarks: 'You forget there's a war going on there or counter-insurgency operations as the optimists call it.'[43] A police reservist, glimpsed through the eyes of a guerrilla, becomes

> an old man trying to relive the lost days of his youth by dressing up and guarding a lonely mission station. Doing his bit for the country. Marunga could imagine the man talking — 'I've fought Hitler and hell, I'm still good enough to show a few munts the wrong end of a rifle.'[44]

That this perception is put into the mind of a superbly fit and highly trained Black soldier who is about to attack the mission shows the sort of irony which Hartmann uses to subvert the discourse.

For the first time in a novel written by a Rhodesian, Blacks who oppose settler rule are not offered as crazy savages. However much the novel disapproves of the guerrilla incursions, both the guerrilla leader, Sixpence, and the main guerrilla figure, Marunga, are shown to be rationally motivated, using arms as the only realistic response to the causal contempt with which society has denied them their dignity. Sixpence revels in his 'houseboy's' name, enjoying the grim tension between his authority as a soldier attacking White Rhodesia and a designation which suggests how Blacks were objectified and transformed as soon as they entered settler space. A vignette of Marunga looking for work before he decides to cross the border makes the point. He approaches a group of women having tea in Highlands.

> 'Oh dear me', one had cooed, 'they're becoming so cheeky these days. It's this silly man Nkomo. Ruining their respect. Here boy, have a sixpence and for goodness sake, stand up straight!' . . . Dismissed as a minor, amusing diversion, sinking with humiliation he had left. Right then he would have cut every white throat in Rhodesia.[45]

In a scene like that we are a long way from the youngsters in Peter Stiff's novel who can be persuaded out of the country only by promises of higher education.

The killing of 'sell-outs' in *The Rain Goddess* were acts of bestial savagery. *Game for Vultures* recognizes that such executions must often have involved agonizing moral choices. A store-keeper, who does not warn the guerrillas that the Rhodesian army has booby-trapped his store, is shot. But his five-year old daughter was shot by some of Sixpence's men and Sixpence, realizing that his hatred of the guerrillas has some validity, pleads with the man to understand his point of view before shooting him. The store-keeper represents people hostile to the nationalists.

> Can you imagine the doubts that will be thrown into the minds of the local people if we let [such a man] go? . . . People are not concerned why a thing happened, they are only concerned with what happened. He let them die, that's all that counts, not why he let them die.[46]

By emphasizing the moral complexity of the incident, Hartmann allows both Sixpence and the store-keeper to emerge with dignity. By registering complexity Hartmann is questioning a discourse which depended for its existence on rigid and simple categories.

A central narrative in *Game for Vultures* is the effect the war has on an inter-racial marriage. Peter Swansey fights with the Rhodesian army; his wife, who is coloured, is the sister of Battin, a guerrilla in Sixpence's section and Swansey gives evidence against him after his capture. Swansey's brother, David, is a sanctions-breaker arranging for war materials to be imported into Rhodesia for the Rhodesian army. By localizing within a marriage the conflict of loyalties the war necessarily provoked, Hartmann refuses to enter into the discursive space where it could be written only as opposition between civilization and savagery. Most of his characters are to a greater or lesser extent confused. After David Swansey has succeeded in getting war materials into Rhodesia, he is forced to recognize the sordid and brutal reality of a war which in England could be distanced by the rhetoric of one side or the other. All the other novels deal with the cruelty of war, but all in subtle or blatant ways assume the wrongness of the freedom fighter's cause. Hartmann with his suggestion that this is a civil war, moves towards a refreshingly compassionate objectivity.

There are, however, limitations in such an approach. *Game for Vultures* seems to suggest that if only Whites had acknowledged a shared humanity with Blacks, the war need never have happened. What such an analysis ignores is a power structure designed to maintain and reinforce the economic status of a White élite. Liberal guilt at the routine racism of White Rhodesia provides no more than a very partial understanding of the motives and ideologies of nationalism. Nevertheless, by centering some of the novel on the Swansey marriage, Hartmann engages with a concrete situation which in its rejection of racial categories is also an acknowledgement that settler discourse has lost any claim it might once have had to name and control settler space.

In 1976 two foreigners published novels about the liberation war. William Rayner published *The Day of Chaminuka* and Giles Tippette, *The Mercenaries*. Fifteen years before in *The Reapers*, Rayner had shown the frustration of nationalist ambitions which would lead inevitably to armed insurrection. In 1976, he had an opportunity to examine the form that revolution had actually taken. In the event he misses the opportunity by shaping his novel around three characters whose atypicality prevents him from engaging in any serious way with the situation he purports to be describing. There is Moyo, the guerrilla leader, whose orthodox Marxism, while being treated with some sympathy, is shown to be irrelevant to the discourses which shape the ideologies of the farm workers in the novel. He is described as a 'young agnostic of Marxist leanings',[47] who is determined to free his people from colonialism as much as from their superstitious delusions. But his passionate invocation of the Chinese revolution as an inspiration for the Rhodesian revolution and the logic and practical rationalism of his rhetoric merely bores and confuses his audience. They are more likely to be controlled by Rufu, the dissident guerrilla in the novel. He claims to be the medium of Chaminuka and preys on the superstitious fears of both peasant and farm worker alike with ritual and paraphernalia. In fact he is no more than a product of a discourse which writes all African religion as Mumbo Jumbo. When he speaks his rhetoric is a curious mixture of the more sanguinary Old Testament prophecies and what Rayner believes is the idiom of Shona mediums. The third character is Holt, a White farmer who maintains his influence on his labour force by organizing fertility dances on the lawn of the farmstead during which he ritually asserts a virile authority over the men. Any typical quality that Moyo, at least, might exhibit is lessened even further by making Moyo Holt's bastard son. Since in terms of the discourse all Blacks are driven by some irrational dread of spiritual power, as soon as Moyo discovers this, Marxism and the war are forgotten and Moyo lives only to protect his father from Rufu.

Rayner's novel usefully evidences how attractive the racial polarities within Rhodesian discourse were even to outsiders who had little reason to be drawn to either side in the Rhodesian conflict. By making Moyo's choice of violence a rational political decision, Rayner is of course breaking radically with the discourse. But by locating superstition as the final basis for political loyalties among Blacks, Rayner allows Rufu's perversion of Shona religion or Holt's bizarre rituals to become appropriate modalities in the conduct of the war. The constituency from which Moyo is attempting to win support is profoundly irrational, understanding only power which derives its authority from the spiritual. They neither want nor understand the freedom and justice he offers them. The novel traces the contest between Holt and Rufu for control of the workers' minds and this can be done only by appropriating the most powerful of Shona spirits. When Rufu is finally killed, Holt assumes the spirit of Chaminuka and Rufu's followers 'moaning with panic' disappear.[48] With Rufu dead and the spirit of Chaminuka in control of a White, the Black discourse is firmly closed. In justice to Rayner it should be pointed out that Moyo does not die and the new discourse opened by nationalist intellectuals presumably remains open but what items it will add to itself is something which the novel is not concerned to trace.

A prefatory note to Giles Tippette's *The Mercenaries* claims: 'All the political and military conditions described here are true, as I have every reason to know.'[49] Tippette must at some point have visited the north-eastern White farming areas and there are accurate descriptions in the novel of the tension such people lived in during the war but since every observation about Blacks in the novel is inaccurate or absurd, I assume he relied largely on Ministry of information hand-outs or speculation among the White farmers themselves for his information about guerrilla tactics and recruiting methods. As such the novel has some interest as it provides an insight into the settler discourse, which is offered with a rare unself-consciousness, modified neither by any critical perception nor personal observation. No Black ever joins the guerrillas voluntarily. This is not surprising since one of the leaders, called Mau-Mau, has filed his teeth in order to more closely resemble his cannibal ancestors, while Mobunzo, his companion, habitually refers to his followers as 'munts'. The Whites in the novel use the word 'wog', while Tippette prefers 'boy', a term which is presumably neutral for him. A sample recruiting incident reads like this:

> Mobunzo called over Lodi, old Emma's nephew. 'Hey, munt!' The boy looked up at him sullenly, Mobunzo grinned. 'You want to be a brave freedom fighter for the people's cause?' When the boy didn't answer, Mobunzo laughed. None of them was worth much, he thought. They'd spend all their time at the training base trying to desert, and, once brought back into Rhodesia . . . they'd fight only out of fear of being shot by their leaders . . . Munts like these, Mobunzo thought, deserved the white man.[50]

A passage like this is written entirely within a discourse which seven years of sporadic fighting and four years of sustained war has done nothing to modify.

Blacks are contemptible even in their own perception of themselves. The majority of Blacks, the vast majority, since Mobunzo and Mau-Mau are egregious, not only deserve the Whites but are only too happy to return to their rule given the first opportunity. Only the ruthless cruelty of a few disaffected men prevents them from living contentedly with the Whites whom their passivity welcomes as an energizing force in their lives.

Tippette's and Rayner's novels can be regarded as eccentric. Neither men were settlers and they could look at the outcome of the war with detachment. For the settler novelists the problem was more difficult. The regime's propaganda machine assured them every day that the war was being won and yet only the more naïve did not realize that a nationalist victory was a possibility. The propaganda made such a victory impossible to contemplate since the ruthless cruelty of both guerrilla armies was endlessly reiterated. There was a crisis of identity. The discourse proclaimed that the Whites were invincible precisely because the Blacks were happily in their place or if they had misguidedly wandered away from it they could soon be put back there. Savage, primitive, contented in their place; buffoons when they sought to escape it — the Blacks were still all of these things, and the Whites controlled them. As Hartmann's novel shows there were Whites who could establish a space where an alternative discourse could be produced but Hartmann was exceptional. It was for many Whites a complex psychological crisis and there was no novelist sufficiently perceptive and skilful to embody that crisis in fiction.

Other reactions were possible. One was a brutal racism which the commentaries of the Rhodesian Broadcasting Corporation actively fostered. If Blacks could be shown as barely human then the discourse of the last eighty or more years could be justified. This is the response of Robert Early's *A Time of Madness* which was published in 1977. Early is the fourth among these novelists who had been a member of the British South Africa Police and was unique among them in being a regular in the Rhodesian army. Despite this experience *A Time of Madness* is as politically ignorant as *The Mercenaries* and the most gratuitously brutal of any of the novels I have considered here.

Early makes his attitudes to Blacks clear although he chooses to express his more doctrinaire racism through the reflections of a missionary priest:

> a thousand years of savage, pagan existence could not be wiped at one stroke. It would take many generations of dedicated men to eliminate the fears and superstitions which were fundamental to the tribal African's make-up.[51]

The implication that 'non-tribal' Blacks are not subject to these 'fundamental' attitudes contradicts the very point that Early wishes to make. In a less confused novel, this could be blamed on the addled mind of Father Antonio whose experience of Blacks inclines him at night to curse God and to 'consign all his teachings to the deepest pits of hell'[52] There is, however, nothing wrong with Father Antonio's mind. Cut-off as he is from settler society, he has had to confirm through bitter experience fixed truths within the settler discourse.

When the priest discovers that his favourite pupil, Gara, is recruiting for the guerrillas and questions him about it, Early observes: 'The blank uncomprehending, slightly idiotic look which has baffled, intrigued and infuriated white men in Africa for hundreds of years, clamped across Gara's features'.[53] Since Gara is holding meetings in a Tribal Trust Land, waving an AK rifle above his head, Early should be the first to appreciate his need for discretion. That would imply rational motive, however, and rationality cannot be attributed to Blacks conditioned by a thousand years of savage existence. 'Wounded buffaloes, charging lions and berserk Africans'[54] are a metonymic set offered in the novel and rational Blacks could not be added to the set without destroying the constancy of its items. Neither of course should an AK rifle be a possible extension and Early gets over that problem by creating a master mind behind the guerrillas who is a Hungarian, Stanislau, working for the Soviet Union. Predictably enough Blacks cannot manage their own revolution.

The novel is structured around the hunts for Gara and Stanislau. Gara and his section murder a farming family, the Ronsons, and not only torture the mother and children before they die but feed the children's limbs to the dogs. The brutality of the murder is used throughout the novel to remove the hunts from any normal moral context and as justification for whatever acts of brutality Kelly, the policeman in charge of the operation, happens to be engaged in. Gara is pursued along and down the Zambezi escarpment; Stanislau is hunted through Victoria Falls hotels and Salisbury night-clubs. To one is attached a brothel, managed by Stanislau's homosexual second-in-command, where soldiers' secrets are coaxed out of them and recorded on listening devices and closed circuit television. Gara's natural space is the bush; communists are decadent effeminates at home only in sleazy cities. The Rhodesians as exemplified in Kelly, are rugged or sophisticated as the occasion demands and control both spaces. A the end of the novel with Gara and Stanislau dead and the nationalists divided into Shona and Ndebele factions, fighting yet again ninety-year-old battles, the entire story simply confirms the resilience of the Rhodesian discourse. Temporarily removed from the constraints in which they are placed within that discourse, Blacks have only ethnic discourses to fall back on. It is a pleasant irony that in 1976, while Early was finishing the novel, the Patriotic Front was formed.

After 1977, however, few Rhodesians could have believed that the discursive space which they had named and controlled possessed its familiar stability. There was little left for the novelists except to turn to fantasy which because it was fantasy did not require any constant relationship with the dominant signifiers. In Lloyd Burton's *The Yellow Mountain* which was published in 1978,[55] it is proposed to build a fence along the entire eastern border equipped with such sophisticated electronic devices that incursion will become impossible. If all the organizations and its discourses in the world which sit in judgement on the settlers can be excluded, then once again Rhodesia will be the happy land it has been for so long.

Communists, the World Council of Churches, the nationalist leadership and the Frontline States will all lie forgotten behind the fence. The only problem is how to raise the money and that is what the novel is about.

A German officer, Krans, discovered oil while drilling for water in the Sahara during the Second World War; he also captured a huge consignment of gold sent by British intelligence to buy the allegiance of desert nomads. The British Treasury is after the gold; an American Company after the oil; the local, corrupt police officer also wants the gold and the situation is further complicated when intelligence officers of Warsaw Pact countries become involved. The most immediate problem is that both gold and the maps of the area where the oil strike was made are hidden in a booby-trapped fort which is used as a training camp for Zimbabwean guerrillas.

With that line-up of opposition any sensible Rhodesian might be expected to call it a day but the Rhodesians of *The Yellow Mountain* are not so pusillanimous. A father and daughter, helped by Krans and a young patrol officer from Beitbridge manage to obtain and escape with both gold and maps. Rhodesians can take on a cross-section of the most powerful forces in the world and through sheer force of will and cunning emerge victorious, even if it is only to retire behind the fence. Once behind the fence fantasy can be laid aside for on the right side of the fence a continuity of discursive practice is allowed to represent its own reality.

There is a fantasy flavour to Peter Armstrong's *Operation Zambezi* which was published in 1979 although it is in part a fictional reconstruction of the raids into Zambia in October 1978.[56] The Soviet ambassador to Zambia is kidnapped, drugged and hypnotized so that when he returns to Lusaka he withdraws his country's support from ZAPU and offers it to ZANU instead. The Rhodesians knew the plot has worked when a shipment of arms bound for Dar es Salaam is diverted to Maputo. Without Soviet support ZAPU will collapse; the Chinese, furious that the Soviets are supporting their client organization, will withdraw their aid from ZANU and both organizations will effectively have been eliminated.

Quite why Rhodesians should rejoice at ZANU's receiving a consignment of arms may puzzle anyone who recalls the horror with which Mugabe's 1980 victory at the polls was regarded by most Whites. The answer lies in part in the ignorance which Rhodesians had towards any nationalist organization from the early days of the Youth League. Neither the press nor radio provided them with any analysis of the parties and in any case it was illegal to name either them or their leaders. Whites consequently reacted to events as they occurred and the raids into Zambia were widely regarded as a response to the shooting down of the Air Rhodesia Viscount a month earlier and it was known that the attack had been carried out by men loyal to Nkomo. The ZAPU leader became, as a result, the epitome of all that was most to be dreaded in the nationalist parties. What is most instructive of settler ignorance in Armstrong's novel is the belief that without Chinese or Soviet backing, the guerrilla threat would wither away. The discourse demanded that Black dissidence had to be inspired from beyond Rhodesia's borders. The courage and ingenuity of Rhodesians, which in *The Yellow Mountain* can capture enough gold to keep Rhodesia cut-off forever from a hostile outside world, can in *Operation Zambezi* manipulate the great powers of the communist world and deny the nationalists their only inspiration.

The last novel I shall look at shows that by 1978 for some novelists at least the horror of the war transcended and destroyed the polarities of heroic Whites and savage Blacks. C. E. Dibb's *Spotted Soldiers* has its genesis as a serial in a South African woman's magazine and is as unpretentious as that provenance suggests. Its widowed heroine is attempting to run a coffee plantation despite the hostility of her neighbours and the scepticism of the army. The man who supports her courageous attempt is a Salisbury attorney and captain in the territorial army, who fortuitously comes into her life. But it is difficult to be completely fatuous when Rhodesia is your only reality — Dibb's grandfather was one of Rhodes's pioneers — and you are writing of a love for a land and the land has been transformed by massacres of Blacks, and suddenly and inexplicably hostile, characterized by Agric-Alerts, ambushes, homestead attacks, and the exhaustion of a people fighting an apparently endless war. She is capable of propaganda clichés like children being lured across the border with promises of education and a *n'anga* smelling out traitors at a camp at Espungabera. But these can be balanced against a compassionate account of one of the children, now man and guerrilla, returning to see his mother, where a fine tenderness of detail allows his humanity to be revealed even while his actions as a guerrilla are deplored. There are also Whites who pay off guerrillas to their neighbours' cost. The discourse no longer exists amidst the confusion of loyalties and motives that give the title to her book. Shakespeare understood that in war the most spotless cause cannot rely on 'unspotted soldiers'. Except for Hartmann's and Trew's novel, all the other novels written about the war depict Rhodesians as a people with a great moral authority on their side. It could not be otherwise when they were fighting for a space which they had appropriated and named and which through that act had created its own discourse and its own moral categories. As I suggested in the quotation from Dibb's novel near the beginning of this chapter, Dibb uses language which still excludes hostile Blacks from any right to that space but in the middle of the war to recognize virtue in Blacks and vice in Whites was in itself acknowledging the existence of a new discursive space.

David Martin and Phyllis Johnson have observed that Ian Smith was never 'an initiator of policy'. He reacted to events and pressures as they arose and seemed incapable of 'predicting possibilities and having a strategy tailored to meet them'.[57] That assessment of Smith's techniques of rule could serve as a comment on the novels looked at in this chapter. None provides new insights into Rhodesia: they instigate no new understanding of either the settlers or the Black world, although for nearly 30 years before Zimbabwean independence, more and more articulate statements by Black leaders had demanded that Rhodesian Whites look at Blacks in a different way. From December 1972, the onslaught of the guerrilla armies provided an almost daily, violent demonstration of the inability of the settler discourse to account for the events in which everyone in Rhodesia was caught up.

Like Smith, the novelists lacked the gift of prediction. What the novels show more clearly than Smith's speeches ever did are the reasons for this fatal lack of understanding. The novelists' world was one of discrete spaces: A white space which was open to appropriate new items for the discourse which named itself progressive; a Black space which belonged to a primitive past and which, because it was closed by the White discourse, was incapable of any new disclosure of what Blacks were within that space or could become if they rejected its boundaries. In the end both the discursive space and the literal geographical space in which racist legislation had over the years embodied the discourse were smashed by war. With Mugabe's victory at the polls both discourse and the Rhodesia which had produced it were simultaneously swept away.

5

Education and the War

PAULOS MATJAKA NARE

The liberation war in Rhodesia assumed a new character at the beginning of 1977. More and more young people started to leave the country to join the guerrillas. In January Manama Secondary School became one of the first schools to move *en bloc* out of the country — a move involving over 300 school children, seven teachers, three nurses and a clergyman. I was one of the teachers. We left in the evening of the first Sunday of the first term of the academic year. Some children in Form I were less than 13 years old. After travelling through the bush in pitch darkness throughout the night, sunrise found us crossing the Shashi River into Botswana *en route* to Zambia. We called it 'going to Geneva'. I still do not know why.

The harassment by the Rhodesian army, hovering above our heads with spotter planes and helicopters, caused untold trepidation. It triggered mixed reactions. Some hid, others cried; while some stampeded, a few students and teachers took the opportunity to hide and eventually returned home. The majority became even more resolute. We had two armed guerrillas in our company. The journey to Francistown was exciting though scathing and cumbersome. With the assistance of the international world, we finally forced our way through from Botswana to Zambia. We all cherished the idea that we would eventually train in guerrilla warfare and return to liberate our country. We were later proved wrong.

EDUCATION

Because all forms of education occur within a given environment, it has not been possible for me to discuss this subject *per se*. Thus besides the actual processes of teaching-and-learning, a consideration has been made of the contextual atmosphere in which these programmes were conducted. Please bear with me in case some of the details sound strange and far-fetched. The fact is that life was strange.

By the end of March 1977 the leadership of the Patriotic Front had made advanced preparations to introduce an Education Department within their

130

structures. Education had become a new and perhaps only meaningful instrument to be used to contain the young boys and girls residing in the numerous refugee camps. Some of them were too young to undergo military training. Accordingly, one day in mid-April I met one of my most perplexing experiences in life. I had already done some preliminary military training at Nampundu Refugee Camp. On this day the President of ZAPU summoned me to Zimbabwe House [Headquarters of ZAPU in Zambia] in Lusaka.

Sitting in a room, with a couple of some top ZAPU officials, the President shocked me with the news that the party had decided to run schools in the camps; and that it was going to be my task to start the ball rolling. I had not expected this. I felt absolutely betrayed. With a touch of ambivalent feelings, and yet given no choice, I ultimately set my hand to it. For a week I was pondering on what strategies to follow in order to succeed.

I knew that the cadres would not be impressed. They would not readily welcome the idea. For them education was not regarded as part of the liberation struggle. After all they had just run away from it at home. It was regarded as a mystic way of capitalist subjugation. After casting about for ideas, I thought it fit to begin with primary education.

Early attitudes
A Monday found me at Victory Camp trying to recruit and convince the residents that education was to become part of our occupations in the struggle. I met with very hostile attitudes. Mr Mareko Madonko and Mr Lephael Nyanga (some of the teachers who had come with us from Halisupi Primary School and Manama Secondary School respectively) gave me a hand in this exercise. I needed their support badly. Our campaign proved to be extremely arduous. We did not only look like fools, but we sounded strange and highly irrelevant, especially to the trained cadres. They called us sell-outs (Selous Scouts). Suspicion and tempers rose so high that some of them threatened to shoot us. At times, in fact, confrontations became so heated that they resulted in physical fighting and assaults among the compatriots. It was shuddering.

It became crystal clear that the task was not going to be easy. One had to be patient and brave to be able to contend with the opposition and resistance. It also called for tact which at times included cajoling. It was not until the ZAPU President visited the camps to allay their anxiety and mixed feelings that we made a breakthrough. As time passed it was rather ironical that even some of the trained personnel came forward to register to attend lessons.

Primary education
Classes were first opened at Victory Camp which was predominantly a female settlement. Once the idea was accepted the next question was, Who were going to be the students and who were to be the teachers? One had to act quickly but adroitly to forestall backpedalling. Thus after failing to get volunteers, we simply decided that everybody who had done Form II was to become a teacher, and the

rest were going to be students — irrespective of age and sex. This approach paid dividends though it later caused problems as the older and bigger students frequently threatened to beat the younger and smaller teachers. This tended to stifle progress.

For expedience the only details we asked for for our records were the individual's home name, pseudonym and highest educational qualification. To ask for more details would have been detrimental. It would have revived and strengthened the suspicious notion that we were Selous Scouts. Unfortunately some of the information we were furnished with by the individuals was false. There was no way in which we could check to verify it. Everybody could hide behind the guise of the confusion inherent in a war situation. Even when we knew that we had been cheated we accepted it to avoid humiliation.

The above formula of approach was later used in other subsequent camps both in Zambia and Botswana e.g. J. Z. Moyo Camp and Selebi-Phikwe Camp respectively. Resistance was more pronounced in J. Z. Moyo Camp because there resided a large number of trained guerrillas; and the untrained cadres envied their superior status. They looked forward to a day when they too would be trained and wield a gun. They wanted to become 'comrades' for this was the password used by the guerrillas.

Classes

It turned out that we had very few teachers and several thousands of students in all camps. Enrolment ranged between 50 and 60 students in a class to be taught by one teacher. With the continuous arrival of children and teachers from Rhodesia these classes hardly stabilized. Numbers fluctuated and levels of acquired knowledge varied from class to class and individual to individual.

Classes commenced either in tents, bungalows made of wood, mud bamboo and thatch, under trees or in barrows. There were hardly any teaching aids in the form of chalk, chalkboards, books, and pens. It was pathetic. To make the situation even more lamentable was the fear of unpredictable attacks and bombardments by the enemy. The large sizes of classes juxtaposed this way were potential targets for bombing. Obviously such circumstances were far from being conducive to effective teaching-and-learning. There were occasions in which we lost cadres because they were either killed or abducted or they had fled from the camps to seek refuge in the neighbouring villages. Some girls even opted for marriages to Zambian villagers. I am sure some of them are mothers in Zambia till now.

Other cadres were only too ready to accept alternative occupations once they were recruited. This was not uncommon. Some students opted to go for military training in spite of their young ages. Teachers opted to go for further studies anywhere as long as they could be moved from these horrible conditions of life. After all they served for no remuneration except food, clothes and some form of military protection. Even these were barely minimal. A need soon arose for the party to select some people to form a core to attend to and deal specifically with problems related to education.

Education Department
The following posts constituted the department:

Mr Josiah Chinamano (late)	Overseer
Mr Phebion Makoni	Secretary
Mr Obert Machalaga	Director
Mr Paulos Matjaka Nare	Schools Co-ordinator
Dr Sikhanyiso Ndlovu	Co-opted Member
Mr M. Mtshana	Co-opted Member

Together with the headmasters of the different schools these constituted the administrative body of the education department. We had to quickly work hard to justify the introduction and existence of the department as a necessary dimension in and for the struggle. To achieve this goal we hurried to attempt to design a curriculum that would neatly address the socio-economic transformation required in the future independent Zimbabwe as we saw it at that time.

The curriculum
Structuring a suitable curriculum was a formidable task for us. Virtually all of us were a product of colonial educational patterns. This orientation limited our capacity for curriculum novelty. For quite some time we were stuck. Change can be stubborn at times.

Eventually we embarked on research, mainly to discover the types of curricula followed in socialist countries. It took long before we could compile a curriculum suitable enough for our purposes. However, by the end of 1977 we had completed curricula for all classes in the primary schools, and a Secretarial Training College.

Another problem soon emerged. There were no resource books to back the implementation of the curriculum. All the resource material we had acquired so far came mainly from Zambia, Rhodesia and Botswana. For us, these were not revolutionary enough. We found ourselves forced to write up and provide notes to guide teachers. We called them 'Schools Resources and Methods'. From time to time teachers were forced to refer to and use otherwise rejected literature from Zambia, Rhodesia and Botswana. This was a typical case of an unforeseen consequence of ambition. Owing to similar constraints we ultimately copied the Rhodesian system of having seven grades in our primary education. Thus in practice a complete departure from the enemy's system proved impossible. Even our timetables were based on our Rhodesian examples and experiences.

The unique feature of our curriculum however was that it deliberately placed emphasis on the poly-technical approach. Bias was for education with production for self-reliance. Consequently, the curriculum was dominated by technical subjects e.g. Integrated Sciences, Agriculture, Metalwork, Woodwork, Building and Leatherwork. Even the teaching of the few academic subjects had to be systematically related to productive activities.

Teachers and students also introduced extra-mural activities in the form of games such as music, football, netball, volleyball, karate and boxing. This helped to fill the gaps within the time tables. This gave the community occupations that averted loneliness and mischievous tendencies. It was here, for instance, that the musical patterns of the popular Black Umfolosi Choir were born. They started with revolutionary songs in the camps.

Given the above factors it was understandable that the curriculum made a deliberate attempt at achieving the following aims:

1.   Equipping learners with productive skills needed to immediately produce commodities to support life in the camps. This practice was spread over all age groups in our refugee camps for their survival.

2.   Preparing the refugees for the future independent Zimbabwe. To achieve this aim some students were sent to various other conventional schools, colleges and universities in the host countries and especially countries of the Eastern bloc in Europe. It was hoped in this way the students would acquire the education and influence we considered compatible with the longed for independent Zimbabwe. Indeed it was our very sincere dream and strong hope that Zimbabwe would adopt and pursue a socialist policy.

3.   Averting boredom and stress inherent in adverse conditions of life for refugees. It was amazing how some teachers developed inimitable charisma of arousing and sustaining students' interest in their work. Again this helped to diffuse tension and latent frustration.

4.   Systematically conscientizing students against suppressive and exploitative types of ruling systems. Political education was introduced for this purpose.

Around November 1977 it became evident that primary education alone could not adequately address the various educational requirements of the different camp inmates. For instance, the primary school teachers were ambitious to improve their qualifications; the army required cadres better qualified than grade seven graduates for more advanced military training. The following facets were thus introduced to meet some of these demands.

Adult education
In the school camps the higher qualified teachers used some afternoons and evenings to teach their less qualified counterparts. This is how secondary education emerged. Eventually some of them were allowed to either go and attend or simply register with Zambian colleges to sit for examinations at different levels of secondary education. Indeed a good number of them obtained certificates in higher levels this way. Enthusiasts even attempted university degrees this way. In turn this practice helped us to convince the Zambian government of the viability of our curriculum and its system in both style and content. Subsequently, their Ministry of Education recognized and agreed to endorse certificates obtained at various levels in our camp schools. No wonder why we produced and brought home a substantial number of certificated teachers, nurses, secretaries, plumbers etc upon repatriation in the 1980s.

It was unfortunate that we had hardly started to map out a curriculum for secondary education when the Lancaster Talks diverted our attention from activities in the camps to thinking about when we would come home. Otherwise the target of our plan was 'education for all, and all for education at all possible levels — including the armed forces'.

Informal education

In all camps there were people, especially adults, who did not fit into formal classes. But in the interest of education for all, and the need for productive activities, they had to learn different skills. Various projects were established. At Victory Camp women engaged in the production of soft textile goods. They made shirts, trousers, jerseys, blouses, skirts, dresses, stockings, gloves etc. At Freedom Camp and McKearn men were involved in producing vegetables, maize, pigs, rabbits, chickens etc. In all these projects methods were dominated by the participatory approach. Because all the end-products were finally consumed by the producers, the participants were motivated and keen to improve them both in quantity and quality. Other similar but appropriate projects were manned by disabled war victims in Kamwala, Kabwata and Kafue.

Kafue Secretarial College

About 30 kilometres south of Lusaka stood a deserted police camp. The Zambian government allowed us to utilize it. In early 1978 the party decided to use the camp as a college to train secretaries. One day, as usual, I visited J. Z. Moyo 3 Camp which was about 700 kilometres from Lusaka. Upon my return to Lusaka I was surprised to find that about 100 classes at Victory Camp had no teachers. To avoid confrontation, the ZAPU President had seized this chance to select the girls who had been teaching and quickly ferried them to Kafue Camp. They were to undergo training as secretaries.

To attain creditable standards of training the party recruited highly qualified tutors from abroad. These were Miss Y. Kamara from Sierra Leone, Miss W. Coussey from Canada, Miss C. Cooker, Miss Chandler and Mr H. Hardy from British Guyana. Only Mrs B. Gwebu was a refugee from Rhodesia. These all worked for salaries. The party paid them out of donations from UNICEF and other well-wishers.

In the absence of any ready-made internal curriculum, the course followed the Pitman syllabus to take off. However, this was later modified progressively to meet our requirements in order to produce the type of secretary we envisaged would fit well in independent Zimbabwe. Hence our compilation of the Kafue Secretarial Training College Syllabus.

Political education

Human survival and the need to liberate Zimbabwe were placed at the top of our educational priorities. People also needed to know exactly why we were at war and why we had to struggle outside our country of birth. While trained guerrillas taught survival tactics, the political commissars carried out deliberate indoctrination processes to cultivate and instil awareness. This way they sharpened a rebellious attitude in all compatriots in the revolutionary camps. For them to appreciate what they were living for they had to know what they were dying for.

EDUCATIONAL PROBLEMS

Logistics

Except for commodities produced within the camps by the refugees, all supplies depended upon the kindness of the donors. At times there were serious shortages. For instance even when some food became available, supplies were minimal. Most of it was either tinned or dried food. This resulted in nutritional imbalances which often resulted in deficiency diseases especially avitaminosis and kwashiokor and other forms of malnutritional diseases. To make it worse all cooking and eating was done in the open. Potential health hazards resulting from contamination of food was prevalent.

For overnight accommodation they crowded in classrooms. In all cases they slept on dusty floors with very scanty, if any, bedding. With scanty supplies of clothing some of them wore tatters or very light clothes even in cold weather. Consequently, diseases related to exposure, dust and crowding were rife. Put together, these maladies caused havoc to life. This in turn had an adverse effect on education.

For purposes of camouflage, and in order to avoid being caught in crossfire during attacks and battles, the Zambian government had located all big refugee camps in bushy remote rural areas. This made communication and supervisory work cumbersome. The risk of being ambushed and attacked by the enemy was very high. Added to transport problems, visits had to be cut to the minimum. No wonder then that the styles of teaching-and-learning gradually tended to drift apart. They differed from school to school and class to class. Meanwhile examinations were set centrally. The end results of the examinations disappointed and demoralized many teachers and students as many children did badly. Latent abilities were badly hampered.

Settled so far away from cities, the refugees depended on pools, streams and rivers for water. Dozens of them died of water borne diseases such as Solwezi disease and celebro-malaria. Sanitation facilities in the form of toilets and pits were absent. Even when efforts were made to provide them they could not cope with the large numbers of people suddenly settling at a place. Camp grounds were often strewn with litter including faeces. These conditions, and many other similar instances, caused anxiety, loss of morale and frustration in the minds of the compatriots. They became homesick.

In the initial stages treatment depended on meagre medical sources supplied by the few guerrillas guarding the camps. They had some kits. It was not surprising that by the time some form of sanitarium was installed a high sense of insecurity would have haunted the refugees. To be sincere, survival depended largely on will-power in these settlements.

Security

Threats and attacks by the enemy were another menace. Indeed such occasions often resulted in stampeding and evacuation of camps — leaving them as deserted ghost settlements. It was not always possible to trace, find and reassemble all the victims back to continue normal lessons thereafter. The presence of a few guerrilla guards in the camps was used by the enemy as an excuse for attacking the civilian camps. This posed a serious dilemma.

Discipline

In a war situation vigilance and discipline are pre-requisites for security and survival. The children in the camps came from different family backgrounds. Their various interpretations of the disciplinary code resulted in conflicts. For example, the word 'comrade' seen through the mind of some children meant that both young and old were equal and identical. This bred contempt of the old by the young at times. In the absence of their real parents and relatives, the children lacked proper guidance and counselling. Strange manners and habits were evolved. Hence at independence we brought youth with practices which were not readily acceptable at home. Meanwhile the cadres enjoyed it. They called it dynamism.

Very often such qualities made the smooth running of classes very difficult. After all some of our teachers had given us wrong details of their qualifications. It was not uncommon to find a person teaching Form II while he had only done grade six. His performance would fail to impress the learners. In turn he would lose their respect and control. Expulsion being out of question, only corporal or other types of punishments were possible. For this purpose each class had a class monitor and two prefects. Otherwise more complicated cases of misdemeanours were referred to and handled by the disciplinary committee whose chairman was the Camp Commander. Very few people allowed their cases to reach this committee. Its verdicts were often severe, harsh and highly unpalatable. They followed military codes.

Another very surprising issue is that refugees tended to have a high propensity for sexual mischief. Their libido seemed to soar to strange heights. This resulted in many pregnancies and births. It disturbed learning and introduced new problems. Eventually we had to open creches in several camps.

Recruitment

Schools provided ready pools of personnel required for various projects and assignments. For example, guerrilla commanders recruited military trainees from among teachers and students; the Director of Education did the same to obtain students to send elsewhere to do various studies. With these different parties vying for personnel from the same source to achieve different goals, it was difficult to avoid chaotic moments in schools. At times classes collapsed and closed down either because they no longer had a teacher or because they became too small.

Public relations

Our financial and material survival depended almost entirely upon donors. They were keen on, and they deserved assurance that their donations were being discharged in accordance with their wishes. Occasionally some of them visited camps and projects to discover whether or not this was the case. To sustain their confidence in order to be assured of their continuous assistance was not always easy.

Finally and fortunately, these problems were soon to be forgotten when in early 1980 the bells of independence called the war survivors back home. The triumph of the liberation struggle then destined us to assemble in the so-called secluded ex-refugee settlements. These settlements later developed into what is today popularly referred to as ZIMFEP (Zimbabwe Foundation for Education with Production) schools.

It is therefore my very sincere conviction that education played a significant role in events that led to the liberation of Zimbabwe.

6

Education and the Liberation Struggle

FAY CHUNG

INTRODUCTION

While land was undoubtedly the key issue in the liberation struggle, many other issues played a significant role. One of these was education. Successive colonial governments had followed a policy of severely restricting educational opportunities for Blacks. In the 1970s Africans still had little access to secondary education. Thus in 1980, for example, only 14.5% of those who entered Grade 1 in 1973 were able to enter secondary education. Even more unpopular was the division of secondary schools into F1 and F2 streams with F1 schools following a similar curriculum to White students which led to the Cambridge School Certificate, and F2 schools following a technical curriculum exclusively designed for Africans. Not surprisingly, F2 schools were regarded as the Rhodesian equivalent of Bantu Education in South Africa and were fiercely resented.

Blacks saw this restriction of educational opportunities as a plot to keep them subjugated. They could not acquire the managerial, professional or technical skills which would allow them to compete with Whites. To make matters worse, the curricula emphasized White achievements and abilities. Blacks needed education which would both qualify them and emancipate them.

THE BACKGROUND TO EDUCATIONAL WORK
DURING THE LIBERATION STRUGGLE

There were few recruits to train as guerrillas in the early days of the war. In the 1960s Zimbabwean youths preferred to go for further studies abroad rather than to train as guerrilla soldiers. Because of the lack of volunteers from inside the country, both ZANU and ZAPU engaged in a policy of forced conscription in Zambia. The Zimbabwean peasant families settled in Mumbwa offered a natural and easily available source of conscripts. Peasant youths, many of them poorly educated or illiterate, were amongst the first to train as guerrillas. The result was that a homogenous group of fighters emerged and became dominant. They were later to be known as the 'Veterans'. Poorly educated and mainly drawn from the Karanga-speakers who had settled in Mumbwa, they developed a sense of pride in their military vocation and a marked disdain for education and distrust of the educated.

However, from the earliest days there was another fertile recruitment ground, and that was from the ranks of young students who had fled from Rhodesia in search of education. These usually travelled by way of either Zambia or Botswana, and both ZAPU and ZANU made it their custom to meet such students at the airport.

Instead of sending them on to colleges and universities, however, the parties whisked them off to military training camps. Many understood clearly that taking up arms against Smith might mean losing their lives, and they sought to escape at the first opportunity. Some ran away after military training, never having intended to fight. Naturally, they were regarded as traitors by those who remained. Some, who were either wiser or more cynical, regarded the ordinary guerrillas as cannon fodder and the educated as the future rulers of Zimbabwe.

But not all of the young students ran away. Many became convinced that it was their national duty to participate in the liberation struggle. One such student was Josiah Tungamirai, who was on his was to university but was commandeered and sent to a military camp. He became Zimbabwe's Airforce Commander after 1980. Such guerrillas valued education and constantly sought opportunities to further it. Wherever they went they initiated classes for their less educated comrades as well as for children. They improved their own education by reading and discussing texts. Classes were organized at the Rehabilitation Centre outside Lusaka and at Morogoro camp in Tanzania. Study groups were set up devoted to the reading and analysis of texts by Marx, Lenin and Mao Tse Tung, which were widely available in the camps. Such studies led to the establishment of Chitepo College in 1976, and education came to be seen as the most critical factor for the success of the armed struggle.

So from the very beginning two disparate groups — peasant youths and educated youths — formed the bulk of the guerrilla forces. For some peasant youths, military training and a military career offered the opportunity of a lifetime, and they became some of the most outstanding fighters and commanders.

This pattern of recruitment began to change, however. Whereas forced conscription was common in the 1960s and early 1970s, by 1973 a flood of willing recruits were pouring into Mozambique and Zambia, many of them secondary school students. Later they were joined by University and College students who preferred to join the guerrilla armies rather than to be conscripted into the Rhodesian army. Students in colleges and universities in neighbouring countries and overseas started to form Party branches and support groups. These young intellectuals were fired with enthusiasm to play a part in the liberation struggle. Many of them were soon to leave their university lecture rooms to join the guerrilla ranks. For its part, ZANU had become by 1973 more stridently left-wing, even going to the extent of calling itself a Marxist-Leninist party. Such rhetoric was intended to attract students to the movement, reflecting the fashion for Marxism-Leninism in Western universities in the 1960s and 70s.

Meanwhile the events of 1974 and 1975 — the Nhari rebellion, the assassination of Herbert Chitepo, the arrest of the 'Veterans' in Zambia — brought about the more direct involvement in ZANU and ZANLA of two groups of supporters who had hitherto remained on the periphery. These were the university intelligentsia and the Zimbabwean businessmen who had successfully established themselves in Zambia. The incarceration of ZANU and ZANLA cadres left a leadership vacuum which had to be filled to save the movement from disintegration. These groups suddenly found an opportunity to take a more direct role.

Thus it was that 1975 and 1976 saw a flood of university lecturers joining the ranks of full-time ZANU cadres. A number of professors and other professionals left secure positions in Britain, the United States, Zambia, other African countries and Rhodesia itself, to go into Mozambique and Tanzania, where they found very young commanders (some even in their teens) in charge of camps overflowing with refugees and recruits. Dozens of young university graduates followed, from Britain, Sierra Leone and Rhodesia. Against this background ZANU began in 1977 a more organized input into education.

THE FORMATION OF THE ZANU DEPARTMENT OF EDUCATION

Up to 1977 education had been a subsidiary responsibility of ZANU's Social Welfare department. In 1977, however, ZANU formally constituted a Department of Education. Its first Secretary was Earnest Kadungure, a trained teacher as well as a veteran guerrilla. He faced a situation in which there were only three qualified teachers and more than 30 000 children and tens of thousands of adults who also wanted to participate in educational programmes. In this crisis, only emergency measures rather than long-term plans were possible. The refugee children not only had no shelter, blackboards, chalk, books or paper, but were also without adequate food or medicine. Many died from a combination of malnutrition and endemic diseases. Kadungure had to seek help from wherever he could find it. In the event UNICEF was the first organization to assist with a grant of US$250 000 used to buy books, pencils, etc. in Dar es Salaam, which were sent to the first schools being established in the camps in Mozambique.

Later in 1977 Dr Dzingai Mutumbuka was appointed Secretary for Education. He was one of the first lecturers to leave his university post to join the struggle. He decided to prepare a long-term education plan which would include not only the provision of primary and secondary education, but also research, curriculum development, teacher training and administrative training. The objective was to establish an education system in the Mozambican camps that would incorporate ZANU's political agenda of national unity and national consciousness; socialism, anti-imperialism, anti-colonialism and anti-racism.

His deputy was Sheba Tavarwisa, one of the first women to join the liberation struggle. A strong leader, she had not only undergone military training, but had also been a pioneer in the early 1970s in transporting arms for ZANLA from Zambia to Mozambique and then into Zimbabwe. Because women were not at first suspected of being guerrillas, it was much easier to utilize women guerrillas to transport arms as well as to politicize the populace to support the guerrilla war. Women such as Sheba Tavarwisa spearheaded the struggle, making it possible for the men to follow after the ground was prepared. She was also one of the first trained teachers to join the liberation struggle. Her ability to organize thousands of teachers and children into orderly schools provided an excellent foundation for Mutumbuka's ambitious plans.

The Education Department's headquarters was first established in Chimoio, where a school — known as Chindunduma, after one of the battles of the first *chimurenga* in 1896 — was set up. Tragically, Chimoio was the object of the Rhodesian attack of 23 November 1977. Chindunduma School and Parirenyatwa Hospital were prime targets of the initial bombing and the subsequent assault by the Rhodesian ground force, intent on killing all survivors. Hundreds of teachers and children were killed as well as many nurses and patients. Those who survived suffered from severe napalm burns and shrapnel wounds. Ironically, the ZANLA military training camp in the same area was not attacked.

The education headquarters then moved to Gondola, where a former farm complex had been made available. Plans which had begun in Chimoio to develop a distant education course continued under Ephraim Chitofu and Peter Tsorai, experienced teachers and headmasters whose schools in Zimbabwe had been closed down as the war began to affect large areas near the border with Mozambique. Inhabitants of such areas, especially those in positions of authority like headmasters, became targets of the Rhodesian forces who accused them of sympathizing with the guerrillas.

The headquarters was later moved to Pasi Chigare, near the Party farm, but this and numerous other camps were bombed in July 1978, making it impossible to continue with educational work there. By this time many school children had experienced as many as six bomb attacks and were beginning to suffer from psychological traumas of various types. Symptoms included incurable hiccups and a strange disjointed and jerky walk. Soon after the July 1978 bombings, hundreds of school children began to fall into nightly trances. This phenomenon only ended when the children were transported to Tete province, then considered to be beyond the range of the Rhodesian planes.

The Mozambique government decided to transport all refugees away from areas bordering on Rhodesia, leaving only guerrillas there. ZANLA had developed a system of underground bunkers which were apparently not identifiable by the Rhodesian reconnaissance planes which circled the camps every night. Throughout the war, the Rhodesians were unable to locate military camps and consistently bombed schools and refugee camps. One of the reasons why refugee camps, and especially schools, were easily spotted by the Rhodesian reconnaissance system was that this depended on infiltrating agents into the camps. Those who went on to military training were a carefully selected group who had to face rigorous interrogation, but those who enrolled in schools merely had to express an interest in furthering their education.

Large trucks arrived to transport thousands of children and their teachers on the more than one-thousand-kilometre journey from the Chimoio area to Tete. A site had been selected near the Matenje river, which provided an essential source of water for the thousands of refugees. Unlike the military camps, which were located very far away from the local population, Matenje Camp was placed very close to the local inhabitants.

Matenje was to be the new headquarters of the Education Department. Far away from the war-front, it was possible to create a more stable education system. Within a few weeks a large camp of grass-thatched pole and *dagga* houses (known as 'postos') and dormitories were built by the teachers and the two thousand children. The main building materials were bamboo and grass, which were in plentiful supply in the area. Beds, tables and benches were also made of bamboo. The camp commander, Cde Chiridza, who was in charge of the construction, displayed an extraordinary organizational ability. Although he himself had only enjoyed primary education, he had gained his very impressive administrative skills in ZANLA where he had served as a military commander at the front. By 1978 he had retired from ZANLA and joined the Education Department. He was able to engender both hard work and aesthetic appreciation as various building teams competed to see which houses and dormitories were the best. An extraordinary spirit of pride and unity developed. The sanitation system which had been chaotic at first now became well-organized with the construction of pit latrines.

It was decided to bring teachers from the other schools at Doroi, Chibavava, Mabvudzi, Nampula, Xai Xai and Chindunduma itself to do teacher-training and administrative courses at Matenje. These activities, together with research and curriculum development, could now take place in a more stable and peaceful atmosphere away from the war-front.

The research and training team included former school heads, such as Ephraim Chitofu, Hoyini Bhila and Tovadini Mwenje. It also included graduates like Fay Chung, who had been teaching at the University of Zambia, Darlington Chitsenga, who had a masters degree in Mathematics from Columbia University, Josephat Nhundu and Stephen Nyengera, who had left the University of Sierra Leone on completion of their studies to join the struggle, and Farai Karonga, who had just completed an honours degree at a British University. There was also a team of graduate and undergraduate students from the University of Rhodesia, including Morgan Borerwe, Simon Masvayi, Khulukane Ndebele, Martin Makomva and Kenneth Munyarabvi. Others had come from universities in neighbouring countries, like Mike Munyati and Irene Mahamba from the University of Botswana.

A number of training courses soon started. A 20-week intensive teacher-training course began, using a combination of face-to-face teaching, distance-education materials, micro-teaching, a case-study, and four weeks of supervised teaching practice. Four such courses were held before the end of the war. The course was known as Teacher Education Part One (TE I). A smaller group was selected to do Teacher Education Part Two (TE II). This was a twelve-month course, with subject specialization. A ten-week administration course was established for those in administrative positions who had completed TE I. The course combined theory and practical exercises. Each student had to choose a practical programme in which to practise his or her theoretical premises. Many of the projects related to health and sanitation, as these were areas where a high standard of administration was obviously necessary.

The secretarial course was a three-months course in which secretarial skills such as note-taking, accountancy, typing and business practice were taught. Research was mainly concentrated on analysis of what was actually taking place in the schools and camps, such as the language used in different age groups, actual practice in the pre-school, the educational levels of the different camps, and so on.

There was also planning for education in semi-liberated zones where the Rhodesian authorities had closed down schools. By mid-1979 ZANU believed that it was appropriate to re-open schools under its own jurisdiction in areas which were seldom entered by Rhodesian forces. A number of educational personnel, including Bassie Bangidza and Emias Munemo, were sent to the war-front to prepare for the re-opening of schools. The plan was never effected, however, as the war came to a sudden end towards the end of 1979 as a result of the Lancaster House negotiations.

Plans were also made for the take-over of the country's education system after independence. Primary education was to be provided for all and secondary education was to be expanded by about 20% per annum. In the event only the plans for primary education were actually followed. The plan to expand secondary education gradually was abandoned, as Government gave in to popular pressure for more secondary education.

Curriculum development concentrated mainly on subjects where it was thought impossible to use Rhodesian textbooks. In Mathematics either Rhodesian or Tanzanian textbooks were used, but new texts were developed for English, Ndebele and Shona as well as History. These were cyclostyled at Matenje, using manually operated duplication machines provided by UNICEF. Nine such texts were developed during this period.

Examinations for all levels from Grade 1 to Upper VI were developed at Matenje and taken in all the schools run by ZANU. Entry into secondary education was by examination, but both Grade 6s and Grade 7s were allowed to sit for the end-of primary examinations. Seventy-five per cent of Grade 7s and 50% of Grade 6s qualified to enter Form 1. Education from pre-school to Form Four was provided at all the schools set up by the ZANU Education Department. However, 6th Form and tertiary education was only available at Matenje. In addition, classes were organized at all refugee and military camps where those who were not directly undergoing arduous military training were able to attend some ordinary classes.

Military camps which offered educational programmes included Ossibissa, Tembue and Pungwe III. Still, education was only a peripheral activity at military camps.

In the formal school camps, classes were small, often with two teachers in charge, because of the number of teachers in training. Team teaching was the common practice. The constant threat of bombing led to the practice by which all teachers left the camp at dawn with their classes and returned at sunset. The 'classrooms' were literally under trees, although some classes built grass shelters. All classes had desks and benches made of bamboo. They were situated around the periphery of the camp, one to two kilometres apart from each other. Supervisors had to walk about half an hour to teach the next class. The idea behind this wide scatter of classes was to avoid direct hit on a considerable number of students at one time. Most of the time Matenje housed 2 000 to 3 000 students, split up into over 80 classes, although for a short period the number rose to over 9 000 students. The strategy appeared to work effectively since, while the Rhodesian reconnaissance system easily identified the camp itself, the camp was always vacated during the day — save for about 20 cooks — and the frequent bomb attacks led to few casualties. For example, at the bombing of Pasi Chigare School only two students were killed, both girls who had been given some household duties in the camp. They were killed because the bombs hit some granite rocks near where they were working and they were struck by the exploding rocks.

Pupils were required to attend five hours of lessons every day as well as to do manual work such as house-building, furniture-making, gardening and cooking for a further four hours a day. Some children went to classes in the morning and to their work stations in the afternoon; others worked every morning and went to classes in the afternoon. The teacher-trainees were required to attend classes from 7 a.m. to 4 p.m., with a short break for lunch. Such was the enthusiasm of these trainees that they nearly all spent long hours studying and doing homework in the evenings, using little home-made diesel lamps for light. Matenje was fortunate in having an up-to-date library of teacher education books of over 3 000 volumes, contributed by a donor and purchased in Britain. This library, run by some sixth-form students, was invaluable to the trainees. Adult education classes, mainly literacy classes, were held for refugees, who lived some kilometres away; the Paulo Freire method was used.

A separate School of Administration was set up in Maputo under the then Secretary-General of ZANU, Edgar Tekere, and Robson Manyika, who was in charge of Manpower Development. Sister Janice Mclaughlin taught at this school. The intention was to train a strong cadre of administrators in preparation for independence. However, the school was operational only for a few months and plans to transfer it to Zimbabwe after independence failed.

Another teacher training programme took place in Denmark under the auspices of Development Aid from People to People (DAPP). Students were sent to Denmark to a DAPP college for a year. The programme proved to be expensive and its results were rather disappointing. Students spent a year doing many different things, with little specialization — an expression of DAPP's philosophy of learning from life rather than from academic instruction.

At the same time large numbers of students were sent to universities in Africa, to the West and to the Eastern bloc. There were several hundred Zimbabweans at the university of Zambia as a result of President Kaunda's determination that Zimbabwe would have more graduates at independence than Zambia had done. Universities in Nigeria and Sierra Leone also took many Zimbabwean students; others went to universities in the surrounding countries, including Botswana, Lesotho, Kenya and Tanzania. Britain and the United States had several thousand Zimbabwean students. It was estimated in 1979 that there were over 4 000 Zimbabwean students in universities outside Rhodesia, leading to a situation where more Zimbabweans graduated outside the country than from the University of Rhodesia itself.

CONCLUSION

Because of the large number of intellectuals and professionals who joined it, ZANU regarded education as an essential part of the liberation struggle. One recalls that when ZANU was first formed in 1963 it was labelled as a party of intellectuals cut off from the masses. There was great emphasis within ZANU on intellectual and professional development which were seen as necessary to overthrow the settler regime. Since 1963, however, ZANU had come to realize the need for mass support for its guerrilla armies. ZANU and ZANLA were successful because they brought together the intellectuals and peasantry.

Tensions constantly existed between the two groups, of course, the one being more scientific in its analysis and orientation and the other more traditional. This tension was reflected in contrasting ideological manifestations, with one group asserting its adherence to democracy, nationalism, modernism, and later Marxism-Leninism, while the larger group of peasants clung to their traditional ideology, dominated by the traditional resistance figures such as Nehanda, Kaguvi, Chaminuka and the ancestral spirits. But these different ideologies co-existed throughout the liberation struggle. ZANU did not try to destroy traditionalism in the way FRELIMO tried to do, but instead tried to win the traditionalists' support for the liberation struggle. The traditional leaders, the spirit mediums, on the other hand, also tried to understand and accommodate modern trends. At a meeting held between the spirit mediums and myself, for example, in early 1978 at Pungwe III military camp, the subject of discussion was the reasons for the participation of such countries as the United States, China and the Soviet Union in the Zimbabwe liberation struggle. Whilst the spirit mediums remained the upholders of traditional values, such as respect for life and preservation of the environment, they were able to accept modern trends such as the use of sophisticated modern weapons and education. The spirit mediums at no time opposed modern education, many of them having received primary education themselves.

7

Healing the War Scars in the Evangelical Lutheran Church in Zimbabwe

NGWABI BHEBE

INTRODUCTION

The Evangelical Lutheran Church in Zimbabwe (ELCZ) took much longer than any other to recover fully from the impact of the liberation war. The major reason for its rather extended period of healing the scars of the war lay in its complicated involvement in both the main war itself and in the subsequent civil war in Matabeleland. It was only on the 29th December 1991, eleven years after the independence of the country and over four years after the Zimbabwe African National Union (ZANU) and Zimbabwe African People's Union (ZAPU) Unity Accord of 1987 that brought peace to Matabeleland, that ELCZ consecrated its first post-independence African Bishop, an event generally considered to mark the end of a long tortuous search for peace in the church. My chapter does not seek to provide an exhaustive description of the complicated events leading to the peace settlement in ELCZ but merely to provide a broad and rough outline of how the church found itself in deep trouble and to explain the efforts mounted to rescue it from possible disintegration.

For the discussion to make sense, I shall try to provide a geographical location, ethnic context and brief historical outline of the church. In this overview I shall attempt also all the time to draw attention to the features of the church and its environment that ultimately rendered it a most highly contested war zone between the various warring forces. As the discussion unfolds I shall all the time keep in sight the Church of Sweden Mission (CSM), the parent overseas organization of the ELCZ, because I believe that the latter's problems and the process of their resolution rested in part in CSM's devolution of power to ELCZ and the former's intimate participation in the humanitarian war programmes.[1]

Map 3

The Evangelical Lutheran Parishes

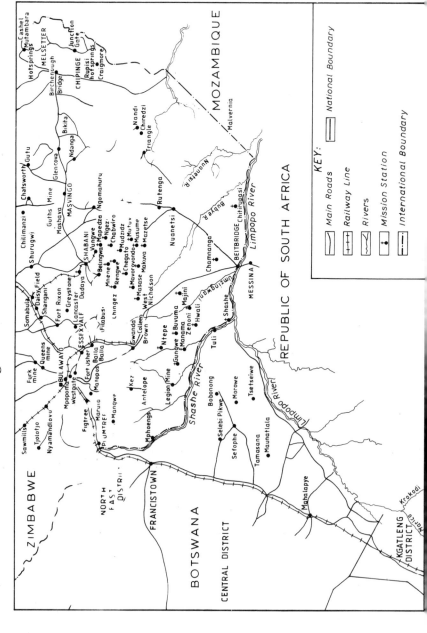

THE GEOGRAPHY, ECONOMIC AND ETHNIC BACKGROUND

ELCZ is largely a rural church, which has only in recent years started to drift to the urban areas, building its congregation and parishes out of the educated young men and women who migrate to the towns in search of employment. Otherwise the church is located in the communal areas of the administrative districts of Mberengwa in Southern Midlands and of Gwanda and Beitbridge in the south of Matabeleland South.

The communal areas lie in a part of Zimbabwe whose altitude varies generally from 1 000 to 4 000 feet above sea level. The area is dry and hot and has a low mean rainfall ranging from less than 16 inches to a mere 24 inches. The communal areas are therefore found in what are classified as Regions IV and V. Region IV is prone to seasonal droughts and severe drought spells during the rainy seasons and it can only be used for growing drought resistant crops and for extensive cattle ranching. Region V's rainfall is too low even for growing drought resistant crops so that it can only be used for extensive livestock grazing.[2] Because of the extensive land alienation that took place in the Mberengwa-Gwanda-Beitbridge districts and elsewhere in Midlands and Matabeleland, when the European settlers took up farms and ejected African families into the adjacent reserves, and because of the rapid human and domestic animal population expansion due to natural increases and influx of the dispossessed immigrants from other parts of the country as well, there developed huge population pressures in the reserves. Thus in 1982 when the national population density of Zimbabwe was 19,3 persons per square kilometre, in the communal area of Mberengwa the density stood at 40–50 persons per square kilometre. To be sure the contrast was even more striking when the communal density was compared with the population density of 0–10 persons per square kilometre in the European farms and ranches in the Mberengwa district itself.

The human and animal overcrowdedness caused accelerated degradation of land and denudation of vegetation, which in their turn have led to ever declining crop yields and also the inability of the communal areas of Mberengwa-Gwanda-Beitbridge to carry and sustain adequate amounts of livestock. Since the 1940s when forced resettlement of African families from White farms was stepped up the inhabitants of communal areas have been plunged into below subsistence food production levels, where they are today wholly dependent on government annual relief programmes. By the sixties and seventies the position had grown worse because of repeated droughts.[3]

The abject poverty and extreme land shortage made the rural people of Mberengwa-Gwanda-Beitbridge receptive to radical messages of the nationalists and the guerrillas and therefore eager to participate and collaborate in the liberation war. They were especially driven to such volatile and aggressive moods not just by frustration of meagre existence but also by their extreme consciousness of what appeared like suffering amid plenty. Everywhere around them there was plenty of wealth and abundant resources to which they were denied any direct access. Both Mberengwa and Gwanda districts are centres of vast mineral deposits and mining activity. The deposits include gold, asbestos, chrome, iron and emeralds. The vast wealth generated by these mines never seemed to come to the people but was instead shared between multinational companies and the colonial state in Harare (Salisbury). Consequently, the peasants always looked for any opportunity to plunder this wealth before it could be transferred from their areas.

Indeed the intense guerrilla activity and its weakening of the colonial security situation in Mberengwa and Gwanda in the late 1970s provided immense opportunity for the peasants, mission teachers, headmasters and local businesspeople to pilfer in a variety of skilful ways the precious emeralds from the Sandawana mines near Chegato, Masase, Musume, Mnene and Mazetese missions. Profitable trade soon flourished between Mberengwa and towns where unscrupulous White smugglers bought the stolen emeralds to sell in South Africa. Most peasants made sufficient incomes during the war from the illicit emerald business to be able to survive while some more astute such as teachers, headmasters, nurses and ordinary businesspeople actually made fortunes that they used to expand their existing enterprises or to become *nouveaux riches*, owning transport and retail businesses. Whenever the guerrillas forced companies to abandon hurriedly their mines, as happened after 1977 at Nyala and Rhonda chrome mines near Musume mission, local people descended swiftly upon any property left behind — especially building and fencing material. Many homes in Mberengwa suddenly assumed a modern outlook using stolen materials. All these seemed concrete rewards for supporting and participating in the liberation war, so that the poor communal people developed strong commitment to the struggle.

The same eagerness to take advantage of the collapsing situation following the escalation of guerrilla activity extended to the White commercial farms. As the farmers abandoned their properties local people moved into the farms with their livestock. Some merely grazed their cattle in the farms while maintaining their permanent homes in the communal villages while others abandoned their homes and became permanent settlers on the farms. By the end of the war the new African government found itself with the problem of how to evict African farm settlers commonly known by the pejorative term of 'squatters'. During the war however such settlements and plundering of mining properties were encouraged by the guerrillas and nationalist leaders because they were considered as ways by which peasants were promoting the aims of the liberation struggle. These peasant actions were seen as some means of undermining the European settlers' economic strength and their hold on the country.

Of course the plundering and destruction of the so-called enemy property was not just confined to secular installations and operations but extended even to the ecclesiastical institutions and individual properties. When mission schools and parish churches, chapels and parsonages were abandoned, some of them were destroyed and their building materials and furniture carried off by the local people. The same thing happened to the property of rich people who were accused of selling out and executed by the guerrillas. Their goods and livestock were stolen or appropriated by their neighbours. The prospect of sharing the wealth of the victims helped to encourage peasant participation in the struggle. The resulting destruction of most ELCZ mission properties, as we shall see, helped to increase the local church's dependence on the CSM, especially during the reconstruction period. Such a development seemed to some people in the local church to be a reversal of the independence process for which they had for a long time striven and they therefore resented it. Thus that was a way in which the war helped to promote significantly the role of CSM in the post-war healing of the wounds.

The attitude of the peasants to the mission stations and their communities must be seen as part of the social inequalities resulting from the educational efforts of the church. The church's educational mission had over the years built up in the midst of rural poverty a middle class of teachers, headmasters, nurses, medical doctors, pastors and evangelists whose bourgeois values, tastes, consumption habits and political awareness and ambitions were inextricably linking these rural areas with the towns. The middle class resided in the parish centres that had every urban outlook and were quite distinguished from their rural-surroundings. The parish centres had modern houses for staff, boarding accommodation and teaching facilities for students, maternity and ordinary in-patient wards and dispensaries, all of which gave a distinctly urban touch to those places because of their modern architecture. In addition there were flourishing businesses that grew next to parishes. The businesses were made up of general stores, groceries, bottle stores, eating houses, butcheries etc.

The parish centres were linked to the towns by means of telephones and buses using these centres as their terminals. The communities of these centres were able to keep abreast of international and national news by means of radio sets and stereos found in almost every teacher's or nurse's house and by means of newspapers delivered almost regularly by the buses. In other words news was absorbed by the parish centre population first and then quickly diffused to the neighbouring rural communities through the out-patients, shoppers and travellers who converged on the mission by the day and returned to their homes in the evenings.

Because of their linkages with the urban areas the mission communities tended to be closely associated with the political movements and organizations of the towns. Before they were banned ZAPU and ZANU were very strong in the missions among staff and students. When the African National Congress led by Abel Muzorewa was formed to oppose British-Rhodesian settlement proposals of 1971/2, many pastors and teachers volunteered to work as mobilizers of local opinion against the settlement proposals. Most noted among radical pastors then were Reverends Elias Masiane of Shashe mission, Arote Vela of Buvuma, Nkane Ramakgapola of Beitbridge and Sibabi Ndlovu of Musume mission, all of whom joined the ANC and continued to work actively for the nationalist struggle long after the British-Rhodesian proposals were rejected. They all became involved in clandestine recruitment of young men and women for the liberation movements based in Zambia. Between 1975 and 1976 all of them were among those arrested, tortured and imprisoned or detained for their political involvements.[4] Thus the middle class communities of the parish centres served to provide nationalist leadership for the rural peasants.

The relationship of the middle class and the peasants was also viewed in terms of the rich and poor, so that the destructive attitude of the peasants towards church property was explicable in that light. Mission workers or employees enjoyed a standard of living far above that of most peasants. Most of the mission workers owned farms and lived in modern houses not only at their work places but in their rural villages, where they set up four-bedroomed brick under zinc/asbestos houses. Quite several of them had saved enough money to start business as bottle store owners, general dealers, or butchers.[5] To many peasants missions did not only represent colonial institutions but parish centres represented an accumulation of wealth and housed a class of rich people that had to be expropriated in line with the redistribution of wealth and property preached by the guerrillas. Such peasant attitudes tended to be strongest around those parish centres whose services were not immediately related to the local communities as was true of Chegato mission that only had a high school but no hospital. Most of the children studying there came from all over Mberengwa-Gwanda-Beitbridge and only a small number from the surrounding villages. When the war closed in on the mission and the staff ran away at the end of 1978 many villagers descended on the parish centre, razed to the ground the buildings, looted and carried off everything that was movable.

The impoverished nature and the sharp class cleavages of Mberengwa-Gwanda-Beitbridge communal areas also combined with their ethnic admixture to influence the response of these areas to the war. Parts of Mberengwa had always belonged to the Ndebele kingdom's tributary area in the nineteenth century, so that although their inhabitants were Shona-speaking, they learnt the Ndebele language and got other cultural traits. The bilingualism increased after the establishment of colonial rule and the displacement of Ndebele communities from their original homeland around Bulawayo. Many Ndebele families migrated to the Gwanda and Mberengwa districts. The process was stepped up further with evictions of the Ndebele from European farms of Mzingwani, Fort Rixon, Somabula, Zvishavane and Mberengwa itself. Mberengwa-Gwanda-Beitbridge communal areas became comprised of the original Karanga and Pfumbi (Shona dialects), Venda and Virwa (Sotho-Tswana dialects) and Ndebele speakers and most of the people were at least multilingual, while the rest were bilingual in that they could speak two or more of the local languages. Therefore, even when the Zimbabwe People's Revolutionary Army (ZIPRA) became closely identified with the Ndebele speakers and the Zimbabwe African National Liberation Army (ZANLA) with Shona speakers, both operated easily in the multilingual complex of Mberengwa-Gwanda-Beitbridge.

During the war ZANLA operated in all communal areas of Mberengwa-Gwanda-Beitbridge and certainly helped ZANU gain more influence than ZAPU. While ZANLA forces fought and built up a large following for their party, ZIPRA units operating there confined themselves mostly to recruiting young men and women for training through ZAPU party officials and by means of abductions. ZAPU influence, which might before the war have been quite strong, was allowed to decline, eroded by ZANLA aggressive politicization programmes. Political divisions in the communal areas therefore remained minimal. After 1980 ZAPU party structures and officials that had been driven underground when nationalist parties were banned in 1964 and forced to operate quietly by the predominant presence of ZANLA combatants during the war, soon burst into the open and competed openly with ZANU for followers. Both parties now resorted to emphasizing ethnic identities, so that Shona speakers were recruited into ZANU while Ndebele speakers went to ZAPU. The Virwa who were thoroughly mingled with the Ndebele tended to follow ZAPU *en mass*. The Venda on the other hand had fewer Ndebele families among them and were therefore divided between ZAPU and ZANU. ELCZ too found itself completely divided similarly and the divisions tended to harden during the civil war in Matabeleland. Because the church mirrored those national divisions, it became virtually impossible to overcome the church divisions before the national peace.

ELCZ: ITS HISTORY, SIZE, PLACE IN SOUTH-WESTERN ZIMBABWE AND ORGANIZATION

In this section I want to show the close, if not intimate, relationships between ELCZ and the rural communities of Mberengwa-Gwanda-Beitbridge. I shall be trying to expose a further facet of why some post-war problems could not be sorted out without reference to the rural communities at large and to the national policies. Indeed I shall be striving to throw further light on the motives behind the unprecedented interest and intervention of a minister, top civil servants, chief education officers, etc in ELCZ quarrels.

In 1976 when the war broke out in southern Zimbabwe and therefore in Mberengwa-Gwanda-Beitbridge districts, ELCZ had been in existence in those districts for almost three quarters of a century. For the greater part of its history it had operated as a rural church (see map 3). It was only in the late 1960s that it began to spread to the urban areas in pursuit of its young men and women who also migrated to towns in search of wage employment. By 1975 therefore ELCZ had congregations and parishes of modest sizes in Kadoma (Gatooma), Harare (Salisbury), Gweru (Gwelo), Zvishavane (Shabani), Bulawayo, Gwanda and Beitbridge. The outbreak of the war accelerated the rural-urban migrations, when many people ran away from the rural war zones and became urban refugees. Even at the height of the war the church still had its majority adherents in the rural areas.

Apart from some insignificant Catholic mission stations in Gwanda and Mberengwa and some scattered congregations of the Zionist and Apostolic faith, ELCZ is the dominant christian church in southwestern Zimbabwe.

ELCZ built up its following and embedded itself in the lives of rural people of southwestern Zimbabwe through the three-pronged evangelization technique — formal education, preaching of the gospel and medical mission. The CSM missionaries who planted the church first arrived in Zimbabwe in 1902 and within a few years had made up their minds that since the field was too large to be covered by White missionaries only they must use African evangelists-teachers, who had the extra advantage of the use of local languages to convert their fellow Africans. Schools were therefore opened to produce bands of evangelists-teachers with a minimum amount of literacy that enabled them barely to read, count and write but were fairly well grounded in elementary scriptures and doctrines as contained in the small catechism of Martin Luther.

Such evangelists-teachers were distributed in villages where they started preaching places that actually served the dual function of schools and churches. During the week children were gathered at those places to be instructed in Bible Knowledge, reading, writing, arithmetic and singing. Those who were older were given extra catechumen classes twice a week on Wednesday and Sunday before the main service. On Sundays the same village schools operated as chapels where services were held and the congregations were frequently the same as the academic and catechumen classes. In other words conversion tended to expand almost at the same pace as the spread of literacy. In time some preaching places were encouraged to grow to parish centres catering for their own surrounding preaching places. In 1918 Mnene, the first mission station, had become a parish with 23 preaching places, 22 evangelists and 170 communicants. By 1923 Masase, the next parish, had also grown and had 13 preaching places and 16 evangelists. In 1932 another parish was started at Gomututu by the famous Swedish pastor, Harald van Sicard. This way the work expanded to include Musume parish.

CSM also expanded tremendously when it got ready-made congregations in Gwanda district in 1928. Some families of the Dutch Reformed Church confession had migrated to Gwanda and started their own congregation at Bethel hoping to receive support from the Dutch Reformed Mission in Masvingo district. Because of the distance the Dutch Reformed Mission decided to transfer Bethel to CSM.

Apart from preaching and teaching, CSM started medical work at Mnene in 1915, which soon acquired government recognition and therefore qualified for state subsidies. Clinics were also started at Musume, Manama and Masase. By 1933 Mnene Hospital was able to treat 1 602 patients while the other clinics were attending to 633 patients annually.

By 1976 when the war broke out the church had grown tremendously as the following figures show. It had 30 parishes, 218 congregations, 33 pastors (all of them local Africans), 107 evangelists and 30 648 members.[6] It is important to note that there was a big discrepancy between the church records' number of Christians annually and the actual number of people who considered themselves Christians. The church only declares Christians those people who are baptised, attend catechumen classes and make a contribution to the church and not any other though they might be baptised. If on the other hand we use the Midlands and Matabeleland South provincial percentages of those who consider themselves Christians to estimate the number of Christians in Mberengwa-Gwanda-Beitbridge by the 1982 national census, we come up with a much higher figure. Out of the total population of over 350 000 in the three districts, well over 180 000 people claimed to be Christians.[7] This figure of course includes some Roman Catholics but also many Lutherans who have reverted to polygamy or have simply stopped going to church for other reasons and have therefore been cancelled from the church registers.

In estimating the magnitude of the influence of ELCZ in Mberengwa-Gwanda-Beitbridge we should look at education and health as well. In 1970, just before the church was forced by government to relinquish its direct running of the primary schools, ELCZ had 175 primary schools and 705 teachers and 24 842 pupils, four secondary schools with 28 teachers and 619 students and a teaching hospital with five teachers and 63 student nurses.[8]

By 1977 the church ran four hospitals with 542 beds, treated an average of well over 60 000 in and out-patients annually and employed a staff of 16 registered nurses, 50 medical assistants and 151 general hospital workers. The church also had nine clinics only four of which handled 13 918 out-patients annually. Apart from Jeka clinic that the government owned near Chegato Secondary School where the church had no medical facilities, the church was entirely responsible for all modern medical requirements of the communal areas in southwestern Zimbabwe.[9]

Clearly ELCZ was not only a big institution but it also influenced the lives of most communal people of Mberengwa-Gwanda-Beitbridge. When these people became involved in the liberation struggle, which took the form of guerrilla warfare, what one writer has described as 'closer to the people than any other form of warfare so far engaged by man, because the people are the target for every operation undertaken by the contending forces, whether political, psychological or military, and because the combatants are themselves of the people',[10] it was inevitable that ELCZ so intimately linked with the people should be involved and suffer all the damages in property, losses of lives including the political and ethnic divisions incurred by the people themselves. It was not only its size and involvement in the lives of the people that decided ELCZ's responses to challenges of the war of liberation, but its organizational structures and relationships with CSM as well. Between 1963 and 1980 CSM tried to grant greater autonomy to ELCZ simultaneously as it acknowledged the financial poverty of the latter by continuing to support its annual budgets. In 1970 all the African schools and health facilities with the mission's immovable and movable property were transferred to ELCZ. It was further agreed that for as long as CSM supported ELCZ the latter would have its books and accounts audited once a year.[11]

Parallel to the devolution of power to the local church was the development of its constitution. The constitution provided for the election of a life-bishop who was assisted by two deans. These headed the Eastern and Western deaneries; the former coincided with the Mberengwa district and the latter with Gwanda and Beitbridge districts. In 1975 the Eastern deanery was made up of 19 parishes four of which (Salisbury, Shabani, Gwelo and Gatooma) were in the urban areas, while the Western deanery had 13 parishes three of which (Beitbridge, Bulawayo and Gwanda) were in towns. Headed by an ordained pastor, each parish was made up of five to 12 or even 15 congregations each of which was under an evangelist.

The basic governing and administrative unit of the church was the parish council made up of the parish pastor, the evangelist, lay delegates from congregations and representatives of the auxiliary groups such as the *Vashandiri* (Bible Women) and *Zvapupu* (Male Witnesses), the Youth Group and Sunday School teachers. The council was responsible for all the spiritual and administrative welfare of the parish. Consisting of all the members of the parish, and meeting at least once a year, the Parish Assembly elected lay delegates to Church Assembly, which also included all the ordained officers of the church. The Church Assembly was the supreme ruling authority of the church and met at least once every two years. It elected members of the Church Council, the highest executive committee of the church.

The Bishop was the chief executive of the church who was supposed to execute all the orders and opinions of the Church Council and the Church Assembly. He ordained all new pastors, inducted his deputy, deans and other church officials and consecrated new churches. Chapels and other buildings were built for divine service. He was supposed to be 'a pastor for pastors and the workers of the church, to visit parishes at least every third year, to see to it that the rules and laws of the church are followed, to function as a chairperson of the Church Assembly, to call a pastors' meeting every second year . . .'[12] In the end the ELCZ Bishop was the single most powerful individual in the church, who headed the whole administrative machinery of the church. He received reports from all chairpeople of the church boards, such as the education board, the medical board, the ministerial board, etc. He was in charge of nearly all the appointments in the church including educational, health, ecclesiastical and general. He supervised the drawing up of the budgets in the church. He was therefore unquestionably the most powerful officer of the church and could choose to influence decisions of the Church Council in subtle ways or even ignore such decisions if they were contrary to his thinking.

CSM not only legally devolved power to the local church but also made efforts to indigenize the clergy and the administration of the educational institutions. By 1977 it had trained 42 pastors and withdrawn nearly all the missionary pastors, except four who were teaching at specialist institutions like the ecumenical seminary, the United Theological College at Epworth, Harare. On June 29, 1975 the Rev. J. C. Shiri, the chaplin and teacher at Chegato Secondary School, was consecrated the first African Bishop of ELCZ. When the war broke out in Mberengwa in 1976, all the missionaries left. In the education field all the teaching staff of 65 and headmasters of the 10 higher primary and secondary schools, still run by the church in 1977, had become indigenous. A similar situation obtained also in the hospitals and clinics where the entire nursing staff including the only medical doctor who was to be killed by what people in the church believe to be Selous Scouts, the secret and murderous arm of the Rhodesian Army, had been localized.

The complete localization of ELCZ removed the possibility of its neutrality in the war of liberation. Swedish missionaries had over the years insisted on abstention from participating in Rhodesian politics by first emphasizing their differences of nationality from the Rhodesian White settlers and secondly by upholding the Lutheran doctrine of the two kingdoms, which taught that citizens must be obedient to their secular rulers because they represented the will of God. Swedish missionaries had therefore in the sixties and early seventies frowned upon the church employees who actively participated in nationalist politics as that was regarded as a form of rebelliousness against, if not actual attack upon the secular rulers. This attitude was to change radically during the war when CSM authorities suddenly found themselves dragged irresistibly into the war by ELCZ.

Whether one agreed with the missionary attitude or not or whether all the Swedish missionaries practised what they preached or not, the merit of their behaviour was that they maintained an official policy that worked as a principle for the church members and guaranteed church unity. Lutherans, whatever their station in the church, knew that African nationalist or White settler politics were disallowed in the church and that political participation was an individual's private affair. Once the missionaries left, the doctrine of the two kingdoms, which Africans had always considered a hypocritical ploy of the Swedish missionaries to prevent the former from working for the overthrow of the oppressive White regime, was discarded. The way was now left open for people to support whatever movement or force operated in the war. Since there were many forces, ranging from the radical guerrilla movements of ZAPU and ZANU through the moderate African National Congress of Bishop Abel Muzorewa, to the Rhodesian government, the church found itself completely torn asunder among all those contending forces.

The divisions further involved the estrangement of the Bishop and his central administration from the main part of the church. Just before the Swedes left in 1975, they had decided, for very sound political reasons and administrative efficiency, to move the headquarters of the church from Mnene to Bulawayo. As communications between the urban areas and the communal areas became dangerous and infrequent during the war, the ELCZ Bishop and his administration too tended to become cut off from the main part of their church. Bishop Shiri later admitted his tenuous relationship with his rural parishes. 'From 1977 to 1979', he wrote in his war autobiography,

> it was very difficult for me to visit parishes openly. I had to make special arrangements with the local authorities who knew the situation well in order to visit some parts of the church. In some parishes I depended on the information sent by pastors to my office and in areas where pastors had left for other centres, I received information from evangelists and christians. Mr Edward Mangenah became my *Mutumwapari* (messenger). He bravely visited affected areas and brought me messages from christians and also from the boys (guerrillas). He discussed church policy with freedom fighters freely. He also carried to them some gifts.[13]

Bishop Shiri cut himself politically also from the rural parishes which were closer to the guerrilla movements in the rural areas than the urban based central administration when he turned his full attention to the urban ecumenical affairs associated with the moderate nationalist politics of the ANC of Muzorewa. From

1978 Bishop Shiri was elected president of the Zimbabwe Christian Council, which was noted for its moderate views concerning the liberation struggle. He even headed the Zimbabwe Christian Council Political Reconciliation Committee, which tried to persuade exiled African leaders to abandon the armed struggle and seek a negotiated settlement.[14]

The alienation of the head office from the rural parishes left the second and third lower levels of ecclesiastical authorities — the pastors and evangelists — to determine the conduct of their parishes and congregations in the war. In the parishes where there were boarding schools, hospitals and clinics the pastors and evangelists cooperated with the local headmasters, teachers and medical staff in meeting the day-to-day demands of the war. Each parish arrived at its own working relationships with the various warring forces with no reference to headquarters or to other parishes and thus again opening up the church to enormous divisions as each unit fell under the permanent influence of either ZIPRA or ZANLA.

THE CHURCH AND THE WAR

We have so far looked at the societies from which the church drew its membership, all the time trying to identify the major features of the church and the communities which determined or shaped their behaviour during the war. We have also indicated some of the ways in which the church and the societies were both influenced by and participated in the war. In this section we should try to focus more fully on the impact of the war on the church concentrating only on those war consequences which affected the peace process in the church.

The three most critical effects of the war which had a lasting impact on the unity of the church were: separation of the Bishop and his central administration from the rural parishes; the accentuation of the regional differences along ethnic lines between the Eastern deanery in Mberengwa and the Western deanery in Matabeleland south; and the inability of ELCZ to survive without financial backing of CSM.

There is a strong opinion in ELCZ which holds that among the many assets and strong qualities which enabled Shiri to win the majority vote in the election of Bishop in May 1974 was his strong nationalist stand favouring the complete transfer of power from missionaries to Africans and the total independence of ELCZ from CSM. The escalation of the war in 1976, which forced CSM to withdraw in a hurry all its missionaries in Zimbabwe, worked in favour of Bishop Shiri's policy of minimization of CSM involvement in ELCZ. Even those missionaries from Sweden who wanted to stay in Zimbabwe in spite of the war were forced to go when CSM stopped sending salaries.[15]

The impact of the war, however, reversed the withdrawal process of CSM. Just under a year after the departure of all the Swedish missionaries ZAPU abducted nearly 700 school children from the Manama mission, an event which touched deeply the hearts of many former missionaries. Both the foreign affairs ministry of

Sweden and CSM immediately felt that those children constituted a section of Zimbabwean refugees in Zambia which required their direct intervention. A missionary was immediately dispatched to Lusaka to go and make an on-the-spot investigation of the welfare of the children. Lutheran parents in Zimbabwe too urged former missionaries to do everything possible in the interest of their children.[16] The immediate result of the abduction of the Manama children was to involve CSM in the humanitarian programmes for refugees in Zambia. On 25 May 1977 CSM granted 11 075 Zambian Kwacha for educational needs as requested by ZAPU and further K1 925 for the purchase of 1 000 bibles. CSM also cooperated with the Lutheran World Federation (LWF) in raising funds for the aid of refugee camps both in Zambia and Mozambique.[17]

When the Lancaster agreement brought partial peace to Zimbabwe, CSM found itself being drawn back to its old mission field first by the reconstruction programme of ELCZ and secondly by the latter's inability to stand on its own. All ELCZ schools except Beitbridge and Mnene primary schools and Musume Secondary school had either been partially or totally razed. The same pattern applied to hospitals and clinics, churches and chapels and personages.[18] CSM found itself having to cooperate with the LWF and having to initiate fresh bilateral agreements with ELCZ to raise funds for the reconstruction programme, for the employment of badly needed medical staff and for the general support of the local church. At a joint meeting held with CSM at Njube Youth Centre in Bulawayo on March 25 1980, ELCZ made plain its need for continued support from CSM. ELCZ said that it was unable to raise money for the running expenses, including salaries for its pastors and other workers, and therefore appealed to CSM for 'a substantial grant for about five years in which time it is hoped that the country and the church could recover from the seven-year old war'.[19]

This acknowledged dependence of ELCZ which coincided with the national euphoria over national independence from Britain called for a rethinking of the relationship between the two organizations. There was need to work out afresh their formal agreement of cooperation so that it could accommodate the independent spirit cultivated by the operational autonomy of the local church during the war on the one hand and the local church's need for continued financial and qualified workers backing from CSM on the other. Indeed in October 1980 CSM invited ELCZ to a formal round conference which would come up with the magic formula in which CSM would continue to support ELCZ without infringing upon the latter's cherished independence.[20]

Bishop Shiri's response to the call sounded not only cautious but showed how he had grown extraordinarily sensitive to anything suggesting encroachment upon the self-rule of his church. Also the Bishop could not ignore his church's dependence upon the CSM for annual subsidies. He therefore welcomed consultations on the future relationship between the sister churches regarding their cooperation in their mission in Zimbabwe. However, he sounded a word of warning that the two partners 'discuss frankly what obstacles can spoil the work and how we can sincerely work together to remove them'.[21] The Bishop had grown extremely sensitive to a relationship which smacked of the dominant-subordinate partnership of the colonial period.

Shiri's views were subsequently echoed by many ELCZ members during a fact-finding tour by two CSM board members on September 15–17, 1981. The two board members visited nearly all the major ELCZ parish centres sounding out people's opinions on the proposed changes in the terms of cooperation between the two churches. It was plain that local Lutherans wanted to be independent from CSM and tended to be extremely embarrassed when their financial dependence upon Sweden was revealed. For instance it was revealed that CSM's contribution to the 1981 ELCZ budget amounted to 74,9%, income from local investments was 12,2%, income from the local congregations was only 9,4% and the rest of the budget was met from pension fees and housing rents. The disparity between the church's local income and its overseas grants was indeed a source of grave worry to the people, as they put it: 'We are proud of our independence but worried about our economy.'[22] Thus in the end people asked CSM to support the local church at least for a limited time while they found ways of developing their capacity for self-sufficiency.

Their spirit was embodied in the new Document of Understanding of 1983, which was couched in a language acknowledging equal partnership between the two churches and the need for continued financial support for the local church by CSM. The fly in the ointment for Zimbabwe Lutherans was the financial accountability by ELCZ to CSM. ELCZ was not only to submit its annual requirements to CSM by the stipulated date of 31st July but the local church could not reallocate funds set aside for specific projects without prior negotiations with its parent body. ELCZ was also required to keep proper financial records and to have them audited regularly. The local church was to provide CSM with its annual financial statements and its audited reports.[23] These demands were a significant erosion of ELCZ's independence and the position was not made any easier by the inability of ELCZ to achieve self-sufficiency. Between 1980 and 1988 local Sunday collections had risen by 700% yet the church still had an annual running deficit of nearly one million Zimbabwean dollars.[24]

Clearly the withdrawal of the Swedish missionaries, the constitutional changes involving the devolution of power from CSM to ELCZ and the war with the outcome of national independence, had heightened the desire for complete independence in the ELCZ leadership. The nominal or neo-colonial independence which CSM underwrote in the Document of Agreement of 1983 therefore simply produced frustration in the local leadership, which frustration soon expressed itself in the local leadership's reluctance to comply with the requirements of making available annual financial reports and audited accounts to the parent body. This soured the relationship between the two churches so much so that CSM resorted to cutting all its financial support for ELCZ. This way CSM became a chief factor to contend with in the healing of the wounds after the war.

A further factor which was also a legacy of the war was indeed the estrangement of the Bishop and his headquarters from both the Eastern and Western deaneries during the war which grew worse during the civil war in Matabeleland from 1982 to 1987. When the Bishop failed to identify himself with the rural parishes and contented himself with 'remote control' through messengers, he exposed himself to severe criticisms by the headmasters, pastors and hospital staff who continued to shoulder the responsibilities of the church and to put up with the war. There was a strong feeling right across the church from east to west that the Bishop and his headquarters staff in the safety of Bulawayo did not understand the war difficulties and therefore gave decisions which were out of keeping with the position in the rural war zones. This was certainly the feeling of headmasters and their staff at Musume Secondary School, who managed to keep the school going throughout the war; also the nursing sister in charge at Mnene Hospital, who maintained excellent working relationships with the guerrillas and saved her hospital from closure.[25]

In the eyes of the church employees in the war zones the Bishop and his administration in their remote sanctuary of Bulawayo were not only oblivious of the war zone problems but they even acted as if they were in collusion with the Rhodesian colonial government. This was indeed the feeling of the medical staff after a temporary closure of three months of Masase hospital due to war pressures in November 1977. The church refused to pay the salaries of the nurses for all those three months. The views of the nurses were expressed through the Medical Board to the Church Council, which insisted that 'the hospital staff both medical and non medical should be paid full salary for three months if they happen to leave the hospital abruptly due to circumstances beyond their control . . . The Church Council should realize that these people are sacrificing their lives.'[26] The Masase affected nurses decided too to address their grievances to Bishop Shiri himself and reminded him that he had not responded to their call to come and see the situation for himself when the hospital was in trouble:

> Before the hospital was closed we requested the pastor in charge to call the Bishop, so as to make the necessary arrangements, that was Tuesday but Bishop did not come. Wednesday we had to give the key to the pastor I/C. All patients had left; also the sister in charge was with you there in town. To this we did not know what exactly you wanted us to do. Above all when you asked those who were available to open the Hospital on the 18th January we were ready for work but did not commence since there was no sister. We want to make ourselves clear to you that you know we are women and did not come to town as all others do when things go wrong. We definitely know this was not the first case in the church. It happened to pastors, sisters, nurses and all others or even for no reason. Our grant came as from July to December. If it is for January the church could pay from Masase surplus as had been recommended by the Medical Board. Even so you did not think that some of the staff members were off duty when they came back there was no work . . . We feel you treated us this way because we are not represented in the Church Council.[27]

The nurses, like many employees in the church, were bitter about an administration which was remote and took decisions which seemed not only callous but bore very little relation to reality. Not only did the church administration withhold salaries of staff when institutions were temporarily shut down but it also continued to demand rents for accommodation and to impose electricity and water charges even when the staff had run away from the missions to escape being killed.[28]

Even more surprising was the arbitrary dismissal of the nursing staff in the Western deanery, a move that appeared as if the church administration was submissively carrying out Rhodesian government regulations without regard for the plight of its African employees who were victims of the war. The following is an example of the dismissal letters written to the nurses at Manama mission:

> The Ministry of Health has from 1st January 1979 reduced the number of staff for which we have been receiving government grants and accordingly we have reduced the staff at Manama hospital. We regret that we will have to give you notice that your employment with the hospital will cease as from 15 January 1979.[29]

There was absolutely no indication which criteria had been used to render some nurses and not others redundant; nor was there any attempt by the administration to visit Manama in order to explain fully the church's action. The nurses naturally felt that they were being treated grossly unfairly as they said it in their letter to the church headquarters:

> We the undernamed nurses hereby notify the Church Council through the Medical Board that we are not satisfied about our dismissal from work for the following reasons:
>
> (1)   We were not given any notice . . .
> (2)   It appears we shall not get any gratuity though we have all worked for more than twenty years in the church.
> (3)   In the letters written to each one of us notifying us to stop work, we have been told that the Ministry of Health says we are over staffed, yet for all these years when we spoke about salary increases, the church always told us that we were working directly under the church.
> (4)   We wonder why the church dismissed us without giving us even a thank you. Instead paid us half salary as if we had done something wrong. We could be happy if this could be clarified to us.[30]

The nurses were grieved at the way the church administration seemed to gladly take up the place of the Rhodesian government 'hatchet man', implementing the latter's war policies designed to disadvantage rural wage employees thought to be collaborating with the guerrillas.[31]

The Bishop and his administration incurred a severely tarnished image. This with the Bishop's participation in the urban ecumenical movements which were associated with the moderate nationalism of Abel Muzorewa's ANC, alienated the church leadership from its rural parishioners, who were proud at the end of the war to have been identified with the radical movements of the liberation struggle. The leadership was looked upon as cowardly and therefore found it difficult to reassert itself or to command unqualified respect of its followers.

The predicament of the leadership was particularly unsalvageable in the Western deanery, where civil war broke out in 1982 when ZANU and ZAPU failed to work together in the new independent government. The civil war threatened to cause a schism between the Eastern and Western deaneries. The possible schism should be understood in the context of Bishop Shiri's long term relationship with the Western deanery, his partiality to the Eastern deanery in the appointments of headquarters personnel and the Western deanery's fear of domination by the Eastern deanery.

Right from the 1974 ELCZ election of the first African Bishop, the Westerners looked upon Shiri as an Easterner and not the Bishop of the whole church. They had not voted for him but had voted for their dean, Rev. A. A. Noko, whom they had fielded to run against the two Eastern candidates — Shiri and Rev. Dr F. K. Gambiza, the present principal of the United Theological Seminary at Epworth, Harare.[32] Westerners became even more concerned when key appointments in the church's head office which were made by the new Bishop and the Church Council, which was also dominated by the Easterners, all seemed to go to Easterners. There came a time when the Bishop, his deputy, the Treasurer and Administrative Secretary were all from the Eastern deanery.[33] The Western deanery must have despaired of ever gaining a significant voice in the affairs of their church because they were in the minority (with only 13 parishes compared with 19 parishes in the Eastern deanery).[34]

The domination in the church by the Easterners also appeared to the Westerners to replicate the national political domination of the Western ethnic groups by the Shona speakers, or in party terms of ZAPU by ZANU. When the civil war erupted in Matabeleland between ZAPU and ZANU there was a strong tendency in the ELCZ for the Western deanery in Matabeleland South province to identify itself with ZAPU while most Easterners identified with ZANU.

By 1989 the church was obviously facing several problems that threatened to break it up. The problems expressed themselves in the reluctance of CSM to continue supporting ELCZ financially; the refusal of Westerners to cooperate with Easterners in the Church Council, Church Assembly and other committees; and the appeal by both ELCZ and CSM officials to the government of Zimbabwe to intervene to save the church.

In response to the feeling by members of the Western deanery that because of their minority status they had no effective say in the running of the church, the Church Assembly decided to draw up a new constitution which was thought to meet complaints of Westerners. It was proposed that instead of the church being made up of two deaneries it must be drastically reconstituted so that it might have three dioceses, coinciding roughly with the two deaneries and the third with the urban parishes. Westerners did not feel happy with that decision because, among many things, Bulawayo with all its church properties which had always formed part of the Western deanery, was being severed from its home. Moreover the Westerners felt that the new dispensation which was being proposed was an imposition from Easterners. Thus from the word go Westerners refused to cooperate with the constitutional committee set up in 1988. When the Bishop and other Easterners appeared to ignore protests and boycotts by Westerners, the latter began a campaign of discrediting the Bishop using the press and through correspondence with CSM. The Bishop and his head office staff were accused of gross financial mismanagement, nepotism, tribalism and arbitrary rule. The chorus was soon joined by a strong faction of pastors from the Eastern deanery who were concerned about the possible schism in the church and attributed all the trouble in the church to the style of leadership of the Bishop. The group of pastors felt strongly that CSM should apparently suspend its financial support for the church until the latter could correct its deficiencies.[35] The concerns of the Eastern pastors and some Westerners regarding the financial position of the church dovetailed with those of the CSM Board, which in December 1988 found it necessary to invite the Bishop and his staff to Uppsala for face-to-face consultations on the finances of the church. For almost a year the Bishop avoided the meeting and only went to Uppsala in November 1989. It appears two reasons persuaded the Bishop to make his visit. First he argued that financial shortages in the church were aggravating church divisions. In his view the financial difficulties had arisen because of the depreciation of the Swedish currency in relation to the Zimbabwe dollar.[36] Secondly, CSM, which normally approved ELCZ annual grants by June had not done so by November 1988.[37]

Perhaps galvanized by its suspicion of financial mismanagement in ELCZ by similar accusations emanating from the Bishop's opponents in Zimbabwe, CSM decided to adopt a tough attitude to ELCZ leadership. The tough stand by CSM was no doubt too intended to Westerners and its Eastern critics. CSM therefore wanted ELCZ leadership to present 'a realistic and true picture of the actual financial situation . . . by presenting Consolidated Annual Accounts for each year 1982–1988, including Balance Sheet and Profit and Loss a/c.' They wanted to see a detailed explanation of how the accumulated deficit in the church had come about. Only after that could CSM start negotiations with the debtors and creditors of the church. Moreover CSM wanted to see all those measures undertaken and carried out by external professional consultants.[38] ELCZ responded by appointing the firm of accountants Price Waterhouse Company whose preliminary report showed that the finances of the church and their management left a lot to be desired. Because of that CSM decided in June 1990 that the Board only authorize any grants to ELCZ if the latter dealt with the following:

(a)   Internal control must be established,
(b)   Negotiation with debtors and creditors must take place,
(c)   A balanced budget of 1990 and 1991 must be prepared.[39]

CSM now took the unprecedented step of communicating directly with the Church Assembly and Church Council of ELCZ because the Board felt that the ELCZ leadership was hiding information from its people and because the leadership was also being deliberately uncommunicative with CSM. CSM was, to be sure, extremely conscious that it was trading on sensitive grounds: 'We feel and know that this is a very painful exercise as we are dealing with your church's internal affairs.' In fact CSM said it would have been easier for them 'to opt out of the picture completely'. But they found themselves bound by existing agreements with ELCZ to continue their partnership with the latter.[40] By September 1990 ELCZ leadership had not only refrained from carrying out a financial reorganization or reconstruction as agreed with CSM in November 1989, but it had not even cared to comment on the findings of the firm of accountants, Price Waterhouse Company. CSM had no option but to suspend completely its grants to ELCZ and also to explore possibilities of paying salaries for its medical missionaries through the government. Such a move would effectively transfer the control of Swedish medical doctors from the church to the government of Zimbabwe.[41] That was what alarmed ELCZ leadership and prompted it to approach the government of Zimbabwe intending to ask the government not to take over control of the missionary doctors.

The approach to government was made by Bishop Shiri himself in company of Rev. Almon Shoko of Tshabalala Township Parish in Bulawayo, Rev. Shava, the Administrative Secretary, and Rev. Jeremiah Shumba, pastor in charge of the Harare parish and through Richard Hove, Minister of Defence and Member of Parliament for Mberengwa East Constituency in October 1990. The Bishop and his delegation admitted that the church was experiencing enormous divisions which the Bishop and his advisors were now failing to solve alone. They informed the minister of the threat of CSM to withdraw their medical missionaries. The delegation too complained about what they called CSM misrepresentation of the church's financial mismanagement. The Bishop therefore wanted the government to be cautious in its dealings with the Swedes about the church's internal affairs.[42]

The Bishop also used that opportunity to lay bare what he considered the problems confronting the church. To him there were political issues and also problems of representation in decision making processes in the church. About appointments to key posts in the administration of the church the Bishop confessed that he had ended up with Easterners only occupying those posts. Besides, the Bishop is reported to have said:

> Previous political affiliations and persuasions were another source of confrontation in the ELCZ ... He advised the minister that the ELCZ was flourishing with the ancient (sic) ZAPU and ZANU PF dogmatics which carried tribal, factional and regional philosophies. The Bishop advised

the minister that he wanted assistance as a matter of urgency to rescue the church from such political undertones ridden by ancient political dogmatics and philosophies.'[43]

The Bishop not only confirmed tribal practices especially in appointments in the church but he seemed frightened by the national political divisions which now threatened to break up the church. Moreover his going to Minister Hove, a Mberengwa ZANU politician and Eastern Deanery Lutheran, revealed the Bishop's own regional and political partiality, which his Western adversaries were quick to spot and, as we shall see shortly, tried to counteract by seeking their own allies in government. In other words the national politics of ZANU and ZAPU, which had just had their dramatic turn-about in the 1987 Unity Accord, including international pressures as represented by CSM, were now being recreated and played out in the Lutheran church. ELCZ too was becoming a national embarrassment in its slowness to follow the national example of pulling itself out of tribal and party conflicts. Apparently even President Robert Mugabe had become concerned about the unflattering reports on ELCZ and its Bishop and had made known his concern to Minister Hove during his tour of the church's medical institutions in 1989.[44]

In Hove's case, his intervention was not only prompted by the adverse newspaper reports and the President's concern, but it seems he was shocked and embarrassed as a Lutheran to witness an example of the conflict in his church on television. The outrageous and mortifying scene followed the replacement of the late Rev. S. C. Ndlovu of Tshabalala Township in Bulawayo by an Eastern pastor, Rev. Almon Shoko. The appointment was made by the Bishop and his Church Council, which now consisted almost entirely of Easterners. On Sunday, the 13th January 1991, the Tshabalala congregation invited a Zimbabwe Broadcasting Television crew, and in full view of the television cameras seized pastor Shoko and threw him out of their chapel. Minister Hove, who saw the scene on television later told a delegation of the Western deanery which he invited to his office on 23rd January 1991, that the conflict had reached 'unacceptable levels of disorder'. He expressed concern that he and many other Lutherans could not allow being exposed to such and more embarrassment and he felt that this should end quickly because it was unacceptable and intolerable for him both as a member of the church and a parliamentary representative of Mberengwa East which is part of the troubled and affected area by this Lutheran order. He concluded by pointing out that the conflict 'had clearly exceeded bounds of the Bishop and his advisors and the Lutheran Church in general'.[45] It therefore now required outside intervention. Indeed it was during the same meeting with the Western deanery delegation that Minister Hove proposed a roundtable conference of the Eastern and Western deanery representatives to discuss and resolve the problems of the church.[46]

Mr Hove further showed his grasp of the church's problems when he proposed issues to be addressed during the roundtable conference. He said the conference should address both structural affairs and the personnel in the leadership of the church and therefore enumerated the issues as follows:

1. People would have to answer . . . questions relating to the authority of an office (the Bishop's). Do we recognise Episcopal Office? Should the Episcopal Office be retained in the ELCZ? Is the problem that of the occupant of this office in the name of Jonas Shiri, or is the problem of both the existence of such an office and the current incumbent?

2. Do we have *one* church in Zimbabwe, or shall we have more than one? This means that people should examine the question of the necessity for the oneness of the ELCZ.

3. The present structures of the church — are they what we need, or are they fictitious and fallacious in our day and age? Are they the sort of thing we need or is their construction unwarranted? The way they are maintained and run is separate from the point of necessity. The Minister emphasised that there is need to differentiate the question of inability to maintain and keep the structures and the need for their existence as structures.

4. Is the ELCZ problem centred on matters of policy which might be incoherent and incomplete accompanied by poor administration?

5. What has caused Lutheran problems, which are they, where are they? Facts must be provided and examined. We need to examine — Do Lutherans vote according to language or region or tribe? We need to look at the ELCZ constitution.[47]

The Western deanery delegation accepted the Minister's intervention, his proposed issues of discussion but expressed grave reservations on whether to trust Bishop Shiri's word that he now wanted to talk to the Western Deanery. The delegation pointed out that in the past they had sent six delegations made up of very respected church members from the Western Deanery to talk to the Bishop about issues affecting the church; in the past too they had even had written agreements with the Bishop, all of which he had either ignored or unilaterally broken. In spite of their distrust of the Bishop, however, they were prepared to participate in any talks organized by Mr Hove merely to give him (Hove) 'a chance and again to afford you with due respect . . .'[48]

Apparently as an insurance against finding themselves in a situation they might be brow beaten into unfair settlements by the Eastern Deanery and ZANU politicians, the Western Deanery delegates sought to enlist the support of Mr Joshua Nkomo, one of the vice-presidents of Zimbabwe and former president of ZAPU. So after meeting with Mr Hove between 11 a.m. and 1 p.m. the Western Deanery delegation moved to Nkomo's home in the evening for a pre-arranged meeting on the same subject. We need to quote extensively the proceedings of that meeting because they afforded the Western Deanery an opportunity to present the problems of the church and their predicament in the church as they really saw and felt them. Because they expected sympathy from Nkomo, who belonged to the same region as themselves and further identified themselves with his former party ZAPU, the delegation could afford to open their hearts and feelings to him.

Rev. Litsietsi Dube, Dean of ELCZ in the Western Deanery, led his group in the discussions. After a word of prayer and an apology for intruding upon the Vice-President's busy time, Dean Dube made the following points:

1   (b)   That the purpose of the visit to V.P. was to inform him personally in his capacity as Vice-President of Zimbabwe and to honour him by not simply letting him hear Lutheran talk from the street, radio, newspapers and television, but from ourselves.

       (c)   Dube gave a detailed historical set up of the ELCZ since the era of missionary administration and that since 1962:

           (i)   There were two ELCZ Deaneries, namely Eastern and Western, being divided by the road from the City of Bulawayo to Beitbridge; Mberengwa and Gwanda being the main Lutheran population centres.

           (ii)   Our first African bishop, Jonas Shiri, comes from Mberengwa and came into leadership in 1975.

           (iii)   After 1981, the division of ELCZ became more than just road demarcations, because now even appointments were done on a tribal framework, even for pastoral workers. Every church organ became tribalized and regionalized. Appointments at ELCZ head office were now turned into Mberengwa office. Dean Dube and his group had then formalized their complaints about their tribal mishap in writing. Bishop Shiri makes himself deaf when it comes to church disagreements.

       (d)   Since 1986, the confrontation now between Bishop Shiri and Western ELCZ escalated and developed into an open tribal confrontation within the Church of God.

           Westerners at that point then wanted creation of two Dioceses, meaning to say there could be an appointment of two Bishops.

       (e)   Voting in the ELCZ Assemblies have been tribalized and sense and reason no longer prevail.

       (f)   There came a situation when the Westerners boycotted ELCZ Church Council on the grounds that people simply went to the meetings to vote as a majority and minority.

       (g)   Only in 1990 January was common ground struck and a 55/50 Church Council created. It was short-lived because the Bishop could not psychologically allow this to flourish.

       (h)   The Bishop wanted to return to the principle of no sense but votes. He called a meeting of Church Assembly to dissolve the Church Council first at Masase in September 1990. We prevented him. Finally in October he made it after the High Court of Zimbabwe could not allow our petition.

(i) We now are subjected to decisions of an ELCZ tribal council. We do not accept this decision.

(j) Now comes the imposed Pastor A. Shoko into Bulawayo. Bishop unmindful about children who do not understand Shona.

(k) Bishop writes to the Dean [of Western Deanery] only when complaining.

(l) Bishop now quarrels with every meaningful Lutheran structure. The general agreement he signed in Sweden in November 1989 has been despised by him.

(m) Sweden has stopped subsidies to ELCZ.

(n) ELCZ hospitals are now undergoing suffering because of ELCZ administration.

(o) Because of these problems, we have been assigned to brief the Honourable Vice-President of Zimbabwe.[49]

Nkomo expressed himself as horrified by the way ELCZ was conducting itself and called for a immediate solution to the conflict. 'There is no such thing as minority and majority before a Church of God,' he said. 'No,' he declared. Aware that Minister Hove was already involved in the mediation process, Nkomo did not put himself forward as a possible mediator but advised the Western group to seek someone who could help them. Obviously the delegation was not only looking for sympathetic hearing but they wanted some intervention from a government minister with ZAPU background apparently to neutralize Mr Hove's influence. After the meeting with Joshua Nkomo the group therefore resolved to approach Minister John Nkomo, a former ZAPU executive member, perhaps to be a co-mediator with Hove.[50]

We have no record of what happened to the efforts to enlist some co-mediation from former ZAPU ministers but it appears that the delegation could not arrange anything within the period agreed with Minister Hove for the first talks to take place and because of commitments made to Hove by the group. The group had agreed that the conference between representatives of the two deaneries should take place within seven days from 23rd January in Bulawayo; that Hove should suggest both the format of the talks and the number of delegates to the conference; that the government should not intervene at that stage, so that Hove was acting in his private capacity and as a member of the Lutheran church; and that Hove be principally responsible for getting everybody to the conference table.[51] These decisions laid the ground for serious talks to resolve ELCZ conflicts.

THE FORMULATION OF A NEW ELCZ CONSTITUTION

Once the two deaneries had agreed to the intervention of Mr Hove, the working out of the new constitution, the testing of its acceptability and implementation took less than a year. Hove's first task was to put together a mediation team that would be acceptable to both deaneries and his strategy of picking upon Lutherans of high standing from both deaneries, but who had no positions in the church worked. He chose Dr Phineas Makhurane, the Pro vice-chancellor of the University of Zimbabwe and soon to be appointed the Vice-Chancellor of the National University of Science and Technology, Dr Eleck Mashingaidze, a diplomat and respected civil servant, Mr Cheda, Permanent Secretary in the Ministry of Legal and Parliamentary Affairs, and Mr July Moyo, Permanent Secretary in the Ministry of Construction. They with Minister Hove himself represented some of the most successful products of the ELCZ school system and were therefore the pride of the church. In the meantime Bishop Shiri now considered leader of the Eastern Deanery, and Dean Litsietsi Dube, leader of the Western Deanery, were each invited to raise a team of 10 negotiators including themselves. Hove's group and the two teams met at the ELCZ Njube Youth Centre in February 1991. Just as an indication of how tense the situation had developed in ELCZ, a participant made the following observation:

> Delegates from the Eastern Deanery did not greet one another or converse and strayed around Njube Youth Centre in an unusual and tense manner before the start of the meeting. Even after commencement of the meeting, the two delegations could not greet one another until 1:00 p.m. when the atmosphere altered for the better.[52]

The upshot of the meeting was to set up a constitutional committee to provide it with terms of reference and to set the date for the next meeting. The committee was asked to focus on the following areas:

(a)   election of Church Council and method to avoid members coming from one deanery.

(b)   division of organs of the church between spiritual and administrative.

(c)   the appointment, functions and terms of office of the deans.

(d)   the Bishop's term of office to be determined.

(e)   rotation of deans in deaneries.

(f)   alternating appointments of Bishops between deaneries.

(g)   Interposing of pastors in deaneries.[53]

The date for the next meeting was set at 23 February 1991 at the same venue. When that meeting took place, it considered progress made by the constitution sub-committee and decided that a final draft constitution be produced for the next meeting scheduled for the 8th to the 9th March 1991.[54]

When the meeting of the 8th to the 9th took place it produced a document which gave a résumé of the proceedings of the negotiating groups and their constitutional sub-committee. The document also contained some of the guiding principles as well as fundamental issues agreed upon as a basis for discussion. It was pointed out for instance that right from the outset

> The two deaneries formally accepted and endorsed the role of the Mediation Committee in assisting the ELCZ to solve the problems presently affecting the church. Both sides and His Lordship Bishop Shiri pledged full cooperation with the Mediation Committee and agreed to be bound by all decisions arrived at.[55]

This was to turn out to be an extremely important principle which often Minister Hove used to keep under firm check members of the negotiating groups who sometimes wanted to backtrack on things to which they had already agreed. It was not uncommon for some members to try to change their minds during the period when the new constitution was being explained to the rest of the church before its formal adoption by the Church Assembly. Such behaviour became common especially among Eastern Deanery negotiators.

The Mediation Committee and the Deanery groups further discussed thoroughly and agreed on the following points and deliberated procedures in the church:

(a)   that the ELCZ should be headed by a Bishop;
(b)   that the *oneness* of the church must be maintained;
(c)   that the Doctrine and other Principles of the Church should be observed;
(d)   that the Church should have clearly defined administrative and deliberative structures or organs such as the Church Assembly, the Church Council, Boards, etc.;
(e)   that the constitution of the ELCZ should be revised to provide for the reorganisation of the church and to enhance greater unity within the church;
(f)   that any problem affecting the church should be discussed and ways be agreed upon to resolve such problems within the context of the unity of the church and spirit of reconciliation.[56]

Finally it was agreed that a team of six people undertake the task of explaining the new draft constitution to the two deaneries at meetings organized by the two deans. The document containing all these agreements was formally signed by all the members of the Eastern and Western negotiating groups, so that they all bound themselves to defend it and the new constitution in their respective deaneries.[57]

The new draft constitution of the church was first explained to the ELCZ Western Deanery Assembly held in Gwanda on 23 March 1991. Its acceptance became a foregone conclusion when Dean Litsietsi Dube who introduced Minister Hove, the main representative of the Mediation Committee, commended it profusely. An observer recorded the dean's speech as follows:

Today is Historical. It is our happiest day. The last six years were full of hatred and disorder in the ELCZ. No proper benefit was made except by Satan. Westerners met for many days and hours. Some people have left the ELCZ because of the six-year old strife. This is now history. We now have to start afresh and the past must go to the archives. Ecclesiastics rightly point out that there is time for everything. Lets respect the biblical assertion. Honour and respect must be given to Richard Hove and his mediation team. The team before us are going to explain the proposed draft constitution. No constitution can be perfect. *What is required is goodwill.* Like the Lancaster House Agreement, it was not perfect but goodwill prevailed. Goodwill is perfect but not a written piece of paper.[58]

After that the meeting proceeded not only swiftly, lasting under three hours, but happily, with Richard Hove explaining the constitution. He prefaced his remarks by pointing out that strife and conflicts in the church had come about 'largely as a result of administration and the nature of the constitution governing it'. He then pointed out the new articles of the constitution which had been added, including the new changes made to old articles. When Hove explained the proposed new voting procedures for elected officers of the church and during deliberations, he received hearty cheers from the meeting. For the first time, according to the new constitution, there would be least domination of the minority Western Deanery by the Easterners because of the cross voting system. Leaders would be voted and retained in power only if they enjoyed at least 30% support from each deanery. During meetings, major contentious decisions would only be adopted if they received the approval of the majority of those present and at least 30% support of members present from each deanery. Another important and new provision of the constitution which also proved extremely popular from the applause of the meeting was that all chairpersons of assemblies of congregations, parishes and the whole church were going to be lay people. For the first time the Bishop would not be chairperson of the Church Assembly but an elected lay person. Professionals would chair the various boards, including education, ministerial, medical etc. Age and experience would be used to decide the eligibility of people to be elected to important offices of the church. One had to be at least 45 or 50 years to qualify for election as Dean or Bishop respectively. It was now a requirement in the constitution that the Bishop and the Deputy should not come from the same deanery. Moreover for the first time the post of Bishop was to rotate between deaneries. Finally the Administrative Secretary and Treasurer of the church could not be recruited from the same deanery. The intention of the constitution was to remove all major sources of conflicts and strife in the church by making sure that no ethnic group or region felt dominated by the other. With those explanations the constitution was unanimously accepted and Minister Hove and his Mediation Committee were praised for a job well done.[59]

The position was very much different when a similar meeting of the Eastern Deanery met at Masvingo a week later. The Eastern Dean was conspicuously less enthusiastic in recommending the draft constitution for adoption. It was obvious that there had been an underground campaign to urge the Easterners to reject the constitution. There was an erroneous but strong feeling that the new draft constitution had been produced by elements in the West who wanted to overthrow Bishop Shiri. Moreover some people who had already put their signatures to the document of acceptance of the constitution now wanted to distance themselves from the constitution. The meeting only made headway when Hove used the privilege of his ministerial position to reveal that it had apparently come to the attention of government through Central Intelligence Organization that certain people in the Eastern Deanery had devoted themselves to mobilizing clandestinely opposition against the draft constitution. He further discredited as grossly immature the behaviour of some negotiators of the draft constitution who now criticized and questioned the document they had approved already. In the end some of those vocal elements acquiesced and it was agreed to take forward the constitution to the Church Assembly for debate and adoption.[60]

The crucial meeting of the Church Assembly to adopt the draft constitution was held in Bulawayo on 26–27 April and was also attended by Rev. Hans S. A. Engdahl, Southern Secretary of CSM, and Rev. M. C. Kuchera, General Secretary of the Zimbabwe Council of Churches. With a few amendments, the constitution was adopted as the new constitution of ELCZ. It was also agreed that the restructuring process with the elections of the new officers of the church should be accomplished within nine months from the date of the Assembly. The old Council was dissolved immediately and replaced by a new one which was charged with the task of overseeing the proposed reorganization of the church. Although evidently serious hurdles lay ahead, the whole Church Assembly was joyful that a new chapter of peace and unity in ELCZ had begun.[61]

By July 1991 many of the new constitutional provisions had been implemented. Congregations, parishes and deaneries had elected their key officers and councils. The Western Deanery which was assigned the task of producing the first Bishop under the new constitution, had nominated its three candidates from whom the Church Assembly would elect the new Bishop; the Eastern Deanery too had made its nominations for the post of Bishop's Deputy. Both deaneries had also selected people from whom the two deans were to be elected. Using a fool proof system of secret ballot voting and the cross voting procedure prescribed by the constitution, on the 4th October 1991 ELCZ elected as its Bishop Rev. D. D. E. Siphuma, a Venda and therefore Westerner from Beitbridge; the Rev. Dr Ambrose Moyo as its Bishop's Deputy; and returned into office the two old deans, Rev. H. Mavunduse of the Eastern Deanery and Rev. Litsietsi Dube for the Western Deanery. The Bishop was consecrated on the 29th December 1991 and Bishop Shiri graciously retired.[62] All the turmoil which had begun during the liberation war finally subsided and ELCZ now looked forward to a future of quiet development and prosperous mission. By the end of the year CSM too had become convinced that peace and tranquillity had at last come to its sister church in Zimbabwe and therefore released its financial aid to ELCZ so that even on the international arena there was a dawn of fresh life for the church.

ELCZ stands out in Zimbabwe as an example of an important religious institution which was permanently scarred by the war and took a long time and effort to recover. The warring forces were divided along ethnic lines and therefore easily divided the church which was already composed of different ethnic groups. The leadership of the church too proved too inept to deal with the crisis, first by seeming to abandon its flock during the war and secondly by aligning itself with one deanery. Especially by its latter behaviour, the leadership exposed itself to serious accusations of tribalism, nepotism, regionalism etc. Once it was closely identified with one part of the church the leadership squandered recklessly all its credibility and appearances of impartiality, which might have enabled it to play a conciliatory role in the war-torn and politically divided church. The leadership of the church seemed too naïve to grasp the fact that African independence whether ecclesiastical or political was only nominal and could be pulled down like a house of cards before a storm by the international forces who controlled the purse strings. It certainly lacked minimal skills of working with aid donors and thought it could defiantly ignore the strings attached to the aid and defy with impunity, apparently in the name of upholding independence, requests for statements of audited accounts. In the end CSM, the major donor of the church, suspended its aid. That pulled the leadership to its knees. It is painful indeed to have to admit that CSM's move against the leadership proved to be the decisive factor in pushing the latter to a negotiated settlement. CSM simply boosted the morale of the opponents of the Bishop and his administration. It is important to emphasize that CSM deeply regretted having to take recourse to such actions.[63] In the meantime the National Unity Accord between ZANU and ZAPU created a propitious atmosphere for the peace settlement in the church. In fact the settlement might have been the decisive factor which persuaded both Joshua Nkomo and John Nkomo against interfering with Hove's mediation efforts and by that also encouraged the Westerners seriously to seek peace with their Eastern brothers. The blessing of the crisis was that the church in its peace settlement came up with a constitution which, with its magnificent principles of cross voting, oscillation of the offices of Bishop and his deputy between the two deaneries, minimum possibility of domination of one ethnic group by another purely on grounds of numerical strengths, must surely be the envy of many churches and states in Africa facing similar ethnic problems. Wounds and their healing have their share of salutary effects after all; and the Lord can employ a crisis to effect His own changes on our institutions.

Things Fall Apart, The Centre Can Hold: Processes of Post-War Political Change in Zimbabwe's Rural Areas

JOCELYN ALEXANDER

Wartime political mobilization led many observers to expect a radical redistribution of land and decentralization of political power in Zimbabwe. The government rhetoric of the early 1980s seemed to confirm these expectations. Despite the advances that have been achieved, however, the reality falls far short of the rhetoric. I will argue that the roots of this discrepancy lie in the processes of political mobilization during the war and in the constraints which a negotiated independence placed on economic and political transformation. Zimbabwe's negotiated independence ensured the survival of a powerful and centralized state. Rhodesian traditions of authoritarian and technocratic planning persisted while constitutional guarantees underpinned a largely unchanged economic system. Though guerrilla mobilization in the rural areas successfully sustained the war and set in motion radical challenges to existing power structures, it failed to produce new political organizations able to resist the manipulations of powerful bureaucracies. The government was able to 'demobilize' the local level political party by excluding it from policy decisions and starving it of resources. Though many party leaders were elected onto local development authorities, these were dependent on government resources and expertise. In some areas, a traditional leadership which based its authority on pre-war power structures re-emerged. Traditional leaders, though often motivated largely by their own ambitions, gained support from a constituency alienated by the government's pursuit of modernizing policies and the marginalization of the local political party.

DEBATES ON WAR-TIME MOBILIZATION

Wartime political mobilization challenged existing structures of authority and sources of legitimacy; it played an important role in creating the possibility of a new basis for rural politics in independent Zimbabwe. Terence Ranger, David Lan and Norma Kriger have presented conflicting interpretations of both the methods and goals of rural mobilization and the social and ideological bases of rural support for guerrillas. I will briefly review their analyses and then discuss some of the implications they have for post-independence rural politics.

Lan has argued that civilian support for guerrillas in the remote Dande area was facilitated by the guerrillas' alliance with spirit mediums.[1] Chiefs had been discredited in Dande as a consequence of their collaboration with the colonial state and subsequently *mhondoro* mediums had become the 'focus of political action'.[2] According to Lan, the *mhondoro*, or lion, spirits are those of the chiefs of the past, they are the source of the land's fertility and of rain and rule over a specific territory or 'spirit province'.[3] During the war, they legitimated the authority of guerrillas by incorporating them as the new 'chiefs'. Guerrillas acquired the chief's prerogative to use violence:

> dead chiefs are the source of the fertility of the territory they are believed to have conquered when alive. By their very nature *mhondoro* are conquerors, warriors, killers. It is through their violence that the fertility of the earth is made available for the descendants.[4]

Their relationship with *mhondoro* mediums 'made the acceptance of the guerrillas easier, quicker, more binding and more profound by allowing this new feature in the experience of the peasantry to be assimilated to established symbolic categories'.[5] In exchange for logistical support, guerrillas gave 'guarantees of access to land, of an end to taxation and of restored political and economic autonomy', in short, they guaranteed a return of the land's 'fertility'.[6] Guerrillas and spirit mediums created a unified opposition by opposing the interests of all Africans as autochthons, and thus as the rightful owners of the land, to the interests of Europeans as 'strangers'.[7] The guerrillas, with the support of the mediums, subsequently handed political authority over to the ZANU-PF village committees. In Lan's analysis, land is a central symbol around which the guerrillas, mediums and support committees rallied.

Terence Ranger has argued that the people of Makoni District acted on the basis of their historical consciousness of grievances, most importantly land alienation and state intervention in agricultural production.[8] He traces the history of peasant consciousness and sees its culmination in support for the guerrilla war. During the war, a revival of support for mediums (as, Ranger argues, symbols of 'the fundamental right of the peasantry to the land') fused with support for the nationalist party of ZANU-PF, thus producing a 'composite peasant/guerrilla ideology'. The 'peasant/guerrilla' programme sought the reconstitution of the 'peasant option', a goal with three main planks: the return of alienated land, an end to coercive state interference in agricultural practices, and access to agricultural services.[9] Grievances related to land alienation and state coercion were central to the successful mobilization of guerrilla support committees.

On the basis of a study in Mutoko District, Norma Kriger has challenged both of these analyses. She argues that they ignore differentiation within rural society along gender, age, wealth and lineage lines and that coercion played a more important role than ideology in mobilizing peasant support committees.[10] Far from seeing support committees as the product of a harmonious confluence of shared grievances and goals, she argues that, where possible (and especially in the case of the sociological category of 'parents'), committees were avoided or were used by less privileged groups to challenge elders, men, ruling lineages, the better off and the better educated.[11] Kriger interprets the patterns of violence in the relationship between guerrillas and civilians as indicating local social tensions rather than as part of the over-arching nationalist struggle. She sees the programme of less privileged groups as more radical than that of the guerrillas who were, as a result of the lack of liberated areas, preoccupied with their own security above all else.

Lan, Ranger and Kriger's differences result in part from contrasts among their perspectives and methodology as well as from contrasts among the districts on which they focused. Lan and Kriger both relied on interviews. Kriger is a political scientist while Lan is an anthropologist with a strong leaning to structuralist analysis. Ranger, a historian, relied largely on archival material and the testimony of local activists. The three areas vary in terms of their experience of the war (both its intensity and its longevity), their geography, their political and religious institutions, and the nature and extent of their incorporation into the colonial economy and polity.

A few examples will illustrate the implications of these differences more clearly. Dande, where Lan worked, is characterized by its isolation, poor communications and its border with Mozambique. The area is unusual for its total lack of land alienation and its high rate of labour out-migration.[12] It was an early area of guerrilla penetration and, historically, the office of the chief has been relatively weak while that of the *mhondoro* mediums has been strong.[13] Lan's structuralist analysis relies heavily on the normative constructs of his informants, especially one particularly articulate spirit medium, and fails to take note of the evidence of frequent divergencies from his ideal model, most notably with regard to the failure of guerrillas to follow the rules of conduct established by mediums.[14]

In Mutoko District, Kriger neglected the role of Methodism in creating support for Bishop Muzorewa's UANC. Towards the end of the war, a strong UANC and auxiliary presence would have contributed to the level of violence and to the ZANLA guerrillas' pre-occupation with identifying sell-outs.[15] Mutoko lacked semi-liberated areas, in contrast to those established in areas such as the remote parts of Nyanga District where David Maxwell conducted research.[16] Kriger also neglects the history of political and social struggle before the 1970s; political violence and social struggle thus appear contingent upon the arrival of guerrillas and not as part of a continuum.

Makoni District, on which Ranger based his case study, was a pre-eminent example of successful peasant production undermined by state interference and land alienation. Guerrilla mobilization based on resurrecting the 'peasant option' may thus have had a particularly strong appeal. Ranger rarely addresses the question of violence directed against civilians by guerrillas or violence among civilians. His analysis treats violence more as a necessary condition of war than as an indicator of social tensions. Ranger stresses the unifying power of the cultural-nationalist appeal; his reliance on government archives and the testimony of local activists leads to a neglect of the divisions within rural communities.

A clear periodization of the war's intensification and of changes in the strategies of the guerrilla armies is an important omission in all three works. Such a periodization might reconcile some of the differences among these interpretations. First, despite their widely divergent experiences, most regions of the country experienced a deterioration in relations between guerrillas and civilians and increase in violence in the last years of the war.[17] Ranger addresses this issue in a later article on banditry in which he argues that the guerrillas suffered a 'crisis of legitimacy' in 1978 and 1979. The growing pressure on guerrillas from auxiliary forces and their own increasing numbers, younger age and inexperience led to demands which their rural supporters considered 'unreasonable'. Guerrillas became a debilitating drain on rural resources: their demands extended to alcohol and access to young women and they used violence more frequently against civilians.[18]

Second, the strategies of guerrilla leaders based outside the country affected mobilization strategies. Though it is difficult to establish how influential external changes in ideology and training were on guerrilla relations with civilians inside Zimbabwe, evidence presented by Sister Janice McLaughlin suggests that spirit mediums were used most extensively in mobilization and recruitment from 1972 to 1974. Subsequently, ZIPA took an overtly hostile attitude to religion in general and to traditional religion in particular. While there was a revival in the use of spirit mediums by some guerrilla groups after the demise of ZIPA, mediums appeared less able to place social controls on guerrillas. Christian missions came to play a more important role, especially as a source of logistical support.[19] As David Maxwell has argued, in some areas missionaries, not mediums, were critical in mediating between guerrillas and civilians.[20]

Thus, distinguishing between different periods of guerrilla relations with rural communities, as well as considering economic, religious and geographical factors, allows at least a partial reconciliation of the pictures painted by Lan, Ranger and Kriger. The point which I wish to stress, due to its critical implications for the postwar period, is that new administrative, political and service structures were rarely established in the course of the war.[21] Instead, as Kriger's work shows most clearly, the organized mediation between guerrillas and rural communities was usually achieved through committees constituted specifically for logistical and security purposes.[22] That is, political organization served primarily military goals and was not used by the guerrillas themselves to achieve social transformation within rural communities. While this was in part due simply to the extreme military pressure brought to bear by the Rhodesian army, it was also a product of the strategies employed by the guerrilla leadership. In his analysis of ANC/SACP strategy, Howard Barrell argues that 'political mobilization remained essentially subject to imperatives of military force'.[23] There are some parallels in the thinking of ZANU and ZAPU.

In regard to ZAPU, Jeremy Brickhill argues that 'the debate within key ZAPU leadership structures in exile had, from the mid-seventies, increasingly posed the political objectives of the party in terms of a strategy to seize power by force'.[24] The so-called Turning Point Strategy formulated in 1978 built on Jason Moyo's 1976 analysis of the struggle. Moyo argued that 'the enemy' was the 'British government and the colonial settler regime in Salisbury' and the goal of struggle was to create a unified front against colonialism and imperialism in order to seize state power by force.[25] Thus the primary means of struggle was military and tensions which might divide opposition to the colonial state were repressed during the war rather than designated as sites appropriate for political struggle. ZANU similarly identified the colonial state as the principal enemy and military struggle as the means of capturing the state. With the exception of the brief reign of ZIPA which did propose establishing 'a formal political structure in order to give better political direction to the armed body that is now fighting inside Zimbabwe' there was little effort to put political struggle on an organizational footing independent of the military.[26]

Nonetheless, as Kriger argues, the arrival of guerrillas in Zimbabwe's rural areas did have transformational effects which reflected a political agenda held by groups within rural communities, not guerrillas or their leaders. This agenda centered on the gender, generation, class and lineage struggles which divided rural communities. It was an agenda which existed alongside — though it sometimes also undermined — the nationalist aim of capturing the colonial state by force.[27] Women and young people tended to play a particularly active role in the war because of the nature of the support tasks, such as cooking food and carrying messages, and because they tended to invoke less suspicion from government security forces.[28] The position which young people and women thus gained allowed them to challenge existing structures of power, setting in motion potentially radicalizing processes. However, these processes were contingent on the exigencies of war and were difficult to sustain subsequently. Once the war ended, the need for support committees fell away. Backed by a strong pressure for a return to 'normality' after the trauma of war, traditional leaders — and male elders in general — reasserted their power.[29] Kriger argues for Mutoko that the only sustainable challenge to rural social structures was that posed by the commoner lineages because their organizational base, the lineage structure itself, was not dependent on the context of war.[30] In short, security pressures, military strategy, and the rapid conclusion of the war prevented the establishment of a civil administration which could institutionalize wartime challenges, particularly those relating to women and young people. 'Partial victories' were achieved but these fell short of transforming 'the system of oppression', as Isaacman has argued is characteristic of peasant protest.[31]

If post-independence rural communities were conflict ridden and the new basis of organization was weak, what of the inherited state and economy? The negotiated transition to independence failed to unseat the Rhodesian state bureaucracies. Important policy-making powers were left in the hands of civil servants strongly influenced by a modernizing and authoritarian ideology.[32] Moreover, the owners of Zimbabwe's wealth were left largely untouched: the rights of property owners were guaranteed for ten years under the Lancaster House constitution and, despite its marxist programme, the new government was keen to assuage the worries of international and local investors.[33] The redistribution of resources was legally and politically constrained.

I will use Chimanimani District as a case study to illustrate the post-independence processes of political demobilization and consolidation of state power and then briefly draw several comparisons with Insiza District in Matabeleland South. I will argue that developments in post-independence rural politics were strongly affected by policy decisions taken by the centralized state with little or no local consultation. The government quickly undermined the autonomy of the local political party by coopting key groups, maintaining central control over development resources, and, in Matabeleland, by military and political repression. People in Zimbabwe's rural areas were largely unable to influence policy-making processes; instead, patronage, squatting and opposition by traditional leaders dominated rural politics. Far from empowering the disadvantaged through democratic bodies, policies reinforced patriarchal authority within communities, thus helping to marginalize women, the young and the poor. Older and relatively wealthy men form the leadership of rural institutions. They receive the majority of state resources and services directed towards the rural areas while, on the whole, women and youth are targeted for specific projects which tend to over-exploit already scarce labour and material resources.[34]

POST-WAR POLITICS IN CHIMANIMANI
'WHO IS TODAY'S GOVERNMENT?'[35]

Due to its location on Zimbabwe's eastern border, Chimanimani District was an active area during the war, especially after 1976. Between 1976 and 1978, David Caute notes that 1053 'contacts' were recorded, the number of functioning commercial farms was reduced from 105 to eight and, in 1978 alone, 24 homesteads were destroyed.[36] ZANLA and ZANU's presence was strongly established by the end of the war. After independence, however, the area quickly returned to peace. The Provincial Commissioner commented in June 1980:

It is remarkable that the District most affected by the war should now be the most peaceful and normal in the Province. It is the district furthest away from assembly [of guerrillas] places and least affected by dissident elements.[37]

The rapid re-establishment of peace indicates how successful the process of post-war disarmament was, a disarmament that was literal for the guerrillas and metaphoric for guerrilla support groups.[38] Nonetheless, the district was rife with competing claims to legitimate authority and to resources, a legacy of the unresolved struggles of the war. Conflicts emerged among government representatives, party leaders and traditional leaders over land, courts, law, taxation and local government.

In 1980 it was through the party's structures that new policies were introduced and popular demands expressed. The party's village, branch and district leadership controlled land allocation and courts in some areas (though often in cooperation or in competition with traditional leaders, some of whom were strong party supporters or party leaders).[39] The relationship between the new government and rural areas was strongly shaped by early interactions between party structures and government representatives charged with communicating and implementing policy.

In June 1980 Chimanimani's ZANU-PF steering committee, made up of the party district chairmen (the committee did not include women, young people or guerrillas), was given the brief of explaining government policies and setting up a District Council. The decision to establish councils was taken by the central government, there was no local consultation. The form the councils took was strongly influenced by the new state's desire to establish democratic and secular local government bodies and to re-establish an administrative presence in the rural areas. Local reactions to the central government's proposals were ambivalent in Chimanimani, as in other districts.[40] After a tour of the District, the ZANU-PF Steering Committee reported strong objections to any imposition of taxes and to the use of the word 'council'. The questions addressed to the Committee during their tour indicated the nature of popular expectations following the war. People asked,

> Whether the District Commissioner was still there and what his role is now that the chairman for the district has been elected? When the money promised the people by Government to rebuild their homes, buy food and clothing shall be coming? When shall land be given to the people? . . . Why the present government is still in use of the old Council Act, Warrant and Advisers which were used by the previous governments? Who is today's government? Why has it been found necessary by the present government to keep in employment the same Policemen and Civil Servants and to use the same government vehicles used by the previous government?

People wanted ex-guerrillas to sit on the commission and wanted government and party officials to hold regular meetings with village and branch committees in order to keep people abreast of policy changes.[41]

The party steering committee members complained of the 'hard job they met' in explaining the government's policy of establishing councils and a taxation system when these had specifically been attacked during the war.[42] Despite popular objections, however, the establishment of the Council proceeded. Wards were delineated by ZANU-PF political commissars on the basis of wartime party districts and candidates were drawn from party ranks. The steering committee, almost wholesale, was elected as the new council.

An elder male fraction of the party seemed to have triumphed: through the council it had achieved legal control over development planning and land allocation. The party's success, however, needs to be qualified in a number of ways. Local level party leaders had failed to secure salaries, in contrast to chiefs and headmen who continued to receive stipends well in excess of even the councillors. Despite party objections, chiefs had been included as ex-officio members on the council. The party had failed to win war reparations for its constituents or a quick and popularly controlled redistribution of land. Party members were further demoralized by a tedious reorganization process in 1982. And, though the party dominated the new district council, the council was dominated by civil servants.[43] As soon as it was able, the government used the council, not the party structures, to communicate policy and channel resources.[44]

Where the party and council failed in their appeals to the government, people tried to realize the promises of the war by acting outside official channels. Though there was little which people could do about many of the government's policy choices — such as the decision not to award war reparations or salaries to local party officials — they could occupy land.[45] The successful occupation of former commercial farms in Chimanimani was favourably influenced by the availability of farms abandoned during the war. Occupations started before 1980 and picked up speed dramatically in 1981 and 1982. Land was often occupied with the authority of traditional leaders or party leaders, though the latter were often also under pressure to promote the official resettlement policy. Spontaneous occupations were also common. Many 'squatters' were later accepted under the accelerated resettlement programme, though rarely where functioning commercial farms were involved.[46]

Squatter occupations expressed not only a dissatisfaction with the speed of resettlement but also a profound and historically based distrust for the extensive bureaucratic regulation in the schemes.[47] In Chimanimani, confusion initially surrounded the resettlement programme. It was not until mid-1981 that a civil servant revealed to the council the necessity of filling in resettlement forms. The councillors 'were not pleased' and described the situation as 'tense' because 'the people's wishes were not being fulfilled.'[48] When the forms arrived they were treated with distrust — only 1400 of 8000 forms were completed. [49] The relevant Local Government Promotion Officer commented:

> Some people refused to fill forms or move on the initial mobilization due to their fear of the permits being revoked and their loss of control on the schemes. Rumors were rampant on government's plans to take the crops grown on resettlement. They didn't trust the government and were suspicious of its motivations.[50]

People sought to avoid government regulations and retain their autonomy, thus expressing aims consistent with their wartime aspirations as well as the extent of distrust of the new government.

Objections to top-down legislation were also expressed with regard to the new court system. As with local government institutions, the post-independence policy called for the introduction of a democratically elected and secular institution.[51] The government's early initiatives on courts were directed towards dismantling the party's so-called kangaroo courts and undermining courts run by traditional leaders. Representatives of the Ministry of Justice attacked chiefs' courts, arguing that they had been corrupt and collaborationist, and the party's courts on the grounds that they were based on beatings, intimidation and lacked respect for the law.[52]

But the new courts were rarely successfully established for a number of reasons. First, the legal restrictions placed upon them were considered inappropriate. For example, some cases (especially in the early 1980s) arose from witchcraft accusations. A Ministry of Justice official sent to Chimanimani District in 1981 explained that these charges were illegal under the Witchcraft Suppression Act. His suggestion that it would be most appropriate for these cases to be referred to the Ministry of Health, which was now responsible for traditional healers, failed to satisfy his audience of councillors and party representatives.[53] Second, presiding officers elected under the new system were often unable to compete with traditional leaders who claimed that running courts was properly their function, regardless of whether they were elected. In practice, it was not unusual for traditional leaders to be elected to courts in the first instance.[54]

DEMOBILIZATION, BUREAUCRATIC CONTROL AND LOCAL ALLIANCES

After the first years of Independence, local struggles over power and resources were strongly influenced by the re-establishment of a powerful state bureaucracy in the rural areas. Most important were the Ministry of Lands, the Ministry of Local Government, and, to a lesser extent, the Ministry of Community Development.[55] Decisions concerning development policy and land reform were taken at the national level, well beyond the influence of district institutions, and the channelling of state resources to rural areas was controlled by centralized sectoral ministries with little sensitivity to (or ability to assimilate) bottom up demands.

Chimanimani's district council, though ostensibly designed to facilitate local participation in planning, lacked both the expertise necessary to formulate plans and the resources to implement them. In general, councils were almost entirely dependent on grants and on the resources and expertise of sectoral ministries. Village development committees (vidcos), established by a presidential directive in 1984, were intended to further decentralize power. But they remained weak in many areas of Chimanimani in part because of the arbitrary nature of the unit itself: the vidco did not build on previous communities and affiliations but was based simply on the figure of 100 households. The vidcos, like the councils, were starved of resources and deprived of an active role in policy-making. They were used largely to implement national level policy initiatives.

Chimanimani's local level party organization lay largely inactive at this time, save for its occasional mobilization for elections, rallies or the collection of membership fees. Party membership remained an important prerequisite to participation in other development bodies but the party itself no longer functioned as an independent voice. In addition, in 1988, the party was effectively shut down for over a year by the reorganizations attendant on the political unity of ZANU-PF and ZAPU. As a political entity capable of expressing local opinion on policy, it had been 'demobilized'.

However, local leaders in Chimanimani's council and vidcos — and this included many party leaders — did benefit from the post-independence expansion of services: they were in a position to profit from the delivery of services and the direct allocation of state resources to rural areas. Councillors influenced the distribution of drought relief and food-for-work jobs, as well as the physical locations of schools and clinics and had access to government representatives responsible for services. Councillors and party officials were often relatively wealthy farmers and thus were able to take advantage of new opportunities to market produce.

An alliance emerged between local patriarchs and certain ministries and politicians which brought benefits to the rural areas. It was, however, a far cry from the aspirations of the war years and the radical rhetoric of the early 1980s. Rather than establishing a dynamic and participatory local government system, the central government set about reconstructing development bureaucracies capable of excluding local bodies from policy-making roles. The government turned from mobilizing people to managing them through bureaucratic control and local alliances.

THE CHALLENGE OF TRADITIONAL LEADERSHIP

The political demobilization in Zimbabwe's rural areas is not unusual in comparison to other African countries. It reflects the difficulty which dispersed, poor, and internally divided rural populations have in influencing governments through political or bureaucratic institutions, especially when they find themselves in competition with other groups such as urban consumers and workers or an agricultural or industrial élite.[56] However, though a process of demobilization and cooption took place in Zimbabwe's rural areas, there was also a re-emergence of what I will broadly refer to as 'traditional leadership'.[57] This leadership drew its power from an ideology and organizational strength made possible, in part, by the independent government's own policies and the divisive legacy of the war.

Traditional leaders had been widely attacked at independence and many commentators predicted their permanent fall from power. The legislation on land, courts, and local g overnment specifically excluded traditional leaders except in an ex-officio capacity. Technical planning ministries attacked traditional leadership as an anachronism that stood in the way of progress.[58] Other analysts saw them as largely irrelevant. Lan depicted chiefs as entirely discredited by their colonial collaboration:

> By accepting their lowly position in the government hierarchy, the chiefs had acquired the authority to receive a monthly salary, to collect taxes, to wear a flamboyant uniform and to little else.[59]

In 1982, Ranger wrote of contemporary Zimbabwe, 'There is room for spirit mediums, some of whom receive ZANU salaries. But there is no room for the old political élite of chiefs and headmen.'[60] Michael Bratton, writing in 1978, confidently predicted,

> One thing that is clear from recent Rhodesian history . . . is that chiefs have lost claim to represent peasants because of their collective decision to join forces with the settlers against Zimbabwean nationalism. Chiefs cannot be rehabilitated. No major administrative role awaits them in Zimbabwe.[61]

Why, then, did they emerge as important actors in independent Zimbabwe's local politics? And why did they increasingly receive recognition from the government?

Though criticism of traditional leadership and predictions of its ultimate demise were widespread, there were powerful resources and alliances on which traditional leaders could draw. The tendency to dismiss them as irrelevant at independence stemmed from an oversimplification and misunderstanding of their role before independence, especially during the war, and from the conspicuous collaboration of some chiefs and headmen. In fact, many traditional leaders had played a supportive role in the war, assuming party positions and working with guerrillas and spirit mediums.[62] In Chimanimani, district records described Headman Gudyanga as a supporter of the freedom fighters. He was elected as ZANU-PF branch chairman in 1980. The Mutambara Chiefs, following a long history of resistance to government intervention, also supported the war. Dandiwa Dandikwe, appointed as chief in the 1950s, was deposed in 1973 after a long non-cooperation campaign. His successor was deposed in 1977 on charges of supporting the war and died in 1978. The current chief, Samuel Mutambara, was jailed from 1974– 1979 for aiding guerrillas and recruiting students to cross the border into Mozambique.[63] Certainly there were many collaborationist chiefs who opposed the war and lost credibility as a result. However, a significant group did not; nor was simply holding a government-recognized traditional office enough to merit condemnation as a collaborator.

One reason why chiefs have on the whole been portrayed as irretrievably collaborationist is the separation drawn between the chief and the spirit medium by writers such as Lan. Lan depicts *mhondoro* mediums as actors ultimately independent of contemporary lineage politics, deriving their legitimacy solely from long dead authochthons. They thus can transfer legitimate authority away from chiefs to other actors such as guerrillas or party committees. However, in many areas mediums of royal ancestors no longer exist while those of other ancestors are directly dependent on the living members of a lineage for patronage and power.[64] For example, in the south-central 'Karanga' areas of Zimbabwe, B. B. Mukamuri found that *mhondoro* spirits had virtually died out while other spirits or aspects of 'traditional' religion were exploited by competing lineages in their attempts to establish political hegemony and control over resources.[65] Ken Wilson notes that chiefs, mediums and ancestral guardians often all belong to the same shallow lineage and that *mhondoro* mediums no longer exist in the Mazvihwa area of Zvishavane District.[66]

Where mediums are dependent on a ruling lineage, or are members of that lineage, their use by guerrillas is not necessarily contrary to the continued power and prestige of traditional leaders.[67] I would argue that the spirit medium is more accurately seen *as part* of a traditionalist faction in rural areas. The office of medium interacts with that of the chief rather than replacing or rising at the expense of the chief.[68] Moreover, spirit mediums did not always support guerrillas nor were they necessarily discredited when they did not.[69] Reynolds cites a case of a man called Mande:

> As a spirit medium and a village headman, Mande was in contact with the comrades frequently throughout the years of the war. He did not help them because he believed his spirit hates bloodshed. He said, 'The comrades were annoyed. My spirit does not allow killing and so I could give neither courage nor power to the comrades for killing.'[70]

Nonetheless, after the war Mande played an important healing role by using his powers to 'cleanse' people returning from fighting in the war or people who had participated in violence locally.[71]

The diverse histories traditional leaders brought to independent Zimbabwe were evident in the party leadership's ambivalence towards them. Though the Chimanimani ZANU-PF steering committee objected to chiefs sitting on the council, they directed their opposition at specific chiefs and not at the office of the chief itself. Party members affirmed the continuing role of the chiefs but seemed unsure of what it should be.[72] In discounting this half-embrace, some writers have miscalculated the potential for a revival of traditional leadership. The tendency to conflate the colonial state with traditional leaders and to assume a complete rejection of traditional leaders by the party committees and mediums is overly simplistic and can explain neither wartime alliances nor post-war developments.

Sympathies within the government also aided a revival of traditional leadership. Immediately after independence, former employees of the Ministry of Internal Affairs lobbied strongly for a continuing role for traditional leaders on the grounds that their hasty departure 'could lead to confusion if not anarchy in the communally occupied areas'.[73] Ministers defended the continued role of chiefs and headmen (and their cost to government of around $1 million per year) on cultural grounds.[74] The Deputy Minister of Justice, on a tour of Chimanimani in 1981, stressed that, despite the new village courts, chiefs were 'still required to officiate in their normal functions as spiritual agents'.[75] Some nationalist politicians strongly backed the attempts of chiefs deposed during the colonial period to regain their offices. In 1981, then Member of Parliament Bishop Joshua Dhube initiated such a campaign in Chimanimani on behalf of 'Chief' Saurombe, a move which garnered him local support.[76]

Another critical factor in the revival of traditional leaders was the demobilization of the political party and the authoritarian and modernizing ethic of the development bureaucracies. By formulating an agenda based on a populist revival of 'tradition' (or neo-tradition), traditional leaders were able to draw on a constituency which found itself threatened by certain of the new agricultural and legal policies. The traditional leaders' mobilization of tradition was not a rejection of all aspects of 'modernization', especially not development policies which allowed better access to markets, but a reaction to the authoritarian implementation of policies which were felt to undermine their authority under the guise of a 'modernizing' agenda. Traditional leaders appropriated a version of the past in a bid to challenge the authority of the state and local development bodies. In this project, mediums played a supportive ideological role by providing a critique of certain policies — e.g., dams and villagization — based on traditional religion. Though traditional leaders may have been partly or largely motivated by their own ambitions, their appeal to tradition gained support from a constituency which perceived state-defined 'modernization' as a threat either to its autonomy, economic interests or social standing and which had no alternative institution through which to express its objections.

The government's first concession to traditional leaders was over the maintenance of their salaries, a move which offended party committees and councillors but which was probably 'a small pay-off for a government that wanted to ensure that chiefs would not oppose it'.[77] The second concession, the promise to return courts to traditional leaders, came in the election year of 1985. It stemmed from the failure of the new village courts to establish control in many areas and the desire to cultivate traditional leaders as a constituency. The courts were legally handed back to chiefs and headmen in 1990.

These moves undermined legislative initiatives intended to accord women new rights: traditional leaders in Chimanimani were unwilling to put into practice such legislation, despite training from the local Ministry of Justice official.[78] Attempts by the new government to put women on an equal footing were not carried out at the local level; instead, patriarchal power was bolstered. Mediums aided in this project as one of the 'mainstay[s] of customary law and traditional culture'.[79] Reynolds also notes the role which mediums and *n'angas* played in re-establishing a patriarchal social order through their cleansing and healing rituals.[80]

The concessions over courts were also important in strengthening traditional leaders' claims to power in other areas, notably land.[81] Traditional leaders frequently overstepped their legal powers with regard to land allocation both within the communal areas and on commercial and resettlement land. Within communal areas, the attempt to give land allocation powers to district councils was never very effective in part simply because of the size of wards. Land was usually controlled through lineage leaders and inheritance practices.[82] The role of traditional leaders as advocates of 'traditional' tenure became increasingly important as a result of a shift in the focus of agrarian policy in the mid-1980s from 'external' resettlement (meaning land redistribution) to the Communal Area Reorganization Policy. The policy emerged from debates within the technical planning bureaucracies. It draws on a long history of intervention in agricultural practices, most notably the Native Land Husbandry Act of 1951.[83] The policy calls for the consolidation of villages, the demarcation of distinct grazing and arable lands and the establishment of limits on stocking levels and land sizes. It had the effect of polarizing the vidcos and councils, which were called upon to implement the policy, and the traditional leaders who resisted the policy by acting as populist proponents of locally controlled land access and communal tenure.[84]

With the marginalization of the local party, traditional leaders also became the most outspoken proponents of continued and popularly controlled land redistribution. Here again, mediums played a collaborative role by supporting the chiefs' claims to ancestral lands. Traditional leaders have used their claim to the right to allocate land to create constituencies among the land hungry and those who resent the bureaucratic controls on resettlement schemes. The Chimanimani District Squatter Control Committee has had repeated problems with traditional leaders who gave land to their followers in vacant and resettlement land, on commercial farms and on state land.[85] Traditional leaders (including mediums) have sometimes had the support of councillors and party leaders in their initiatives to claim land. In response, the government has employed a combination of heavy handed tactics — such as jailing recalcitrant village heads or destroying squatter settlements — and compromise.

Compromises have been achieved through granting access to land bordering communal areas on terms set by the government. For example, the Dzingire resettlement scheme in the south of Chimanimani is on land that had been intermittently occupied with the authority of or by traditional leaders for decades.[86] The dispute was finally resolved, with government mediation, when the land owners agreed to turn over the contested 300 hectares for resettlement provided the settlers became tea out-growers on the estate and gave up their cattle holdings.[87] In another case, Chief Mutambara in the north of the district successfully gained at least temporary control of grazing land (which he claimed on ancestral grounds) on what was supposed to be a Model B resettlement scheme by negotiating with provincial officials.

These compromises have been dependent on the availability of at least some commercial land. As Chimanimani District neared the end of the first decade of independence, it was faced with a severe land shortage which threatened to provoke a crisis in relations between leaders and people in communal areas on the one hand and private land owners and the government run Squatter Control Committee on the other.[88] The use of commercial land as a way of controlling rural radicalism — as a 'reform sector' used to 'defuse social tensions'[89] — may falter in the context of land scarcity, a growing commitment to private land ownership and the rise of technical planning bureaucracies to the exclusion of patronage and political influence.

In sum, the government successfully demobilized the party by depriving it of resources and influence over policy. Many party leaders took up posts on state-dependent development authorities with which government bureaucracies formed alliances in exchange for conceding limited control over development resources. The government attempted to keep the allegiance of traditional leaders by maintaining their salaries, by conceding power over courts to them and by making some marginal concessions on land demands. The groups most obviously left out of these power structures are women, young people and the resource-poor who are unable to take advantage of increased marketing opportunities and services or to make headway in the male elder-controlled land allocation processes. However, it should be noted that, where conflicts among leaders are severe, these groups are able to exploit the competing leaders' attempts to cultivate constituencies. For example, traditional leaders faced with strong challenges from vidco chairmen are more amenable to making land allocations as it creates a group of clients on whose allegiance they can draw.

DEMOBILIZATION THROUGH REPRESSION: INSIZA DISTRICT

The experience of the Matabeleland Provinces differs dramatically from the rest of the country. Insiza District, located in Matabeleland South, will be used as a case study to illustrate those differences which have affected local political and development structures and land redistribution. Two factors favoured Chimanimani: first, in the early 1980s, local leaders achieved limited land redistribution through the actual occupation of abandoned farmland, thus forcing a then weak and largely sympathetic bureaucracy to increase the speed and scope of resettlement. Second, local institutions which were considered both loyal and legitimate gained access to development resources and services by influencing ministries and politicians.

In Insiza and much of southern Matabeleland, the large-scale occupation of land by communal area residents was not common in the early 1980s. As a consequence of ZIPRA military strategy, relatively few commercial farms were abandoned in the 1970s.[90] The squatter population was made up largely of former mine and farm workers who faced eviction.[91] Squatting was also less common because of the perceived shortage in grazing, rather than arable, land: communal area people sought to take advantage of vacant or state land by simply driving cattle onto it.[92] 'Poach-grazing' did not prove to be as effective a means of claiming land because it did not involve the construction of houses or the planting of crops. Cattle can simply be herded off land or impounded. Moreover, in the early eighties, there was no alternative to the crop production-based resettlement model (Model A). Whereas Model A schemes were acceptable in Chimanimani, though state controls were resented, they were greeted with a wholesale rejection in Insiza.[93]

During the early and mid-1980s the quantity of state land and thus, potentially, resettlement land increased dramatically as 'dissident' violence and drought drove ranchers from the land, much as the guerrilla attacks had in the 1970s war in Chimanimani.[94] This land was not settled, however, because of the 'security situation' and conflicts over resettlement models. Instead, the land purchased in this period was given over to the state farm parastatal and leased to individuals — many of whom were civil servants — for cattle ranching.[95]

Because of the political conflicts which erupted soon after 1980, local party and traditional leaders could not effectively influence ministries or lobby politicians for patronage. Instead, local leaders were subject to harassment and violent attacks. Many were driven out of the rural areas, others were abducted, killed or forced to resign.[96] Councils made up of government 'nominees' were imposed in many areas, including Insiza, and even these were subject to attack and did not function for long periods of time.[97] The negotiation for resources and the establishment of alliances common in Chimanimani was only possible to a very limited extent in Insiza.

The return of peace and relative political freedom following the Unity Accord of December 1987 enabled the revival of councils and the return of some ZAPU activists. Debates over access to land and development strategies started anew and brought the issue of unsettled state land to the fore. But the late 1980s differed dramatically from the early 1980s: local leaders faced well-consolidated development bureaucracies, and the political sympathies and high expectations of the immediate post-independence period no longer held sway. Political mobilization and negotiation with state institutions thus faced far greater obstacles in Insiza at the end of the first decade of independence than they did in the Chimanimani District of the early 1980s, though the availability of land and perceived need for client-building may lead to some compromises.

CONCLUSION: RURAL POLITICS, WAR AND AGRARIAN REFORM

Zimbabwe's experience illustrates the difficulty of achieving agrarian and political transformation in the absence of a more positive disruption of the previous state and economy.[98] Though existing power structures in rural areas were challenged during the war, the conditions were not created for new structures to become firmly established. Women and young people, in particular, were unable to sustain the enhanced status they had achieved during the war. After independence, local party leaders found themselves and their claims pushed aside by bureaucracies that still wielded much of their previous power. Many party leaders were elected onto councils and vidcos. Though this allowed them access to patronage, they were put in the difficult position of having to implement policies which they played a negligible role in formulating. The party's programme was strongly constrained on the central issue of land redistribution by constitutional protections for private property. The actual redistribution of land depended more on wartime attacks on White farmers and on squatter occupations than on claims made through political or development structures.

Perhaps the most surprising development in rural politics after the war was the re-emergence of the traditional leadership. Traditional leaders' increasing authority (in some areas) and their increasing recognition from the government calls into question both the extent to which they were discredited by their colonial collaboration and the extent to which patriarchal power was undermined during the war. Ironically, the modernizing agenda and authoritarian practices of the development bureaucracies helped to create a disaffected constituency upon which the traditional leaders were able to draw.

In sum, the post-independence state used the tactics of local alliance building, bureaucratic control, and, in the case of Matabeleland, military repression to manage wartime aspirations and post-war challenges to state authority. The measure of democratization and redistribution of resources that has been achieved falls short of the expectations expressed by party committees and nationalist politicians at independence. The Rhodesian legacies of centralized bureaucracies and economic inequality, in combination with the conflict-ridden wartime mobilization process, allowed the post-independence state to reassert central control.

9

In Memory: A Heritage of War in South-western Zimbabwe

RICHARD P. WERBNER

The liberation war and its aftermath in the counter-insurgency campaign against 'dissidents' in Matabeleland left a heritage that is powerful and uneasy. There are social wounds of terror and violence which survivors recreate in their memories and which they are unwilling or unable to forget. These memories have to be understood, their force and their nature need to be recognized, if the present significance of the liberation war and its aftermath is to be appreciated in any depth. My own knowledge of the importance of such traumatic memories comes primarily from a large Kalanga family, Lupondos,[1] based in Bango Chiefdom in South-western Matabeleland, about whom I have written a social biography, *Tears of the Dead*.[2] I first lived with members of Lupondo's family in 1960–61, and during that fifteen-month period, with the sensitive help of Saul Gwakuba Ndlovu and Timon Mongwa, in turn my research assistants, I recorded the life histories of family members.

When I returned to Lupondo's family in 1989 and asked the present elders, the generation of Lupondo's sons and their wives, about the years since we had last been together, they spoke passionately about the wartime brutality they had endured. Each side in the war — whether it was in the liberation war, especially in the final years towards the end of the seventies, or in the post-Independence counter-insurgency war at its height in 1983 and 1984 — terrorized them. Remembering that, they told me of their grief in bereavement, of how they had suffered torture, how they had been violated, and not merely physically.

I found a great change both in the accounts family members gave me of their lives and also in the personal stories they told among themselves at feasts and beer drinks or, more privately, at night around a hearth in the compound. They made physical and personal ordeals the focus of many of their current stories. In the past before the wars, they had woven a world of family understandings around stories of quarrels. Instead, they were recreating another world in its place, after the wars, by telling of how they survived in the face of the suffering which war and its aftermath brought them.

192

In this change, some older women told of how, unarmed yet driven to resistance in defence of their homes, they had acted with that heroic quality, usually attributed distinctively to men, of *chibindi*, 'fierceness, reckless courage'. But most of their ordeal stories were about heroes or heroines as victims of physical brutality, terror and superior force. They were terrorized by the armed forces or, in the case of labour migrants, as ex-combatants accused of going to South Africa to train to be 'dissidents', by the police. Even more revealing is the fact that certain ordeals remained largely outside the personal discourse in which family members recreated their experience as shared memory. The unspoken and, perhaps after the atrocities of the post-Independence war, the unspeakable were the ordeals of the family members as guerrillas. 'Freedom fighters', remarked the teenage younger brother of one, 'don't like to talk about the war and their fighting. They sometimes sit alone or with others not talking, and they don't want to tell others about their experiences, which grieve them and trouble their thoughts so much they just want to forget.'

Virtually all of the former guerrillas from Lupondo's family who came home after the liberation war ended in 1980, had to flee from the countryside during the ensuing counter-insurgency war. Like other ex-freedom fighters, who had fought under Nkomo in ZIPRA, the former guerrillas from Lupondo's family became prime targets, among others, for torture and beatings. To be an able-bodied young man was, by that very fact, to be guilty. It was simply too dangerous for the former guerrillas to stay home. Their lives were at risk in the countryside. Towns in Zimbabwe, Botswana and South Africa became their refuge. After the counter-insurgency war, despite the government's withdrawal of troops, the declaration of an amnesty in 1988, and the end to any immediate threat to their lives, some of them remained uneasy about coming home. Almost none of them were home during my return visit in 1989; most were in South Africa working as labour migrants. Their absence was due in good measure also to the impoverished state of the countryside, following the looting of crops, cattle, and personal goods and, most recently, the run of bad years and severe drought.

But how did these former guerrillas remember the liberation war? What were their memories of how they fought and what they were fighting for? My attempt to discover the answers was largely, if not totally, unsuccessful. The failure arose from the very predicament I sought to understand: the heroism of the guerrillas, their glories, and their wartime suffering had been marginalized, blocked from the personal discourse shared with people at home. Nevertheless, I put my questions about the war to neighbours and friends of the former guerrillas from Lupondo's family. What they told me expressed their anger and frustration at being impoverished and brutalized in their own country after having fought and won a war 'to free the country so that we could live well and rule ourselves'. I found that unemployed former guerrillas expressed much resentment at not getting work in Zimbabwe, because they had taken it for granted that one aim of fighting the war to win control of the country was to secure jobs in Zimbabwe for the people, above all the freedom fighters. It was not solely a matter of being able to earn a decent wage, but of truely coming home after having suffered abroad.

And how did the people who had remained at home see their predicament? Peace had come at last to their chiefdom of Bango in 1988, the year before my return. But the elders of Lupondo's family said they were not yet truely at ease, that they still felt anxious, tense in their very guts. 'We worry that the war will come back', many said. Feeling outraged, they had been virtually helpless to defend themselves and yet, they insisted, they remained unvanquished.

'We have been burnt, but we have come through the fire alive', one elder remarked. She went on to say that she was deeply glad that I had returned, but she thanked God that I had gone, for had I remained she was sure I would have been killed. Family members and neighbours saw their suffering in the light also of widely known stories of mass murder and other atrocities by the Fifth Brigade in different parts of Matabeleland. What they conveyed to me was their sense that the horror was beyond anything they had thought possible, anything that they could have imagined before.

During the liberation war, the Rhodesians had made the violation of the person into a deliberately savage form of psychological warfare. Their sadistic tactics were intended to turn the people's own sense of humanity against them in physically loathsome perversions.[3] In many parts of the country, for example, the Rhodesians displayed the bodies of dead guerrillas, and forced people to look at the degradation. As Bob North of the Rhodesian Intelligence Corps told a reporter shortly after the liberation war:

> Body displays. A nasty but effective operation. See, the locals were told by the terrs [guerrillas] that they were immortal, so we'd leave a few bodies lying around of terrs that we'd killed in contacts, in the locals' huts and kraals [homesteads]. If we had a high hill which could be seen for miles around, we'd stick a body up it. Good deterrent. Or a helicopter would fly over kraals carrying a netful of dead bodies for everyone below to see.[4]

By contrast to the Rhodesian soldiers, the elders of Lupondo's family saw the ZIPRA guerrillas as 'the boys of the country', their children. Nevertheless, the guerrillas also committed previously unimaginable atrocities. In the past, during peace-time, the elders had voiced suspicions of sorcery as part of an ongoing and controlled family debate about moral character and social obligation. But witchcraft fear became something monstrous in wartime. The guerrillas launched a brutal campaign against sorcery, a campaign which was out of the control of family elders but which was driven by the paranoia of young strangers unfettered by the responsibilities of close kinship.

The guerrillas were themselves fearful of attack no less than betrayal by the very people on whose behalf they fought. In part, this may have been due to the Rhodesians 'dirty tricks', or 'Psyops' (Psychological Operations), which included the use of cyanide. The poisoning was spread through treated clothing distributed to unsuspecting guerrillas by African collaborators.[5] Guerrillas feared the attack from sorcerers as food poisoners and the betrayal by *batengesi* 'sell-outs' as agents or informers of the Rhodesians. The two things were not easily separated: the sorcerer and the sell-out were often equated in practice or were labels different people used for the same victim of suspicion.

Guerrillas rarely, if ever, fought in their own home areas. The advantages of local knowledge were held to be more than offset by the dangers of being known and being subject to the pull of prior loyalties. In trying to protect themselves and the people also, the guerrillas waged their brutal campaign against sorcery on the basis of suspicions, the guerrillas' own and those which people admitted upon being interrogated in private, one by one. On that basis, the guerrillas punished suspected sorcerers, sometimes by severe beating, sometimes by torture to death. Elsewhere in Zimbabwe, and elders of Lupondo's family did not mention this to me, young boys and girls as trusted helpers, who carried food, messages, and intelligence for the guerrillas, were also blamed by elders for spreading false accusations and making innocent people suffer at the hands of guerrillas.[6] This appears to have primarily happened in areas further east where guerrillas used quite different tactics.[7]

In peace-time witchcraft accusations were levelled at perceived deviants. It was a measure of the unnatural monstrousness of the wartime campaign against sorcery that its victims included some of the most esteemed members of Lupondo's family. Among these victims were Lupondo's senior son, Dzilo, his wife and daughter. The atrocity of Dzilo's death was a memory that members of Lupondo's family could not put to rest. They wanted me to realize how senseless his death was, and I found it painful to listen and become, like them, a grieving witness. Dzilo was killed in the Bango school by ZIPRA (Zimbabwe People's Revolutionary Army) guerrillas when the liberation war was reaching its height, roughly in 1978. He was tortured and butchered to death for hiding his mother-in-law whom the guerrillas blamed for their comrade's death by food poisoning and sorcery. Dzilo's mutilated body was left to hang through the night soaking that Bango schoolroom with his blood. On the same day, the guerrillas also mutilated and killed his wife and daughter. His mother-in-law they wrapped in plastic and burnt alive. Fearing the arrival of Rhodesian troops and the danger of being caught in the crossfire or being tortured to reveal the guerrillas' movements, Lupondo's family could not give the dead a decent burial.

In death, Dzilo became, for his family and the people immediately around his home, what is called *ngozi*, a restless and vengeful presence, innocent yet wronged, aggrieved and dangerous to the living. None of his surviving family had been allowed to mourn him by shedding the tears for their loss in a wake that would have freed them of his presence as a ghost and sent his soul back to rest among *midzimu*, the shades as divinities of the dead.

Family members gave me accounts of Dzilo's death which revealed their strong ambivalence towards the guerrillas. Among these accounts was one by the widow of Dzilo's brother, Buka. On the one hand, she told very painfully of the terror the guerrillas struck in committing the atrocity of Dzilo's death. On the other, she recalled their respect for her husband, Buka. The guerrillas addressed him as father. The widow also recalled the guerrillas' concern to take responsibility for other family members as his children. She spoke of the guerrillas' care for the helpless orphans of the murdered Dzilo, and their warning about the imminent danger from the arrival of the Rhodesian Army. Later, when she told me about the guerrillas during the recent counter-insurgency war, she also recalled their careful warning of the danger from looting by soldiers.

There was no such ambivalence in what family members recalled about the soldiers in the liberation war or in the post-Independence counter-insurgency war, especially the soldiers of the notorious Fifth Brigade. Each of these forces was an unmitigated evil, although the Fifth Brigade was felt to be an evil even greater than the Rhodesian Army. Indeed, the violence of the 'dissident' war was believed to be yet more senseless and unassimilable than that of the liberation war.

The end of the liberation war and Independence for Zimbabwe in 1980 brought a brief interlude, more a fleeting ceasefire than a peace in the province of Matabeleland South where Lupondo's family lived. The ex-guerrillas left the army, and many returned home in that year and the next. The period immediately after Independence became a time of sporadic violence between opposed forces of ex-combatants. It was also a time of attacks by bands of ex-combatants against civilian targets, including White farmers, still in control of vast areas of Matabeleland despite the liberation war. The hostilities advanced struggles for power which had been waged during the liberation war, but not resolved.

As is well-known, two separate guerrilla armies, the Zimbabwe People's Revolutionary Army (ZIPRA) led by Joshua Nkomo and the Zimbabwe National Liberation Army (ZANLA) under Robert Mugabe, fought the liberation war. They made an uneasy alliance towards the end of it but, as Martin and Johnson reported:

> There had been difficulties between ZANLA and ZIPRA from the outset, and at two joint training camps . . . there had been clashes and a considerable number of ZIPRA guerrillas had been killed. There had been differences over political education, strategy and methods of mobilization.[8]

The two forces were unlike in so many ways, and perhaps most importantly in ZIPRA's greater emphasis on the build-up of a regular or more conventional army outside the country. In accord with their differences, they had rival sources of support: among others, the Russians heavily backed ZIPRA and the Chinese, ZANLA.

All the guerrillas in Lupondo's family joined ZIPRA. They joined it as most others did in the region immediately around Matabeleland and centred on its major city, Bulawayo, ZIPRA had its main base in Zambia along Zimbabwe's north-western border from which it recruited guerrillas primarily, though not exclusively, from western Zimbabwe. Apart from English, and for some their first language was Kalanga or Venda or even Tswana, the lingua franca of these guerrillas was Sindebele. The rest of the country, dominated by speakers of distinct Shona dialects from numerous colonial tribes, provided most of the guerrillas for ZANLA, which was by far the larger of the two armies. Neither of the armies was homogeneous, ethnically or racially, and each of the armies espoused the causes of unity against colonial domination and of freedom for all, irrespective of race, tribe or gender. But the recruiting of the armies on a regional basis was itself a process that polarized people who came to be identified by language as Shona or Ndebele. The nationalist struggle thus fed and in turn was fed by its antithesis, the polarization of two quasi-nations or super-tribes, the 'Shona' against the 'Ndebele'.

The powerful reality of that polarization was and is a creation of present politics, not a mere survival of pre-colonial chiefdoms. Nor is it to be explained away as simply a consequence of a colonial policy of divide and rule according to which White settlers invented two hostile tribes, for their own purposes. Such invention, elaborated in settler mythology and settler state propaganda, was perhaps a necessary but certainly not a sufficient basis for the polarization.[9] Quasi-nationalism, like the nationalism with which it breeds, is a movement of ideas and practices that stages its often cruelly violent moments within the formation of the nation-state in the twentieth century. If energized by a myth of being prior to the nation-state, of revenging old scores left as unsettled from ancient hostilities, quasi-nationalism is nonetheless made in and by the struggle for power and moral authority in the nation-state. Nor should quasi-nationalism be confused with ethnicity, which operates differently in different situations, irrespective of any dominant cleavage dividing the nation.

The catastrophe of quasi-nationalism is that it can capture the might of the nation state and bring authorized violence down ruthlessly against the people who seem to stand in the way of the nation being united and pure as one body. In such times, agents of the state, acting with its full authority, carry out the violation of the person. It is as if quasi-nationalism's victims, by being of an opposed quasi-nation, put themselves outside the nation, indeed beyond the pale of humanity. They are dealt with ferociously not merely for the sake of political dominance by one part of the nation over another, but importantly also for the sake of the moral renewal of the nation as a whole. The attack by the forces of the state on the victims' own bodies, in the present instance, by starvation and torture, even to death, seems to fulfill the objective of purifying and cleansing the body of the nation.

One of the extreme measures of the late Rhodesian state, from 1973 onwards, was 'collective punishment', imposed under the Emergency Powers, directed against whole communities as supporters of guerrillas, and including the use of curfews and in some cases the closure of schools and stores.[10] Using the same Emergency Powers, the new nation-state brought back 'collective punishment'.

Early in 1983, the government unleashed an army of mostly Shona-speaking soldiers, ex-ZANLA guerrillas who came from outside Matabeleland. Among them was the élite force known as the Fifth Brigade, 'with unswerving loyalty to the Prime Minister. Its chain of command by-passed the intermediate levels observed by the rest of the army.'[11] The unleashed army, if of the National Army in name, was quasi-national in intent and practice. It was a punitive army which, along with the police, behaved like an occupying force come down upon an alien people to strangle them into submission, and if need be by starving everyone, women, children, and the old indiscriminately. The terror brought back the most brutal methods of the Rhodesians but were more ruthless and far more devastating.

A popular name for this period of counter-insurgency, *Gukurahundi*, is revealing. According to a school text-book, written from a ZANU point of view to teach the nationalist lesson of history to the children of Zimbabwe, 'ZANU President Mugabe named 1978 the 'Year of the People' and 1979 *Gore reGukurahundi*, the 'Year of the People's Storm'.[12] 'Rain after threshing, early spring rains' is the pre-war translation in the Standard Shona Dictionary.[13] *Gukurahundi*, as Mugabe named it, was the culmination of the people's war, the year when the storm of the nationalist struggle brought the victory of majority rule; the Lancaster House agreement, ending the war, was signed in December 1979. That was the *Gukurahundi* of nationalism, with its promise of moral renewal in the image of spring rains.

The name took on a different force, however, transferred in place and time to the region around Matabeleland and the war from 1983 onwards. For people of Bango, it was a Shona name that meant, 'The sweeping away of rubbish', and they explained to me that the 'rubbish' the Shona soldiers intended to sweep away were the people of Matabeleland themselves. 'Rubbish', *malala*, is used among Kalanga for the pollution of death. 'Those MaShona wanted to finish off all the people of Matabeleland' was the expressed opinion of many at Bango. It is significant that the intent of the attack was perceived, not simply in terms of old scores — and I was told by members of Lupondo's family that the Shona soldiers took loot from them, Kalanga, calling it 'the cattle stolen from our forefathers by you Ndebele' — but also in terms of a moral renewal, the purification of the country from rubbish. The Fifth Brigade, known too by the people of Bango as *Gukurahundi*, was perceived to be, as one of Lupondo's sons said, 'evil without humanity'. The *Gukurahundi* of nationalism gave way to its monstrous twin in the *Gukurahundi* of quasi-nationalism.

Some of the nightmarish quality in the experience of family members during the later *Gukurahundi* came from a virtually Surrealist re-enactment of certain parts created in the liberation war. The Fifth Brigade soldiers were the merciless enforcers of collective punishment by the state, re-enacting the part of the Rhodesian forces, yet they represented themselves also as having the moral authority of freedom fighters, and they demanded displays of support of the kind they had known as freedom fighters. Such displays had been made during the liberation war in the night-long rally, known as *pungwe* in Shona and much used by ZANLA, and rarely if at all by ZIPRA.[14] In the *pungwe* the guerrillas led the people in discussions and in singing songs of liberation, to which the people clapped hands and responded with supporting choruses. The *pungwe* was a means of political education meant to mobilize the people and raise their consciousness in the nationalist struggle. In their revival of the *pungwe*, or rather their introduction of it to people who had not known it before, soldiers of the Fifth Brigade acted as if they were the true makers of Zimbabwe as a nation. They were the heroes about whom and for whom were sung the popular Shona songs of *Chimurenga*, as the liberation war is known in Shona. In accord with that, the people they came to discipline were compelled to re-enact the parts of choruses supporting the freedom fighters — they had to learn the Shona songs, although few spoke Shona, and they had to clap while singing them in rallies that lasted the whole day. For the sake of making the people submit to their discipline, which also entertained the soldiers as something of a sport to watch, they pitted women from the chorus against each other as if they were gladiators. The women had to beat each other down, using poles. If the *pungwe* had taught some people the lessons of nationalism, the revival of the *pungwe* was political education of another kind entirely; it was a parody further alienating the people from their own state and raising their consciousness of quasi-nationalism and their awareness of the role of their own state in the polarization of Shona and Ndebele.

One of the surviving widows, Baka Lufu, gave me a grim account of *Gukurahundi*, testifying to these lessons of alienation and distrust, and she concluded:

> We may die but we can never forget. When we sleep, we wake up remembering . . . the suffering we endured . . . Did we really live? We can never forget that life that captured us. No, we can never forget. How can we ever forget?

These questions and the many others Baka Lufu put, reflecting upon the experience of surviving *Gukurahundi*, were rhetorical, to some extent. How could one manage to share food? How could one join in burying others? How could one avoid betraying others to the enemy, when the betrayal meant protecting oneself and one's own immediate kin? The answers were implied, up to a point. Baka Lufu was speaking to me at home, surrounded by some of her favourite kin, children, grandchildren, and immediate neighbours. She addressed herself to them as well as to me, asking, even urging, their agreement as witnesses who knew and understood from their own experience the self-evident truth. But Baka Lufu's questions were more than merely rhetorical in the sense of being simply for stylistic effect and thus not demanding a reply, spoken or tacit. My companion and guide to her homestead, a youth about to marry into Lupondo's full brother's family, having fathered his girlfriend's child, was the son of a woman Baka Lufu had beaten, under duress from the soldiers, to the ground. It was a matter of some embarrassment to her. She admitted it freely, but with a rather uncomfortable, nervous laugh; and in talking about it, she seemed to be asking my guide, too, to agree that any other woman would have done the same, under the circumstances. If she wanted the truth she told to be taken as self-evident, she could not help but know that it was actually a contested truth. Her questioning, like the rest of her telling of the ordeals of *Gukurahundi*, had a force of self-justification in the continuing rehearsal, among intimates, of how the survivors had conducted themselves during the wars. Such questioning, understood within ordeal stories, was significant after the catastrophe of war for the reconstruction of character and the redefinition of the person as a moral being, no less significant than was the telling of quarrel stories after personal misfortune and moral disturbance in peacetime.

The significance of questioning such as Baka Lufu's went beyond even that, however. Being an active member of an Apostolic church, Baka Lufu represented the fact that she and others had survived as if it were a proof that God had protected them for the sake of their innocence. But her questioning seemed to me to be addressed to herself, at least as much as to others; it revealed an inner disquiet, an irresolvable doubt, and it conveyed the anxiety, perhaps the guilt, of a predicament she shared with other survivors of the catastrophe of *Gukurahundi*. It was the predicament of having to go on living as usual, taking things for granted once again, despite their experience of having had certain taken-for-granted truths of human existence called into question. The very fact that they had survived and at such cost, when so many others had died, threatened their efforts to recreate the old once taken-for-granted peace-time world and to renew its truths through their everyday practice.

Having survived one guerrilla war after another, members of Lupondo's family bore the lasting marks of collective punishment and terror on their bodies and in their memories. After the amnesty, although some did say they felt free once again, free 'as a bird on the wind', in Baka Lufu's words, they remained wary. They could neither forget nor forgive the atrocities of the wars. Nor could they make sense of their suffering in the liberation war by its part in making their country free of alien domination. The later war against them by their own state had cast the significance of their suffering in doubt. They had known the danger that the state becomes when it empowers quasi-nationalism, when it fixes collective guilt upon people as a quasi-nation within the nation and terrorizes them as the dehumanized enemy within. Whether it would ever become possible for them to look forward to the future without a sharp regard for that danger remained an open question.

Following the liberation war and its aftermath, among many of the people of Matabeleland, and not merely among members of Lupondo's family, there was a widespread experience of senseless loss and anxious bereavement, often due to kin dieing in atrocities and without decent burial or wakes. It was well known that there were mass graves into which people had disappeared, leaving no trace for their kin. The need to be cleansed from wartime acts of violence and violation was also widely felt.

One response in Matabeleland, both in the towns and in the countryside, was a remarkable increase in the number of mediums known as *sangoma* in Sindebele or *changoma* in Kalanga. A great revival took place around these mediums. With it came a fresh surge of attention to their specially costumed embodiment of the dead, their revelatory messages warning people against forgetting the past, their fixing of blame for sorcery and responsibility for neglect of the dead, their herbal prescriptions for cleansing and protection, their dancing and drumming, their blood sacrifices and other ritual acts of therapy.

This is not the place for a full account of what mediums dream, say and do or of what the cult practice is. Very generally, the *sangoma* cult is a cult in which participants seek protection against sorcery and ask for healing through restored communication with the dead. Its revival reveals three important tendencies: first, the growing importance of memorializing war and the violation of the person; second, the interaction of family members in this cult, whether in town or in the country; and third, the emerging inter-ethnic significance of transcultural healing. My aim in the rest of this discussion is to consider these tendencies. It is worth saying also that in speaking of a revival I do not seek to imply that the *sangoma* cult had temporarily been in retreat but rather that it is simply a religious movement greatly invigorated by efforts to revive the past.

Let me first consider the growing importance of the revival for memorializing violence, aggression, and the violation of the person. The *sangoma* mediums I saw on my first visit were alien witchdoctors who danced aggressively, brandishing weapons, such as spears and axes, sometimes threatening onlookers. Costumed as warriors, they enacted a counter-aggression to attacks by sorcery. Since then, however, and I cannot say when the change took place, it has become common for mediums to wear a mantle of red cloth (in Sindebele, *ilembu elibomvu*). The red is for blood, the blood of violence and war, I was told. The significance of this has come in part from a contrast in colours, red and black. The contrast has emblazoned a changing opposition between cults: on the one hand, the *sangoma* cult and, on the other, the regional cult dedicated to God Above, Mwali.

Black is said to be for the rain that God lets sow the earth when it is free of pollution, such as comes from the shedding of blood and other violations of the person. The peace and the welfare of the land along with its people have been the overriding concerns of the Mwali cult.

Somewhat opposed concerns and interests have prevailed at times in the *sangoma* cult. The *sangoma* cult has been associated with Ndebele as conquerors. At least one of its mediums, embodying a warrior chief of the past, Mtuwane Dhlo-Dhlo, has spoken on behalf of 'the kingdom of the Ndebele people'; he has claimed the authority to call for war or its end.[15] During the revival of the *sangoma* cult and perhaps for a considerable period before that, certain mediums of the *sangoma* cult and their supporters have made attempts to create a merger, or at least a close link between their cult and that of Mwali. They have gone to great lengths, against resistance from within the Mwali cult, to turn its great pilgrimage centres, containing the shrines of highly prestigious and very widely attended oracles, into places for authoritative communication by *sangoma* mediums also. They have tried to use those sacred central places in ways that memorialize war and the violation of the person.

Among the close kin of Lupondo's granddaughters, the medium most directly involved has been the one embodying an exemplary figure, Hobani. Hobani was an important messenger between the Mwali cult and the Chief Bango of his time. Still remembered as a martyr, having been shot in the back by an American at a Mwali cult shrine during the rebellion of 1896, Hobani exemplified the unarmed, innocent victim of war whose murder left his kin suffering from a vengeful, aggrieved presence as *ngozi*. Not long after the end of my recent visit, his kin sought to make a major sacrifice and consult Hobani through his medium at a cardinal shrine of Mwali; their intent was 'to return him back home', appeasing the *ngozi*.

A similar concern was paramount when one of Lupondo's granddaughters, Baka Ngoma, became a *sangoma* medium after the liberation war, in 1982. Having been afflicted by throbbing headaches, severe pains across her whole body, and swollen legs so badly enlarged she could hardly move from her house in Bulawayo, Baka Ngoma, accompanied by her mother, Baka Lufu and her brother, consulted diviners.

Neglect of the dead and failure to give them due recognition caused Baka Ngoma's affliction, the diviners indicated. In particular, her suffering came because of the wrong done her father's brother and her own step-father, Dzilo. It was a wrong that made his ghost a vengeful and aggrieved presence, *ngozi*. The atrocity of his death, unmourned in any wake, haunted his family. In their divinations, they remembered that he had intended to leave one of his cattle for a child of his younger brother, whose widow Baka Lufu he had inherited.

The consultations disclosed, according to Baka Lufu:

> Their forefathers [her children's] were saying that we cast them aside into the open and that we are no longer concerned about them. And Dzilo [her husband's older brother] had spoken saying, 'When I die, you will take out a beast for the child of my younger brother.' Then having become *ngozi* [a vengeful ghost] he was grieving in his heart that his death was not known and recognized. It was a very bad thing, and that is how we came to do it just as he had spoken. His beast was slaughtered from the pen, and she [Baka Ngoma] was made to suck the blood while it was still fresh. Then it was said, 'Today the changoma has come back to your homestead, to the homestead of its father.'

The remembered events concerned 'tears', both literally and figuratively in Kalanga terms. Literally, they were the tears shed by the living when they cried in mourning their loss. Figuratively, the tears were embodied in cattle and everything that came to the living from the dead. By acting upon one aspect of their concern with memory, the figurative embodiment, and putting it right, the intent of family members was to act upon and right the other aspect, the literal expression of loss. In terms of their intent, also, sucking the sacrificial blood fresh from a black beast of Dzilo's, and by his pen, brought the *changoma* back as a spirit within Baka Ngoma and within Dzilo's homestead.

In Baka Ngoma's dreams came songs of her own from the dead. It was a communication characterizing her as a medium. The refrain of one of these songs, which she later sang in Sindebele and then translated into Kalanga for me, was: 'The sangoma sleeps in the river, suffering.'

This conveyed an image of suffering brought on by abandonment, by people becoming remote and neglectful when they should be caring, remembering their late forefathers.

Distinct voices of the past, 'the voices of the people of old', spoke through Baka Ngoma as a medium. They were, in turn, those of her paternal grandfather, Lupondo himself, her great grandfather, and her maternal grandfather, but not the voice of Dzilo. It was through the sacrifice that family members worked upon the memory of Dzilo's death and his grieving presence as ngozi. They proved that they acknowledged him in death as a kinsman having claims upon them; that they did know and recognize him, despite having been forced to bury him without the respect due to him. But the very fact that they could not and would not forget him and his death meant that they could appease but not fully free themselves of his grieving presence.

Secondly, as the revival expanded, it mobilized people and their resources not only in the country but also in town. Performances were held wherever mediums and their kin lived or died, now and in the past. A medium, such as Baka Ngoma, whose *changoma* was brought back from the dead in the countryside, 'back to the father's homestead', was expected to make offerings each year at that home. But she could and did do so also in the city. If originally beer offerings had to be brewed from the family's own grain and in the vicinity of their own homes, in town it came to be acceptable also to offer factory-brewed beer bought from the bars.

In demands on time, money, and services, the revival tested brothers and sisters and other close kin. They had to give a powerful and highly valued proof of their responsibility and co-operation across town and country. Often, the kinsmen who enabled women to become mediums were the brothers who as labour migrants sent their sisters goods from South Africa for sale in Bulawayo and who were regarded as keeping their sisters' needs in mind, while they themselves were based in the countryside. Such a brother was Lufu, who paid for Baka Ngoma's costume and most of her ritual paraphernalia, at the time of her initiation. His donation, like that of other responsible kin, was an endorsement of moral claims across town and country, for it enabled his town-based sister to become a figure having a voice, indeed, several voices, of moral weight and authority in both places.

This view of the medium's importance calls for some qualification. Baka Ngoma told me that after the *midzimu*, the divinities or shades of the dead, have gone, following a consultation, she never knows what they have said, and she has to hear about that from other people. Like all *sangoma* mediums, she had to speak during drum-induced trance in a representative capacity, and not as herself or in her own right. Another qualification needs to be mentioned, also. At least in Lupondo's family, no two mediums have come from the same group of brothers and sisters, so that in terms of the representation of moral weight and authority, each medium has been representative in and for a distinct part of the family.

Virtually the whole of Lupondo's family in Matabeleland got caught up in the *sangoma* revival, in one way or another. Besides Baka Ngoma, several of Lupondo's granddaughters permanently resident in town and at least one grandson also became mediums. Even family members belonging to churches opposed to mediums found they had to take part. They did so by paying for the costly costumes (Zimbabwe $300, at least, or roughly £100 sterling), by caring for novice mediums during their year-long training and treatment, by attending the mediums' performances, by testifying to the past as it was manifested in present affliction, and by meeting the other obligations of kin to mediums as the embodiment of their grandfathers, great-grandfathers, or even more remote ancestors.

The revival thrived on and, in turn, fostered handicrafts, the production of petty commodities, and petty trade. It was of one piece, in other words, with that informal economic activity upon which so many granddaughters of Lupondo relied to supplement their husbands' earnings as workers. In the circulation across town and country, ritual objects were revalued as 'curios' to be commercially traded for cash; they were then turned into traditional gifts for recovering or repairing the past and thus for healing and protecting the present. Family members bought the mediums' costumes and paraphernalia, the red cloths (Z$14), axes (Z$7), staffs (Z$10.50), ostrich headdresses (Z$30), skirts (Z$55), leg rattles (Z$10.50), drums (Z$10.50), baskets (Z$3.95), shells (each Z$0.25 or Z$0.50), beads, python and other snake bones, herbal roots and clays from the smart display cases of a store in a modern office block on a main street near the city centre of Bulawayo. The store trades under the name of Tim's Jewelry Services and Curios.

Since the end of the liberation war in 1979 its owner, Timothy Ncube, a businessman and not himself a medium, has travelled widely, collecting virtually all of his 'curios' from remote parts of the countryside for resale in the city. Throughout the growing revival, his trade in 'curios' as ritual costumes and paraphernalia has fluctuated seasonally, his shop assistants told me, according to the flow of people between town and countryside. The demand has been greatest around the holiday seasons, such as at Christmas, when people, coming home to the countryside from the city, 'hear that they have problems', as the shop assistants put it.

Finally, the revival has had considerable inter-ethnic significance. For Lupondo's family, the *sangoma* cult was exotic. It came to them from Ndebele. Although even at the time of my first visit some Kalanga had long before borrowed it, family members turned to it then, in the early 1960s, merely to seek remote and alien witchfinders. At that time, it was not a cult to which anyone in Lupondo's family belonged. Family members first joined, becoming mediums, during the revival.

Family members met their concerns by re-establishing communication with the dead through an exotic cult focused upon aggression and associated with Ndebele and their stereotype of being war-like. As a consequence, family members tied the healing recovery of the past to the reconstruction of their identities in the present. They did so in response to certain recent changes. Among these were their new experiences of living in the midst of ethnic strangers and marrying them, of speaking Sindebele in the city, and even in the countryside, as the region's lingua franca and as the main language for many of their children, and of being identified with Ndebele in the quasi-nationalism of the liberation war and its violent aftermath.

The healing they received and offered through the cult was even more broadly transcultural, however. It was drawn from therapeutic practices and prescriptions which had become widespread beyond Ndebele. The cult was open to patients irrespective of their ethnic origins. Among Baka Ngomas patients in Bulawayo were Kalanga, Ndebele and Shona, and the ease with which she conversed with them in their own language was impressive. In this sense, therefore, participation in the revival, at least by some members of Lupondo's family, can be understood as at once an appropriation of Ndebele identity and a transcendence of it.

Through the revival, voices of the past have been made to speak in the present in order to testify to a truth, deeply felt by many family members, that certain memories have to be kept alive, honoured and never forgotten. Among these are memories of suffering and loss, of lapses from humanity, of the failures of kin, and not merely their triumphs in success or achievement.

Notes

General Introduction

1. An excellent summary of much of the work already done on the war and on Zimbabwean society can be found in the opening pages of Jocelyn Alexander's chapter in this volume.

2. N. Kriger, *Zimbabwe's Guerrilla War: Peasant Voices* (Cambridge, Cambridge Univ. Press, 1992); K. Manungo, 'The Role Peasants Played in the Zimbabwe War of Liberation, with Special Emphasis on Chiweshe District' (Ohio, Ohio University, Ph.D. thesis, 1991); T. Ranger, *Peasant Consciousness and Guerrilla War in Zimbabwe* (London, James Currey; Harare, Zimbabwe Publishing House, 1985); R. Werbner, *Tears of The Dead: The Social Biography of an African Family* (Edinburgh, Edinburgh Univ. Press; Harare, Baobab, 1991).

3. I. Staunton (ed.), *Mothers of the Revolution* (Harare, Baobab, 1990).

4. D. Lan, *Guns and Rain: Guerrillas and Spirit Mediums in Zimbabwe* (London, James Currey; Harare, Zimbabwe Publishing House, 1985); A. Moyo and C. Hallencreutz (eds.), *Church and State in Zimbabwe* (Gweru, Mambo, 1988).

5. P. Reynolds, 'Children of tribulation: The need to heal and the means to heal war trauma', *Africa* (1990), LX.

6. J. K. Cilliers, *Counter-Insurgency in Rhodesia* (London, Croom Helm, 1985); H. Ellert, *The Rhodesia Front War* (Gweru, Mambo, 1989); P. Moorcraft and P. McLaughlin, *Chimurenga: The War in Rhodesia 1965–1980* (Marshalltown, Sygma/Collins, 1985).

7. K. Flower, *Serving Secretly: An Intelligence Chief on Record* (London, Murray; Harare, Quest, 1987); P. Stiff, *See You in November: Rhodesia's No-holds Barrred Intelligence War* (Alberton, Galago, 1985).

8. R. Reid Daly and P. Stiff, *Selous Scouts: Top Secret War* (Alberton, Galago, 1982).

9. P. Stiff, *Selous Scouts: Rhodesian War — A Pictorial Account* (Alberton, Galago, 1984).

10. B. Moore-King, *White Man Black War* (Harare, Baobab, 1989).

11. The most illuminating study of White Rhodesia during the war is that by D. Caute, *Under the Skin: The Death of White Rhodesia* (London, Allen Lane, 1983); a recent history is P. Godwin and I. Hancock: *Rhodesians Never Die: The Impact of War and Political Change on White Rhodesia, 1970–1980* (Oxford, Oxford University Press, 1993).

12. Two of Ngwabi Bhebe's research students, Josiah Tungamirai and Janice McLaughlin, have had access to the ZANLA files and make use of them in their chapters in these volumes. Josephine Nhongo is currently working on an Oxford M. Litt. making use of material relating to women in the ZANLA files.

13. Jeremy Brickhill was able to work on the ZIPRA files before their seizure by the police and draws upon them for his chapter in *Volume One*.

14. A. Nyathi with J. Hoffman, *Tomorrow is Built Today: Experiences of War, Colonialism and the Struggle for Collective Co-operatives in Zimbabwe* (Harare, Anvil, 1990). There is one invaluable book by a *chimbwido*, P. Chater, *Caught in the Crossfire* (Harare, Zimbabwe Publishing House, 1985).

15. D. Martin and P. Johnson, *The Struggle for Zimbabwe: The Chimurenga War* (Harare, Zimbabwe Publishing House; London, Faber, 1981), is often cited as having established this 'official version'.

Introduction

Society in Zimbabwe's Liberation War: Volume Two

1. D. Lan, *Guns and Rain: Guerrillas and Spirit Mediums in Zimbabwe* (London, James Currey; Harare, ZPH, 1985); I. Linden, *The Catholic Church and the Struggle for Zimbabwe* (London, Longman, 1980).

2. 'So That Our Youngsters Will Know' (Gwanda, J. Z. Moyo School History Project, n.d.).

3. 'Southern Africa: A smuggled account from a guerrilla fighter', *Ramparts* (Oct. 1969), VIII, (iv).

4. M. Daneel, *ZIRCON: Earth-keeping at the Grassroots in Zimbabwe* (Pretoria, Sigma Press, 1991), 6.

5. M. Daneel, 'Healing the Earth: Traditional and Christian Initiatives in Southern Africa', 'Conference on Religion in Post-Apartheid South Africa' (Utrecht, Sept. 1991), 2, 5, 12, 13, 15, 16.

6. J. McLaughlin, 'The Catholic Church and the War of Liberation' (Harare, Univ. of Zimbabwe, Dept. of Religious Studies, Classics and Philosophy, Ph.D. thesis, 1991), 572, 580, 582.

7. Daneel, 'Healing the Earth', 15.

8. D. Maxwell, 'The Roasting of Chief Gambiza: The Anatomy of a Hwesa Succession Dispute', 'African Research Seminar' (Oxford Dec. 1991); D. Maxwell, 'A Social and Conceptual History of North-East Zimbabwe, 1890–1990' (Oxford, University of Oxford, Faculty of Modern History, D.Phil. thesis, 1994).

9. Daneel, *ZIRCON*.

10. Daneel, 'Healing the Earth', 17, 18.

11. Ngwabi Bhebe, *ZAPU and ZANU Guerrilla Warfare and the Lutheran Evangelical Church in Zimbabwe* (Mambo, in press).

12. McLaughlin, ''The Catholic Church and the War of Liberation', 544, 547.
13. *Ibid.*, 563.
14. R. Weiss, *Zimbabwe and the New Élite* (London, British Academic Press, 1994).
15. McLaughlin, 'The Catholic Church and the War of Liberation', 583.
16. Daneel, 'Healing the Earth', 20.
17. T. Ranger, 'The Politics of Prophecy in Matabeleland' 'Colloquium on African Religion and Ritual' (Satterwaite, April 1989).
18. Daneel, 'Healing the Earth', 21.
19. Two books stand out as offering a gendered perspective. These are I. Staunton (ed.), *Mothers of the Revolution* (Harare, Baobab, 1990); N. Kriger, *Zimbabwe's Guerrilla War: Peasant Voices* (Cambridge, CUP, 1992). But neither apply to the period of the war the sort of systematic analysis of changing gender relations which is offered by recent treatments of the earlier colonial period. See D. Jeater, *Marriage, Perversion and Power: The Construction of Moral Discourse in Southern Rhodesia, 1894–1930* (Oxford, Clarendon, 1991); E. Schmidt, *Peasants, Traders and Wives: Shona Women in the History of Zimbabwe, 1870–1939* (London, James Currey, 1992).
20. Heike Schmidt has recently delivered a conference paper which sets out her developed ideas — 'Women as Victims, Women as Heroines: Beyond Dichotomies in the Analysis of Gender and War in Southern Africa', *Journal of Southern African Studies* conference on 'Paradigms Lost, Paradigms Regained' (York, Sept. 1994). Josephine Nhongo is working towards a thesis on the experience of Zimbabwean women during the war in ZANLA camps in Mozambique. Eleanor O'Gorman is working towards a thesis on the experience of women during the war in Chiweshe T.T.L.
21. McLaughlin, 'The Catholic Church and the War of Liberation', 477, 488.
22. C. Mazobere, 'Christian theology of mission', in C. Banana (ed.), *A Century of Methodism in Zimbabwe, 1891–1991* (Harare, Methodist Church, 1991), 172.
23. K. Manungo, 'The Role Peasants Played in the Zimbabwe War of Liberation, with Special Emphasis on Chiweshe District' (Ohio, Ohio State University, Ph.D. thesis, 1991), 184–193.
24. Alexander has treated these issues fully in 'The State, Agrarian Policy and Rural Politics in Zimbabwe: Case Studies of Chimanimani and Insiza Districts, 1950–1990' (Oxford, University of Oxford, Faculty of Politics, D.Phil. thesis, 1993).
25. Werbner has treated the question of violence in southern Matabeleland more fully in *Tears of the Dead: The Social Biography of an African Family* (Edinburgh, University of Edinburgh Press, 1991; Harare, Baobab, 1992).
26. Daneel, 'Healing the Earth', 24.
27. Banana (ed.), *A Century of Methodism*, 208.
28. P. Reynolds, 'After war: Healers and children's trauma in Zimbabwe', *Africa* (1990), LX, (i), 1–38; T. Ranger, 'War, violence and healing in Zimbabwe', *Journal of Southern African Studies* (1992), XVIII, 698–707.

Chapter 1
Religion in the Guerrilla War: The Case of Southern Matabeleland

1. The archival research on which this chapter is based was done by Terence Ranger; the oral interviews were carried out by Mark Ncube and Terence Ranger. Mark Ncube transcribed and translated the Sindebele interviews; Terence Ranger transcribed the English ones. Full texts are available in the Bulawayo Records Office. It should be emphasized that our research has *not* been focused on the guerrilla war. Terence Ranger is writing a history of the Matopos between 1898 and 1964 to be entitled *Voices from the Rocks*. We hope to write a joint book on the twentieth century history of the Mwali cult in Matabeleland. The evidence presented in this chapter is, therefore, not the product of intensive research on the war.
2. D. Lan, *Guns and Rain: Guerrillas and Spirit Mediums in Zimbabwe* (London, James Currey; Harare, ZPH, 1985).
3. M. F. C. Bourdillon and P. Gundani, 'Rural Christians and the Zimbabwe liberation war', in C. Hallencreutz and A. Moyo (eds.), *Church and State in Zimbabwe* (Gweru, Mambo, 1988). See also the chapters by David Maxwell and Sister Janice McLaughlin in this volume.
4. T. Ranger, 'Whose heritage? The case of the Matobo National Park', *Journal of Southern African Studies* (1989), XV, 217–49; T.Ranger, 'The Origins of Nationalism in Rural Matabeleland: The Case of Wenlock' (Oxford, mimeo, 1990).
5. Dr Richard Werbner has kindly provided us with the gist of his own interviews with Chief Bidi during this period.
6. T. Ranger, 'The Politics of Prophecy in Matabeleland' 'Colloquium on African Religion and Ritual' (Satterwaite, April 1989).
7. J. Nkomo, *Nkomo: The Story of My Life* (London, Methuen, 1984), 14.
8. T. Ranger, 'The Politics of Prophecy in Matabeleland'.
9. Interview with Mrs V. Lesabe, Bulawayo, 24 Aug. 1988.
10. *Ibid.*
11. M. L. Daneel, 'Healing the Earth: Traditional and Christian Initiatives in Southern Africa' (Utrecht, Paper presented at a conference on 'Wholeness, Healing and Resistance: The Role of Religion in Changing South Africa', 1991).
12. M. Gelfand, *An African's Religion: The Spirit of Nyajena* (Wynberg, Juta, 1966); M. L. Daneel, *The God of the Matopo Hills: An Essay on the Mwari Cult in Rhodesia* (Mouton, The Hague, 1970).
13. Interview with Minye Ncube and Melusi Sibanda, Bembe, 23 July 1989.
14. Daneel, *The God of the Matopo Hills*.
15. Interview with Mrs Mpofu, Matopo Communal Area, 27 July 1989.
16. Group interview with 30 men and women, Kumbudzi, Matopo Communal Area, 10 Sept. 1988.
17. P. J. Wentzel, *Nau DzabaKalanga: A History of the Kalanga* (Pretoria, Univ. of South Africa, 3 vols., 1983); C. van Waarden (ed.), *Kalanga: Retrospect and Prospect* (Gaborone, The Botswana Society, 1991).

18. Interview with Mrs Lesabe.
19. *Ibid*.
20. H. Aschwanden, *Karanga Mythology* (Gweru, Mambo, 1989).
21. Interview with Mark Dokotela Ncube, Wenlock, Gwanda, 30 Aug. 1990.
22. Interview with Japhet Ngwenya, Tshatshani, Matobo, 30 Aug. 1988.
23. *Ibid*.
24. T. Ranger, 'The Politics of Prophecy'.
25. Interview with Dumiso Dabengwa, Harare, 9 July 1991.
26. M. Clarke, 'In Search of the Shrine of the Mambo' (Oxford, paper presented at a seminar, 1991).
27. T. Ranger, 'The Politics of Prophecy'.
28. J. O'Reilly, *The Centenary of Empandeni* (Bulawayo, Bulawayo Province, 1987).
29. *Mission Work of the Mariannhill Missions in Zimbabwe: 1896–1980* (Bulawayo, Bulawayo Province, 1980), 13.
30. Fr. Pius Ncube, 'Report on the Second Raid on St Joseph's Mission — Semokwe', file 'History of Empandeni', Empandeni Archives.
31. *Mission Work*, 22.
32. Such encounters are described in the Jesuit periodical, *Zambezi Mission Record*, in 1907, 1912, 1914 and 1915.
33. *Mission Work*, 22.
34. *Ibid.*, 12.
35. O'Reilly, *Empandeni*, 27, citing Fr. Bausenwein.
36. *Mission Work*, 24–6.
37. Fr. Ncube, 'Report on the Second Raid on St Joseph's Mission'.
38. *Mission Work*, 36–8.
39. Fr. Andrew Bausenwein, 'Special Events in 1978', 13 Oct. 1978, in file 'Annals of Empandeni', Empandeni Archives.
40. J. S. Gordon, 'Outline of Report on Problems Experienced in 1976 and Continuing in 1977', among papers deposited in 1991 by Rev. Enock Musa, Musa Papers, Bulawayo Records Centre.
41. E. Musa to A. M. Ndhele, 27 Nov. 1976, Musa Papers, Bulawayo Records Centre.
42. E. Musa, 'For Private Investigation by Capable People Who Have the Know-how and Sympathy and No Exaggeration', Nov. 1976, Musa Papers, Bulawayo Records Centre.
43. Gordon, 'Outline of Report on Problems Experienced in 1976 and Continuing in 1977', Musa Papers, Bulawayo Records Centre.
44. J. S. Gordon to Senior Assistant Commissioner, Bulawayo, 25 Jan. 1977, Musa Papers, Bulawayo Records Centre.

Chapter 2
Christianity and the War in Eastern Zimbabwe: The Case of Elim Mission

1 H. Cox, *The Seduction of the Spirit: The Use and Misuse of People's Religion* (London, Simon and Schuster, 1974), 193.
2 P. A. Kaliombe, 'Doing Theology at the Grassroots: A Challenge for Professional Theologians', Second General Assembly of the Ecumenical Association of African Theologians, Nairobi 1984, cited in T. O. Ranger, 'Religious movements and politics in Sub-Saharan Africa', in *African Studies Review* (1986), XXIX, (ii), 52–53.
3 N. Bhebe, 'The Evangelical Lutheran Church in Zimbabwe and the war of liberation', in C. Hallencreutz and A. Moyo (eds.), *Church and State in Zimbabwe* (Gweru, Mambo, 1988), 163–194. T. O. Ranger, 'Holy men and rural communities in Zimbabwe, 1970–80', in W. J. Sheils (ed.), *The Church and War* (Oxford, Blackwell, 1983), 443–61; M. Bourdillon and P. Gundani, 'Rural Christians and the Zimbabwe liberation war: A case study', in C. Hallencreutz and A. Moyo (eds.), *Church and State in Zimbabwe*, 147–161; Janice McLaughlin, 'The Catholic Church and the War of Liberation' (Harare, University of Zimbabwe, Dept. of Religious Studies, Ph.D. thesis, 1991).
4. T. O. Ranger, 'Religion and witchcraft in everyday life in contemporary Zimbabwe', in Preben Kaarsholm (ed.), *Cultural Struggle and Development in Southern Africa* (London, James Currey, 1991), 150.
5. I. Linden, *The Catholic Church and the Struggle for Zimbabwe* (London, Longman, 1980).
6. R. Werbner, 'In Memory of Dzilo's Death', in R. Werbner, *Tears of the Dead: The Social Biography of an African Family* (Edinburgh, Edinburgh Univ. Press; Harare, Baobab, 1991). J. Brickhill, 'Overcoming the Traumas of Violence in Zimbabwe', Seminar given at St. Anthony's College, Oxford, 22 Nov. 1990. P. Reynolds, 'Children of tribulation: The need to heal and the means to heal war trauma', *Africa* (1990), LX, (i), 1–38.
7. Interview with Fr Peter Egan, Hatfield, 28 Dec. 1988.
8. Interview with Fr David Weakliam, The Priory, White Friars Street, Dublin, 12 Sept. 1990; 'Policy Document, Carmelites of the Irish Province in Rhodesia' (Gweru Diocese Archives, 1978). This policy dealt mainly with the issue of priests' security, leaving them free to work out relationships on the ground.
9. Interview with Fr Paddy Stornton, The Priory, Dundrum, Dublin, 11 Sept. 1990.
10. Elim Archives, Cheltenham, henceforth EAC., file, Reports and Notes on South Africa and Rhodesia; J. C. Smyth and L. Wigglesworth, 'Report of Delegation's Visit to Rhodesia and South Africa', 13 June–6 July.
11. P. Thompson, *The Rainbow or the Thunder*, (London, Hodder and Stoughton, 1979), 66.
12. Diary in the possession of Brenda Griffiths, 27 Apr. 1976.
13. P. Thompson, *The Rainbow or the Thunder*, 46.

14. Diary in the possession of Brenda Griffiths, 27 Apr. 1976.
15. EAC., file Elim Missionaries L-T to 1966, Letter from A. and A. Renshaw to Missionary Secretary, Elim HQ, Feb. 1966. One missionary couple wrote on the issue of U. D. I. 'It has been said that this country is ruled by a few hundred White people who keep the Africans like slaves. This is completely untrue! . . . The Government action enjoys the support of a large number of Africans as well as Europeans who want to see the best for their country. We who are British citizens feel like hiding our heads in shame ₐt the vindictive actions of the leaders of our homeland'.
16. EAC., file Dr Brien, Letters from Dr Cecil Brien to Rev. S. Gorman, Elim HQ, London, 26 Mar. and 31 Mar. 1964.
17. EAC., file, Dr Brien, Letter from M. and C. Brien to Pastor and Mrs Gorman, Elim HQ, London, 5 June, 1962.
18. P. Thompson, *The Rainbow or the Thunder*, 46.
19. B. R. Wilson, *Sects and Society: A Sociological Study of Three Religious Groups in Britain* (London, William Heinemann Ltd., 1961), 89.
20. Diary in the possession of Brenda Griffiths, 5 Nov. 1976 and 30 Nov. 1976.
21. Transcript of television interview between Brian Barron with Peter Griffiths, Elim Mission, Rhodesia, B.B.C. Television News, 24 Feb. 1977, in *Elim Evangel*, 12 Mar. 1977.
22. EAC., file, Reports and Notes on South Africa and Rhodesia, General Meeting of the Missionary Conference with the Delegation in Attendance, 19 June 1976.
23. Diary in the possession of Brenda Griffiths, 4 Aug. 1976.
24. *Rhodesia Herald*, 18 and 21 April 1977. Diary in the possession of Brenda Griffiths, 18 April 1977. Griffiths was thanked by priests and nuns for his contribution.
25. Diary in the possession of Brenda Griffiths, 2 Dec. 1976.
26. EAC., file, Reports and Notes on South Africa and Rhodesia, General Meeting of the Missionary Conference with the Delegation in Attendance, 19 June 1976. J. C. Smyth and L. Wigglesworth, Report of Delegation's Visit to Rhodesia and South Africa, 13 June–6 July.
27. EAC., file, Rhodesia-Zimbabwe, Letter from ZANLA Forces 1 to Elim Missionaries, July 1977.
28. Interview with Pastor Pious Munembe, Elim Mission, 19 April 1989. EAC., file, Reports and Notes on South Africa and Rhodesia; J. C. Smyth, Final Report of Visit to Rhodesia, July 1977.
29. Interview with Pastor Pious Munembe, Elim Mission, 19 April 1989.
30. *Manica Post*, c.30 Aug. 1977.
31. D. J. Maxwell, 'A Social and Conceptual History of North-East Zimbabwe, 1890–1990' (Oxford, Department of History, Oxford University, D.Phil. thesis, 1994), Chapters 3 and 4.
32. EAC., file, Phil and Mrs Evans, Letter from P. and S. Evans to L. Wigglesworth, Elim HQ, London, Aug. 1976.
33. Diary in the possession of Brenda Griffiths, 27 Feb. 1977, 28 Mar. 1977, 3 Nov. 1976, 31 Mar. 1976.

34. EAC., file, Reports and Notes on South Africa and Rhodesia, J. C. Smyth, Final Report of Visit to Rhodesia, July 1977.
35. EAC., file, Reports and Notes on South Africa and Rhodesia, J. C. Smyth and L. Wigglesworth, Report of the Delegation's Visit to Rhodesia and South Africa, 13 June–6 July 1976.
36. EAC., file, Reports and Notes on South Africa and Rhodesia, J. C. Smyth, Final Report of Visit to Rhodesia, July 1977.
37. Interview with Pastor Pious Munembe, Elim Mission, 19 April 1989.
38. Interview with Pastor Ephraim Satuku, Elim Mission, 14 Aug. 1987.
39. I. Linden, *The Catholic Church and the Struggle for Zimbabwe*, 246.
40. EAC., file, Reports and Notes on South Africa and Rhodesia, J. C. Smyth, Preliminary Report of Katerere Visit, July 1977, 3.
41. EAC., file, Reports and Notes on South Africa and Rhodesia, J. C. Smyth and L. Wigglesworth, Report of Delegation's Visit to Rhodesia and South Africa, 13 June–6 July 1976. 'We also met the African leaders and they too emphasised strongly the need for more obvious black-white relationships and the need for more black involvement . . . They mentioned the military presence and suggested no social contact should be made.'
42. EAC., file, Reports and Notes on South Africa and Rhodesia, J. C. Smyth, Preliminary Report of Katerere Visit, July 1977, 2. Diary in the possession of Sister Joy Bath, 8 June and 20 Oct. 1976. Diary in the possession of Brenda Griffiths, 27 Aug. 1977.
43. Diary in the possession of Brenda Griffiths, 9 May and 6 Aug. 1977.
44. P. Thompson, *The Rainbow or the Thunder*, 85–86.
45. EAC., file, Reports and Notes on South Africa and Rhodesia, J. C. Smyth, Preliminary Report of Katerere Visit, July 1977, 4.
46. EAC., file, Rev. and Mrs Lynn, Letter from R. and J. Lynn to L. Wigglesworth, Elim HQ, Cheltenham, 31 Jan. 1978.
47. Diary in the possession of Brenda Griffiths, 27 July 1977.
48. EAC., file, Miss Wendy White, Letter from Sister Wendy White to Elim HQ, Cheltenham, Nov. 1977.
49. EAC., file, Miss Wendy White, Letter from Sister W. White to Elim HQ, Cheltenham, April 1978. File, Zimbabwe Reports 1984–88 and some older papers, R. B. Chapman, Sequence of Events Surrounding the Contemplated Closure of Emmanuel Secondary School, 3 May 1978; and P. D. Griffiths, Report on Visit to Rhodesia on 19 and 20 April 1978.
50. Interview with Pastor Pious Munembe, Elim Mission, 19 April 1989. EAC., file, Miss Wendy White, Letter from W. White, to Elim HQ, Cheltenham, April 1978.
51. EAC., file, Reports and Notes on South Africa and Rhodesia, J. C. Smyth, Rhodesia Report, June/July 1978. P. Thompson, *The Rainbow or the Thunder*, 151-53.
52. EAC., file, Zimbabwe Reports 1984–88 and some older papers, Special Meeting of the Emmanuel Secondary School Staff, 13 June 1978.
53. EAC., file, Reports and Notes on South Africa and Rhodesia, J. C. Smyth, Rhodesia Report, June/July 1978. See also *Sunday Telegraph*, 25 June 1978.

54. M. Meredith, *The Past is Another Country. Rhodesia: U.D.I. To Zimbabwe* (London, Deutsch, 1980), 342.

55. R. Reid Daly and P. Stiff, *Selous Scouts: Top Secret War* (Alberton, Galago, 1982). B. Cole, *The Elite. The Story of the Rhodesian Special Air Service* (Amanzimoti, Three Knights, 1984).

56. Interview with Colin Kahuni, Eastlea, 12 April 1991. Interview with Peter Griffiths, Mount Pleasant, 9 July 1991. In 1978, an official in the British Foreign Office called Patrick Laver, told Griffiths that Robert Mugabe had 'unofficially' apologized for the massacre. Mugabe further stated that he had called the platoon commander responsible back for disciplining, but the guerrilla in question had refused to return. This point is also made by David Caute whose book contains a vivid description of both the scene in the Vumba after the massacre and the international repercussions. D. Caute, *Under The Skin: The Death of White Rhodesia* (London, Allen Lane, 1983), 253–58.

57. Recorded sermon preached by Peter Griffiths, Woolwich, Britain, 1985.

58. EAC., file, Reports and Notes on South Africa and Rhodesia, J. C. Smyth, Rhodesia Report, June/July 1978.

59. Interview with Pious Menembe, Elim Mission, 19 April, 1989.

60. Interview with Pastor Ephraim Satuku, Elim Mission, 14 Aug., 1987.

61. Letters in the possession of Peter Egan, Letter from Mary Brien to Father Peter Egan, 10 Mar. 1980.

62. Letter from Cecil and Mary Brien to Father Peter Egan, 18 April 1980.

63. Letter from Cecil Brien to Father Peter Egan, 21 Aug. 1979.

64. EAC., file, Reports and Notes on South Africa and Rhodesia, J. C. Smyth, Rhodesia Report, June/July 1978.

65. *Ibid.*

66. EAC., file, Reports and Notes on South Africa and Rhodesia, J. C. Smyth and L. Wigglesworth, Report of Delegation's Visit to South Africa and Rhodesia, 13 June–6 July 1976.

67. EAC., file, Miss Wendy White, Letter from W. White to Elim HQ, Cheltenham, Mar./April 1977. File, Reports and Notes on South Africa and Rhodesia, J. C. Smyth and L. Wigglesworth, Report of Delegation's Visit to Rhodesia and South Africa 13 June–6 July.

68. EAC., file, Reports and Notes on South Africa and Rhodesia, J. C. Smyth, Final Report of Visit to Rhodesia, July 1977.

69. EAC., file, Reports and Notes on South Africa and Rhodesia, J.C. Smyth, Preliminary Report of Katerere Visit, July 1977. File, Miss Wendy White, Letter from W. White to Elim HQ, Cheltenham, July 1977.

70. EAC., file, Reports and Notes on South Africa and Rhodesia, J. C. Smyth, Final Report of Visit to Rhodesia, July 1977.

71. Letters in the possession of Brenda Griffiths, Letter from Phil Evans to Peter and Brenda Griffiths, 27 May 1978.

72. Turner file, in possession of T. O. Ranger, Report on Symposium: Driefontein 17–19 May (R.C .B.C. News Sheet, 15 Aug. 1977).

73. Catholic Institute of International Relations (henceforth CIIR.), London, file, Silveira House, 'Annual Report of Silveira House', 1978, 2.
74. See D. J. Maxwell, 'A Social and Conceptual History of North-East Zimbabwe'.
75. Interview with Fr Tony Clarke, the Priory, Mutare, 21 April 1989.
76. I. Linden, *The Catholic Church and the Struggle for Zimbabwe*, 262.
77. Interview with Bishop Donal Lamont, Terenure College, Dublin, 8 Sept. 1990. Interview with Fr David Weakliam, the Priory, White Friars St., Dublin, 12 Sept. 1990.
78. Interview with Pastor Pious Munembe, Elim Mission, 19 April 1989.
79. EAC., file, Reports and Notes on South Africa and Rhodesia, J. C. Smyth, Final Report of Visit to Rhodesia, July 1977.
80. *South Wales Evening Post*, 15 Sept. 1977. Griffiths told the paper in an interview that the guerrillas left them alone and seemed to have found 'alternative sources of supply'.
81. Interview with Augustine Wellington Mabvira (Comrade Rangarirai Mwana We Povo or Comrade Ranga), Elim Mission, 31 May 1988.
82. Interview with Pastor Pious Munembe, Elim Mission, 19 April 1989.
83. *Ibid.*
84. Interview with Comrade Ranga, Elim Mission, 31 May 1989.
85. Personal correspondence from Comrade Ranga, 5 Mar. 1990. Sister J. McLauglin, 'Avila Mission: A turning point in church relations with the state and with the liberation forces', this volume. Personal communication, Janice McLaughlin.
86. Interview with Pastor Pious Munembe, Elim Mission, 19 April 1989.
87. G. P. Kahari, 'The history of Shona protest song: A preliminary study', in *Zambezia: The Journal of the University of Zimbabwe* (1981), XIX, (ii), 82–89.
88. *Ibid.*, 99.
89. *Ibid.*, 89.
90. Conversation with Pastor Pious Munembe.
91. Interview with Herbert Turai, Comrade Sam Zvaitika, Chitungwiza, Aug. 1988.
92. EAC., file, Rev. and Mrs McCann, Letter from S. and P. McCann to L. Wigglesworth, Elim HQ, Cheltenham, 1 Jan. 1977.
93. Letter from R. and J. Lynn to L. Wigglesworth, Elim HQ, Cheltenham, 31 Jan. 1978., file, Rev. and Mrs Lynn, EAC.
94. M. Bourdillon and P. Gundani, 'Rural Christians and the Zimbabwe liberation war', 56.
95. Interview with Emmanuel Nyarumba, Elim Mission, 16 April 1988.
96. Written reminiscences of Calista Chikafa, 1988; *Ibid.*
97. Interview with Pastor Pious Munembe, Elim Mission, 19 April 1989.
98. Interview with Gwara Nyambuya, Elim Mission, 13 Aug. 1987. Interview with Emmanuel Nyarumba, Elim Mission, 16 April 1988.
99. EAC., file, Reports and Notes on South Africa and Rhodesia, J. C. Smyth, Preliminary Report on Katerere Visit, July 1977, 1.
100. Interview with Michael Mudzudza, Elim Mission, Nov. 1987.

101. D. J. Maxwell, 'A Social and Conceptual History of North-East Zimbabwe'.
102. T. O. Ranger, 'Religion, development and African Christian identity', in K. Holst Peterson (ed.), *Religion, Development and African Identity* (Uppsala, Scandinavian Institute of African Studies, 1987), 37, 46.
103. M. Gelfand, *The Spiritual Beliefs of the Shona* (Gweru, Mambo, 1982), 5.
104. *Ibid.*, 129–41.
105. Interview with Fr Peter Egan, Hatfield, 28 Dec. 1988.
106. Interview with Diki Rukadza, Medium of Nyawada, 21 Jan. 1989.
107. D. J. Maxwell, 'Local politics and the war of liberation in north-east Zimbabwe', *Journal of Southern African Studies* (1993), XIX, (iii), 361–86.
108. Personal correspondence from Comrade Ranga, 13 July 1990.
109. Interview with Brother Ignatius Moore, the Priory, Dundrum, Ireland, 10 Sept. 1990.
110. Interview with Dr Robert MacCabe (Father Luke), the Priory, Dundrum, Ireland, 10 Sept. 1990.
111. Interview with Cyprian Pasipanodya and Camillo Mudondo, Bumhira School, Nyamaropa, 3 June, 1991.
112. Interview with Dr Robert McCabe, 10 Sept., 1990.
113. Interview with Fr David Weakliam, the Priory, White Friars Street, Dublin, 12 Sept. 1989.
114. Interview with Comrade Ranga, Elim Mission, 31 May 1988.
115. I. Linden, *The Catholic Church and the Struggle for Zimbabwe*, 272.
116. Interview with Brother Ignatius Moore, the Priory, Dundrum, Ireland, 7 Sept. 1990.
117. Interview with Pastor Pious Munembe, Elim Mission, 19 April 1989; Interview with Pastor Ephraim Satuku, Elim Mission, 14 Aug. 1987. EAC., file, Reports and Notes on South Africa and Rhodesia, J. C. Smyth, Final Report on Visit to Rhodesia, July 1977; Interview with Archibald Maziti (Comrade Howard Shaka), Dakota Barracks, 25 July, 1991.
118. Diary in the possession of Brenda Griffiths, 14 Sept. 1976.
119. *Ibid.*, 15 Oct., 1976.
120. National Archives of Zimbabwe (NAZ.), Outletters from Native Commissioner, NUC., 2/3/3, 1918. The N. C. wrote: 'No European would consent to transport grain up to Mt. Nani privately as the road is very bad'. Outletters 17 Jan. 1925., S603, The N. C. wrote 'At present it is impossible to get to Nyamaropa Reserve or within several miles of it by wheeled vehicle.'
121. EAC., file, Reports and Notes on South Africa and Rhodesia, J. C. Smyth and L. Wigglesworth, Report of Delegation's Visit to Southern Rhodesia and South Africa. Diary in the possession of Brenda Griffiths, 28 July 1977.
122. Diary in the possession of Brenda Griffiths, 4 Aug. 1976, 7 Oct. 1976. Diary in the possession of Sister Joy Bath, 7 June 1976. Headmen Chifambe and Mungezi were killed and another unnamed one in the Ruangwe area. Mungezi was unpopular for collecting contour ridge fines.
123. Diary in the possession of Brenda Griffiths, 4 Aug. 1976, 28 July 1976. Diary in the possession of Sister Joy Bath, 24 June 1976.

124. EAC., file, Reports and Notes on South Africa and Rhodesia, J.C. Smyth and L. Wigglesworth, Report of Delegation's Visit to Rhodesia and South Africa, 15 June–6 July 1976.
125. EAC., file, Phil and Mrs Evans, Letter from P. Evans to L. Wigglesworth, Elim HQ, Cheltenham, 1 Dec. 1976. Evans wrote: 'We have been on the edge of one of the biggest security force operations to date . . . Its been a little like London airport with planes and helicopters flying around.' He noted that the operation had been reported as successful.
126. EAC., file, Reports and Notes on South Africa and Rhodesia, J. C. Smyth, Preliminary Report of Katerere Visit, July 1977, 1.
127. Personal correspondence from Comrade Ranga, 13 July 1990.
128. Interview with Pastor Pious Munembe, Elim Mission, 19 April 1989.
129. Here ZANLA are equating their fire power with the image of the Kaerezi (Gaerezi) River in flood. The song was transcribed by Laiza Chikutirwe.
130. N. J. Kriger, *Zimbabwe's Guerrilla War: Peasant Voices* (Cambridge, CUP, 1992).
131. EAC., file, Miss Wendy White, Letter from Wendy White to Elim HQ, Cheltenham, Mar./April 1977.
132. Interview with Richard Simbi, Elim Mission, 4 Aug. 1988.
133. Interview with Comrade Sam Zvaitika, Chitungwiza, Aug. 1987.
134. Interview with Pastor Ephraim Satuku, Elim Mission, 14 Aug. 1987.
135. Interview with Father Tony Clarke, the Priory, Mutare, 21 Apr. 1989.
136. EAC., file, Rev. and Mrs P. McCann, Letter from S. and P. McCann to L. Wigglesworth, Elim HQ, Cheltenham, 1 Jan., 1977. File, P. and Mrs Evans, Letter from P. Evans to J. C. Smyth, Elim HQ, Cheltenham, 31 Jan. 1977.
137. EAC., file, Miss Wendy White, Letter from W. White to Elim HQ, Cheltenham, April 1978. Diary in the possession of Brenda Griffiths, 1 Dec. 1976.
138. Terence Ranger has written extensively on the founding of popular Christianity in Manicaland. See T. O. Ranger, 'Religion, development and African Christian identity', 29–57.
139. D. J. Maxwell, 'A Study of The Roman Catholic Church — From Rhodesia To Zimbabwe 1959–1986', (Manchester, Manchester University, B.A. Honours thesis, 1986), 55–60.
140. J. Kerkhofs, 'The Church in Zimbabwe: The Trauma of Cutting Apron Strings', in *Pro Mundi Vita Dossiers* (Jan. 1982), 28.
141. CIIR., file, The Church, 'Report of the National Pastoral Consultation', 22–23 April 1980, 2.
142. CIIR., file, Zimbabwe Council 1, Report on the Pastoral Effort of the Catholic Church in Zimbabwe in 1982. ZCBC. News Sheet, Mar. 1983, 2.
143. Leonardo Boff, *Church Charisma and Power: Liberation Theology and the Institutional Church* (London, SCM, 1985), (ix).
144. Interview with Father David Weakliam, the Priory, White Friars St., Dublin, 12 Sept. 1990.
145. Elim Hospital, Katerere, Dr A. P. Smyly, Progress Report For Oxfam, 19 Feb. 1984.

146. EAC., file, Zimbabwe Reports, 1984–88. D. Bucher, Report on the Visit to Southern Africa, 5.

147. P. D. Griffiths, 'The harvest of the Vumba massacre', *Elim Evangel* (18 June 1988), 158. Recorded sermon preached by P. D. Griffiths, Woolwich, Britain, 1985.

148. R. Werbner, 'In Memory of Dzilo's Death'. Church of England Newspaper, CWN., Series, 23 Feb. 1990 gives the example the evangelist Stephen Longu. An ex-combatant, he was converted on entering a Harare mission tent which he had planned to petrol bomb.

149. T. O. Ranger, 'The Meaning of Violence in Zimbabwe', ms. 1991, 10.

150. Interview with Michael Mudzudza, Elim Mission, 8 Nov. 1987.

151. P. Reynolds, 'Children of tribulation: The need to heal and the means to heal war trauma', in *Africa* (1990), LX, (i), 12–14.

152. *Ibid.*, 12, 14.

153. EAC., file, Vumba press cuttings, R. B. Chapman, 'Was it a Waste on the Misty Mountains of Rhodesia', ms, nd.

154. P. D. Griffiths, 'The harvest of the Vumba massacre', *Elim Evangel* (18 June 1988).

155. Interview with Bishop Donal Lamont, Terenure College, Dublin, 8 Sept. 1990.

156. Interview with Pastor Pious Munembe, Elim Mission, 19 April 1989.

157. EAC., file, Reports and Notes on South Africa and Rhodesia, J. C. Smyth, Rhodesia Report, June/July 1978, 8.

158. EAC., file, Vumba press cuttings, 10 Aug. 1979. W. R. Jones, Secretary General of the Elim Movement wrote to the National Front expressing their distaste. Martin Webster of the National Front was unrepentant. See letter from M. Webster to W.R. Jones, Elim HQ, Cheltenham, 20 Aug. 1979.

159. Interview with Pastor Pious Munembe, Elim Mission, 19 April 1989.

160. Victor Kwenda, Buriro/Esizeni Reflection Centre Seminar, 26–27 Sept. 1981. Cited by T. O. Ranger in 'Holy men and rural communities in Zimbabwe, 1970-1980' in W. J. Sheils (ed.), *The Church and War, Vol. 20* (Oxford, Blackwell, 1983) , 460.

161. I. Linden, *The Catholic Church and the Struggle for Zimbabwe*. Linden's analysis of the Bishops' pastorals finds them consistently ecclesiocentric rather than advocating a preferential option for the poor and oppressed. The Kairos Document also known as *Challenge to the Church, A Theological Comment on the Political Crises in South Africa* (Gweru, Mambo, 1985).

162. T. O. Ranger, 'The Meaning of Violence in Zimbabwe', ms, 1991, 20.

163. Interview with Br. Adamson S. J. , 3 Jan. 1989. Cited by J. McLaughlin, 'Taking Sides: A Case Study of St. Paul's Mission Musami', ms, 1989, 24.

164. R. Werbner, 'In Memory of Dzilo's Death'.

165. The two examples above are just verses from the songs. They were collected by Shupikai Chikutirwe.

166. T. O. Ranger, 'Missionaries, migrants and the Manyika', in LeRoy Vail (ed.), *The Creation of Tribalism in Southern Africa* (London, James Currey, 1989).

Chapter 3
Avila Mission: A Turning Point in Church Relations
with the State and with the Liberation Forces

1. Interview with a former member of the Special Branch, Harare, 20 Dec. 1988.
2. D. J. Maxwell 'A Social and Conceptual History of North-East Zimbabwe, 1890–1990' (Oxford, University of Oxford, Dept. of History, D. Phil. thesis, 1994). See also D. Maxwell 'Christianity and the War in Eastern Zimbabwe, The Case of Elim Mission', this volume.
3. D. Martin and P. Johnson, *The Struggle for Zimbabwe: The Chimurenga War* (London, Faber; Harare, ZPH, 1981).
4. The ZANU Archives contain the full syllabi of both the 'National Grievances' course and the Red Army lessons as well as the Whampoa syllabus used by ZIPA.
5. Interview with Alexandra Kanengoni (Comrade Gora), Ministry of Education, Harare, 18 Jan. 1989. Also informal discussions with Fay Chung, Sam Geza, Dzingai Mutumbuka and many former Vashandi members.
6. At a history seminar held at the University of Zimbabwe in September 1990, Jeremy Brickhill put forward the thesis that the majority of ZAPU recruits came from a working class background.
7. Interview with Bishop Donal Lamont, Terenure College, Dublin, 18 April 1989.
8. D. Lamont, *Speech From the Dock* (Essex, Kevin Mayhew, 1977).
9. *Ibid.,* 72.
10. Interview with Mr. Wilson Martin Chiutanye ('Heavy Duty' Avila Mission, Nyanga, 24 June 1990.
11. D. Lamont, *Speech From the Dock*, 74 ff.
12. Interview with Bishop Lamont. Interview with Bishop Patrick Mutume, ZCBC Offices, Harare, 26 Jan. 1989.
13. Interview with Bishop Mutume.
14. Ranger, 'Holy men and rural communities in Zimbabwe', 443–61.
15. Interview with Bishop Lamont.
16. Interview with Bishop Mutume.
17. Interview with Special Branch Officer.
18. Interview with Sr. Susan McGrath, PBVM, Nagle House, Marondera, 23 Aug. 1990.
19. I. Linden, *The Church and the Struggle for Zimbabwe* (London, Longman, 1979), 225.
20. Lamont, *Speech From the Dock*.
21. I. Linden, *The Church and the Struggle for Zimbabwe*, 251. This incident is also reported in Martin and Johnson, *The Struggle for Zimbabwe*.
22. Interview with Bishop Mutume. According to Bishop Lamont, Evans killed himself playing Russian roulette a few years later.
23. *Ibid.*
24. *Ibid.*

25. P. Mutume, 'Insights from the second chimurenga', in C. F. Hallencreutz and M. Palmberg (eds.), *Religion and Politics in Southern Africa* (Uppsala, The Scandinavian Institute of African Studies, 1991), 144.

26. Interview with Mr Constantine Munyaka, Crossdale School, Nyanga, 25 June 1990.

27. Interview with Bishop Lamont and Bishop Mutume.

28. Interview with Fr. Maximan Muzungu, ZCBC Offices, Harare, 19 Dec. 1990.

29. Interview with Kanengoni; Also interviews with George Rutanhire, Parliament, Harare, 18–19 July 1989; Hudson Kundai, Ministry of Youth, Masvingo, 31 July 1989.

30. Interview with Kundai.

31. ZANU Archives, Enterprise Road, Harare, F. Commissariat; 'National Grievances', Serial II; 'Division in our Nation', Serial IV; 'Mental Enslavement'.

32. D. Lan, *Guns and Rain: Guerrillas and Spirit Mediums in Zimbabwe* (Harare, ZPH, 1985). Interviews with many ex-combatants indicate that traditional religion was most influential from 1972 to 1974, declining later for a variety of reasons, support from Christian missions being one.

33. J. McLaughlin, 'The Catholic Church and the War of Liberation' (Harare, University of Zimbabwe, Ph.D thesis, 1991).

34. Interview with Kundai.

35. Interview with Bishop Mutume.

36. Informal discussions with Sam Geza and Augustine Mpofu.

37. Interview with Air Vice-Marshall Perence Shiri, Air Force, HQ, Harare, 1 June 1989.

38. Interview with Major-General Constantine Chiwenga (Comrade Dominic Chinenge), Army HQ, Harare, 6 Feb. 1989.

39. J. Mclaughlin, 'The Catholic Church and the War of Liberation', Chapter 7.

40. Interview with Mrs Letitia Afonso (Sr. Helen Nyakupinda), Shurugwi, 23 Aug. 1989.

41. ZANU Archives, State House, Harare, F. Ops. Chitepo; Chitepo: Op. Report, 17 Jan. 1978, by B. Chakamuka , 2.

42. Interview with Muzungu.

43. *Ibid.*

44. *Ibid.*

Chapter 4
Rhodesian Discourse, Rhodesian Novels and the Zimbabwe Liberation War

1. I first discussed novels about the liberation war in 'The treatment of the Rhodesian war in recent Rhodesian novels', *Zambezia* (1977), V, (ii), 177–202. Some passages from the novels which I cited in this article appear again here as well as some plot summaries and analysis which still seem to be valid. I would like to acknowledge my indebtedness to Donal Mackay for helping me to develop a different analytical approach to the texts.

2. W. A. Ballinger, *Call it Rhodesia* (London, Mayflowerdell, 1966), 315–19.

3. C. E. Dibb, *Spotted Soldiers* (Salisbury, Leo Publishers, 1978).

4. R. Brown, *When the Woods Became the Trees* (London, Michael Joseph, 1965), 19.

5. *Ibid.*, 110.

6. *Ibid.*, 33.

7. *Ibid.*, 136.

8. *Ibid.*, 238.

9. In the sequel to *When the Woods Became the Trees, A Forest is a Long Time Growing*, the priest explains his crucifixion as a diversionary tactic. Since the whole narrative of the earlier novel has moved towards this symbolic point, I suspect this is an afterthought on Brown's part.

10. M. Wilson, *Explosion* (London, Robert Hale, 1966), 22.

11. *Ibid.*, 27.

12. *Ibid.*, 140.

13. *Ibid.*, 69–70.

14. J. G. Davis, *Hold My Hand I'm Dying* (London, Michael Joseph, 1967), 530–1. At the time I shared a house with one of the defence team and was able to see just how little information had been given to the local press.

15. *Ibid.*, 433.

16. *Ibid.*, 432–3.

17. *Ibid.*, 434.

18. *Ibid.*, 373.

19. *Ibid.*, 9.

20. *Ibid.*, 183.

21. *Ibid.*, 431.

22. *Ibid.*, 446.

23. *Ibid.*, 611.

24. A. Burgess, *The Word for Love* (London, Michael Joseph, 1968).

25. D. Carney, *The Whispering Death* (Salisbury, College Press, 1969), 9.

26. *Ibid.*, 73.

27. A. Trew, *Towards the Tamarind Trees* (London, Collins, 1970).

28. *Ibid.*, 13.

29. *Ibid.*, 14.

30. *Ibid.*, 64.

31. Wilbur Smith, *The Sunbird* [1972], (London, Pan, 1974), 74.

32. *Ibid.*, 231.

33. *Ibid.*, 20.

34. L. van der Post, *A Story Like the Wind* (London, Hogarth Press, 1972), 10–11.

35. *Ibid.*, 438.

36. *Ibid.*, 444–5.

37. M. Cutlack, *Blood Running South* (London, Collins, 1972), 172.

38. *Ibid.*, 160.

39. *Ibid.*, 53.

40. *Ibid.*, 95–6.

41. P. Stiff, *The Rain Goddess* (Salisbury, Jacaranda, 1973), 26.
42. *Ibid.*, 39.
43. M. Hartmann, *Game for Vultures* (London, Heinemann, 1973), 19.
44. *Ibid.*, 168.
45. *Ibid.*, 41.
46. *Ibid.*, 87.
47. W. Rayner, *The Day of Chaminuka* (London, Collins, 1976), 149.
48. *Ibid.*, 221.
49. G. Tippette, *The Mercenaries* (New York, Delacorte, 1976).
50. *Ibid.*, 287.
51. R. Early, *A Time of Madness* (Salisbury, Graham, 1977), 33.
52. *Ibid.*, 34.
53. *Ibid.*, 32.
54. *Ibid.*, 37.
55. L. Burton, *The Yellow Mountain* (Salisbury, Regal, 1978).
56. P. Armstrong, *Operation Zambezi* (Salisbury, Galaxie, 1979).
57. D. Martin and P. Johnson, *The Struggle for Zimbabwe: The Chimurenga War* (London, Faber, 1981), 98.

Chapter 7
Healing the War Scars in the Evangelical Lutheran Church in Zimbabwe

1. My paper must be read in conjuction with Professor Carl Hallencreutz's recent brief but authoritative account of the evolution of the Swedish ecclesiastical and secular involvement in Zimbabwe and its war of liberation. See Carl F. Hallencreutz, 'Religion and War in Zimbabwe and Swedish Relationships', paper presented to the Research Seminar on Religion and War in Zimbabwe and Swedish Relationships, arranged by the Department of Theology, University of Uppsala, in cooperation with the Royal Academy of Letters, History and Antiquities, Stockholm, Uppsala, 23 March–28 March 1992.
2. G. Kay, *Rhodesia: A Human Geography* (London, London University Press, 1970), 20–21.
3. A good discussion of the plight of Africans in communal areas in Regions IV and V and the degradation of this environment is that by J. R. Whitlow, 'Environmental constraints and population pressures in the tribal areas of Zimbabwe', *Zimbabwe Agricultural Journal* (1980), LXXVII, (iv), 173–181; J. R. Whitlow, 'Land uses, population pressure and rock outcrops in the tribal areas of Zimbabwe Rhodesia', *Zimbabwe Rhodesia Agricultural Journal* (1980), LXXVII, (i), 11; J. R. Whitlow, 'An assessment of the cultivated land in Zimbabwe Rhodesia, 1972 to 1977', *The Zimbabwe Rhodesia Science News* (Oct. 1979), XIII, (x), 233–238.

4. Interviews with: Ephraim Maposa at Zvishavane, June 4, 1987; with Rev. Nkane Alfred Ramakgapola at Bulawayo, Sept. 29, 1987; Rev. Elias Kalibe Masiane at Bulawayo, Sept. 29, 1987.

5. Two Musume headmasters, Chegato headmaster, and many teachers owned shops in the local business centres.

6. E[vangelical] L[utheran] C[hurch] A[rchives], (ELCA) Matopo House, Bulawayo: Evangelical Lutheran Church in Zimbabwe Statistics, 1978, 8; Evangelical Lutheran Church Statistics, 1979, 8.

7. *Zimbabwe 1982 Population Census: Main Demographic Features of the Population of Midlands Province* (Harare, Central Statistics Office, Jan. 1989), 3, 27–28; *Zimbabwe 1982 Population Census: Main Demographic Features of the Population of Matabeleland South Province* (Harare, Central Statistics Office, Sept. 1989), 3, 27–28.

8. Hugo Soderstrom, *God Gave Growth: History of the Lutheran Church in Zimbabwe 1903–1980* (Gweru, Mambo Press, 1984), 181.

9. ELCA, Matopo House, Bulawayo, Evangelical Lutheran Church in Rhodesia Statistics for 1977.

10. Arthur Campbell, *Guerrillas: A History and Analysis* (London, Arthur Baker Ltd, 1967), xi.

11. S[venska] K[yrkan] M[ission] S[styrelses] A[rkiv] (SKMSA), A628, 'Document of Understanding Signed Ruben Josefsson, Uppsala, July 21, 1971 and S. Strandvik, Bulawayo, August 25, 1971', 1–3.

12. Soderstrom, *God Gave Growth*, 127; see also ELCA, Matopo House, Bulawayo, Five Year Plan, ELCR, 1975.

13. C. Shiri, *My First Decade as Head of the ELCZ, 1975–1985* (no publication details), 59–60.

14. *Ibid.*, 244–246; C. F. Hellencreutz, 'A council in crossfire: ZCC 1964–1980', in C. F. Hallencreutz and A. Moyo (eds.), *Church and State in Zimbabwe* (Gweru, Mambo Press, 1988), 89–101.

15. Tord Harlin's Personal Collection, Uppsala, Tore Bergman, 'Report to the Board of the Church of Sweden Mission', August 28, 1976, translated for me by Anna-Lena Forsberg, Department of Archaeology, University of Uppsala, 5–6.

16. SKMA A6221, Kalfors to Cabinet, February 7, 1977; Bo Kalfors to Cabinet, February 8, 1977; Bo Kalfors to Heineback, February 15, 1977; Tord Harlin, 'Konfidentiellt, Till SKM, Report Fran Tord Harlin Resa Till Sodra Africa Den, 21 Mars–6 April 1977'; A7221, SKM, 'Rapport till missionstyre Isen', March 4, 1977.

17. Tord Harlin's Personal Collection, Uppsala, Neldner to Harlin, April 27, 1977; Tore Bergman to Edward Ndlovu, June 1, 1977; Tore Bergman to Neldner, June 1, 1977; Telex LWS, June 1, 1977; Neldner to Tore Bergman, July 5, 1977.

18. SKMA A6244, L. Sifobela, Research Project in Rhodesia, 16th July–28th September and resumed from 13th December, 1979, written on December 31, 1979; J. C. Shiri, Memorandum 'The Institutions Damaged During the War of Liberation, Church and Chapels', May 5, 1980.

19. SKMA, A6244, Minutes of the CSM–ELCZ Joint Consultation Meeting held at Njube Youth Centre, Bulawayo, Zimbabwe, on 25 March, 1980.

20. SKMA, A6281–178/79, T. Bergman, 'A Short Summary of the Address of the ELCZ Church Council Meeting, 3rd October, 1980; Terms of Cooperation Between the CSM and the ELCZ', June 24, 1981.
21. SKMA, A6281–178/79, Bishop J. C. Shiri to Mr T. Bergman, January 15, 1981.
22. SKMA., A502–13/81 'Report from T. Bergman and O. Joelson From the Visit to the ELCZ Regarding Matters Related to the Forthcoming Consultation in Zimbabwe, September 15th to 17th 1981'.
23. 'Document of Understanding Between the Evangelical Lutheran Church in Zimbabwe (hereafter ELCZ) and the Church of Sweden (hereafter CS)', May 25, 1983.
24. Minutes of the 32nd Meeting of the ELCZ Meeting, Appendix III, Rev. Mavunduse, Treasurer, 'Treasurer's Report to CA 32 at Chegato'.
25. Interviews: Sr. C. Guramatunhu, Matron at Mnene Hospital, Harare, 16 August 1987; Kenny Nyati, Headmaster of Musume, 25 March 1987; Mapolisa, Store owner at Mnene, April 7, 1987; Ananias Shumba, Acting Headmaster of Masase at Chegato, 7 April, 1987; Ephraim Maposa, Former Headmaster of Musume Secondary School, at Zvishavane, 4 June 1987.
26. ELCA, Matopo House, Minutes of the ELCR Medical Board Meeting held at Bulawayo on 30 May 1978.
27. ELCA, Matopo House, Mrs C. A. Dube, Mrs F. F. A. Shumba, Mrs E. Moyo, Mrs T. C. Moyo, Mrs M. Moyo, Mrs E. W. Hove to the Bishop, Masase Hospital, August 7, 1978.
28. ELCA, Matopo House, Minutes of the ELCR Church Council held at Bulawayo, 18 May 1979.
39. ELCA, Matopo House, S. Shoko to Mrs T. Mate, January 4, 1979.
30. ELCA, Matopo House, Mrs M. Noko, Mrs A. Silamulela, Mrs R. Madongo, Mrs T. Mlauze, Miss S. Malamane, letter written at Tuli, Bethel School, Gwanda, nd.
31. Group interview with Nurses Mrs T. Mathe, Mrs A. Silamulela, Mrs M. Noko, Mrs S. Malula at Manama Hospital, 8 June 1987; Rev. Ezekiel Gwate at Gwanda, 9 June 1987.
32. It is quite clear from the vote cast that the Westerners gave all their 51 votes to Noko, while the Easterners avoided losing the election by giving merely all their votes (66) except two to Shiri, see SKMA A6203, Strandvik's memo, 1974.
33. Bishop was Shiri, his Deputy Dean M. Moyo, Treasurer Rev. H. Mavunduse and Administrative Secretary Rev. N. Shava, all from the Eastern deanery.
34. ELCA, Matopo House, 'Five Year Development Plan, 1975', 3.
35. Rt. Rev. Dr J. C. Shiri, 'Opening Address — Church Assembly No. 32 at Chegato 18–21 January 1990', Appendix II of Minutes of the 32nd Meeting of the ELCZ Church Assembly Held at Chegato Mission from 18 to 21st January 1990.
36. Ibid., 5.
37. Statement from the ELCZ-SM Consultation, November 23–24, 1989, 2.
38. Ibid., 3.

39. Author's Personal Collection, Rev. Dr Biorn Fjarstedt and Bishop Bertil Gartner to The Church Assembly and Church Council of the Evangelical Lutheran Church in Zimbabwe, June 26, 1990.
40. *Ibid.*
41. Author's Personal Collection, Biorn Fjarstedt, Director, to the Rt. Rev. Dr Jonas Shiri, September 19, 1990.
42. Author's Personal Collection, 'Evangelical Lutheran Church in Zimbabwe Church Dispute Under Discussion, 23 January 1991', 2–3.
43. *Ibid.*, 5.
44. *Ibid.*, 9.
45. *Ibid.*, 3.
46. *Ibid.*
47. *Ibid.*
48. *Ibid.*, 7–8.
49. Author's Personal Collection, Meeting at Vice-President's Official Residence in Gunhill, Harare, 23 January, 1991.
50. *Ibid.*, 3.
51. Author's Personal Collection, 'Evangelical Lutheran Church in Zimbabwe Dispute Under Discussion', 11.
52. Author's Personal Collection, ELCZ Meeting at Njube, February 2, 1991, 1.
53. Author's Personal Collection, Minutes of the Meeting on the ELCZ held at Njube Centre on Saturday, 2 February, 1991.
54. Author's Personal Collection, Minutes of the Meeting on the ELCZ held at Njube Centre on 23 March 1991.
55. Author's Personal Collection, Agreed Summary of the Proceedings of the Mediation Progress in the Evangelical Lutheran Church in Zimbabwe, 9 March 1991, 2.
56. *Ibid.*
57. *Ibid.*, appendix.
58. Author's Personal Collection, Western Deanery Assembly, Chronicled and Recorded Minutes of the ELCZ Western Deanery Assembly held in Gwanda Parish on 23rd March 1991 starting at 10:30 am and concluding at 1:20 pm of the same day, 3.
59. *Ibid.*, 3–10.
60. Personal observations.
61. Author's Personal Collection, 'Report from the ELCZ Church Assembly 26–27 April 1991 in Bulawayo, Zimbabwe, by the Southern Secretary of CSM', as observer; Minutes of the 35th Meeting of ELCZ Church Assembly held at Njube Lutheran Youth Centre from 26–27 April, 1991.
62. Author's Personal Collection, Minutes of the ELCZ Church Council Meeting No. 143 held at Njube Youth Centre on 4th October 1991. Minutes of the ELCZ Church Assembly No. 36 held at Njube Youth Centre on the 4th October 1991.
63. Author's Personal Collection, Biorn Fjarstedt, Director to the Rt. Rev. Dr Jonas Shiri, September 19, 1990.

Chapter 8
Things Fall Apart, The Centre *Can* Hold: Processes of Post-war Political Change in Zimbabwe's Rural Areas

1. D. Lan, *Guns and Rain: Guerrillas and Spirit Mediums in Zimbabwe* (Harare, Zimbabwe Publishing House, 1985).
2. *Ibid.,* 136.
3. *Ibid.,* 31–5.
4. *Ibid.,* 152.
5. *Ibid.,* 165.
6. *Ibid.,* 148, 167.
7. *Ibid.,* 172.
8. T. Ranger, *Peasant Consciousness and Guerrilla War in Zimbabwe* (London, Currey, 1985).
9. Ranger, *Peasant Consciousness and Guerrilla War in Zimbabwe*, 182–3, 197, 212–13 and *passim*, Chapter 5.
10. N. Kriger, 'Struggles for Independence: Rural Conflicts in Zimbabwe's War for Liberation' (Cambridge, Massachusetts Institute of Technology, Ph.D. thesis, 1985) and N. Kriger, 'The Zimbabwean war of liberation: Struggles within the struggle', *Journal of Southern African Studies* (1988), XIV, 304–22.
11. N. Kriger, 'Struggles for Independence', 276–413. Kruger's thesis has been published in revised form as *Zimbabwe's Guerrilla War: Peasant Voices* (Cambridge, Cambridge University Press, 1992).
12. Lan, *Guns and Rain*, 149, notes these conditions but fails to pursue the implications for his analysis. For example, if, as Lan assumes, 72,3 per cent of the men of Dande were employed away from home, what effect did this have on the support committees which must have relied heavily on women? One might also ask why the appeal to the 'lost lands' was so powerful in Dande when it is an area notable for its lack of land pressure (despite evictions of people into the area) and also unusual in terms of the relatively minor state interventions into agricultural production.
13. M. F. C. Bourdillon, '*Guns and Rain*: Taking structural analysis too far?', *Africa* (1987), LVII, 270, points out that this was the case long before the outbreak of war. He takes issue with the causal connections Lan makes between the incorporation of chiefs into the settler administration, their loss of legitimacy and the increasing political authority of mediums.
14. See Bourdillon, '*Guns and Rain*: Taking structural analysis too far?', 263–74; M. Sithole, 'Review', *Journal of Modern African Studies* (1987), XXV, 697–701; J. Comaroff, 'Reviews', *Africa* (1988), LVIII, 256–7.
15. Discussions with Terence Ranger on the road between Harare and Bulawayo, July 1991.
16. Kriger refutes David Maxwell's charge that Mutoko was especially violent as a result of its accessibility to security forces. She argues that proximity to Salisbury and tarred roads were less critical than proximity to army bases in

contributing to pressure from security forces. Nonetheless, the areas of Mutoko where Kriger worked do seem to have been qualitatively different in terms of pressure from security forces than those in which Maxwell worked. Discussions with David Maxwell; D. Maxwell, 'Christianity and the war in Eastern Zimbabwe: The case of Elim Mission' in this volume; Discussions with Norma Kriger, Harare, July 1991.

17. See, for example, N. Bhebhe, 'The Evangelical Lutheran Church in Zimbabwe and the war of liberation: 1975–1980', in C. Hallencreutz and A. Moyo (eds.), *Church and State in Zimbabwe* (Gweru, Mambo Press, 1988), 163–94 and the accounts in I. Staunton (ed.), *Mothers of the Revolution* (Harare, Baobab, 1990).

18. T. Ranger, 'Bandits and guerrillas: The case of Zimbabwe', in D. Crummey (ed.), *Banditry, Rebellion and Social Protest in Africa* (London, Currey, 1986), 386–90; also see Ranger, *Peasant Consciousness and Guerrilla War in Zimbabwe*, 212.

19. See the contributions by Sr. Janice McLaughlin in this volume and David Moore in N. Bhebe and T. Ranger (eds.), *Soldiers in Zimbabwe's Liberation War, Vol. I* (Harare, University of Zimbabwe Publications, 1995); Ranger, 'Bandits and guerrillas'.

20. D. J. Maxwell, 'Christianity and the war in eastern Zimbabwe: The case of Elim Mission', in this volume; and see M. Daneel, 'Healing the Earth: Traditional and Christian Initiatives in Southern Africa' (Utrecht, Paper presented at a conference on Healing, Ecology and Religion in a Post-Apartheid South Africa, 1991), 17–20, on the role of independent African churches.

21. D. Dabengwa, 'ZIPRA in the Zimbabwe war of national liberation' in N. Bhebe and T. Ranger (eds.), *Soldiers in Zimbabwe's Liberation War*; F. Chung, 'Education and the Liberation Struggle' in this volume.

22. Staunton (ed.), *Mothers of the Revolution* also illustrates the point.

23. H. Barrell, 'The Historicist Conspirator, His Detonators and Bellows: The ANC of South Africa and the Political-Military Relationship in Revolutionary Struggle' (Oxford, Paper presented at a conference on Violence in Southern Africa, 1991), 3.

24. J. Brickhill, 'Daring to storm the heavens: The military strategy of ZAPU, 1976–1979', in N. Bhebe and T. Ranger (eds.), *Soldiers in Zimbabwe's Liberation War*.

25. *Ibid.*

26. I would argue that the focus on military struggle was the result of an ideology of national democratic revolution and the repeated failure of negotiations to end the war on terms the nationalist leadership would accept rather than the result of a Marxist-Leninist historicism as Barrell argues for the South African case. See David Moore, 'The Zimbabwe People's Army: Strategic innovation or more of the same', in N. Bhebe and T. Ranger (eds.), *Soldiers in Zimbabwe's Liberation War*.

27. For example, Dumiso Dabengwa argues that towards the end of the war the problems guerrillas faced in settling civil disputes was undermining their

228 SOCIETY IN ZIMBABWE'S LIBERATION WAR

ability to operate militarily. One of the reasons ZIPRA was trying to set up liberated zones was so that a civil administration could handle these disputes separately. Comments at the Conference on the Zimbabwean Liberation War, Harare, July 1991.

28. See Kriger, 'Struggles for Independence', Chapter 8 and *passim*, Section 2; F. Chung, 'Education and the Liberation Struggle'.

29. See Lan's discussion, 212–13.

30. Kriger, 'Struggles for Independence', Chapters 7 and 8, especially pp. 323–45. Even in the case of lineages, challenges remained dependent on local political constellations. Guerrillas supported and worked with royal lineages where they held numerical superiority and popular legitimacy. The guerrillas' interest in lineage disputes was 'peripheral and stemmed from their concern to win support from the majority'; it stemmed not from a political programme but from an overriding need to decrease their vulnerability. Kriger, 'Struggles for Independence', 345.

31. A. Isaacman, 'Peasants and Rural Social Protest in Africa', (U.S., Social Science Research Council, 1989), 87.

32. Michael Drinkwater argues this is the most significant legacy of the colonial period. See his 'Technical development and peasant impoverishment: Land use policy in Zimbabwe's Midlands province', *Journal of Southern African Studies* (1989), XV, 288.

33. See, *inter alia*, D. Gordon, 'Development strategy in Zimbabwe: Assessments and prospects', in M. Schatzberg (ed.), *The Political Economy of Zimbabwe* (New York, Praeger, 1984), 119–43; R. Libby, 'Development strategies and political divisions within the Zimbabwean state', in Schatzberg (ed.), *The Political Economy of Zimbabwe*, 144–163; I. Mandaza, 'The state in post-White-settler colonial situation', in I. Mandaza (ed.), *Zimbabwe: The Political Economy of Transition* (Dakar, CODESRIA, 1986), 21–74.

34. See S. Moyo, 'The Zimbabweanisation of Southern Africa's Land Question: Lessons or Domino Stratagems?' (Harare, Zimbabwe Institute of Development Studies, draft, 1990).

35. The following sections are based on research conducted in 1988 and 1989 while I was a Research Associate in the Department of Political and Administrative Studies at the University of Zimbabwe. Interviews with 'local leaders' in the political party, traditional hierarchy and development committees and councils as well as with district officials of the Ministries of Lands and Local Government were conducted in Chimanimani and Insiza Districts. Interviews with officials were also carried out at provincial and national levels. This research was supplemented with a review of district records and with archival research in Harare. For a fuller treatment of some of the themes presented here see my 'Tradition, modernization and control: Local and national disputes over authority and agrarian policy in Zimbabwe', in M. Drinkwater and K. Wilson (eds.), *A Question of Perspective: Re-interpreting Environmental and Social Relations in Zambia and Zimbabwe* (London, Currey,

in press) and 'The Unsettled land: The politics of land redistribution in Matabeleland South, 1980–1990', *Journal of Southern African Studies*, in press.

36. D. Caute, *Under the Skin: The Death of White Rhodesia* (Harmondsworth, Penguin, 1983), especially pages 271–83. See also D. Martin and P. Johnson, *The Struggle for Zimbabwe* (London, Faber and Faber, 1981), 223–4.

37. Provincial Commissioner, Mutare, to the Secretary for District Administration, Harare, 8/7/80.

38. The metaphor of 'disarmament' is from Howard Barrell, personal communication, Oxford.

39. Because some traditional leaders held party posts it is somewhat misleading to draw a clear distinction between the two. Nonetheless, and especially in the case of courts and land allocations, competition between the two groups was commonly noted and keenly felt. Also see Kriger, 'Struggles for Independence: Rural Conflicts in Zimbabwe's War for Liberation', 429–30.

40. See Ranger, *Peasant Consciousness and Guerrilla War in Zimbabwe*, 294–6 and Kriger, 'Struggles for Independence', 438–29, 446–8.

41. Third Meeting for the Formation of the Melsetter District Council held at the District Commissioner's Conference Room, Melsetter (Chimanimani), 15/9/80, appended sheet entitled, 'Minutes of Trips Made Throughout the District to Brief People on the Formation of the Melsetter District Council'.

42. Minutes of the Second Meeting for the Formation of a District Council in Melsetter, District Commissioner's Conference Room (Chimanimani), 25–26/6/80.

43. See R. Murapa, *Rural and District Administrative Reform in Zimbabwe* (Bourdeaux, Centre D'Etude D'Afrique Noire, 1986).

44. On the decline of the party also see Kriger, 'Struggles for Independence', 485–95.

45. See J. Herbst, *State Politics in Zimbabwe* (Harare, Univ. of Zimbabwe, 1990), 78–9 on the nature of land as a 'political good'.

46. The dramatic case of the forced sale of a farm in Headlands was an exception to the rule. The evictions of squatters in Chipinge were more representative of government policy. See Ranger, *Peasant Consciousness and Guerrilla War in Zimbabwe*, 305–6 on the Headlands case. For Chipinge, see especially Moven Mahachi's justification for the squatters' eviction in terms of the foreign currency earning capacity of coffee, tea and the dairy industry in *The Herald*, 23 Dec. 1983; Information also from interviews with the Provincial Planning Officer, Mutare, 24/11/88 and the Provincial Administrator, Mutare, 24/11/88.

47. See B. H. Kinsey, 'Emerging policy issues in Zimbabwe's land resettlement programmes', *Development Policy Review* (1983), I, 190.

48. Minutes of the Mabvazuwa District Council, Chimanimani, 27/5/81.

49. Minutes of the Mabvazuwa District Council, Chimanimani, 30/7/81.

50. Interview, Local Government Promotion Officer, Chimanimani, 31/10/81.

51. See Kriger, 'Struggles for Independence', 471–3.

52. See Bishop Joshua Dube's comments in 'Report for a Meeting held at Ngangu Stadium, Melsetter (Chimanimani), 9/8/80'; attacks on 'kangaroo courts' made in parliament, Parliamentary Debates, 3/2/81; and an attack on the chiefly institution by Minister of Lands, Moven Mahachi, in 'Minutes of a Meeting at the District Commissioner's Conference Hall, Melsetter (Chimanimani), 27/2/81'.

53. 'Minutes of a Meeting with the Deputy Minister of Justice and Constitutional Affairs, Melsetter (Chimanimani), 21/7/81'.

54. Kriger,'Struggles for Independence', 473, notes that five of the eight headmen who survived the war in her study area were elected to court positions. I also found that many traditional leaders had been elected to run courts after independence and that, where they had not, it had only been a matter of time before the 'official' court was undermined.

55. See C. Stoneman and L. Cliffe, *Zimbabwe: Politics, Economics and Society* (London, Pinter, 1989), 93–4.

56. See Isaacman, 'Peasants and Rural Social Protest in Africa'; C. Young, 'Africa's colonial legacy', in R. Berg and J. S. Whitaker (eds.), *Strategies for African Development* (Berkeley and Los Angeles, Univ. of California Press, 1986); R. Bates, *Markets and States in Tropical Africa: The Political Basis of Agricultural Policies* (Berkeley and Los Angeles, Univ. of California Press, 1981).

57. The term is unsatisfactory. I am referring not only to the salaried chiefs and headmen and recognized kraal or village heads but also to the many who are unrecognized and occupy rungs lower or only loosely affiliated to the 'official' chiefs and headmen. It is also problematic to use the term 'traditional' because it denotes something which is timeless and unchanging when, in fact, the role of 'traditional' leaders has changed dramatically through Rhodesia and Zimbabwe's history. I will use the term nonetheless for lack of a better shorthand.

58. See Zimbabwe, *Communal Lands Development Plan: A 15-Year Development Strategy* (Harare, Ministry of Lands, Resettlement and Rural Development, 1985).

59. Lan, *Guns and Rain*, 146.

60. T. Ranger, 'Survival, Revival and Disaster: Shona Traditional Elites Under Colonialism', (Paris, Paper presented to the Round Table on Elites and Colonialism, July 1982), 14.

61. M. Bratton, *Beyond Community Development: The Political Economy of Rural Administration in Zimbabwe* (Gwelo, Mambo Press, 1978), 50.

62. Local elected officials and civil servants certainly felt chiefs retained legitimacy and authority in many areas. Interviews, District Council Chairman, Chimanimani, 10/88; Senior Administrative Officer, Chimanimani, 20/10/88; Regional Agritex Officer, Chimanimani, 4/11/88. Also see Daneel, 'Healing the Earth'; A. Ladley, 'Just Spirits? Chiefs, Tradition, Status and Contract in the Customary Law Courts of Zimbabwe' (unpub. ms, 1990), 8, fn 48. Lan and Ranger both cite examples of traditional leaders playing a supporting role.

63. Ministry of Local Government PER 5 and PER 4 (Chiefs and Headmen) files, kept in the Chimanimani District Administrator's offices and Interview, Senior Administrative Officer, 20/10/88, Chimanimani. It is possible that the post-independence Ministry of Local Government has been overly generous in its descriptions of traditional leaders' war records in an effort to justify government appointments.

64. In Chimanimani, mediums were not involved at all in conferring office or tended to serve the purpose of approving selections made through the consultations of elders. For example, the Gudyanga headmanship does not require a medium to confer office. In the case of the Ngorima chieftaincy, the family of the conspicuously collaborationist previous chief was prevented from continuing to inherit the chieftaincy by a council of elders who nominated a popular nephew of the previous chief (a man who had been elected to the post of presiding officer and who had supported the liberation war). In the case of the Mutambara chieftaincy, the question of collaboration, opportunistic use of mediums and disputes among the houses involved in nominating the chief was most pronounced. In the early 1970s, the incumbent, Dandiwa Dandikwe, fell out of favour not only with the government but also with other elders and contenders to the throne. Other elders challenged the medium who Dandiwa Dandikwe claimed represented the proper spirit and who also backed his claim to the throne. After the government removed him from office, his younger brother, Ngani James, became acting chief with the backing of the government, another medium and other elders. His younger brother, Samuel's accession to the chieftaincy was secured after an agreement reached among the elders and sanctioned, after the fact, by a medium. See the Ministry of Local Government PER 5 and PER 4 files kept in the Chimanimani District Administrator's office. David Maxwell, personal communication, has found in Nyanga that claimants to a chieftaincy are able to mobilize mediums on their behalf, indicating the medium's dependence on or at least intense interaction with the candidate.

65. B. B. Mukamuri, 'Rural Environmental Conservation Strategies in South-central Zimbabwe: An Attempt to Describe Karanga Thought Patterns, Perceptions and Environmental Control' (Harare, unpublished paper, ENDA-Zimbabwe, 1987).

66. K. Wilson, 'Research on Trees in the Mazvihwa and Surrounding Areas' (Harare, unpublished paper prepared for ENDA, 1987).

67. S. Makanya, personal communication, a former ZANLA guerrilla who operated in the Mberengwa area, argues guerrillas simply relied on locally gathered information to establish which leaders — be they mediums, traditional leaders or others — were trustworthy and influential.

68. I am indebted to Terence Ranger for his comments on the relationship between the offices of chief and medium.

69. Bourdillon, '*Guns and Rain*: Taking structural analysis too far?', 270; and see P. Reynolds, 'Children of tribulation: The need to heal and the means to heal war trauma', *Africa* (1990), LX, 1–38.

70. Reynolds, 'Children of tribulation', 10.
71. *Ibid.*, 13.
72. See discussion in 'Minutes of the First Meeting Held for the Formation of a District Council in Melsetter, 11/6/80' and Report by the District Commissioner, Melsetter, in his correspondence with the Provincial Commissioner, Manicaland, 27/6/80. Kriger, 'Struggles for Independence', 448, notes that in 17 of 53 cases councils objected to chiefs sitting on the council. The number is surprisingly low if we assume chiefs had become totally discredited.
73. District Commissioner, Melsetter (Chimanimani) to Provincial Commissioner, Manicaland, 27/6/80; Provincial Commissioner, Manicaland to Secretary for District Administration, Harare, 8/7/80.
74. Kriger, 'Struggles for Independence', 475–9.
75. 'Minutes of a Meeting with the Deputy Minister of Justice and Constitutional Affairs, Melsetter (Chimanimani), 21/7/81'.
76. See correspondence in Headman Saurombe's PER 4 file, kept at the District Administrator's Office, Chimanimani.
77. Kriger, 'Struggles for Independence', 479.
78. Interview, Magistrate, Chimanimani, 3/11/88.
79. Daneel, 'Healing the Earth', 5.
80. Reynolds, 'Children of tribulation'.
81. It should be noted that the government's concessions on courts did not preclude continued competition among traditional leaders for control of the limited number of official courts. Those excluded (because they were not recognized by government or because there was more than one claimant in a ward) tended to run a court anyway or encourage non-cooperation with other institutions in protest. This was one of the more serious causes of conflict among local leaders in Chimanimani.
82. Kriger, 'Struggles for Independence', 477, notes that in some areas, the council at no point interfered in land disputes.
83. See Drinkwater, 'Technical Development and Peasant Impoverishment', 187–305, especially 289–292 and 303–305.
84. JoAnne McGregor's study of Shurugwi District provides a counter example. Traditional leaders adopted modernizing technology and practices largely, she argues, because they made economic and ecological sense in Shurugwi. She writes, 'Shurugwi has the reputation of being modern and developed and people are proud of this, including the 'traditional' leaders'. See J. McGregor, 'Local Management and Control of Woodland' unpub., 1991. Her study has now been submitted as a D.Phil thesis to Loughborough University.
85. Interviews, Senior Administrative Officer, Chimanimani, 20/10/88 and Regional Agritex Officer, Chimanimani, 4/11/88.
86. See the 1965 delineation report for the Dzingire area for an outline of the origins of this problem. 'Report on the Dzingire Community: Chief Muusha, Ngorima Tribal Trust Land, Melsetter District', in C. J. K. Latham, Senior

Delineation Officer, Delineation Reports: Tribal Trust Lands in the Melsetter District (Nov. 1965), 19–21, National Archives of Zimbabwe.

87. See Minutes of the Squatter Control Committee, Chimanimani, 30/9/88; *Manica Post*, 3 Feb. 1989; *The Chronicle*, 5 Mar. 1989; *The Herald*, 2 Aug. 1990.

88. Since 1985 the scarcity of resettlement land has presented a problem. Interview, Senior Administrative Officer, Chimanimani, 20/10/88 and Chimanimani District Five Year Plan, draft document, 1985.

89. A. de Janvry, *The Agrarian Question and Reformism in Latin America* (Baltimore, Johns Hopkins, 1981), 272. De Janvry, in pages 264–5, contrasts the reform sector to the 'non-reform' sector which remains at the centre of the economy.

90. ZIPRA's 'Southern Front', in which Insiza falls, formed part of a transit route through which casualties, supplies and recruits were moved to and from Botswana. ZIPRA deliberately tried to avoid drawing a heavy Rhodesian army presence into the area by not, for example, attacking White ranchers. Interview, Jaconia Moyo, former ZIPRA Security Officer, Bulawayo, July 20, 1991. Collet Nkala reported that only seven ranchers were killed on their land in the 1970s war in Matabeleland. 'Peace returns — but militias are now jobless', *Parade* (April 1989), 43.

91. Interview, Resettlement Officer, Filabusi, 7/10/88. This pattern was also reported to hold true for Matabeleland North, *The Herald*, 31 Jan. 1989.

92. See reports in *The Herald*, 22 and 26 Oct. 1981.

93. Interview, Chief Vezi Maduna (former council chairman), Avoca, 14/4/89 and see reports of the Deputy Minister of Lands Mark Dube's tour of Matabeleland, *The Herald*, 4 and 5 June 1982.

94. For figures see *Matabeleland South Provincial Development Plan* (Bulawayo, Provincial Development Committee, 1985); *Matabeleland South Provincial Development Plan, 1989/1990* (Bulawayo, Provincial Development Committee, 1989); *Matabeleland South Provincial Development Plan, 1988/1989* (Bulawayo, Provincial Development Committee, 1988).

95. The policy was publicly defended by Minister of Lands, David Karimanzira, in *The Herald*, 10 Dec. 1988 after revelations appeared in the press concerning Matabeleland South Provincial Governor Mark Dube's use of a resettlement scheme in Beitbridge. See *The Herald*, 18 Nov. 1988. In Insiza, 13 farms were leased to 33 individuals and syndicates, including civil servants. Mberengwa Rural Council, List of Lessees as of 10 September 1987.

96. Lawyers' Committee for Human Rights, *Zimbabwe: Wages of War, A Report on Human Rights* (New York, Lawyers' Committee for Human Rights, 1986).

97. The District Administrator was appointed as 'manager' in Insiza in mid-1983. The council was entirely ZAPU when it was disbanded while the government claimed the new council was almost entirely ZANU-PF. See Minutes of the Provincial Governor's Meeting with the Insiza District Council and Representatives of Government Departments, Filabusi, 29/3/84; *Zimbabwe Project News Bulletin* (3 June 1983), XXVIII.

98. For a comparison of the Zimbabwean and Angolan cases see M. McFaul, 'Southern African Liberation Movements and Great Power Interventions:

Towards a Theory of Revolution in an International Context' (Oxford, Univ. of Oxford, D.Phil. thesis, 1991), especially pp. 188–249, 315–55.

Chapter 9
In Memory: A Heritage of War in South-western Zimbabwe

1. I use pseudonyms to protect the identity of family members.
2. Richard Werbner, *Tears of the Dead* (Edinburgh, Edinburgh Univ. Press, 1991; Harare, Baobab, 1992).
3. On mutilation displayed as propaganda see Julie Frederikse, *None But Ourselves: Masses versus Media in the Making of Zimbabwe* (Harare, Zimbabwe Publishing House, 1982), 123; and on the deliberate violation of taboo, see *Ibid.*, 131.
4. *Ibid.*, 128.
5. Terence Ranger, 'The Meaning of Terror in Zimbabwe', Workshop on Terror and Counter-Terror, Trinity College, Cambridge, March 1991; Jeremy Brickhill, personal communication, 24 April 1991.
6. Terence Ranger, *Peasant Consciousness and Guerrilla War in Zimbabwe* (Harare, Zimbabwe Publishing House; London, James Currey, 1985), 292; P. Reynolds, 'After war: Healers and children's trauma in Zimbabwe', *Africa* (1990), LX, 11.
7. On differences between ZIPRA forces in the west and ZANLA forces in the east, see Ranger, 'The Meaning of Terror in Zimbabwe'.
8. D. Martin and P. Johnson, *The Struggle for Zimbabwe: The Chimurenga War* (Harare, Zimbabwe Publishing House; London, Faber, 1981), 243.
9. For the modern history of ethnicity see T. Ranger, *The Invention of Tribalism in Zimbabwe* (Gweru, Mambo, 1985).
10. J. C. Colliers, *Counter-Insurgency in Rhodesia* (London, Croom Helm, 1985), 16–17.
11. Lawyers Committee for Human Rights, *Zimbabwe:Wages of War* (New York, The Committee, 1986), 33.
12. G. Seidman, D. Martin and P. Johnson, *Zimbabwe: A New History* (Harare, Zimbabwe Publishing House, 1982), 129.
13. M. Hannan, *Standard Shona Dictionary* (Salisbury, College Press in conjunction with the Literature Bureau, 1959), 228.
14. Frederikse, *None But Ourselves*; J. Nkomo, *Nkomo: The Story of My Life* (London, Methuen, 1984), 162.
15. This is my reading of the evidence in Ranger, 'The Politics of Prophecy in Matabeleland' (Conference paper, Satterwaite Conference on African Religion, April 1989). See also the chapter by Ranger and Ncube in this volume where the evidence is interpreted differently.

Bibliography

Alexander, Jocelyn. 'The State, Agrarian Policy and Rural Politics in Zimbabwe: Case Studies of Chimanimani and Insiza Districts, 1950–1990' (Oxford, University of Oxford, Faculty of Politics, D.Phil. thesis, 1993).

_____. 'The unsettled land: The politics of land redistribution in Matabeleland South, 1980–1990', *Journal of Southern African Studies*, in press.

_____. 'Tradition, modernization and control: Local and national disputes over authority and agrarian policy in Zimbabwe', in M. Drinkwater and K. Wilson (eds.), *A Question of Perspective: Re-interpreting Environmental and Social Relations in Zambia and Zimbabwe* (London, Currey, in press).

Armstrong, P. *Operation Zambezi* (Salisbury, Galaxie, 1979).

Aschwanden, H. *Karanga Mythology* (Gweru, Mambo, 1989).

Ballinger, W. A. *Call it Rhodesia* (London, Mayflowerdell, 1966).

Barrell, H. 'The Historicist Conspirator, His Detonators and Bellows: The ANC of South Africa and the Political-Military Relationship in Revolutionary Struggle' (Oxford, unpubl., 1991).

Bates, R. *Markets and States in Tropical Africa: The Political Basis of Agricultural Policies* (Berkeley and Los Angeles, Univ. of California Press, 1981).

Bhebe, N. 'The Evangelical Lutheran Church in Zimbabwe and the war of liberation', in C. Hallencreutz and A. Moyo (eds.), *Church and State in Zimbabwe* (Gweru, Mambo, 1988).

_____. *ZAPU and ZANU Guerrilla Warfare and the Lutheran Evangelical Church in Zimbabwe* (Mambo, in press).

Boff, Leonardo. *Church Charisma and Power: Liberation Theology and the Institutional Church* (London, SCM, 1985).

Bourdillon, M. F. C. '*Guns and Rain*: Taking structural analysis too far?', *Africa* (1987), LVII.

Bourdillon, M. F. C. and Gundani, P. 'Rural Christians and the Zimbabwe liberation war', in C. Hallencreutz and A. Moyo (eds.), *Church and State in Zimbabwe* (Gweru, Mambo, 1988).

Bratton, M. *Beyond Community Development: The Political Economy of Rural Administration in Zimbabwe* (Gwelo, Mambo Press, 1978).

Brickhill, J. 'Overcoming the Traumas of Violence in Zimbabwe' (Seminar given at St. Anthony's College, Oxford, 22 Nov. 1990).

Brown, R. *When the Woods Became the Trees* (London, Michael Joseph, 1965).

Burgess, A. *The Word for Love* (London, Michael Joseph, 1968).

Burton, L. *The Yellow Mountain* (Salisbury, Regal, 1978).

Campbell, Arthur. *Guerrillas: A History and Analysis* (London, Arthur Baker Ltd., 1967).

Carney, D. *The Whispering Death* (Salisbury, College Press, 1969).

Caute, D. *Under the Skin: The Death of White Rhodesia* (London, Allen Lane, 1983).

Chater, P. *Caught in the Crossfire* (Harare, Zimbabwe Publishing House, 1985).

Chennells, Anthony. 'The treatment of the Rhodesian war in recent Rhodesian novels', *Zambezia* (1977), V, (ii).

Cilliers, J. K. *Counter-Insurgency in Rhodesia* (London, Croom Helm, 1985).

Clarke, M. 'In Search of the Shrine of the Mambo' (Oxford, paper presented at a seminar, 1991).

Cole, B. *The Elite: The Story of the Rhodesian Special Air Service* (Amanzimoti, Three Knights Press, 1984).

Comaroff, J. 'Reviews', *Africa* (1988), LVIII.

Cox, H. *The Seduction of the Spirit: The Use and Misuse of People's Religion* (London, Simon and Schuster, 1974).

Cutlack, M. *Blood Running South* (London, Collins, 1972).

Daly, R. D. and Stiff, P. *Selous Scouts: Top Secret War* (Alberton, Galago, 1982).

Daneel, M. 'Healing the Earth: Traditional and Christian Initiatives in Southern Africa' (Conference on Religion in Post-Apartheid South Africa, Utrecht, Sept. 1991).

_____. *The God of the Matopo Hills: An Essay on the Mwari Cult in Rhodesia* (Mouton, The Hague, 1970).

_____. *ZIRCON: Earth-keeping at the Grassroots in Zimbabwe* (Pretoria, Sigma Press, 1991).

Davis, J. G. *Hold My Hand I'm Dying* (London, Michael Joseph, 1967).

Dibb, C. E. *Spotted Soldiers* (Salisbury, Leo Publishers, 1978).

Drinkwater, Michael. 'Technical development and peasant impoverishment: Land use policy in Zimbabwe's Midlands province', *Journal of Southern African Studies* (1989), XV.

Early, R. *A Time of Madness* (Salisbury, Graham, 1977).

Ellert, H. *The Rhodesia Front War* (Gweru, Mambo, 1989).

Flower, K. *Serving Secretly: An Intelligence Chief on Record* (London, Murray; Harare, Quest, 1987).

Frederikse, Julie. *None But Ourselves: Masses versus Media in the Making of Zimbabwe* (Harare, Zimbabwe Publishing House, 1982).

Gelfand, M. *An African's Religion: The Spirit of Nyajena* (Wynberg, Juta, 1966).

_____. *The Spiritual Beliefs of the Shona* (Gweru, Mambo, 1982).

Godwin, P. and Hancock, I. *Rhodesians Never Die: The Impact of War and Political Change on White Rhodesia, 1970–1980* (Oxford, Oxford University Press, 1993).

Gordon, D. 'Development strategy in Zimbabwe: Assessments and prospects', in M. Schatzberg (ed.), *The Political Economy of Zimbabwe* (New York, Praeger, 1984).

Hellencreutz, C. F. 'A council in crossfire: ZCC 1964–1980', in C. F. Hallencreutz and A. Moyo (eds.), *Church and State in Zimbabwe* (Gweru, Mambo Press, 1988).

––––––. 'Religion and War in Zimbabwe and Swedish Relationships' (Paper presented to the Research Seminar on Religion and War in Zimbabwe and Swedish Relationships, Department of Theology, University of Uppsala, in cooperation with the Royal Academy of Letters, History and Antiquities, Stockholm, Uppsala, 23 March–28 March 1992).

Hannan, M. *Standard Shona Dictionary* (Salisbury, College Press in conjunction with the Literature Bureau, 1959).

Hartmann, M. *Game for Vultures* (London, Heinemann, 1973).

Herbst, J. *State Politics in Zimbabwe* (Harare, Univ. of Zimbabwe, 1990).

Isaacman, A. 'Peasants and Rural Social Protest in Africa' (U.S., Social Science Research Council, 1989).

de Janvry, A. *The Agrarian Question and Reformism in Latin America* (Baltimore, Johns Hopkins, 1981).

Jeater, D. *Marriage, Perversion and Power: The Construction of Moral Discourse in Southern Rhodesia, 1894–1930* (Oxford, Clarendon, 1991).

Kahari, G. P. 'The history of Shona protest song: A preliminary study', in *Zambezia: The Journal of the University of Zimbabwe* (1981), XIX, (ii).

Kay, G. *Rhodesia: A Human Geography* (London, London University Press, 1970).

Kerkhofs, J. 'The church in Zimbabwe: The trauma of cutting apron strings', in *Pro Mundi Vita Dossiers* (Jan. 1982).

Kinsey, B. H. 'Emerging policy issues in Zimbabwe's land resettlement programmes', *Development Policy Review* (1983), I.

Kriger, N. J. *Peasant Perspectives on Zimbabwe's War of Liberation: Diverse Agendas Under Guerrilla Coercion* (Cambridge, in press).

––––––. 'Struggles for Independence: Rural Conflicts in Zimbabwe's War for Liberation' (Cambridge, Massachusetts Institute of Technology, Ph.D. thesis, 1985).

––––––. 'The Zimbabwean war of liberation: Struggles within the struggle', *Journal of Southern African Studies* (1988), XIV.

––––––. *Zimbabwe's Guerrilla War: Peasant Voices* (Cambridge, Cambridge Univ. Press, 1992).

Ladley, A. 'Just Spirits? Chiefs, Tradition, Status and Contract in the Customary Law Courts of Zimbabwe' (unpub. ms, 1990).

Lamont, D. *Speech From the Dock* (Essex, Kevin Mayhew, 1977).

Lan, D. *Guns and Rain: Guerrillas and Spirit Mediums in Zimbabwe* (London, James Currey; Harare, Zimbabwe Publishing House, 1985).

Lawyers Committee for Human Rights, *Zimbabwe: Wages of War* (New York, The Committee, 1986).

Libby, R. 'Development strategies and political divisions within the Zimbabwean state', in Schatzberg (ed.), *The Political Economy of Zimbabwe* (New York, Praeger, 1984).

Linden, I. *The Catholic Church and the Struggle for Zimbabwe* (London, Longman, 1980).

Mandaza, I. 'The state in post-White-settler colonial situation', in I. Mandaza (ed.), *Zimbabwe: The Political Economy of Transition* (Dakar, CODESRIA, 1986).

Manungo, K. 'The Role Peasants Played in the Zimbabwe War of Liberation, with Special Emphasis on Chiweshe District' (Ohio, Ohio University, Ph.D. thesis, 1991).

Martin, D. and Johnson, P. *The Struggle for Zimbabwe: The Chimurenga War* (Harare, Zimbabwe Publishing House; London, Faber, 1981).

Matabeleland South Provincial Development Plan (Bulawayo, Provincial Development Committee, 1985).

Matabeleland South Provincial Development Plan, 1988/1989 (Bulawayo, Provincial Development Committee, 1988).

Matabeleland South Provincial Development Plan, 1989/1990 (Bulawayo, Provincial Development Committee, 1989).

Maxwell, D. J. 'A Social and Conceptual History of North-East Zimbabwe, 1890–1990' (Oxford, University of Oxford, Faculty of Modern History, D.Phil. thesis, 1994).

———. 'A Study of The Roman Catholic Church — From Rhodesia To Zimbabwe 1959–1986', (Manchester, Manchester University, B.A. Honours thesis, 1986).

———. 'Local politics and the war of liberation in north-east Zimbabwe', *Journal of Southern African Studies* (1993), XIX, (iii).

———.. 'The Roasting of Chief Gambiza: The Anatomy of a Hwesa Succession Dispute' (African Research Seminar, Oxford, Dec. 1991).

Mazobere, C. 'Christian theology of mission', in C. Banana (ed.), *A Century of Methodism in Zimbabwe, 1891–1991* (Harare, Methodist Church, 1991).

Meredith, M. *The Past is Another Country: Rhodesia: U.D.I. To Zimbabwe* (London, Deutsch, 1980).

McFaul, M. 'Southern African Liberation Movements and Great Power Interventions: Towards a Theory of Revolution in an International Context' (Oxford, Univ. of Oxford, D.Phil. thesis, 1991).

McGregor, J. 'Local Management and Control of Woodland' (unpub., 1991).

McLaughlin, J. 'Taking Sides: A Case Study of St. Paul's Mission Musami' (ms, 1989).

———. 'The Catholic Church and the War of Liberation' (Harare, Univ. of Zimbabwe, Dept. of Religious Studies, Classics and Philosophy, Ph.D. thesis, 1991).

Mission Work of the Mariannhill Missions in Zimbabwe: 1896–1980 (Bulawayo, Bulawayo Province, 1980).

Moorcraft, P. and McLaughlin, P. *Chimurenga: The War in Rhodesia 1965–1980* (Marshalltown, Sygma/Collins, 1985).

Moore-King, B. *White Man Black War* (Harare, Baobab, 1989).

Moyo, A. and Hallencreutz, C. (eds.), *Church and State in Zimbabwe* (Gweru, Mambo, 1988).

Moyo, S. 'The Zimbabweanisation of Southern Africa's Land Question: Lessons or Domino Stratagems?' (Harare, Zimbabwe Institute of Development Studies, 1990).

Mukamuri, B. B. 'Rural Environmental Conservation Strategies in South-central Zimbabwe: An Attempt to Describe Karanga Thought Patterns, Perceptions and Environmental Control' (Harare, unpubl. paper, ENDA-Zimbabwe, 1987).

Murapa, R. *Rural and District Administrative Reform in Zimbabwe* (Bourdeaux, Centre D'Etude D'Afrique Noire, 1986).

Mutume, P. 'Insights from the second chimurenga', in C. F. Hallencreutz and M. Palmberg (eds.), *Religion and Politics in Southern Africa* (Uppsala, The Scandinavian Institute of African Studies, 1991).

Nkomo, J. *Nkomo: The Story of My Life* (London, Methuen, 1984).

Nyathi, A. and Hoffman, J. *Tomorrow is Built Today: Experiences of War, Colonialism and the Struggle for Collective Co-operatives in Zimbabwe* (Harare, Anvil, 1990).

O'Reilly, J. *The Centenary of Empandeni* (Bulawayo, Bulawayo Province, 1987).

van der Post, L. *A Story Like the Wind* (London, Hogarth Press, 1972).

Ranger, T. O. 'Bandits and guerrillas: The case of Zimbabwe', in D. Crummey (ed.), *Banditry, Rebellion and Social Protest in Africa* (London, Currey, 1986).

———. 'Holy men and rural communities in Zimbabwe, 1970-1980' in W. J. Sheils (ed.), *The Church and War, Vol. 20* (Oxford, Blackwell, 1983).

———. 'Missionaries, migrants and the Manyika', in LeRoy Vail (ed.), *The Creation of Tribalism in Southern Africa* (London, James Currey, 1989).

———. *Peasant Consciousness and Guerrilla War in Zimbabwe* (London, James Currey; Harare, Zimbabwe Publishing House, 1985).

———. 'Religion and witchcraft in everyday life in contemporary Zimbabwe', in Preben Kaarsholm (ed.), *Cultural Struggle and Development in Southern Africa* (London, James Currey, 1991).

———. 'Religion, development and African Christian identity', in K. Holst Peterson (ed.), *Religion, Development and African Identity* (Uppsala, Scandinavian Institute of African Studies, 1987).

———. 'Religious movements and politics in Sub-Saharan Africa', in *African Studies Review* (1986), XXIX, (ii).

———. 'Survival, Revival and Disaster: Shona Traditional Elites Under Colonialism', (Paris, Paper presented to the Round Table on Elites and Colonialism, July 1982).

———. *The Invention of Tribalism in Zimbabwe* (Gweru, Mambo, 1985).

———. 'The Meaning of Terror in Zimbabwe', Workshop on Terror and Counter-Terror (Trinity College, Cambridge, March 1991).

Ranger, T. O. 'The Meaning of Violence in Zimbabwe' (ms, 1991).

———. 'The Origins of Nationalism in Rural Matabeleland: The Case of Wenlock' (Oxford, mimeo, 1990).

———. 'The Politics of Prophecy in Matabeleland' (Colloquium on African Religion and Ritual, Satterwaite, April 1989).

_____. 'War, violence and healing in Zimbabwe', *Journal of Southern African Studies* (1992), XVIII.

_____. 'Whose heritage? The case of the Matobo National Park', *Journal of Southern African Studies* (1989), XV.

Rayner, W. *The Day of Chaminuka* (London, Collins, 1976).

Reid, Daly. R. and Stiff, P. *Selous Scouts: Top Secret War* (Alberton, Galago, 1982).

Reynolds, P. 'After war: Healers and children's trauma in Zimbabwe', *Africa* (1990), LX.

_____. 'Children of tribulation: The need to heal and the means to heal war trauma', *Africa* (1990), LX, (i).

Schmidt, E. *Peasants, Traders and Wives: Shona Women in the History of Zimbabwe, 1870 –1939* (London, James Currey, 1992).

Seidman, G. Martin, D. and Johnson, P. *Zimbabwe: A New History* (Harare, Zimbabwe Publishing House, 1982).

Shiri, C. *My First Decade as Head of the ELCZ, 1975–1985* (no publication details).

Sithole, M. 'Review', *Journal of Modern African Studies* (1987), XXV.

Smith, Wilbur. *The Sunbird* [1972], (London, Pan, 1974),

Soderstrom, Hugo. *God Gave Growth: History of the Lutheran Church in Zimbabwe 1903–1980* (Gweru, Mambo Press, 1984).

'So That Our Youngsters Will Know' (Gwanda, J. Z. Moyo School History Project, n.d.).

'Southern Africa: A smuggled account from a guerrilla fighter', *Ramparts* (Oct. 1969), VIII, (iv).

Staunton, I. (ed.), *Mothers of the Revolution* (Harare, Baobab, 1990).

Stiff, P. *See You in November: Rhodesia's No-holds Barrred Intelligence War* (Alberton, Galago, 1985).

_____. *Selous Scouts: Rhodesian War — A Pictorial Account* (Alberton, Galago, 1984).

_____. *The Rain Goddess* (Salisbury, Jacaranda, 1973).

Stoneman, C. and Cliffe, L. *Zimbabwe: Politics, Economics and Society* (London, Pinter, 1989).

Thompson, P. *The Rainbow or the Thunder* (London, Hodder and Stoughton, 1979).

Tippette, G. *The Mercenaries* (New York, Delacorte, 1976).

Trew, A. *Towards the Tamarind Trees* (London, Collins, 1970).

van Waarden, C. (ed.), *Kalanga: Retrospect and Prospect* (Gaborone, The Botswana Society, 1991).

Weiss, R. *Zimbabwe and the New Élite* (London, British Academic Press, 1994).

Wentzel, P. J. *Nau DzabaKalanga: A History of the Kalanga, 3 Vols* (Pretoria, Univ. of South Africa, 1983).

Werbner, R. *Tears of The Dead: The Social Biography of an African Family* (Edinburgh, Edinburgh Univ. Press; Harare, Baobab, 1991).

Whitlow, J. R. 'An assessment of the cultivated land in Zimbabwe Rhodesia, 1972 to 1977', *The Zimbabwe Rhodesia Science News* (Oct. 1979), XIII, (x).

_____. 'Environmental constraints and population pressures in the tribal areas of Zimbabwe', *Zimbabwe Agricultural Journal* (1980), LXXVII, (iv).

_____. 'Land uses, population pressure and rock outcrops in the tribal areas of Zimbabwe Rhodesia', *Zimbabwe Rhodesia Agricultural Journal* (1980), LXXVII, (i).

Wilson, B. R. *Sects and Society: A Sociological Study of Three Religious Groups in Britain* (London, William Heinemann Ltd., 1961).

Wilson, K. 'Research on Trees in the Mazvihwa and Surrounding Areas' (Harare, unpublished paper prepared for ENDA, 1987).

Wilson, M. *Explosion* (London, Robert Hale, 1966).

'Women as Victims, Women as Heroines: Beyond Dichotomies in the Analysis of Gender and War in Southern Africa', *Journal of Southern African Studies* conference on 'Paradigms Lost, Paradigms Regained' (York, Sept. 1994).

Young, C. 'Africa's colonial legacy', in R. Berg and J. S. Whitaker (eds.), *Strategies for African Development* (Berkeley and Los Angeles, Univ. of California Press, 1986).

Zimbabwe 1982 Population Census: Main Demographic Features of the Population of Midlands Province (Harare, Central Statistics Office, Jan. 1989).

Zimbabwe 1982 Population Census: Main Demographic Features of the Population of Matabeleland South Province (Harare, Central Statistics Office, Sept. 1989).

Zimbabwe, *Communal Lands Development Plan: A 15-Year Development Strategy* (Harare, Ministry of Lands, Resettlement and Rural Development, 1985).

Zimbabwe: Wages of War, A Report on Human Rights (New York, Lawyers' Committee for Human Rights, 1986).

Newspapers and Magazines

Daily Mail	U.K.
Parade	Harare
Sunday Telegraph	U.K.
The Bantu Mirror	Salisbury
The Chronicle	Bulawayo
The Herald	Harare
The Manica Post	Mutare
Zimbabwe Project News Bulletin	Harare

Index